GL●BAL SQU■RE

Edited by
Matthew Gutmann, Brown University
Jeffrey Lesser, Emory University

The Global Square series features edited volumes focused on how regions and countries interact with the rest of the contemporary world. Each volume analyzes the tensions, inequalities, challenges, and achievements inherent in global relationships. Drawing on work by journalists, artists, and academics from a range of disciplines—from the humanities to the sciences, from public health to literature—The Global Square showcases essays on the histories, cultures, and societies of countries and regions as they develop in conjunction with and contradiction to other geographic centers.

Each volume in The Global Square series aims to escape simplistic truisms about global villages and to provide examples and analysis of the magnitude, messiness, and complexity of connections. Anchoring each book in a particular region or country, contributors provoke readers to examine the global and local implications of economic and political transformations.

1. *Global Latin America: Into the Twenty-First Century,* edited by Matthew Gutmann and Jeffrey Lesser

Global Latin America

Global Latin America

INTO THE TWENTY-FIRST CENTURY

EDITED BY

Matthew Gutmann
Jeffrey Lesser

UNIVERSITY OF CALIFORNIA PRESS

University of California Press, one of the most distinguished university
presses in the United States, enriches lives around the world by advancing
scholarship in the humanities, social sciences, and natural sciences. Its
activities are supported by the UC Press Foundation and by philanthropic
contributions from individuals and institutions. For more information, visit
www.ucpress.edu.

University of California Press
Oakland, California

Library of Congress Cataloging-in-Publication Data

Names: Gutmann, Matthew C., 1953- editor. | Lesser, Jeff, editor.
Title: Global Latin America : into the twenty-first century / edited by
    Matthew Gutmann and Jeffrey Lesser.
Description: Oakland, California : University of California Press, [2016] |
    "2016 | Series: Global square ; 1 | Includes bibliographical references
    and index.
Identifiers: LCCN 2016009428 (print) | LCCN 2016011042 (ebook) | ISBN
    9780520277724 (cloth : alk. paper) | ISBN 9780520277731 (pbk. : alk.
    paper) | ISBN 9780520965942 (ebook)
Subjects: LCSH: Latin America—Foreign relations. | Regionalism—Latin
    America. | Globalization—Latin America. | Latin America—Social
    conditions.
Classification: LCC F1415 .G565 2016 (print) | LCC F1415 (ebook) | DDC
    327.8—dc23
LC record available at http://lccn.loc.gov/2016009428

Manufactured in the United States of America

25   24   23   22   21   20   19   18   17   16
10   9   8   7   6   5   4   3   2   1

In keeping with a commitment to support environmentally responsible and
sustainable printing practices, UC Press has printed this book on Natures
Natural, a fiber that contains 30% post-consumer waste and meets the
minimum requirements of ANSI/NISO Z39.48–1992 (R 1997) (*Permanence of
Paper*).

*To our global children, Maya, Liliana, Lianna,
Jonathan, Aron, and Gabriel*

CONTENTS

LIST OF FIGURES

INTRODUCING THE GLOBAL SQUARE
BOOK SERIES

Matthew Gutmann and Jeffrey Lesser

Global Latin America is the first volume in the University of California Press's GLOBAL SQUARE BOOK SERIES. Over nine volumes, THE GLOBAL SQUARE will focus on how regions and countries interact with the contemporary world. The chapters in each book will draw on specialists in various areas: from academia to journalism, from environmental sciences to public health. The histories, cultures, and societies of particular countries and regions are far from flat as they develop in conjunction with and contradiction to other geographic centers.

Readers will see how countries that gain dominance in the world always do so in relation to broader, non-national historical characteristics, resources, ambitions, and opportunities. No major region or country is isolated, and the ways in which Brazil or Turkey or South Africa is tied to the globe are not identical, by design or execution. The standing of a country or region vis-à-vis its global partners and competitors, its ambitions and anxieties, needs to be documented and analyzed in each case.

By looking at particular regions and countries, we hope that readers will be provoked to examine the global and local implications of economic and political transformations. As the Group of 20 (G20) major economies in the world replaces the Group of 8 (G8) as representative of contemporary world leadership, THE GLOBAL SQUARE BOOK SERIES anticipates a world where the four largest economies in the world will soon be China, the United States, India, and Brazil.

These shifts in economic dominance will have implications well beyond those currently imagined. GLOBAL SQUARE books seek to capture the dynamic and complex geographies and cultural politics developing from one region out around the rest of the world. The world as our grandparents knew it is being turned upside down, and new centers of power and influence are increasingly found in new locations within our GLOBAL SQUARE.

ACKNOWLEDGMENTS

As editors, we would like to extend our gratitude to the contributors of essays, interviews, manga, and poems to this book. They accepted our request to write from Latin America *out* and to address themselves to a broad public, something academics too often find an insurmountable challenge. We know readers will appreciate these creative interventions as much as we do.

Several people were integral to the project, including our PhD students who worked as project assistants: Susan Ellison and Bryan Moorefield at Brown University were essential in helping to prepare the book in its earlier stages; and Andrew Britt at Emory University researched and drafted the part introductions and helped us prepare the final manuscript. Thanks as well to Brown University students Yelena Bide for transcription and translation and Lauren Papalia for translation; and to Emory University PhD student Suma Ikeuchi for translation. We appreciate the participation of many chapter authors in a workshop on this volume, as well as two outside commentators, Dorothy Hodgson and Richard Locke.

University of California Press Executive Editor Naomi Schneider was instrumental in bringing about this book and the GLOBAL SQUARE series; we are delighted that *Global Latin America* is the first in the series that we will edit with her guidance. Naomi's assistant, Will Vincent, was a model of efficiency and grace, and copy editor Sheila Berg lent a perfectly balanced red pen. This book has been improved by the comments of outside reviewers, including Miguel Centeno and Kris Lane and others who remained anonymous.

Our thanks for funding generously provided by the Watson Institute for International and Public Affairs at Brown University, the Samuel Candler Dobbs Chair at Emory University, and the University of California Press. These resources made preparing the book for publication much easier.

Special thanks to Cathy and Eliana, whose delight in our book together has made this project all the sweeter.

Finally, we dedicate this book to our children, who, we feel fortunate, are practically cousins, too. Between them, Maya, Liliana, Lianna, Jonathan, Aron, and Gabriel have already lived many years in Brazil, Ecuador, Ireland, Israel, Italy, Kenya, Mexico, Paraguay, and Spain, as well as the United States. Together they represent the intense and extensive engagement of Latin America with the rest of the world, just as collectively they embody the countless interconnections that we have tried to gather in the pages of *Global Latin America.*

Chasing Che

INTRODUCTION TO *GLOBAL LATIN AMERICA*

Jeffrey Lesser and Matthew Gutmann

The puzzle that inspired *Global Latin America* was, Why did we find Che Guevara's image everywhere we went in the world? Why was a Latin American revolutionary of the 1950s and 1960s so popular among so many people around the globe in 2016? Why was Che easily the most famous Latin American outside the region? Sure, images of the bearded face and beret were often devoid of deep meaning, but there was his image, and we wanted to make sense of it. Trying to understand global Che led us to the larger meanings of global Latin America.

Jeff thought Che was following him in a hipster coffeehouse in Oaxaca City, Mexico, shouting the slogan, "Café para todos." Matt realized that he was following Che when he interviewed Zhu Wenbin, a professional matchmaker who each weekend works the crowds of parents in Shanghai's People's Park looking for a mate for their daughter or son. When Matt asked Mr. Zhu why he wore Che on his cap (see figure 1.2), he laughed and said he thought it looked good on him. Who knew that Che would become a beacon of sartorial splendor among Mexican baristas and Chinese matchmakers?

Jeff and Matt together followed Che to yet another part of the world, to Palestine, where we saw many young men playing soccer in their Che T-shirts in Ramallah and elsewhere on the West Bank. Well known among rebellious youth when he was alive, Che Guevara became truly famous after he died. Ernesto (Che) Guevara was born in Argentina in 1928 and played a leading role in the 1959 Cuban Revolution. He tried to launch another revolution in the Congo in 1965, before he was killed by CIA-backed troops in La Higuera, Bolivia, in 1967. A former medical student in Argentina, Che may be known to some readers for a famous road trip immortalized in the movie *The Motorcycle Diaries*. That film stars the man who might be the most globally

FIGURE O.I. Cartoon of Che Guevara from a coffee shop in Oaxaca, Mexico.

famous Latin American in 2016, Gael García Bernal, interviewed by the journalist Alma Guillermoprieto in the final chapter of this book.

Today, Ernesto Guevara has become Che, the Guerrilla Fighter Action Figure; Che, the Target of Capitalist Conspiracy; Che, the Hipster Hunk; and Che, the Ultimate Rebel with a Cause and Champion of the Underdog. *Global Latin America* thus took shape as we asked ourselves, What is it about Che that led him to take root anywhere, even while representing something different almost everywhere? What allowed a single image to be filled with different meanings? Chasing the vagabond rebel Che reminded us of Latin America's enormous impact on the globe in ways political, social, economic, and cultural.

Interactions between peoples, economies, and cultures from different parts of the world are nothing new. Global migrations, exchanges, and communications have been taking place since humans emerged from Africa

FIGURE 0.2. Palestinians wearing Che Guevara T-shirts.

Credit: Picture taken by Justin McIntosh, August 2004. This file is licensed under the Creative Commons Attribution 2.0 Generic license. https://commons.wikimedia.org/wiki /File:Palestinians_wearing_Che_Guevara_tshirts.jpg

millennia ago. As the Mexican anthropologist Lourdes Arizpe has noted, "We humans are the most wandering species on earth." In the twenty-first century, Latin America is a central player in every kind of global interaction and all manner of tensions between global and local economies, populations, and politics.

CONQUEST, COLONIALISM, AND CHRISTIANITY

We are often more familiar with the impact of the world *on* Latin America than with the impact of Latin America on the world. The three C's— Conquest, Colonialism, and Christianity—provide a tortured, if better-known story, about how some parts of the world have exercised control over other parts. When Columbus "discovered" the New World in the late 1400s and the Spanish and Portuguese Conquest of the Americas began, indigenous peoples all over the continent began living under colonial rule. They had to contend with strange languages, religions, and diseases.

Demographers estimate that, depending on the region, within decades of Columbus's arrival, as many as 90 percent of the indigenous peoples died as a result of violence and smallpox and other diseases. Millions of inhabitants living on the vast lands that later came to be called *Latin* America ceased to exist (or were never born), and with their demise the memories of their histories and cultures often disappeared. The Christianization of the Americas resulted in the often-forced conversion of most indigenous peoples and the millions of Africans brought to the region as slaves. Newly imposed brutal working conditions transformed the lives of the conquered and enslaved subjects. This was the situation for hundreds of years, from the early 1500s until the wave of independence movements that began in Haiti in 1803 and picked up steam across the continent in the next decades. Yet even independence did not end the three C's—as new powers, from Asia, the Middle East, and North America, have continued to seek to dominate the region.

Latin Americans have always been intertwined in wholly uneven global relationships that have encompassed every aspect of their lives. As teachers about Latin America, Matt and Jeff know a great deal about the influence of Europe and the United States on Latin America, and in our classes we often focus on the ambition of outsiders to exploit what the Uruguayan journalist Eduardo Galeano famously called "the open veins of Latin America." Gold, bananas, oil, labor, and more gold have filled the coffers of many a foreign company at the expense of the peoples residing between what is today the U.S. Southwest and Patagonia north of Antarctica.

Although the significance of Latin America for the rest of the world is not new or sudden, it is ever more apparent. The impact that Latin America has had in the other direction, even though unmistakable, has never been as familiar a narrative. This volume, like the others in the GLOBAL SQUARE series, seeks to remind us that regions are not just victims but also global players.

Latin America in 2016 is home to emerging global powers. In 2016, even despite massive downturns economically, Brazil had the seventh largest economy in the world and Mexico was poised to break into the top ten. Latin America is tightly bound to regions from Asia to Africa, from the Middle East to Europe, through commerce and trade, migration, and the arts. In political and economic terms, Argentina, Brazil, and Mexico are world leaders, part of the Group of 20 (G20) countries that have greatly expanded membership beyond the old geopolitical leadership of Europe, Japan, and the United States.

In Realpolitik, Latin American leaders from Argentina's Carlos Menem to Brazil's Luiz Inácio Lula da Silva to Venezuela's Hugo Chávez have proposed that they are uniquely able to help to resolve global problems, from conflicts in the Middle East to energy to climate change to participatory democracy. Heavy manufacturing in Latin America is reshaping global auto, weapons, and airplane industries. Environmental measures in the enormous Amazon region, positive and negative, are central to global discussions of climate change. Truth commissions formed to document the abuses of past dictatorships in Latin America have become vital reference points for similar efforts from South Africa to Rwanda to Cambodia.

Power has also moved in other, new directions. China has begun to play a larger role economically and financially in Latin America and the United States a reduced one. Trade between China and Latin America went from around $12 billion in 2000 to $289 billion in 2013. Trade between the United States and Latin America, in comparison, went from $380 billion in 2000 to $850 billion in 2014. This is important in its own right, and it is also a good indication of the sway of Latin America in China today, as shown in chapters in this book on the arts (Maisonnave) and the environment (Neill and Macedo).

Today Latin America is a model, in ways good and bad, in public health. For example, when Brazil's government turned the tables on the global pharmaceutical industry and refused to pay what the companies wanted to charge for HIV antiretroviral therapies, the rest of the world not only took note, but many followed suit. Brazil's steps toward the prevention and treatment of sickle cell anemia are creating new global prototypes. Medicines first developed by indigenous healers from the Andes and Mesoamerica, once mocked as backward and unscientific, are now intensively studied by pharmaceutical corporations.

Global Latin America is for students, business leaders, policy makers, and global travelers interested in better understanding Latin America's deep entanglements with and influence on our interdependent world. Chapters by academics, politicians, activists, journalists, scientists, and artists shine light on Latin American history, society, and culture. For those who want to appreciate the diversity and global relevance of Latin America in the twenty-first century, this volume collects some of the top scholarship and social analysis about global Latin America today and historically.

THE WORLD IS NOT FLAT

The authors and editors of *Global Latin America* do not subscribe to a self-serving view popular in the United States that argues that factors like information technologies and rapid transportation have for the first time in the history of humanity "flattened" the global landscape. We do not see "impact" as the end of unequal international relationships or as the creation of new level playing fields on which young and globalized entrepreneurs compete simply on some objective notion of merit.

The naive "the world is flat and a free marketplace" position, most famously argued by the *New York Times* columnist Thomas Friedman, is seductive for many reasons. Based on the expansion of the gross numbers of the middle class in places like India, Korea, Mexico, and Brazil, many want to believe that we are headed away from rampant global inequalities and toward a future that is more prosperous, equitable, and just. Yet the Flat Worlders are too sanguine about persistent and growing poverty and disparities of all kinds. Widening fault lines in the twenty-first century represent more jagged social lives and an ever fiercer scramble for resources, including basic natural resources like water, that many in Europe and the United States might have sworn were globally abundant.

Flat Worlders might point to our story of Che as evidence of a new world order, of how one image, often missing its historical meaning, is replicated in so many places and in so many ways. See? Since all sorts of people endorse Che, we must all be the same. It is a nice pie-in-the-sky story of one big happy global middle class, with the Internet and laptops and cell phones linking humanity around the globe. But simplistic truisms about upwardly mobile global villages and heartfelt sentiments that wish gaping inequalities were no longer characteristic of the world do not stand up to the magnitude and messiness of actual global connections. Che's image, then, is not evidence of a generalized, flattened world but of a more specific world that we are calling Global Latin America.

The chapters in *Global Latin America* present a nuanced and grounded assessment by showing that people often understand the globalized world in local ways. Indeed, they often engage in global activity without perceiving it as such because they have taken something as simple as a smart phone and changed its significance, for example, from a communications tool to a bank. Each chapter is packed with concrete examples showing widening fissures and the emerging social struggles that challenge them.

Global Latin America listens to the voices of citizens on the ground and those who have governed, people who are country specialists and regional generalists, anthropologists, biologists, poets, and other critically engaged observers of emerging global trends. Readers will see that even with a seem-

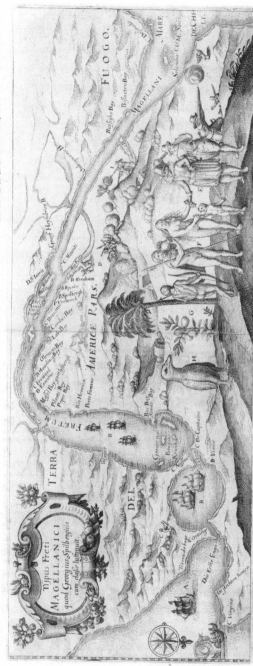

FIGURE 0.3. "Delineatio freti Magellanici." Plan of the Strait of Magellan with south at the top. Includes European men with muskets or guns greeting native Americans, scenes of hunting and warfare, spears, bow and arrow, drinking vessel, birds, dwellings, ships, fruit tree, compass rose, and some topographical details. Courtesy of the John Carter Brown Library at Brown University.

ingly enlarged middle class, Latin America has been far from flattened. Indeed, the region has as many peaks as it did historically, as the divide between haves and have-nots continues to expand. Most of all, *Global Latin America* shows a new appreciation for the contention that Latin Americans and Latin American nations have as much impact on the rest of the world as the other way around, and that Latin America's global connections are creating local futures everywhere on earth.

WHAT'S INSIDE GLOBAL LATIN AMERICA?

The first part of the book, "The Latin American Past in the Global Present," begins with an original interview with Chilean former president Ricardo Lagos as he contemplates the relation between past and present in Latin America. As many readers will know, a 1973 military coup d'état in Chile led by Augusto Pinochet was backed by the U.S. government of Richard Nixon. On 11 September of that year, the democratically elected government of Salvador Allende was overthrown and the country plunged into years of brutal dictatorship. More than any other individual, Ricardo Lagos represented the opposition to the Pinochet dictatorship, never more than when on national television in 1988 he pointed his finger at the television camera and denounced the "tortures, murders, and human rights violations" of the dictatorship. (A photograph of this famous finger is reproduced in chapter 1.)

In his interview with Matthew Gutmann, President Lagos considers the history of colonialism in Latin America, the region's contemporary relationships with Africa, and the export of global Latin American democracy and social change not only to other parts of the Global South but also to Europe and the United States. He argues that these factors were essential in creating a vibrant Latin America whose voice in the world is unmistakable and powerful. Like other chapters in the volume, the interview with President Lagos highlights a contemporary appreciation for multiculturalism as a positive social, economic, and cultural characteristic that allows many Latin Americans to see themselves as especially able to integrate with diverse populations across the globe. The president's idea about heterogeneity, what the Mexican philosopher and politician José Vasconcelos called "the cosmic race" in 1925, is an example of the positive interpretation of racial and ethnic mixing. Yet mixing (both real and imagined) has been anything but smooth or problem-free. Even so, it is often used as a counterexample of the cultural and social uniformity and conformity preached and practiced elsewhere.

Perhaps no Latin American in 2016 stands out more than the Argentine pope Francis, whom the anthropologist Nancy Scheper-Hughes met in 2015. A chapter written with the historian of religion Jennifer Scheper Hughes draws out the impact of the first Latin American (and Global South) pope, including the past and future role of women in the Catholic Church. At the same time, they delve into the impact of Argentina's Dirty War on Pope Francis and by direct extension on the world in the twenty-first century.

In "Fidel Castro: The First Superdelegate," the historian Greg Grandin updates a provocative piece he wrote originally for TomDispatch.com, in which the outsized impact of an island not too far from Miami is shown to be as long-lived as it is irksome to those presiding in the halls of Washington, DC. For more than fifty years, Cuba has figured more prominently in U.S. politics than almost any other nation, and Fidel Castro excelled at influencing (even if often negatively) more U.S. policy decisions than almost any other leader in the world.

Interspersed throughout the volume are poems by the scholar-poet Renato Rosaldo, whose work reminds us that this particular art form has had a global impact, brilliantly exemplified by the Chilean poet-diplomats Pablo Neruda (1904–73) and Gabriela Mistral (1889–1957) and the Mexican poet-diplomat Octavio Paz (1914–89). Remarkable for their engagement in politics as well as letters (how many diplomats from the United States are famous for their poetry?), each of the three also won the Nobel Prize in Literature. (See Ilan Stavans's chapter for more on Latin American literature, politics, and the world stage.) In his first poem, "Cruces de fronteras / Border Crossings," for example, Rosaldo traces how Mexicans cross borders that earlier in history crossed them, drawing on popular imagery and personal accounts, both comic and tragic. In later poems in this volume, he captures and unleashes the illegal, the profane, and the confidential secrets of global Latin America.

The sociologists Gabriel Hetland and Peter Evans next describe how democratic practices developed first in Brazil are today implemented in cities far outside Latin America. This is noteworthy in its own right, especially given the habit of politicians and policy wonks in Western Europe and North America to preach about democracy even when they do not practice it. Hetland and Evans overturn this claim and demonstrate why the world is learning from Latin America when it comes to citizen rights and participation in governance and political decision making.

We come back to Che Guevara at the end of this part with an excerpt from the original Japanese biography of Che that uses manga, a transnational graphic style that emerged from Japan. Kiyoshi Konno and Chie Shimano illustrate how images ebb and flow around a Latin American guerrilla fighter whose biography is far less recognizable than his face and grin.

Tongues and Feet

Part 2, "Tongues and Feet," begins with an exploration of languages by the sociolinguists Paja Faudree and Daniel Suslak. Most readers will know that when the Portuguese and Spanish invaded and occupied what became Latin America, they brought and imposed their own languages. This is why Portuguese is today the language of Brazil and Spanish is used in most of the other nineteen countries of the region. While it might appear that language use has been a one-way process for centuries, Faudree and Suslak show the impact of *Brazilian* Portuguese and *Latin American* Spanish on Portugal, Spain, and the rest of the world and how indigenous languages from Latin America have also influenced and shaped other languages across the globe.

In the first of two chapters on the reception of Latin American music in other parts of the world, the anthropologist Michelle Bigenho reveals, through "love, protest, dance, and remix," why exoticism and nostalgia are part of the appeal of Latin American music for world audiences. So, too, the politics of contemporary social movements and more long ago sounds conjuring up days of slavery and colonialism.

Undoubtedly the most global of sports, *fútbol/futebol*/soccer was, as described in the chapter by the historian Brenda Elsey, "created in England but perfected in South America." The mutual influence of one part of the world on another, in terms of player rosters and style of play, has been circuitous: after a century of international matches it is often hard to trace who started what change in the game and where. What Elsey does show is how Latin America has transformed the racial, gendered, and class character of global football.

Of all the things that those in the United States might take for granted, food from "South of the Border" surely ranks high. The literary critic Sarah Portnoy and the historian Jeffrey Pilcher take us into the world of the raw and the cooked, sensory material that considers how Mexico, Peru, and Korea come together in the food truck movement of Los Angeles and what this means for global Latin America. Tacos, for example, have become a staple in the United States, Italy, Brazil, and China, and Latin American cuisine has only just begun to leave its mark on taste worldwide.

Science, Technology, and Health

In part 3, the world is turned on its head as the environmental biologists Christopher Neill and Marcia Macedo discuss how natural resources like soybeans have become a de facto twenty-first-century legal currency. And that currency in a sense is none other than water: what Brazil has in abundance and China so badly lacks has made soybeans a transpacific trade staple. And, of course, the amount of Brazilian soybeans sold to others globally depends on how much water there is, which is dependent on how many Amazonian forests remain in the future.

If anyone thinks that the effect of Latin America on the rest of the world refers primarily to its impact on the United States and Europe, the sociologists Wendy Wolford and Ryan Nehring give us an important example of development projects shared between Latin America and Mozambique. Using insights gleaned from their study of South-South foreign assistance projects, we learn of Latin American experts and the transfer of technical knowledge to this Portuguese-speaking African country.

Few readers will fail to recognize Latin America as the origin of much of the world's illegal drug trade, from cocaine to cannabis. But drugs' Latin American origins need to be questioned. The historian Paul Gootenberg provides an insider's glimpse into how street drugs and illicit economic ties around the globe have created a demand that Latin America has fulfilled over the past several decades. As drug reforms spread globally, we would do well to learn more about this part of the history of global Latin America.

Communities

Part 4 showcases Latin American models of belonging that are not exclusively national or ethnically based. For example, the children of indigenous Central American migrants to the United States often learn Spanish as a local language in places like Atlanta and Houston. The low cost of communications has meant that families once permanently separated by migration now have daily spoken and visual connections "back home," creating new communities in which actions are expressed without direct face-to-face experience. Who would have thought in 1975 that migrants from Central America would Skype back to their villages of birth to participate in local decisions about road repairs and who should be elected mayor? At the same time, new configurations of everything from sexuality to religion move back and forth across space.

Nobel Peace Prize laureate Rigoberta Menchú addresses what indigenous peoples in the Americas have contributed to knowledge and well-being in the world overall. Far from accepting the label of victim, Menchú shows in her award speech how social movements among native peoples in Latin America have responded to centuries of colonialism, racism, and impoverishment with determined social movements demanding rights and community control. She also spells out clearly the enormous contributions of indigenous peoples to human understanding, from the zero value in mathematics to the creation of great works of engineering and art.

In the following two chapters, anthropologists look at two distinct yet interrelated populations and social relationships. Denise Brennan explores how people around the world have looked to Latin American sex worker organizing as a model for labor efforts in their own countries. From links to nongovernmental social support organizations to public health institutions across the continent, sex workers in Latin America have demonstrated how through knowledge and activism their rights and well-being can be won and expanded.

Next, Florence Babb examines how tourists look to Latin America for their personal edification and amusement, including but of course not limited to sex workers. For many readers of *Global Latin America*, tourism may be the means of connecting with the region, and it is often as tourists that they see the influence of their homelands on Latin America rather than vice versa. One way Babb reverses our orientation is to look closely at preconceptions about Latin America and how these may reflect as much about where people come from as where they visit.

In a whirlwind tour of his own, one of Brazil's leading intellectuals, Ruben Oliven, provides a keen sense of the multiple meanings of global and local communities from a Latin America–outward perspective. Race, economics, religion, and inequalities of all kinds provide the backdrop for this chapter that situates Brazil, and by extension all of Latin America, in a dynamic global context, full of aspirations and challenges. Oliven helps us to understand why it is worth paying attention to Latin America as the tenor and scope of protest and demands for inclusion are shared globally.

Art Moves the World

The impact of Latin America on global art can be seen in everything from music to graffiti to photography. This volume, however, focuses on familiar and less expected arenas. The final part of *Global Latin America* shows how far the image of Latin American culture has changed from Carmen Miranda–like women dancing with tropical fruit on their heads. Although we still see stereotyped narco drug lords on television and in the movies, where Latin American culture begins and ends is no longer nearly so clear as it once might have been.

The literary scholar Ilan Stavans analyzes Latin American literature's "boom heard round the world" by detailing the multiple personal and aesthetic connections between legendary Latin American authors—Gabriel García Márquez, Mario Vargas Llosa, Carlos Fuentes—in Europe and in virtually every corner of the literary world. Yet Stavans worries that the very worldliness of Latin American authors might be smoothing too many of Latin America's wrinkles out of the region's fiction, something he calls "the drawback of internationalization."

Without a doubt, more people in more places around the world have learned what they know about Latin America from *telenovelas,* the region's hyperpopular and influential "soap operas." *Telenovelas* are not exactly the same as the soaps in the United States—they last for months and not decades; they are shown at night, not during the day, and as a consequence, they are watched by men as well as women. Originally from Ecuador, the social scientist Hugo Benavides investigates the huge global market in *telenovelas* in locales as far flung as Africa and the Middle East. Why they are so well liked similarly reveals as much about global viewers as about Latin America.

Next, the Brazilian journalist Fabiano Maisonnave explores the bossa nova singer Lisa Ono's popularity in China. Singing the archetypical Brazilian music from a bygone era, Ono is in fact better known in East Asia than she is in her native Brazil. And that is the point: Latin American music goes through a global metamorphosis so that Chinese audiences come to believe a Brazilian musician is from Japan, singing in a foreign language (in this case Portuguese) that could be English as well as anything else. And the musical voyage lingers on.

We close with an original interview by the renowned Mexican journalist Alma Guillermoprieto with the Mexican movie star Gael García Bernal. From *Amores Perros* to *Y tu mamá también* and *The Motorcycle Diaries* to the

Jon Stewart–directed *Rosewater,* García Bernal has changed how people around the world see Latin America, and this chapter changes how we understand the influence of cinematic global Latin America. Idealistic, rebellious, genial, and always entertaining, this Mexican actor is, like Latin America, rooted in but defined by far more than nationality.

The central premise of *Global Latin America* then is quite simple: Those in the rest of the world have much to learn from Latin America. Readers from the United States and Europe may find that the authors of this volume present much more sophisticated answers to pressing challenges than those that come from Washington, Paris, London, and Berlin. As editors, we hope that these chapters will lead you to share our appreciation of how differently things can and should look when viewed from Latin America out toward the rest of the globe.

PART ONE

The Latin American Past in the Global Present

INTRODUCTION

MANY OF US THINK OF time as moving in a linear direction from a *before* in the past to a *now* in the present and toward a *then* in the future. Imagine the neat simplicity of a time *line:* from left to right, from past to present. The title of this part challenges the linear trajectory from a regionally specific, Latin American *then* to a regionally uninhibited, global *now*. In Latin America, as elsewhere, the shape of time and the borders between a historical past and a contemporary present are not necessarily as they first seem. With tones ranging from the poetic to the presidential, these chapters introduce us to global Latin America and the blurry boundaries between past and present and between here and there. In the process, they offer a refreshed and refreshing map of globally extended networks and globalized interdependencies with Latin America at the center.

Coined in 1930, the term *globalization* has come into common use only over the past thirty years. Many describe the proliferation of institutions and individuals operating on a transnational scale as unequivocally new and unprecedented. Yet global connections, as the long history of a globally connected Latin America shows, are not products of the recent past. Many chapters in this volume situate Latin America at the crossroads of centuries of transoceanic global links. That history includes the region's pivotal role in the development of modern social, political, and economic forms of world historical importance. Try thinking about the trajectories of empire, slavery, and capitalism *without* Latin America. Nonetheless, *Global Latin America* is not a history textbook narrating the old if undeniably significant history of the region.

"The Latin American Past in the Global Present" begins at the end, so to speak, with contemporary developments that originated within Latin

America but have made a splash elsewhere. In particular, these chapters lift up regionwide sociopolitical innovations from the scale of global institutions and national governments to everyday life. Some observers may balk at this proposition; relatively recent histories of dirty wars and dictatorships might suggest that Latin America has little success in governance in the twenty-first century. A number of authors here invert that thinking, offering examples that compel readers to reckon with the instructive good that has emerged (and continues to develop) out of conflict and hardship.

As a fitting opening to *Global Latin America,* this part introduces us to examples of globally pioneering activity. We hear from Ricardo Lagos, Chile's president from 2000 to 2006, who sat for a conversation with the anthropologist Matthew Gutmann in 2014. President Lagos gives insights on far-reaching topics, from climate change to *mestizaje.* Specialists will relish Lagos's insider commentary, including snippets from one-on-one conversations with other global political and intellectual leaders.

The sociologists Gabriel Hetland and Peter Evans complement Lagos's assessment of the challenges and opportunities facing the region with four case studies of regional social innovation. Newcomers to Latin America will learn much from these narratives about novel forms of local democratic engagement, responses to environmental degradation, and patterns of rural mobilization. Together, Lagos, Hetland, and Evans help to counter enduring stereotypes of Latin America as a place mired in the past. They show, for instance, that the passage of time has not left memories of dirty war and dictatorship from the 1960s and 1970s buried in oblivion. By reckoning with those histories, Latin America's transitions to democracy have become meaningful referents for projects of increased political participation, reconciliation, and accountability worldwide.

Readers of this part will encounter towering and iconic figures from global Latin America's past and present. The anthropologist Nancy Scheper-Hughes and the historian Jennifer Scheper Hughes profile the first Latin American pope, Francis, born Jorge Mario Bergoglio in Buenos Aires in 1936. In addition to compelling, firsthand accounts of the development of liberation theology in Latin America, Scheper-Hughes and Scheper Hughes deliver an impassioned plea for the pontiff to continue remaking the Catholic Church in a relatively more radical image. Then there is Fidel Castro, subject of the historian Greg Grandin's chapter, which traces on a time line the roles of Cuba and Cuban American exiles in U.S. presidential politics. Though recent efforts have led to a further defrosting of the ties between the United

States and Cuba (currently under the leadership of Fidel Castro's brother Raúl), Grandin's piece reminds us that U.S. politicians have long found ways to mobilize versions of Castro to suit their own ends.

Depicting the most recognizable symbol of global Latin America, the authors and illustrators Kiyoshi Konno and Chie Shimano show how Ernesto "Che" Guevara has become an icon for rebellion across spectrums of geography and ideology, from Marxist revolutionaries fighting global capitalism to disgruntled adolescents defying heavy-handed parents.

Combining fresh ideas with unfamiliar narratives, these chapters spur us to look at time and history through the lenses of the Latin American past and the global present. We are obliged to challenge simple vectors between the past and the present and the certainty of a seemingly more modern and better future just down the line. We find precedent for such alternative ways of thinking in the cyclical cosmology of the Mexica Aztec Empire, which rose and fell in modern-day Mexico in the century before the Europeans arrived in Tenochtitlan (today's Mexico City) in 1521. We find that same cyclical time as we read and reread the Nobel Prize–winning Colombian author Gabriel García Márquez's *One Hundred Years of Solitude,* which traces the porosity of time over seven generations of the Buendía family. For those familiar with and new to Latin America alike, "The Latin American Past in the Global Present" encourages expansive thinking about the passage of time and the borders that serve both to separate and to connect *before, now,* and *then.*

This and all part introductions were written by Andrew Britt.

ONE

Looking at the Past and the Future without Fear

AN INTERVIEW WITH RICARDO LAGOS

Matthew Gutmann

How has Latin America had a significant impact around the world, economically, politically, culturally?[1]

Ricardo Lagos: The most important contributions of Latin America to the world have not necessarily been in the social sciences but instead in literature, in painting, in music, perhaps even in the kitchen. From Mexican tacos distributed throughout the United States to the most sophisticated, contemporary Peruvian cuisine, right? What I mean is that, as Carlos Fuentes liked to say and Mario Vargas Llosa[2] says, too, the intellectual and cultural worlds have played a larger role in making Latin America what it is than its politicians have.

However, I would say that, despite this, Latin America has undergone a learning process. And we have learned, first, that many of the theories taught abroad have to pass through the sieve of our own reality. Beginning with John Maynard Keynes's *General Theory of Employment, Interest and Money* (1936)—Keynes called his theory "general," although it was only general for countries like those in which Keynes lived and not for the rest of the world. Second, in many cases when these theories pass through the sieve of our own reality they become, instead of a general theory, one that is particular to the developed world. It has been hard for us to understand this because, in many instances, we want to mechanically apply ideas from the social sciences. If one tries to mechanically apply Max Weber, we find that Weber was thinking about a German reality that is very different from our own.

Then what can the rest of the world learn from the process that Latin America has gone through in understanding and applying external theories?

From the economic perspective, two interesting phenomena occurred. First, the phenomenon of the transition from dictatorships to democracies, although even in democracy we have learned that if there aren't sensible macroeconomic policies in place, then the economy will give us a hard time. I have always said that the most important thing about Alfonsín [Raúl Alfonsín, president of Argentina, 1983–89]—who was undoubtedly one of the most respected democrats because he was able reestablish democracy in Argentina[3]—is that his government suffered from poor economic management, which obliged him to end his presidency six months early. The result was that we began to take macroeconomics much more seriously. And if you think about it carefully, although the Washington Consensus[4] was in fashion at the time, we also learned that the Washington Consensus only mentioned us in relation to the "trickle down" effect and the need for public policies. It was one thing to implement solid macroeconomic policies, but it was also important to understand that the Washington Consensus was not useful in helping us improve the social situation of our people.

That said, it is also important to note that because we had the Tequila Crisis,[5] the currency depreciation crisis in Brazil, the currency depreciation crisis in Argentina after Carlos Menem [president, 1989–99]—each of these crises caused a regional crisis—and we had so many crises that we learned the importance of having an effective financial system. Perhaps this explains why our financial systems were able to resist the 2008 financial crisis. I don't know if this means that we were able to teach the world something, it's just to say that we had learned from previous crises how to execute the necessary tasks in the new one.

And today we can say that we didn't cause this crisis. We can declare ourselves innocent of this, the biggest of all the crises. Also, as a result of previous crises—and this is an advertisement—we learned how to implement countercyclical policies. We learned that if we Latin Americans have to depend on soya prices, petrol prices, copper prices, and other commodities whose prices fluctuate greatly, there was also another possibility. The possibility to have the so-called structural surplus budget. By this I mean that the fiscal budget should use structural determinants of income, like taxes, as a fraction of potential GDP [gross domestic product] established by an independent technical committee. These policies mean that when commodity prices are low, we spend as though the cost were the long-term cost, which is much higher. However, when the price is very high we spend less because the long-term price is lower.

In Chile, we applied these policies in 2000, 2001, and 2002, when the price of copper was only 60 cents per pound but we used the price of 89 cents. When this same pound of copper reached a price of $3.00, we could spend as though it cost $1.19, both established by the Committee. And why am I telling you this? Because when the 2008 crisis came along, the Chilean government had savings of about 40, 50 percent of our yearly GDP, and we could therefore implement countercyclical policies and spend more. We spent 4 percent of GDP supporting the neediest sectors, simply withdrawing from our savings; we didn't have to ask for financial support from anywhere else.

And these savings were not the result of the Chicago Boys[6] either?

Right, because it wasn't the Chicago Boys who implemented them. So, we have to talk about the Chicago Boys, who dominated the scene especially during the dictatorship [1973–90] when it was relatively easy to justify their policies. When you explain their policies, when you decide to open your economy as we did in Chile, for example, and you go from 170,000 textile workers to 30,000, well that has an enormous impact from the perspective of employment, and one that happens in less than a year, in the 1980s. So, I would say that our policies were part Washington Consensus and part of the reestablishment of democracy, which is when we realized that many aspects of the Washington Consensus were just common sense. However, there were assumptions that were not common sense and did not work.

For example, even if the trickle-down effect existed, it was in the very long term and was therefore not compatible with our immediate problems. Now, what we did learn was how to create well-targeted social policies, although in those years the International Monetary Fund and the World Bank did not like these words. In 1990, as minister of education, I realized that in the majority of schools along the coast there were only girls or very few boys above the age of fourteen, because the boys went to work with their fathers in the boats. However, in other parts of Chile, such as the Valle Central, I encountered schools where there were only boys because all the girls over fifteen went with their mothers to harvest fruit.

There wasn't anywhere for them to work. So, based on these experiences, I said, "Why don't we create a program for people who are extremely poor? We will offer a grant that will allow parents to support themselves a bit better so that children won't have to go fishing with their fathers or harvesting with their mothers." This experience—"grant" is a big word for such a small amount of money, but it was enough to incentivize parents to keep their children in school. Later, in 1993, Cardoso [Fernando Henrique Cardoso, president of Brazil, 1995–2003] named Paulo Renato de Souza as his minister of education, and Paulo Renato asked me, "What can I learn from Chile?" And I told him about this experience. That was the origin of Brazil's Bolsa Escola program. Bolsa Escola then spread to other countries.

Another example is when we decided that to address the issue of extreme poverty we would create a program called Chile Solidario, where we would work with the poor to teach them their rights. Through this experience we discovered that it is one thing to say that we are going to create laws to protect the rights of the poor and quite another that the poor understand that there are laws that work in their favor.

Has this been a model outside of Latin America as well?

Chile Solidario? I would say yes, through the World Bank, which decided to disseminate the model. It is funny: the World Bank told me they wanted to celebrate, in quotation marks, the ten-year anniversary of Chile Solidario at a large forum that did take place at the World Bank. Simply because they understood that it had been a really worthwhile program. Now, why had it been worthwhile? When you are president and you issue an invitation to the presidential palace, everyone comes. And there were people from the Right, from the Left, and I said, "Gentlemen, we know who the poor are in Chile, we know where they live, so what do we do to end poverty?" Some said, "Send them a check," others said, "Send them social workers," and it was a big debate. In the end, I decided that sending a check would be insulting to people's dignity; it wasn't just about clientelism, it was about people's dignity, so we chose the social workers. We chose a different way of working.

The result: a social worker would visit each family and tell them, "I'm here to teach you what rights you have as a result of your social situation." As a woman once told me, "I never knew that, as a result of my poverty, I had certain rights. I didn't dare go to the municipality and say, "Help me, I'm poor." So, I think that one could say that from the economic and social perspectives, we have learned a lot.

Of course, there was also the financial crisis and the G7 that Chirac [Jacques Chirac, French president, 1995–2007] timidly wanted to turn into the G14, so he would invite the BRICs, Brazil, India, and China. Well, it became the G20 after the 2008 crisis. I still find it picturesque that it was

President [George W.] Bush who first called the G20 together in Washington, D.C. I don't think that there was anything further from his mind before the crisis than the notion of having a G20 rule the world. But the depths of the crisis necessitated a much wider world.

What about the role of Argentina, Brazil, and Mexico representing the other Latin American countries? Do you think this has been special in the G20 or not?

Yes and no, yes and no. I think that in many cases, we have had to contribute to criticisms of the Washington Consensus, because after the crises the issue was the need to revive the world economy. The 2009 G20 in London was very good when, in half an hour, the group agreed that the International Monetary Fund, which had capital worth $250 billion, should become $750 billion instead. Because now the developed countries needed the Fund to save Europe. Right? Something that had been impossible to achieve during the past twenty years—that to arrive at the $750 billion, the Special Drawing Rights [supplementary foreign exchange reserve assets managed by the IMF] would be $250 billion. China supplied $50 billion of these funds because China is interested in special rights that may eventually allow it to become the international currency of the future, instead of the dollar.

The 2009 G20 was decisive because similar policies existed between the United States and Europe to revive the economy. But it was in Pittsburgh in 2010 when those policies were developed. Obama was still saying, as he does today, although perhaps a bit more timidly, that we needed to reactivate the economy and Merkel [Angela Merkel, German chancellor, 2005–] was saying that the problem was inflation and austerity was the answer. And this provoked the end, I think, of a common politics in the G20 and it lost its relevance, its ability to face the crisis. And it was then, unfortunately, that Latin America, despite being in favor of Obama's policies—it didn't express this viewpoint with a single voice, with enough force. If you push me a little bit, I would say that we haven't really taken full advantage of our position in the G20 where, if we have three countries, we technically make up 15 percent of the group.

DEMOCRACY AND DEMOCRATIC MODELS

Politically, we obviously talk a lot about Latin America when we speak about democracy, about democratic models. Many political analysts who study Latin America suggest that it is an example for the rest of the world, including in the sense of showing how to end dictatorships and arrive at a democracy, to achieve real democratic participation. What do you think?

I think two things. One, the ways in which we moved from dictatorial systems to democracy worked well in some cases, but it is certainly a slow process. If we take the case of Chile, I mean, the context in which these changes happen are very different. I liked to say to my Spanish friends, "You waited until Franco[7] had died." We achieved the transition while our Franco was still alive and commander in chief of the army. So it was a little different, right? But, that said, each context is different. In Argentina, the context was different because the transition happened in the context of the implosion resulting from the Falkland Islands disaster.[8] In our case, the transition happened based on Pinochet's constitution because it called for a plebiscite,[9] and we thus defeated him in a plebiscite included in his own constitution. Chile is different.

Today in Chile, the man who was the head of Pinochet's secret police has been sentenced to four hundred years in jail, and he's still in prison. In other words, there is also something to show. The commissions created by Aylwin [Patricio Aylwin, president of Chile, 1990–94], the Rettig Report, published by the National Commission for Truth and Reconciliation, well, those who worked on that later went to work with Mandela [Nelson Mandela, president of South Africa, 1994–99]. Aylwin's commission was first. But what the South Africans did was something that wasn't done in Chile, that if you admitted to your crimes, you gained automatic amnesty. That's an important point. If I go and I admit that there was torture, that you tortured, that I tortured, they can't incriminate me. So, for admitting the truth, you gained amnesty. It wasn't like that in the Chilean case because the courts could sentence you.

During my presidency, we appointed a presidential commission on political prisoners and torture—it is important to note that very few countries in the world have done investigations into political prison and torture. There are commissions on political killings, on the detained-disappeared, but there are so many people who were imprisoned and tortured. It's hard. It opens wounds. How do I do it? What we decided to do was say that the commission would establish the truth about what had happened, but it wouldn't bring people to justice. It's one thing to establish the truth and say, yes, you were tortured and we must therefore remove your criminal record on Interpol because you were in prison not as a criminal but because you were politically persecuted by the dictatorship. Very well. Now, if you want justice in regard to what you testified about before the commission, you have to go to and testify in court, and the court has the power to bring the torturer to justice if necessary. Do you understand the distinction?

This distinction allowed us to create a report on political prison and torture, which is a form of teaching. Now, reading the document, reading the report, it's a trip through hell. There are details about the places where people were detained, and these places are classified according to the kinds of torture that took place in them, because there were different kinds of torture in each place. But, in this sense, I think that the democratic models that emerge are also different. Today I would say that it is in a country like Brazil where you have the most democracy and the least democracy, when you choose a union leader as your president. I don't think that anybody thought that, fifteen years after democracy was established, Lula [Luiz Inácio Lula da Silva, 2003–11] would be the president of Brazil, or Dilma [Dilma Rousseff, 2011–], a woman and former militant of a guerrilla group. Or that you would have in Chile, sixteen years after Aylwin, that is, after the transition, a woman elected twice as the president of Chile.

And keep in mind that in Chile there wasn't serious debate around the idea that a woman could be president. I think why it happened is because there were two women who were in the best position to succeed me. Both had been members of my cabinet.

In Latin America there have been many women presidents. Not in the United States yet.

Not yet.

And why would that be?

Because they chose a black man first, an African American. I think that the 2008 elections were going to be a first because it was either going to be an African American or a woman. So, there was an important step. Now, I think that in Latin America a few of these women such as Evita Perón [1919–52] in her time, then Isabelita Perón [1974–76], both were wives of President Perón. The wives of former presidents. One could say something similar, more respectfully, about Cristina Fernández de Kirchner [president of Argentina, 2007–]. But I think that, in any case, Latin America has been able to advance more quickly in this sense.

Another generation, no?

Another generation, a generation for which the coup was what was in history books. And they were shocked to see what they saw, the movie *No*[10] and all of those stories. So, the question that one poses is, in what moment do countries feel mature enough or strong enough to look at the past without fear, not to hide anything under the carpet? The Spanish are only recently daring to look into what happened during the Civil War. These days you can't travel the world without democratic credentials, without the credentials to say, "In my country we have a democracy, I'm a product of democracy, I was elected president, I didn't force my way into power." And I think that this is an important step forward. Now, how are things going to progress in the future? It's hard, it's hard. Why? Because these new generations aren't scared because they didn't live through the fear of the dictatorship and, therefore, they demand a lot more. It's a different way of approaching things.

Look, the coup d'état happened in 1973, and 20 years after the coup, in 1993 with Aylwin as president, very few in the media dared to show or write about the past. And 25 years after, in 1998, the media were still careful to present the real picture. After 30 years (2003), I thought that we had to do something to remember what happened in the Palace and we opened the door of La Moneda,[11] through which they had carried out Allende's body, and in spite of that fact, the media showed a little bit more of the 1973 events. But 40 years after the coup: an explosion on TV, suddenly there were *telenovelas, radioteatros,* there was everything. And they showed images that Chileans had never seen on public TV before. Why did Chilean society, 40 years after the coup, dare to look at the coup through different eyes?

THE FAMOUS FINGER: "WAS THAT *IT*?"

I've told this story a few times. I was with my grandchildren at an *asado,* a barbecue, and suddenly one of them says to me, "Hey, Grandpa, what is this story about the finger and Pinochet?" Well, I'm a little tired of the story, and so I told them, "It's on YouTube." And they said, "Oh, on YouTube, let's go watch it on YouTube!" They were excited to watch the video.

But then you could see the disappointment in their faces when they looked at me and said, "Grandpa, was that *it*? Getting annoyed with someone on TV isn't anything special. Everyone gets annoyed on TV." Can you

FIGURE 1.1. During a television appearance in 1988, President Lagos took the risk of pointing his finger in accusation against the Chilean dictator Augusto Pinochet. Internet reproduction from TV broadcast.

believe that's what they told me? But it's the context[12] that changes all the meaning.

Do you think that there is something to learn from Latin America in regard to the practice of democracy, about genuine and not only formal participation?

Well, that's a really important topic. Two things. One, in many of our countries we've already been able to establish state financial support for candidates in elections. And, as a result, they passed laws about this, and I remember very clearly when I asked a deputy from the lower house of Congress how much was spent in the last election. He told me, and I then questioned him, if he could really run with so little money. "Yes, it was enough," he said. "I didn't need to raise any extra money." And in the last presidential elections, for example, this worked and it worked relatively well. There is private money, but there's more than that, too.

The subject of participation is perhaps more difficult. Why? Because you have a rising middle class. If you go around the world saying proudly that you eliminated poverty, or that poverty has decreased significantly, well, those who raised themselves out of poverty consider themselves middle class and they have other demands, other needs. And they thus demand participation. So, if you go around the world saying, "Look here, today of the students in higher education or high school, seven out of ten are first generation." Well, those seven have computers and the rest of it, they have a different set of demands from those that there were twenty years ago. How do we satisfy these demands? How do you find a civilized way to resolve these demands so that it is not necessary to go to the Plaza to protest? Because, until now, the only way to make demands was to go the Plaza to protest.

What about the student movement?

What happened in Chile was shocking, especially because of the force that the movement had. And this force was due to two factors. First, it was more a movement of the middle classes than the working classes. The majority of protests didn't involve the very poor, because they were entitled to fellowships that paid their tuition. And second, when it occurred to the students one weekend to say, "We are going to march this weekend so that our parents can come with us to our protest." Well, it ended up being a huge civic party because the parents went, of course, and they brought the babies because there wasn't anyone to leave them with, and others came with their grandmothers. And you were there, and you saw people in jeans, in uniforms, in everything. But you also saw people with different demands.

So the question was, what demands are going to arise? Is it going to be possible to say, look, if a law passes in Parliament, I want us, the people who are the owners of popular sovereignty, to be able to revoke the law because we don't like it? In a few well-established democracies, if you can gather a significant number of signatures on a petition you can demand a binding plebiscite and revoke the law. Wow. Wow. I want to see the legislation of a congress that knows that the people can revoke the laws it passes. Wow. In Peru, for example, or in Venezuela's constitution, halfway through your presidency, in Peru halfway through your term as mayor, the people can demand a revocation of your mandate. Now, the way one governs becomes completely different. Because each political reform has an impact on the way you govern.

If I know I was elected president for six years and that three years into my term the people can revoke my presidency, well, I'll wait to pass contentious reforms until after the three years. In other words, governance takes on a different form, right? It's not free. You can't just come along and make a decision—it sounds really democratic that halfway through your presidency you can have your power revoked. But it has political consequences. It's going to lead to a different way of governing.

President Peña Nieto [Enrique Peña Nieto, Mexico, 2012–] told me, "You have to pass all the reforms in your first year because in the next five you have to implement them. Otherwise, you're a failure." And he's tried, no? To pass reforms very quickly. So, you realize that it's a complicated topic. OK. What is participation going to look like? Which political institutions will emerge? And Latin America has offered a few, no? Well, Hugo Chávez's [president of Venezuela, 1999–2013] constitution in Venezuela established that halfway through your presidency you can— and I think that now, many of the protesters and whatnot, they are thinking more about revoking Maduro's [Nicolás Maduro, president of Venezuela, 2013–] mandate after three years than actually going to vote now.

May we talk more about how all of this might be meaningful for the rest of the world?

I think that if there are these kinds of institutions in the rest of the world, Latin America will have something to export. Note that the PT [Workers' Party] in Brazil introduced participatory budgeting at the municipal level long before the PT won the presidency with Lula. This was already a trademark of the PT in the municipalities that they controlled, like Porto Alegre. So they asked businessmen, "Aren't you scared of Lula?" Many of them said, "No, because now I have participation in local government when before nobody asked me anything."

Now, this little machine, the Internet, also allows face-to-face, no? In Santiago, on the website of my foundation we have a thing called the Quinto Poder. Obviously, this is because the press is the Fourth Estate, so the Internet is the Fifth Estate. Well, in the Quinto Poder, there was, for example, a discussion that cyclists—where there aren't bike lanes, they can ride on the sidewalk, right? "Well," one mayor said, "no, they can't ride on the sidewalk because there are people walking on sidewalks." And there was a debate. And then the cyclists said, "Next Saturday, we are all going to ride our bikes to go protest to the governor." Well, to everyone's surprise over one thousand cyclists arrived at his office. I don't need to add that the deputies quickly sent a bill to resolve the problem.

It's one thing for people to be annoyed and talking on social media, on Twitter. But it's another when you say things face-to-face. When people said, "Why don't we protest on our bicycles?," and others saw the physical magnitude of the protest, well, there was a change. In other

FIGURE 1.2. Che Guevara image on the cap of a man in Shanghai, 2013. Photo by Matthew Gutmann.

words, I think this is an example where perhaps in Latin America, as a result of having arrived later to the discussion about transitions from dictatorships to democracy, we have been able to keep an open mind and keep advancing toward greater participation. I would say that this is an area in which Latin America is rather advanced, in regard to civil participation.

CHE

I'm looking for a photograph to ask you a very different kind of question. I took this photo in Shanghai last fall, and it prompts me to ask you why Che's image, his symbol, is so widely seen all over the world?

Because Che embodied rebellion. Lots of people embody rebellion and, precisely because he was a rebel, he was successful, but also a practitioner who was president of the Central Bank of Cuba.

That's a part of his story many people don't know about.

But people do know that he was up there with Fidel at the pinnacle of power. And they do know that once he arrived at the pinnacle of power he said, "I've completed my task in Cuba, now I'm going to the Sierra Maestra, to another Sierra Maestra, to participate in the revolution in Africa." So, he went to Africa, and then to other places, and he ended in Bolivia; we all know how his story ended. Those of us who are older know where we were when Kennedy was assassinated; we also know where we were when we heard of Che's death in Bolivia. I was climbing a staircase as the recently appointed director of the School of Political Science, and the president of the students told me, "They killed Che in Bolivia!" I couldn't believe it.

I think that above and beyond the photo, the icon, is another theme. That famous photo. There are lots of stories about the photo, how it happened, why is he in it? The photo is about utopia, rebellion, and the need to take risks. It's clearly not only about what happened to him because when he ends up as an image on T-shirts around the world, it's not just the photograph. It's Che's history. Che the romantic. It's the romance of it.

Does that apply to Latin America more generally?

There are lots of romantic parts. Think about what the rest of the world thought of Fidel Castro's revolution at the end of the 1950s, beginning of the 1960s. The Cuban Revolution clearly captured the world's imagination. Afterward, it took different directions, other paths.

Well, if you are a revolutionary you have to die young.

It's good that he knew to die at the age of thirty-three.

MESTIZAJE

What can we learn from Latin America about el mestizaje?

Oh, how interesting. But is there only one Latin America in this sense? Or are there various? Was *mestizaje* in Brazil, between whites and blacks, the same as in other parts of Latin America, *mestizaje* of the Indians and the Spanish? I've always noticed the drastic difference between the indigenous population and the white population in Peru, for example. It's the same in our country as well. But not with as much force. And I think that this is because all those who consider themselves white, or have Spanish last names, know that they have some Mapuche blood. As Carlos Fuentes said, we are all immigrants in Latin America because the first immigrants arrived through the Bering Strait. And now they are saying that there were others who came from the South, no? Through Antarctica. Otherwise it would be hard to explain how human beings were in Puerto Montt 14,000 years before Christ. They say it would have taken longer to arrive in Puerto Montt through the Bering Strait, and they've started to uncover evidence that Antarctica was attached to South America and they therefore arrived from there on an ice bridge.

We do know that these people arrived 15,000 years ago, and they obviously didn't have passports, but they arrived, and then the Spanish came later. And then the Afro-Americans arrived as slaves, 400 to 350 years ago. And that's when the mixing started, and it was related to how people adapted themselves. Then there's that famous scene when the Spanish conquerors say to Atahualpa, "This is the Bible. God speaks in this book." And the guy grabs it, puts it to his ear and says, "I can't hear anything." It's dramatic, this clash of two cultures, they were so stunned. That's how the two came together.

Here in the United States, the colonialists didn't come to conquer or to evangelize. They arrived simply to have the right to a religion, a right they didn't have in their country. And therefore there was no interest in evangelizing the natives. Here the natives ran away. And they were also massacred.

And it is a *mestizaje* that is also about the Spanish that you speak. That's why the Real Academia Española accepts *argentinismos, chilenismos,* and the rest of it. But there is only one language. It is different in Portuguese. Many books that are published in Portuguese are translated into "Brazilian." That is, the language spoken in Brazil today is different from that spoken in Portugal. They are different books. But in the Spanish case, the Spanish is the same. And what is Latin America for the rest of the world? We speak through the arts of our poets, novelists, musicians, and painters.

CLIMATE CHANGE

Climate change is a challenge that you have dedicated many years to, and it's a topic that is immensely important in the world. I want to know whether there are green paradigms in Latin America from which we can learn in other parts of the world?

I think that the first Latin American issue has to do with something particular to Latin America, which is deforestation. I mean, of the total global emissions 20 percent is from deforestation, but in Latin America 49 percent of total emissions come from deforestation. And I'm going to tell you something that is even more unbelievable. All of the carbon emissions produced by the Brazilian economy, that is, its GDP, are 800,000 tons of carbon dioxide. Deforestation accounts for 1,000,000 tons. That is, deforestation in Brazil contributes more to carbon dioxide emissions than the emissions produced by the Brazilian economy. It's unbelievable. What I do think is that Latin America could take a big step to become a sort of soft power to the rest of the world, to say, "Look, I've reduced deforestation." Why? Because reducing deforestation means that, especially in the Brazilian case, deforestation has been undertaken mostly to create space for agriculture or big hydroelectric dams or mining. Of course, Brazil's leadership is fundamental because of the theme of the Amazon. It's true that ten South American countries possess a part of the Amazon, but the Amazon's true number one is Brazil. Brazil is the star, right? There is clearly a network of Amazonian countries, but the star is Brazil.

Now, on the other hand, Latin America as a whole clearly has to play a role in the issue of climate change. I think that in order to advance, Latin America also has to stop pretending that countries that aren't the most developed have the right to keep emitting whatever we like because I think that in the future this won't be very feasible. That is, we are all going to need to contribute, especially a continent that is economically successful, for which things are going well. The question of the twenty-first century is going to be, "Tell me: how much do you pollute? You go around the world proudly saying, 'Look, I've got a per capita of $15,000, and at this rate, I'll soon achieve $20,000 per citizen.' What are your greenhouse gas emissions per capita?" That is going to be the mark of your civility or incivility.

And has Latin America been a pioneer in any way with regard to climate change?

I think that in terms of technological innovation, Latin America hasn't contributed much. There have been some processes of adaptation in Latin America, adaptation to natural phenomena that aren't necessarily related to climate change. Now, will there be a process of adaptation to climate change or only relief efforts? The Caribbean countries obviously have a lot to say on that topic because for them relief efforts are really important, right? But I also think that countries like the United States are going to have to start undertaking more relief efforts. Someone told me that

Hurricane Sandy had a bigger impact in the United States than one thousand climate change conferences. It caused people to say, "It looks like this climate change might actually be serious," right?

We'll see if any of this means anything.

LATIN AMERICA'S CULTURAL WEALTH

Let's return to Latin America's literature, paintings, language, music, and telenovelas. What has Latin America's impact been? A few days ago Gabriel García Márquez died [17 April 2014], which makes it all the more poignant to try to understand these questions.

I think that is true. I think it's true that there is great wealth in Latin America and that this wealth has been exported, like Che, for example. This wealth, and perhaps Che has to do with this as well, is part of a romantic culture. The romance of the man who sells bars of ice, or mirrors, whatever the case may be. Artisans and all that. I think that Latin America has a great wealth in that sense.

I don't think García Márquez invented magical realism [see Stavans this volume]. Instead, he was a magician because of his ability to write about reality. It's a different thing. Because he imagined the things he imagined. Let me tell you a story about a dinner that we had. García Márquez told us that he had a friend who read his works before they were published, and when he finished the novel *The General in His Labyrinth,* about Simón Bolívar, his friend says, "Hey, people are going to say you are lying because you say that the general, alone, abandoned by everyone, isn't able to sleep, so after his meal he goes for a stroll, and he is walking along, awaiting the next day when he will be able to travel to the Caribbean by boat along the Magdalena River, when he sees a full moon rising between the trees. Who told you, Gabo [affectionate nickname for García Márquez], that there was a full moon that night?"

"I just came up with it," García Márquez replies. "Who is going to refute that there was a full moon?" "Did you know that there was a full moon that night?" "No, no, I didn't," he responds. "But the world knows whether there was a full moon or not." "Who knows that?" "The Royal Observatory of Greenwich, in the United Kingdom. Write to them." So, García Márquez told us that he wrote to the Royal Observatory to ask whether on that day in 1831 there had been a full moon. And in those days, one sent letters, and the answer took time. Waiting for the postman to arrive, he said that he was like a groom awaiting his bride. He would approach the window every time he saw the postman to see whether there was a letter for him. But it was only electric bills and that kind of thing. After about forty days, he received an envelope: "Royal Observatory of Greenwich." He didn't dare open it, but finally he did. There had been a full moon that night!

Perhaps we Latin Americans are, for some reason, richer in this sense of romantic culture and in regard to the other things we talked about earlier.

NOTES

1. This interview with President Lagos was conducted on 21 April 2014, in Providence, Rhode Island, by Matthew Gutmann. The conversation was transcribed and translated by Yelena Bide and edited by Matthew Gutmann and Ricardo Lagos.

2. Carlos Fuentes (1928–2012) was an essayist and novelist from Mexico who was part of the *boom* generation of Latin American authors in the 1960s and 1970s. The Peruvian Mario Vargas Llosa (1936–) also occupied a key role in the *boom* generation and was recognized for his fiction and nonfiction with the Nobel Prize in Literature in 2010.

3. Alfonsín won the presidency in 1983 as a member of the Radical Party, becoming the country's first democratically elected majority president in nearly forty years. His administration took power from a brutal military junta that relinquished its grip in the face of a devastated economy, military defeat in the Falkland, or Malvinas, Islands, and mounting popular opposition. Alfonsín played a central role in the opposition movement, helping to found in 1977 the Permanent Assembly for Human Rights. As president he established the National Commission on the Disappearance of Persons to investigate crimes under the military dictatorship.

4. The Washington Consensus originated as a set of ten policy prescriptions offered by the English economist John Williamson in 1989 to steer what U.S. and international financial institutions (most based in Washington, DC) saw as necessary stages for economic growth. Including recommendations for financial and trade liberalization, privatization, and deregulation, the framework espoused intensified integration into the international economy and macroeconomic stability. This neoliberal view of economic growth has shaped approaches to development in Latin America and other regions over the past three decades, though many economists and politicians have levied strong critiques against the Consensus philosophy as the best approach for so-called developing countries.

5. In December 1994 the Mexican government devalued its national currency, the peso, in response to political instability and warning signs of capital flight. The

devaluation sparked a financial crisis that pulled the country into a recession with soaring inflation and a peso at half of its original value. Also known as the "Peso Crisis," the Tequila Crisis sent shockwaves throughout Latin America and other emerging markets and prompted the United States and the International Monetary Fund to offer a bailout package.

6. The "Chicago Boys" were a crew of economists from Latin America trained mostly at the University of Chicago (under Milton Friedman and Arnold Harberger) and the Pontifical Catholic University of Chile. With roots in the U.S. State Department's "Chile Project" of the 1950s, the influence of this group rose especially during the early years of General Augusto Pinochet's reign (1973–90), when the new government adopted the Chicago Boys' neoliberal program of deregulation, privatization, and other free market policies.

7. After successfully overthrowing a republican government in the brutal Spanish Civil War from 1936 to 1939, General Francisco Franco (1892–1975) established a totalitarian state that lasted until his death. Franco's successor, Prince Juan Carlos (grandson of Spain's former king), initiated Spain's transition to a constitutional monarchy in the late 1970s.

8. In April 1982 the military junta in Argentina sent soldiers to invade the Malvinas, or Falkland, Islands, a remote colonial outpost of Britain. The effort to resuscitate the flagging regime through an anti-imperialist and nationalist campaign elicited a surprisingly strong reaction from Margaret Thatcher's government. The ten-week conflict ended in humiliation for the dictatorship in Argentina, which subsequently yielded to civilian rule.

9. Mass opposition to Chilean dictator Pinochet mounted throughout the 1980s. Pressure from the democratic movement forced concessions from Pinochet, who called for a plebiscite—a vote by all members of the nation—on his rule in October 1988. Chileans voted down another term for Pinochet by 54.6 percent.

10. A 2012 film directed by Pablo Larraín and starring Gael García Bernal about advertising tactics used in the plebiscite of 1988.

11. La Moneda is a block-long palace and seat of the president of the Republic of Chile. As President, Lagos opened some of the inner courtyards to the public in 2000, as soon as it was inaugurated, and restored Morandé 80, a door on the side of the palace that symbolizes a democratic Chile. It was this door that was opened in 2003.

12. The specific context here was Lagos's 25 April 1988 appearance on the program *De cara al país,* one of the few sites for public political discourse and opposition in Pinochet's Chile at the time. Lagos, who had become leader of the recently created Partido por la Democracia (PPD), levied direct criticism against Pinochet's abuses of power and urged support for a "No" vote in the 1988 plebiscite that would ultimately lead to the dictator's removal from office.

TWO

The Conversion of Francis

THE FIRST LATIN AMERICAN POPE AND THE
WOMEN HE NEEDS

Nancy Scheper-Hughes and Jennifer Scheper Hughes

ON 12 MARCH 2013 Cardinal Jorge Mario Bergoglio of Buenos Aires entered the Vatican papal conclave in Rome with a heavy heart. He had just resigned as cardinal archbishop of Buenos Aires and had already chosen a simple room in an Argentine retirement center for Catholic clerics when he was suddenly summoned to the Vatican following the scandalous resignation of Pope Benedict XVI (b. Joseph Ratzinger).[1] Instead, he would be sequestered with 114 other cardinals until they reached a divinely inspired consensus about who would be the next spiritual and political leader of an estimated 1.2 billion Catholics, 40 percent of whom live in Latin America.

Two days before the opening of the papal conclave, Cardinal Bergoglio took a solitary walk through Rome's historic district dressed incognito in the black cassock of a simple village priest. On seeing an old friend, Father Thomas Rosica, Bergoglio grabbed his hand, saying, "Please, pray for me." When the acquaintance asked him if he was nervous, Bergoglio replied that indeed he was. Whoever was chosen pope would inherit a bloody, holy mess.

First there was the fallout of decades of papal malfeasance in refusing to acknowledge and respond appropriately and adequately to a clerical child and adolescent sexual abuse scandal that was global, relentless, and continuous (Scheper-Hughes and Devine 2003; Scheper-Hughes 2011).[2] Then there was the "Vatileaks" scandal when Pope Benedict's butler released secret papal documents and communications bearing on the intrigue, cronyism, power struggles, bribes, and money laundering within the most secret banking system in the world, the Vatican Bank .

Finally, there were problems inside the Curia, the Vatican's "royal court" of high-ranking cardinals who oversee church law and Catholic doctrine. Published reports described a dysfunctional gay, homophobic lobby within the Curia. The Vatican double standard requires its gay prelates to be celibate or to be discreet and silent except for taking their sins to the confessional. Together, these events and dilemmas led to the abdication of Pope Benedict, a scholarly and fiercely conservative prelate who owned up to being a poor administrator.[3]

Prior to his papacy, Joseph Ratzinger headed the Congregation for the Doctrine of the Faith, the modern-day heir of the Inquisition. As the guardian of Catholic orthodoxy, Ratzinger was known as "God's Rottweiler" in his defense of the papacy and his close friend and papal predecessor, Pope John Paul II (b. Karol Józef Wojtył). Both men were Central Europeans who came of age during World War II and rose to preeminence in the church during the Cold War. Their worldview was Eurocentric and focused on the evils of Communism and the godless Soviet Union. Both were deeply troubled by a new Marxist-inflected revolutionary theological turn, "liberation theology," within sectors of the post–Vatican II church in Latin America.

Ironically, the two future popes had participated in Vatican II, which was led by Pope John XXIII, who sought to "open the window and let in fresh air" and to reposition the church in the modern world. Rather than being inspired, they became obsessed with the "errors" and "excesses" unleashed by Vatican II, and their papacies were marked by an attempt to reverse reforms that they found excessive. They did not like the inclusion of secular Catholic scholars in discussions of delicate topics such as the celibacy of priests, the ordination of women, contraception, and abortion. And they disapproved of activist priests participating in liberation theology base communities in Latin America that questioned the close ties of the traditional Latin American hierarchy with oppressive ruling classes.

Although liberation theology was never the dominant or hegemonic Catholic theology in Latin America,[4] it was a strong and visible social movement that realigned clergy and nuns in support of the poor and those who spoke on their behalf during civil wars in Central America and military dictatorships in South America in the 1970s and 1980s. Prominent liberation theologians, such as the diocesan priests Leonardo Boff in Brazil and Gustavo Gutiérrez in Peru, wrote influential books that returned Catholic theology to its origins and the roots of Christianity. With the writings of the early desert fathers and the Gospels and teachings of Jesus of Nazareth, they brought renewed attention to a focus on the poor, the lowly, the sick, the stigmatized, and the marginalized. Liberation theology was a uniquely Latin

FIGURE 2.1. The Council Fathers seated during the Second Vatican Council. Photo by Lothar Wolleh. This file is licensed under the Creative Commons Attribution 2.0 Generic license. https://commons.wikimedia.org/wiki/File:Second_Vatican_Council_by_Lothar _Wolleh_003.

American theological revolution that defined Catholicism as a religion of the oppressed.

At the 1968 Medellín Conference of Latin American Bishops, liberation theologians took their message further into what this might mean in terms of everyday pastoral practice. The bishops pledged themselves to a new spiritual-social contract, called the "preferential option for the poor." This contract required a structural realignment of the Latin American church away from its colonial moorings and its favoritism toward the power elites, the landowning and industrial classes. They called for ecclesiastical base communities in favelas and shantytowns where Catholic clergy and laypeople would read and discuss the scriptures as political as well as theological texts. Poverty and hunger were recast as "structural violence" and as social sins to be challenged and expunged. Liberation theology reconciled Christianity and Marxism at a time when right-wing dictators overthrew democratic socialist political leaders with the help of the CIA and the U.S. Congress. From Medellín in 1968, a new liberation theology reoriented the entire Christian project from the northern to the southern hemisphere, untethered the church from the colonial-imperial apparatus to which it had tied itself for more than a millennium, reconciled Christianity and Marxism, and charted a path of redemption for a morally and theologically comprised religion for the Latin American Catholic Church.

While in some circles liberation theology was seen as a shift in the cultivation of a critical, sociological, spiritual imagination, in Nicaragua and Guatemala during the 1980s liberation theology became a veritable call to arms against military dictators. This feet-on-the-ground, "barefoot" theology introduced new exemplars in a generation of beloved "red bishops": Dom Hélder Câmara in Recife; Samuel Ruiz in Chiapas; Sergio Méndez Arceo in Cuernavaca; and the martyr-bishop of El Salvador, Óscar Romero.

Less recognized was the central role of Latin American women theologians, such as the Argentine Marcella Althaus-Reid and the Brazilian ecofeminist Ivone Gebara, and women catechists, often illiterate, almost invariably poor, who organized, led, and mostly populated the ecclesiastical base communities. The feminist theologians, while in sympathy with the liberation theology of Leonardo and Clodovis Boff and Gustavo Gutiérrez, identified a lacuna in the failure of the progressive theologians to recognize and acknowledge the suffering of women, including those who were designated as "sinners" and "indecent" because they were single mothers, traditional midwives, or sex workers who had nowhere else to turn during times of extreme scarcity and crisis. Some of these "deviants" became prominent leaders in liberation base communities.

In response to the wars on "indecency" by the military juntas of the 1960s through 1980s, the Argentine liberation theologian Marcella Althaus-Reid proposed an "indecent theology" that confronted the political trinity of Pope, Nation, and Catholic Family that underpinned the ideology of right-wing military regimes in Latin America. She wrote, "The resurrection [of Christ] was not a theme for our generation. . . . *Los desaparecidos* [among them, kidnapped women and their babies] was our theme."

In Recife, Brazil, Sister Ivone Gebara, a Catholic nun and one of Latin America's leading feminist theologians, wrote and taught from the perspective of ecofeminism and liberation theology. For nearly two decades, Gebara was a professor at ITER, the liberation theology seminary in Recife. Gebara's theology emerged from her work with poor women in the slums and favelas of Recife in the late 1960s during the military dictatorship years. In her first book, *Longing for Running Water: Ecofeminism and Liberation,* Gebara articulated what she called a "theological anthropology" embedded in the struggles of everyday life. The garbage in the street, the nonexistent or inadequate health care, and, above all, the reproductive crises faced by poor women led Gebara to argue for "religious biodiversity," one that was inclusive of women's suffering and needs. She saw reproductive rights for women as linked to environmental and economic sustainability and to the creation of a dignified life.

The papacies of John Paul II and Benedict XVI fought tooth and nail against this Latin American theological "heresy." The two previous popes saw the new Latin American radical theology as a threat to papal authority. They argued that liberation theology was no theology at all but a political project that focused on the "here and now" rather than a spiritual project concerned with the soul and its afterlife. However, liberation theology's greatest threat to papal authority was its empowerment of women as theologians and at the grassroots level as community leaders, catechists, and pastoral counselors and representatives of the new church.

Pope John Paul II and Cardinal Ratzinger, later as Pope Benedict, actively dismantled Latin American liberation theology. In 1984, just as the Brazilian military dictatorship was ending, Ratzinger issued his "Instruction on Certain Aspects of the 'Theology of Liberation,'" which listed the many doctrinal errors and excesses of Vatican II, including its dedication to building a church of the poor.

Thus, in 1985, the Vatican silenced the Brazilian liberation theologian Leonardo Boff and forced Dom Hélder Câmara into retirement. When in October 1989 Ratzinger closed ITER, Dom Hélder's liberation theology seminary, several hundred seminarians, nuns, laypeople, and peasants traveled by foot from the impoverished, drought-ridden interior of Pernambuco to protest, and one of us (Jennifer Scheper Hughes) joined the demonstration. The powerful social movement that was called liberation theology was eventually destroyed, as theologians were disciplined, if not silenced, and young clergy were encouraged to take up a populist and artificial charismatic Catholicism to contest the growth of Pentecostal churches in Latin America. One of the last straws was the attack on the feminist theologians who had never really been incorporated within the male-dominated hierarchy of liberation theology. They were marginalized even by their male colleagues, who, with the exception of Dom Hélder, found them scandalous for addressing in public the sexuality of women in the context of a kind of "green" feminist theology.

Professor Gebara achieved notoriety when the Vatican silenced her for two years in 1995. Her difficulties began in 1993 with an interview she gave to the Brazilian news magazine *VEJA,* in which she said, rather off-handedly, that abortion was not necessarily a sin for poor women. Given the extreme poverty of many women in Brazilian favelas, too many births would only result in more hardship for the mothers and their other children. Moreover, Gebara said to the journalist, overpopulation puts increased stress on natural resources, including decreased access to potable water, one of her main concerns. For these reasons, Gebara called for greater tolerance for women's reproductive rights and needs. The article in its day went viral via television rather than social media. Complaints were raised, and following many discussions throughout 1994, the president of Brazil's Catholic Conference of Bishops of Brazil, Dom Luciano Mendes de Almeida, judged that the case against Gebara as a heretic was closed, citing her deep commitment to, and understanding of, the suffering and pain of poor women. However, the Vatican's Congregation of the Doctrine and Faith disagreed and began an investigation of Gebara's theological writings, interviews, and teaching modules. On 3 June 1995, Gebara was instructed to refrain from speaking, teaching, and writing for a period of two years, during which time she was exiled to France for theological reeducation. Today Professor Gebara is struggling with illness, but she remains totally dedicated to her feminist theology.

ENTER JORGE BERGOGLIO—A VATICAN IN SHAMBLES AND A CATHOLIC CHURCH DIVIDED

Cardinal Bergoglio approached the 2013 papal conclave with anxiety. He had come close to being chosen pope in the 2005 papal conclave that elected Cardinal Joseph Ratzinger. Bergoglio withdrew from the competition and threw his support to Ratzinger when he learned that opponents in Argentina were undermining his candidacy by circulating damning documents about his history as provincial superior of the Jesuits during Argentina's infamous dirty war (1976–83). It was a time of terror when militants and radicals, students and labor leaders, journalists and psychiatrists, priests and nuns who worked and lived with the poor in base communities were kidnapped, interrogated under torture, and disappeared. Those who proved to be useless informants were drugged and thrown semiconscious into the Atlantic Ocean and the Rio Plata, as were others regardless of whether they provided information. The "method" was sanctioned by high-ranking Argentine Catholic prelates as a dignified death, a death at sea. It was a sacrifice of some questionable lives to preserve the *Proceso,* the National Process of Reorganization to make Argentina conform to a right-wing fascist version of Catholicism. Among the tens of thousands of victims were 150 Catholic priests who refused to bend, as well as hundreds of nuns, lay catechists, and religious persons who embraced liberation theology.

Jorge Bergoglio's complex political history begins in 1973 when, as a recently ordained Jesuit priest, he was appointed provincial superior of the Argentine Jesuits at the absurdly young age of thirty-six. Jesuits are the muscular scholars of the Roman Catholic Church. Ordination requires more than a decade of intellectual and spiritual training, often culminating in two doctorates, one in theology and one in another chosen field. It is unheard of that a man so young and inexperienced could be appointed provincial superior of the Jesuits anywhere in the world.

The Vatican put pressure on the superior general of the Jesuits in Rome to stop Argentine Jesuits from following the path of the Jesuits in Central America, Brazil, Chile, and Peru in resisting military regimes. Thus, the left-leaning head of the Jesuits was removed and Father Bergoglio took his place without the support of most of his religious order in Argentina. Given the close relationship between church and state in Argentina, there also must have been some negotiation over Bergoglio's appointment with the declining Peronist government and the Argentine military, waiting in the wings.

Father Bergoglio was a pious priest of conservative political views. He was not a popular superior among the Jesuits, and he was forced out of office in 1979, when he was assigned to serve as rector of the Colegio Máximo in Buenos Aires, where he taught theology. In 1986 he was exiled to Germany under the pretext of completing a second doctoral thesis. On his return to Argentina in June 1990, his period of imposed reflection and penance was not over. The former Jesuit superior was again sent into exile, this time to the city of Córdoba, Argentina, where he spent two solitary years in a small guest house at the Jesuit rectory.

This period, we suggest, was the beginning of the conversion of Bergoglio. During his enforced solitude, Father Bergoglio rarely spoke to anyone. He was even cut off from the other Jesuits with whom he was living. He was coming to terms with his (self-defined) rigid, authoritarian personality that had contributed to his decision to dismiss the two "disobedient" liberation theology Jesuits, Father Franz (Francis) Jalics, his former theology teacher, and Orlando Yorio, who had refused to give up their ecclesiastical base community in a poor parish of Buenos Aires. Bergoglio's decision put the men in mortal danger. Once removed from the protection of the Society of Jesus, the Jesuits were kidnapped, along with several other liberation catechists, by the agents of Admiral Emilio Massera and taken to the Escuela de Mecánica de la Armada (ESMA), where for six months they were tortured and interrogated, then rescued in the nick of time by Father Bergoglio's intercessions in person with both General Videla and Admiral Massera. Bergoglio walked out of the second meeting with Massera saying definitively as he left, "I want them to appear." Soon after, the two Jesuits were removed from their cells and dropped from a plane in a field on the outskirts of Buenos Aires, where they were found drugged, dazed, and in poor physical condition. The others who were kidnapped with them were dropped into the sea. This story has been told many times.

REMEMBER THE WOMEN: THE FIRST CONVERSION OF JORGE BERGOGLIO

Less noted is the failed response of the former Jesuit superior on learning of the disappearances of three women. Two of them were French nuns, originally catechists (catechism teachers) to the mentally "deficient," which included their devoted care for Jorge Videla's young son who had severe and irreversible developmental problems. A third *desaparecida* was Father Bergoglio's former boss and mentor, Esther Ballestrino de Careaga, a chemist in the factory where the future pope worked as a student in 1953–54, just before he decided to enter the priesthood. Over time, the spiritual formation of the nuns and Esther Ballestrino de Careaga changed as it was shaped by liberation theology. They spoke of "an option for the poor," while criticizing General Videla's option for "power, blood, and fire." Videla's secretary-general broke the news of their kidnapping on 13 December 1977, a week before all three were drugged and thrown into the Atlantic Ocean. The bodies of two of the women washed up on shore, to be buried in pauper graves. They were later exhumed and identified by members of the Argentine forensic team.

Several weeks before she and her daughter were kidnapped, Esther Ballestrino contacted Father Bergoglio asking for help when she learned that her daughter, a university student, had been targeted by the military. Bergoglio agreed to come to the family's home and remove and hide any books that might be seen as questionable or subversive. One of the books Bergoglio took away with him was *Das Kapital*. He warned Esther to be prudent, to drive carefully, to wear dark sunglasses, and to be as inconspicuous as possible. This assistance proved to be not so helpful. Both the daughter and, later, her mother were kidnapped. While her daughter was released and survived, Esther was dropped into the ocean.

After his period of seclusion in Córdoba ended, Bergoglio was given another chance and appointed auxiliary archbishop of Buenos Aires in 1992. He emerged as a strong and popular spiritual leader and an effective politician. He moved quickly up the ladder from archbishop to cardinal in 1998. A new Bergoglio began to emerge during this time, a more tolerant and humble prelate, not without contradictions but clearly on a different path. He visited poor *villas* and barrios, he tended to the needs of young clerics, and he became involved in social action on behalf of marginal people, including migrants, street children, and asylum seekers. He collaborated in the founding of a nongovernmental organization (NGO) dedicated to the rescue of displaced refugees and trafficked persons. In 2000, Archbishop Bergoglio made the most difficult voyage of his life, when he paid a visit to Father Jalics in Germany. By all accounts, it was an emotional encounter. Both men wept, embraced and (presumably) forgave each other, and co-celebrated the Mass.[5] However, Pope Francis has not yet made amends to the memory of the Argentine women who died for their faith under his watch.

THE FIRST LATIN AMERICAN POPE

By the time Bergoglio was summoned to Rome for the papal conclave the political climate had changed. The demand for a new dispensation, a petite reformation of the Roman Church and its Curia, was on the top of the agenda. There was talk of selecting a pope from the South: Latin America, Africa, or Asia. However, Cardinal Bergoglio did not enter the conclave as one of the papal finalists. But after a mere twenty-four hours of deliberation the conclave settled on him. When asked if he accepted the vote, Bergoglio did not give the expected ritualized reply, "Accepto." Instead he said, "I am a great sinner; trusting in the mercy and patience of God in suffering, I accept."

When he appeared on the balcony of Saint Peter's Basilica as the new pope, the well-wishers gathered below in Saint Peter's Square were confused. They did not recognize him. But once they heard that the new pope would be known as Pope Francis, they sent up cheers: "Viva Francesco! Viva Francesco!"

Like John Paul II, Francis was a first: the first Latin American pope, the first pope from the Global South, the first Jesuit pope, and the first pope to name himself after Saint Francis, who was never a pope at all. Both of these outsider popes were or are positioned to make decisive public roles in global transitions. The Polish pope, John Paul II, gave his blessing to Solidarność, contributing to the end of the Soviet Union. The Argentine pope has already played a key role in negotiating behind the scenes the dialogues between President Barack Obama and Raúl Castro that promise an end to the U.S. Cold War in Cuba and U.S. meddling with socialist agendas in other Latin American nations.

The Catholic world quickly warmed up to Pope Francis, who was praised for his simplicity, humility, and common touch. The new pope refused all the trappings of popery: the throne and the palace, the lace and rose slippers. This pope wore well-worn black shoes that he carried with him from Buenos Aires. He liked to travel by bus and subway and to cook his own meals. He joined Vatican workers for lunch in the Vatican cafeteria.

His manner is informal, his language colloquial. He soon became famous for his off-the-cuff zingers, especially in the air and between his travels. "I don't know what comes over me," Pope Francis told Antonio Spadaro, the Jesuit editor in chief of *La Civiltà Cattolica,* in August 2013. The pope had just returned from his first and wildly successful international trip to Brazil for World Youth Day. "I did not recognize myself when I responded to the journalists asking me questions [about gay clergy] on the flight from Rio de Janeiro." He famously told the journalists, "If someone is gay and he searches for the Lord and has goodwill, who am I to judge?" He spoke in Italian, but he used the English word *gay* rather than *homosexual.* Another papal first.

What does this auger for Catholics, non-Catholics, and secularists alike? Does "Who am I to judge?" mean that the pope will support gay marriage or that he sees gay priests as sinners who need to seek penance and practice sexual abstinence? When he tells a divorced woman who is sad about not taking Holy Communion, "Go ahead and take it, you have done nothing wrong," is Pope Francis inviting divorced Catholics to participate in all the sacraments, including remarriage? When he affirms the science of evolution and the Big Bang theory of creation, will he rethink the church's ban on new reproductive technologies and stem cell research? When he says that poor women should not have to "breed like rabbits," is he questioning *Humanae vitae,* the papal encyclical that condemned contraception and abortion, or is he demeaning the "second sex" as breeders?

Is Francis a populist pope who is promising bread and circuses to the masses at Mass? Or are his off-the-cuff zingers an attempt to rattle the nerves of the old guard Curia and its conservative and pampered cardinals? Is he offering an open window and breath of fresh air in the style of Pope John XXIII, or is he masking the stale air trapped inside the Vatican? Many Vatican watchers suggest that Pope Francis is a good politician who is trying to please all sides. On the one hand, he clears the way for a possible sainthood for the martyred leftist Archbishop Romero of Salvador. On the other hand, he nominates for sainthood Father Junípero Serra, the despised colonizer of native Californians (Scheper-Hughes 2015).

So, who is Francis? What can a Latin American Argentine pope do for Latin America and for the world?

ONE POPE FOR MANY CATHOLICISMS

Despite the unifying symbol of the Vatican and its pontiff, Latin American Catholics are an unruly lot. There are many versions of Catholicism, with diverse histories and religious traditions. Mexican Catholic piety, forged by the religious and ritual labors of its mestizo population, has little in common with Caribbean Catholic spirituality, shaped as it was by African populations laboring within the constraints of a slave society. Catholicism in Central America, the Andes, and the Amazon has distinct roots that mix Roman Catholicism with indigenous and African religions. Although Brazil, with close to 127 million Catholics, has more Catholics than any other country, many of them are independent and "secular" Catholics. Brazilians term this group "Católico lite," or cultural Catholics (similar to Jews in Latin America). They are Catholics who devote themselves to the rituals and traditions, the saints and the pageantry, but shrug their shoulders at the dogma. Poor Catholic women in the favelas of Brazil pay scant attention to the Vatican prohibitions on contraception and abortion: what do celibate men,

FIGURE 2.2. Pope Francis drinks mate offered by a pilgrim in St. Peter's Square. Photo courtesy of Associated Press.

poor things, know about birthing and raising babies?, they often wonder. The pope can preach a universal doctrine, but it will be differently received. Broad generalizations about the impact of an Argentine pope on Latin America and the world must be parsed through local and regional histories and contexts.

Catholics received the new pope differently in Brazil than in Argentina. Three and a half million Brazilians gathered on Copacabana Beach to watch Francis drive by in his pope mobile. The crowds were euphoric. The pope was seen as *agradável,* personable, intimate, unpredictable, and, most of all, *animado,* full of vitality. "Did you see how he responded to the crowds, how he accepted a gourd of *chá mate* [yerba mate] and slurped it up? He is a man in love with life." Brazilians from the shantytowns thought that they could teach the new pope about their social needs and realities. He was seen as flexible and teachable.

Their president agreed with them. A few weeks earlier, President Dilma Rousseff met with Pope Francis in the Vatican, and she emerged from the thirty-minute conversation to congratulate Argentines on being very lucky to have a pope of their own while jesting that nonetheless God, as everyone knows, is a Brazilian. Although Dilma suffered torture at the hands of Brazil's military dictatorship, which overlapped with Argentina's brutal dirty war, she praised Pope Francis as a charismatic leader and a pope who would speak on behalf of the poorest and the weakest classes and who has the capacity to be moved. His election, she said, was reason for Brazilians, Argentines, and all Latin Americans to be proud. He was good news for Latin America, and good news for the world at large.

In Argentina, however, the new pope's reception was more complex and measured. Familiarity was an obstacle to unmoderated adulation. While some were willing to overlook Bergoglio's shortcomings, and there were certainly celebrations in the street with people shouting, "¡Un Papa Argentino!," some of his former Jesuit colleagues refused to acknowledge the new pope as one of their own. They knew Bergoglio close up and over time and had mixed reactions. The Argentine church remains bitterly divided between an old guard embodied in popular youth movements such as Catholic Action, Acción Católica, and the Catholic Scouts, Opus Dei, and the Legionnaires of Mary and those progressive Catholics who remain faithful to the liberationist church.

The Argentine Catholic Church has always played a strong hand in government affairs, from the church's fights with Juan Perón over the legalization of divorce and prostitution, for which he was excommunicated (and later reconciled), to the church's silence and tacit support of the military junta of President Videla. Then-Archbishop Bergoglio described disputes he had with Presidents Néstor and Fernández Kirchner and over gay marriage in a letter to Carmelite nuns as "a clear rejection of the law of God, engraved in our hearts."

There are two versions of the new pope. The first is found in a carefully orchestrated series of biographies, conversations, and dialogues with Jorge Mario covering the period before and after he became Pope Francis. These are romantic hagiographies that describe a man on his way to sainthood. They deny the critique of Bergoglio's behavior during the dirty war and describe him as a consistent, modest defender of the poor. In his book, *Bergoglio's List* (2014), Nello Scavo dared to compare Jorge Bergoglio to Oskar Schindler, who saved the lives of more than a thousand mostly Polish Jewish refugees during the Holocaust by employing them in his factories. The second and opposing version, a series of essays and books by journalists and the pope's most relentless critic, his bête noir, Horatio Verbitsky,[6] is that Bergoglio was a lackey of the generals during the dirty war (Verbitsky 2006). This view is historically incorrect, and even Verbitsky has retreated somewhat.

We suggest a third view, one of Pope Francis as a "man of tortured complexity" (Vallely 2013) who saved some individuals, but he was no Schindler. His interventions were so discreet, so specific, so late in the game, so personalistic (saving this one but not that one), that it left the pope himself deeply guilt-ridden (Scheper-Hughes 2013).

Even thirty years after the dirty war, in 2010, under the new democratic dispensation, when Bergoglio, now archbishop of Buenos Aires, was called as a witness in the criminal trial of eighteen officers who had worked at ESMA, the Naval Mechanics School, including Admiral Massela, although not a defendant in the case, he was extremely evasive. In his formal deposition he said that he had warned his two Jesuit subordinate elders to abandon their liberation base community work in the slums because some sectors of the military and the official church hierarchy saw their activities as subversive. When they refused his authority as their superior he told the priests that their disobedience meant they could no longer be Jesuits. Bergoglio's responses to questions about his actions on behalf of the French nuns and his former boss, Esther, were perplexing. What did Bergoglio have to lose in giving information recorded in official church archives? The archbishop was not on trial. When asked about the existence of church archives bearing on the deaths of the French nuns and of Esther de Careaga, Bergogio replied, "I suppose so, but I don't know for sure." When asked where these files were located, he said they were in the central archive of the Conference of the Catholic Bishops. "Who supervises the archives?" "I do," Bergoglio said. Could he possibly locate the file? Bergoglio replied, "I can look for it, but I am not sure I can find it."

When asked what he did to rescue his former mentor, Esther de Careaga, when he learned that she had been disappeared, Bergolio said that he tried to locate a family member but they seemed to be in hiding. Had he contacted any public officials about their disappearance? No, because the case fell under the jurisdiction of the archbishop of Buenos Aires, and at the time he was only the provincial of the Jesuits. You knew Ms. de Careaga well? Yes, Bergoglio said. *Bastante,* quite well. Elsewhere in his testimony Bergoglio said that Esther "was a good woman." The question hanging in the air was, "Was this all you could do?"

Bergoglio's confession, like his conversion, is incomplete. His defense that he was young and inexperienced is not convincing. The excuse that he, like Pope Benedict, is not a good administrator is also unconvincing. He has been an administrator for most of his religious life. His defense that he was rigid but that he was neither a right-winger nor a saintly goody two-shoes—just "a poor guy" who made some errors—is as close as Bergoglio gets to making an apology. But he did not sound like a "poor guy at loose ends"[7] when he visited ESMA Commander Emilio Massera demanding that he make the two disappeared Jesuits "appear." He sounded firm and convincing. Massera responded positively. Without that intervention the Jesuits would surely have been selected for extermination by the ESMA executioners. The problem was one of the adequacy and timing of his response to the state of terror.

We suggest that as Pope Francis, Jorge Bergoglio is in the process of spiritual, moral, and political conversion, one that is incomplete. All is naught if he fails to forge a new social contract or a new covenant, as Hannah Arendt defined it in the *Human Condition*. This new covenant is with women, remembering and honoring the female victims of the dirty war who were killed for being "sluts" and their infants kidnapped at birth and given to friends of the junta to raise and to purify the nation while the Argentine church stood by, doing nothing to save them. The failure of the future pope to save his mentor and his good friend, Esther Ballestrino de Careaga, is a case in point.

If Bergoglio was not a Schindler, neither was he a Pope Pius XII, who refused assistance to Jews during the Holocaust. His was a weak response to a major catastrophe. He worked behind the scenes for a small number of Argentine people at risk of being disappeared. He arranged passports and visas and hid some political suspects in his Colegio, describing them as theology students or visitors. He warned those who had been identified to be careful, to be vigilant, to not glance out of their home or car windows, to walk with their heads down, and so on. But he did not condemn the military dictatorship. He did not raise his voice at Mass. He did not threaten to excommunicate the generals. He did not seem to recognize the enormity of the crime, even when his loyal female friend Judge Alicia Oliveria urged him to speak out. The future pope told her that this was not easy to do.

As head of the Argentine Conference of Bishops between 2005 and 2011, Bergoglio resisted pressures to issue a formal apology for the church's actions during the dirty war. Finally, in October 2012, Argentina's bishops, under Bergoglio's leadership, issued a strangely worded apology for failing to protect their flock adequately during the dictatorship. But the "apology" blamed *both* the right-wing generals and the left-wing guerrillas for the years of bloodshed, a grossly inaccurate depiction of what happened. Pope Francis has yet to acknowledge, let alone apologize to, the families of the disappeared. Until his death (in Argentina) Father Yorio held Bergoglio responsible for his kidnapping.

We could use the same words that Francis used in referring to the private lives of gay Catholics, Who are we to judge? Not one of us knows how we might have behaved under the tyranny of the Argentine junta, how we might resist or hide from responsibility during what the anthropologist Michael Taussig might term a culture of terror, and space of death, one that destroyed civil society, solidarity, and decency, when one's own existence, as well as that of those for whom one is responsible, is at stake. Sometimes complicity is very direct, but more often it is indirect, as, for example, in attempts to negotiate with the terrorist, with the dictator, as Father Bergoglio did on behalf of the disappeared Jesuits. Sometimes complicity is disguised as a Realpolitik of letting some go, so that many others might live.

Bergoglio had exemplars in liberation theology priests, nuns, and bishops whose conversion to action during other political and human rights crises was swift and appropriate. As his fellow Jesuit Jon Sobrino states, Jorge Bergoglio was "no Óscar Romero," referring to the archbishop of El Salvador who was murdered by CIA-influenced counterinsurgents in San Salvador on 24 March 1980. Neither was he a Dom Hélder Câmara, the tiny archbishop of Recife, who became an outspoken critic of the military dictatorship (1964–85), daring to suggest that structural violence, poverty, and hunger were sins of the state.

Like Bergoglio, Óscar Romero and Dom Hélder Câmara were exposed to strong fascist tendencies as young priests. But Romero's and Câmara's conversion to liberation theology in response to the threat posed by violent military regimes was immediate and complete. They and other radical prelates broke ranks with the power brokers, defied the government, and publicly criticized the military. For example, Archbishop Romero, once allied with the traditional elites, began driving through city dumps searching among the trash for the tortured and eviscerated victims of the death squads. His sermons became fiery to the extent that Pope John Paul II decided to remove him from office. But the letter of dismissal never reached Romero, who was celebrating Mass when assassins murdered him.

Bergoglio/Francis is trying to do the impossible—to straddle a space in-between, between the legacy of the old colonialist, patriarchal church and the church of liberation theology. This strikes us as a project that will ultimately fail, leaving a legacy of a church at war with itself.

THE FINAL CONVERSION OF POPE FRANCIS

As a political spiritual leader Francis has negotiated a détente between Cuba and the United States. He has welcomed atheists to the table in the task of peacemaking. He has begun to make peace with former theological enemies. He initiated a rapprochement with eighty-five-year-old Father Gustavo Gutiérrez of Lima, Peru, the father of liberation theology, and he lifted the ban on the beatification of Óscar Romero, the first step to sainthood, describing Romero as "a man of God." He also ended the Vatican investigation of feminist Catholic nuns by praising the work that the good sisters do in educating the poor, housing the homeless, and visiting the imprisoned. These important gestures augur well for the global Catholic community and for the family of man. But there is a disturbing and glaring absence at the center of his new papacy: the family of women. He has not reached out to Catholic women theologians.

At present Pope Francis is at a critical juncture. He declared radical feminism one of the most serious dangers facing the modern Catholic Church. Here, Francis is at risk of repeating the same dangerous error, his fear of liberation theology priests. He risks turning feminist theologies of liberation and their works of mercy on behalf of suffering mothers and children into theological errors and mortal sins. Without a new covenant with women, can Francis respond adequately to his fellow Jesuit Jon Sobrino's challenges to him: to fix the unbearable and untenable situation of women vis-à-vis the church, to recognize and value the indigenous peoples of world, and to love Mother Earth?

Thus far, Francis has not heard the "sigh of the oppressed" from women who are turned away from public clinics and doctors throughout Latin America by the Roman Catholic bans on contraception enshrined in the laws of most Latin American countries. Some are the victims of domestic violence, others of police brutality against their adult sons, and still others are living on the edge of a reproductive cliff. We know them all too well in the favelas of Brazil and in the mestizo villages of Mexico, and we know the consequences of coerced births in the head counts of tiny graves with white wooden crosses and in the municipal ledgers that tally the deaths of mothers and infants.

Pope Francis says that the church needs to divert its obsessive preoccupation with sexuality, contraception, and divorce as these are negative and divisive issues; better to put them aside. But in so doing the pope is ignoring the doctrinal millstone that is tied around the necks of women and their doctors. In stigmatizing the writings of Latin American women theologians, by referring to them as following "radical feminist themes incompatible with the Catholic faith," he is invalidating the work of serious women scholars, portraying them as irresponsible, naive, or worse, as dangerous thinkers. Here, Pope Francis comes close to his earlier suspicion of the liberation theologians he failed to understand or to protect during the dirty war.

The new prefect of the Congregation of the Doctrine of the Faith, Gerhardt Mueller, has declared that "the war between liberation theology and Rome is over" and that liberation theology should be recognized as "among one of the most important currents in 20th century Catholic theology."[8] The time is right for a rapprochement with women theologians like Ivone Gebara, a nun with two doctoral degrees and a dozen books bearing on poor women in Pernambuco, Brazil. Sister Gebara was silenced in 1995 for suggesting off the record that a poor woman with five children and an absent father who accidentally became pregnant after a one-night stand with a gas station attendant and who took a night-after pill had not committed a mortal sin. If the scientist in Pope Francis can embrace the mystery of time and the Big Bang, he can delve into the anthropological ambiguity of the embryo, as a potential life but not yet ensouled until the quickening, a biblical view of pregnancy still held by women in the rural northeast of Brazil (Scheper-Hughes 2013). In inaugurating the Year of Mercy (2016–17), Pope Francis announced an opening, a year in which women could be forgiven for the previously "unforgivable" sin of abortion. This imposes a double bind on women and their marital or domestic partners. Must they both admit to committing a grievous sin in order to receive forgiveness? While abortion is not nothing, morally speaking, it is often the only path allowing women to let go of an embryo that would become an infant that they cannot nurture. An embryo, my Brazilian shantytown informants insist, is not yet a child; it is a *creatura,* a creature, equal to a bird or to a tadpole, all of whom deserve respect.

In taking the name of Saint Francis, Jorge Mario might reflect on the close relationship between Saint Francis and Saint Clare, who shared an intimate intellectual and spiritual relationship in cofounding the mendicant and the cloistered Franciscan orders. Francis's strong, equitable relationship with Clare as his spiritual *companheira* was necessary to the founding of Franciscan theology in praxis, a dynamic theology, rooted in voluntary poverty, that embraced all creatures, humans and animals. Francis often referred to himself and to his barefoot friars as "mothers" rather than as men. We would like Pope Francis to follow his patron saint and to think of himself as "la Mamma" as well as "il Papa."

We have followed Jorge Bergoglio/Pope Francis as he strives to remake himself as a progressive, transformative, charismatic populist who remains a theological conservative with respect to the public roles and private needs of women worldwide. We suggest a solution, one with a long and distinguished pedigree, the intellectual, theological, and administrative companionship of women to church leaders beginning with the close female friends and disciples of Jesus, including the three Marys—Jesus's mother, Mary the mother of James, and Mary Magdalene, incorrectly identified as a prostitute rather than as the generous and influential woman of means that she was. The pope's avatar, Saint Francis of Assisi, consulted throughout his public life with Clare, founder of the Franciscan Order of Poor Clares. Pope Francis needs the wisdom of strong women to help him navigate the other half of the world—shall we call it the invisible 50 percent—the part of the world that still perplexes him and without which he cannot succeed in his reformation of the Catholic Church in Latin America and in the world.

REFERENCES AND SUGGESTED READING

Althaus-Reid, Marcella
    2000 *Indecent Theology: Theological Perversions in Sex, Gender and Politics.* New York: Routledge.
Ambrogetti, Francesca, and Sergio Rubin
    2010 *Pope Francis: His Life in His Own Words.* New York: New American Library.
Boff, Leonardo
    1988 *Saint Francis: A Model for Liberation.* New York: Crossroad.
Camara, Javier, and Sebastián Pfaffen
    2014 *Aquel Francisco.* Córdoba, Argentina: Raíz de Dos.
Castro, Fidel
    2006 *Fidel & Religion: Conversations with Frei Betto on Marxism & Liberation Theology.* North Melbourne, Australia: Ocean Press.
Fichelstein, Federico
    2014 *Fascism, Populism, and Dictatorship in Twentieth Century Argentina: The Ideological Origins of the Dirty War.* Oxford: Oxford University Press.
Gebara, Ivone
    2002 *Out of the Depths: Women's Experience of Evil and Salvation.* Minneapolis, MN: Augsburg Books.
Griffin, Michael L., and Jennie Weiss Block, eds.
    2013 *In the Company of the Poor: Conversations with Dr. Paul Farmer and Gustavo Gutiérrez.* New York: Orbis Books.
Kulish, Nicholas
    2013 "Full Statement from Jesuit Kidnapped by Argentine Junta on New Pope." *New York Times.* http://thelede.blogs.nytimes.com/2013/03/15/full statement-from-jesuit-kidnapped-by-argentine-junta-on-new-pope/.
Scavo, Nello
    2014 *Bergoglio's List: How a Young Francis Defied a Dictatorship and Saved Dozens of Lives.* Charlotte, NC: Saint Benedict Press.
Scheper-Hughes, Nancy
    [1979] *Saints, Scholars, and Schizophrenics: Mental Illness in Rural Ireland.*
    1999 Berkeley: University of California Press.

1993   *Death without Weeping: The Violence of Everyday Life in Brazil.* Berkeley: University of California Press.

2011   "So, Finally, What's a Catholic to Do When Her Church Is Corrupt and Moribund?" *CounterPunch* 18.18: 1, 5–8.

2013a   "Can God Forgive Jorge Mario Bergoglio?" *CounterPunch.* www.counterpunch.org/2013/03/20/can-even-god-forgive-jorge-mario-bergoglio/.

2013b   "No More Angel-Babies on the Alto do Cruzeiro." *Natural History Magazine.* www.naturalhistorymag.com/features/282558/no-more-angel-babies-on-the-alto-do-cruzeiro.

2015   "Witness to a Troubled Sainthood: Junipero Serra and a Failed Theology." *CounterPunch.* www.counterpunch.org/2015/10/07/witness-to-a-troubled-saint-making-junipero-serra-and-the-theology-of-failure/.

Scheper-Hughes, Nancy, and John Devine

2003   "Priestly Celibacy and Child Sexual Abuse." *Sexualities* 6.1: 15–39.

Vallely, Paul

2013   *Pope Francis: Untying the Knots.* New York: Bloomsbury Academic.

Vatican Congregation for the Doctrine of the Faith

2012   "Doctrinal Assessment of the Leadership Conference of Women Religious," 18 April. www.vatican.va/roman_curia/congregations/cfaith/documents/rc_con_cfaith_doc_20120418_assessment-lcwr_en.html.

Vatican Insider

2013   "The War between the Liberation Theology Movement and Rome Is Over," 21 June. www.lastampa.it/2013/06/21/vaticaninsider/eng/the-vatican/the-war-between-the-liberation-theology-movement-and-rome-is-over-dzCNBPTKbXUDZDoJswurLP/pagina.html.

Verbitsky, Horacio

2006   *El silencio: De Paulo VI a Bergolglio. Las relaciones secretas de la Iglesia con la ESMA.* Buenos Aires: Editorial La Página.

NOTES

1. Benedict XVI was the first pope to resign in six hundred years. Pope Gregory XII renounced his papacy in 1415 amid a great schism in which two other "antipopes" in Europe were vying for the papal chair. Before him, in 1045, another Benedict, Pope Benedict IX, resigned after selling his papacy to his godfather. The retirement of a pope raises theological questions about the role of the "Holy Spirit" in guiding the selection of the pope. A pope's resignation casts doubt on papal, let alone divine, *infallibility.*

2. In 1991 Scheper-Hughes was invited to address a closed meeting in Saint Johns, Newfoundland, of public officials, police, educators, clergy, parents, and victims of sexual abuse by Catholic clergy and teachers following the publication of the *Royal Commission of Inquiry into the Newfoundland Criminal Justice System to*

Complaints (of clerical sexual abuse). The allegations of abuse went back to the 1950s, and the sense of betrayal by the church was enormous. See http://bishopaccountability.org/reports/1991_Hughes_Mount_Cashel/1991_Hughes_Volume_1_Royal_Commission_of_Inquiry_Report.pdf.

3. As soon as Francis became pope, he was given a secret report commissioned by his predecessor, Benedict XVI, on the leaks and scandals that had plagued his papacy.

4. The possible exceptions are Nicaragua during the Sandinista revolution and Brazil during the election of President Luiz Inácio Lula da Silva in 1989. In both instances the influence of liberation theology was a powerful political factor.

5. A full statement by Father Franz Jalics on his arrest and detention was published on 15 March 2013 on the *New York Times* blog. See Kulish 2013.

6. Verbitsky's book, published only in Spanish, *El silencio: De Paulo VI a Bergoglio. Las relaciones secretas de la Iglesia con la ESMA,* is the most complete assault on the complicity of Father Bergoglio.

7. Javier Camara and Sebastián Pfaffen (2014) quote Bergoglio as saying that he is no saint and describes himself during his period in Córdoba as "just a poor guy" at loose ends.

8. "Doctrinal Assessment of the Leadership Conference of Women Religious," issued 18 April 2012, by the Vatican Congregation for the Doctrine of the Faith. www.vatican.va/roman_curia/congregations/cfaith/documents/rc_con_cfaith_doc_20120418_assessment-lcwr_en.html.

THREE

Fidel Castro

THE FIRST SUPERDELEGATE

Greg Grandin

"LONG ERE THE SECOND CENTENNIAL ARRIVES," Walt Whitman predicted in 1871, "there will be some forty to fifty great States," among them Cuba. It was a common enough belief. From Thomas Jefferson onward, many Americans thought that, as Secretary of State James Blaine said in 1881, "Cuba must necessarily become American."

Based on its current population, if the island had become a U.S. state, it would hold about the same weight in deciding American presidential elections as does Ohio. History, of course, took a different turn; yet, over the last five decades, Cuba could still count one superdelegate.

Fidel Castro was not seen in public for several years after July 2006, when a near-fatal stomach illness forced him into semi-retirement. In the United States, however, he remains a contender, at least in terms of the hold he has on the imagination of candidates running for the White House. Here's a short history of Castro's long run in U.S. presidential politics.

1960. John F. Kennedy, flanking his Republican opponent, Vice President Richard Nixon, on the right on matters of foreign policy, was the first presidential candidate to brand Fidel Castro an "enemy." In August 1960, having just accepted the Democratic nomination, JFK told a Miami gathering of American veterans that, for the "first time in our history, an enemy stands at the throat of the United States." The Cubans, he declared, are our "enemies and will do everything in their power to bring about our downfall." During the campaign, he repeatedly hammered Nixon on Cuba, demanding that the Eisenhower White House cut off trade to the island and provide aid to "fighters for freedom" to overthrow Castro.

In fact, months before Kennedy's August speech, President Dwight D. Eisenhower had already authorized the funding of a campaign of paramilitary sabotage in Cuba, as well as the training of a small army of Cuban exiles to overthrow Castro. Republicans had no problem with what today goes by the name "regime change," having already orchestrated two successful coups—in Iran in 1953 and Guatemala in 1954—against governments they perceived as hostile to U.S. interests. They just preferred to do it quietly.

As Eisenhower's vice president, Nixon was obligated not to reveal his administration's secret foreign policy plans, so he could only lamely respond to Kennedy's taunts. Cuba, he insisted, was not "lost." Nixon knew that the White House had started training Cuban exiles, and he was probably aware that the CIA was working on a plan to poison Castro's cigars, but the vice president could only barely allude to such knowledge, which just made him sound complacent. "The United States," Nixon said, "has the power, and Mr. Castro knows it, to throw him out of office any day that we would choose to." Kennedy, of course, won the election. As president, he carried out the Republican invasion plan, the botched Bay of Pigs operation. When that failed, Kennedy authorized "Operation Mongoose," a broad-spectrum covert operation that used sabotage, assassinations, and psychological warfare in hopes of sparking an uprising against Castro. He also imposed a trade embargo on Cuba. A stickler for legality, JFK held off signing the decree cutting off trade with the island until his press secretary, Pierre Salinger, could purchase him a cache of 1,200 Petit Upmann Cuban cigars.

1964. Castro, who by one recent count has survived more than six hundred assassination attempts, never allowed a free vote in Cuba. "The revolution," he once reportedly remarked, "has no time for elections." But he made time for those held in the United States. In 1964, the Havana daily *Revolución* condemned both President Lyndon Johnson and his Republican challenger Barry Goldwater, writing that the two candidates reflected the "structural degeneration" of American democracy. But in the weeks leading to the election, Castro, fearing Goldwater's "extremism" and convinced that Johnson would pursue a "policy of moderation," stepped up his anti-imperialist, anti-U.S. rhetoric, hoping to spark a backlash in the president's favor. Johnson won in a landslide, without the need for a (back)hand from Fidel.

1968. Decades before Willie Horton, there was Fidel Castro—and France's president, Charles de Gaulle, whose criticism of U.S. policies in Western

Europe and its war in Vietnam had earned him the enmity of many Washington opinion makers. Richard Nixon, this time running as the challenger against Johnson's vice president, Hubert Humphrey, sponsored a TV ad flashing images of those two tribunes of "anti-Americanism," the odd-coupled "axis of evil" of that American moment, while promising that he would restore U.S. authority at home and abroad.

The Vietnam War, and the demonstrations it provoked, dominated popular debate, and Cuba played only a small role in the campaign. Still Nixon and his running mate, Spiro Agnew, knew who to blame for the protests that dogged them. Agnew regularly condemned student antiwar protesters as an "effete corps of impudent snobs" who "have never done a productive thing in their lives." He continued, "They take their tactics from Fidel Castro and their money from Daddy." Agnew used that Castro line whenever he could as part of his pitch for the blue-collar vote. After invoking Castro to silence protesters at a Florida university event, he even suggested that student dissent was a "disease," assuring the audience, "When Dick Nixon becomes president of these United States we are going to find that that disease comes under some kind of treatment pretty quickly."

1972. Impending defeat in Vietnam made talk of cooperation and compromise—not confrontation—the order of the day, as President Nixon ran for reelection on his national security adviser Henry Kissinger's dramatic diplomatic openings to Moscow and China. Perhaps afraid that the Kremlin leaders would cut a deal and abandon him, Castro made a number of overtures in the middle of the presidential campaign that caught the White House off guard. There was even talk of Kissinger making a "secret visit to Havana," as he had earlier that year to Beijing. But Nixon's powerful right wing, unable to stop the advance of Kissinger-style "appeasers" when it came to the Soviet Union, China, or even Hanoi, was not about to roll over on Cuba.

By now, three elections after Kennedy had first outflanked Nixon on Cuba, anti-Castroism had become a veritable obsession on the carnivalesque right where an alliance of Cuban exiles, John Birchers, Young Americans for Freedom, law-and-order anticommunists, Soldier of Fortune mercenaries, and CIA spooks held sway.

So even though Nixon studiously ignored Cuba during the campaign, the Far Right, including the *National Review*'s William Buckley, began to whisper that the Democratic nominee, George McGovern, had actually cut a secret deal with Castro. McGovern dismissed the rumors as the work of a "bitter," "paranoid," and "despicable" conservative movement that wouldn't be happy with any candidate who wasn't to the "right of Genghis Khan."

There was, at the time, about as much intelligence establishing a covert relationship between McGovern and Castro as there would be linking al-Qaeda to Saddam Hussein—or Barack Obama to an Islamic madrassa. Yet Nixon did try to oblige. His "plumbers"—the secret team that broke into the Democratic National Headquarters at the infamous Watergate Hotel complex—were largely made up of anti-Castro Cuban exiles. It had been organized by Bay of Pigs veteran CIA agent E. Howard Hunt, who said that one of the reasons for the burglary was to look for evidence establishing a connection between Castro and McGovern. Nixon won in a landslide, but Watergate eventually took him down.

1976. Castro played an important role in the Republican primaries in this election. Challenged by Ronald Reagan from the Right, Gerald Ford, the House majority leader who had gained the presidency when Nixon resigned, tried to act tough. He flew to Puerto Rico and told Castro to keep his hands off the American colony, but that bizarre demand had nothing on the Gipper. Before he began to criticize Ford on Cuba, Reagan was trailing by double digits in the Florida polls. But by making Castro an issue, the challenger turned the primary into a horse race, losing the state to an incumbent president by just a few points. Reagan swept Dade County and its Cuban American vote, prompting a Ford campaign adviser to comment sardonically that his boss might as well "recognize Cuba immediately."

"The Cuban threat is a geopolitical version of the miracle of the loaves and fishes," noted the *Washington Post*—the gift that keeps giving. Reagan lost his challenge but would be back as Ford went down to Democratic challenger Jimmy Carter.

1980. Reagan played his Dade County strategy large: In the Republican primaries, he called for a blockade of Cuba in retaliation for the Soviet invasion of Afghanistan, which made about as much sense as attacking Iraq in response to 9/11. His main opponent, ex-CIA director George H. W. Bush, called Reagan's proposal a "macho thing," pointing out that "Cuba didn't invade Afghanistan." But such a fact-based campaign position was a nonstarter. After Reagan beat Bush 2 to 1 in the Florida primary on his march to the nomination, Bush, signing on to the ticket as vice president, made his peace with Reagan's voodoo diplomacy. In the election campaign, Castro—perhaps forgetting the reverse psychology he had applied in 1964—praised President Jimmy Carter for supplying financial aid to Nicaragua's leftist Sandinistas and called Reagan a "threat to world peace." Reagan, of course, took Florida in the general election and trounced Carter. As his cabinet was getting settled in the White House, Secretary of State Alexander Haig told his boss, "You just give me the word, and I'll turn that fucking island into a parking lot." Reagan demurred, choosing to take the far smaller, more defenseless Caribbean island of Grenada instead—and sparing Cuba for his next and last presidential campaign.

1984. Reagan accused Democratic presidential nominee Walter Mondale of neither rejecting nor denouncing Jessie Jackson for—as a candidate for the Democratic nomination—having visited Havana and, according to Reagan, having "stood with Fidel Castro and cried: 'Long Live Cuba.' 'Long Live Castro.' 'Long Live Che Guevara.'" (What Reagan didn't say was that Jackson had used the visit to negotiate the release of several political prisoners and that he had also shouted "Vivas" to the United States, as well as to Martin Luther King Jr.) "I don't admire Fidel Castro at all," Mondale responded, "but Jesse Jackson is an independent person. I don't control him." In November, Reagan won every state except Minnesota.

1988. Vice President George H. W. Bush invoked the possibility of a nuclear attack from Cuba to justify his support for Reagan's much-ridiculed Star Wars anti-missile defense system, but he didn't need Castro to take out the inept Democratic candidate Michael Dukakis and win the presidency. Ronald and Nancy Reagan's astrologer, Jeanne Dixon, did predict that a crisis in Cuba during Bush's first summer in office would give the new president a chance to move out of Reagan's shadow and "consolidate his nation's confidence."

1992. Following the collapse of the Soviet Union, many observers thought the time was finally opportune to normalize relations with Havana. But Florida has 25 votes in the electoral college, and Miami's Cuban exiles—about 600,000 (out of a state population of, as of 2008, just over 800,000 Cuban migrants) live in crucial Dade County—remained a powerful domestic lobby. Touched by the spirit of JFK, challenger Bill Clinton headed for Miami in April 1992 to excoriate George H. W. Bush for not "dropping the hammer down on Castro and Cuba." Clinton even endorsed the punitive Cuban Democracy Act, which Bush (finding himself outflanked to his vulnerable right) signed shortly thereafter. Along with subsequent legislation that Clinton, as president, would back, the act tightened Washington's long-standing embargo on Cuban trade. This only served to cut Washington out of what would be the island's post–Cold War political and economic opening to the rest of the world. Clinton took 20 percent of Florida's Cuban Americans, lost the state to George H. W. Bush, but won the White House.

1996. Clinton, as president, stayed on point against Republican challenger Robert Dole, running to his right on Cuba, though he did admit in a TV debate that "nobody in the world agrees with our policy on Cuba now." During his first term, Clinton had drawn close to Miami's anti-Castro Cuban lobby, taking political advice from Hillary Clinton's Cuban-immigrant sister-in-law, María Victoria Arias. This time, Florida was his, and he doubled his percentage of Cuban American votes.

2000. In October, by a vote of 86 to 8, the Senate passed legislation easing the embargo, allowing food to be sold to Cuba. Castro criticized the legislation for being paternalistic and not going far enough in normalizing commercial relations. George W. Bush condemned it. Al Gore refused to comment. Angry at Janet Reno's return of Elián González, the young Cuban refugee rescued by fishermen after most of his companions, including his mother, drowned trying to make it to the United States, Florida's Cuban Americans abandoned the Democratic Party en masse in November. Along with Naderites and Palm Beach Jews-for-Buchanan, Bush got just enough votes to deadlock the election. Castro offered to send observers to oversee a recount.

2004. During a visit to Brazil in October, Secretary of State Colin Powell made an offhand remark that Cuba was no longer a major threat to Latin America. "We don't see everything through the lens of Fidel Castro," he said. John Kerry thought he saw an opening and pounced. He claimed he found it "shocking that the Bush administration is telling the world that Fidel Castro no longer poses a problem for this hemisphere." Perhaps after a mere forty-four years and twelve presidential elections, the Castro bounce was wearing off. Bush won Florida with a million more votes than he had received four years earlier.

2008. This, his thirteenth, will most likely be Castro's last presidential election.[1] After a photo surfaced indicating that one of Barack Obama's Texas volunteers (who is Cuban American) had hung a Cuban flag superimposed with an image of Che on a wall behind her desk, the conservative blogosphere right-clicked a collective ah hah! Considering the temptation of Democratic candidates to call for a hard line against Cuba as a low-cost, high-return way of establishing their national security creds, the Obama campaign responded with remarkable restraint, simply terming the flag "inappropriate." Hillary Clinton, looking more like the hapless Kerry than the wily Bill, promptly attacked Obama for saying that he would meet with the ailing revolutionary. "We're not going to just have our president meet with Fidel Castro," she said. "I don't want to be used for propaganda purposes."

It's been nearly fifty years since Richard Nixon said that the United States could get rid of Fidel Castro whenever it wanted. Castro, of course, is still around, though not for lack of effort on Washington's part. The Cuban government calculates that some 3,500 Cubans have died over the past five decades as a result of U.S.-supported paramilitary operations against the island. In recent years, Castro's continued survival, not to mention the disaster in Iraq, may have forced on our policy makers a somewhat more modest appreciation of Washington's ability to bring about regime change.

Still, the Castro factor has yet to disappear. John McCain recently called on his supporters to sign an online petition to "stop the dictators of Latin America," though he didn't say exactly whom such a petition should be delivered to. It has since been removed from his campaign's webpage. The dictators in question apparently include Hugo Chávez of Venezuela and Evo Morales of Bolivia as well as Castro. "They inspire each other," McCain told a gathering of Bay of Pigs veterans in Miami's Little Havana. "They assist each other. They get ideas from each other. It's very disturbing."

Last month [February 2008], Castro announced that he would not seek reelection as Cuba's president. But that hasn't stopped him from weighing in on the contest in the United States, predicting that a Clinton-Obama ticket would be "unbeatable." "Will Castro's nod to Hillary and Obama," ran a *Fox News* header reporting the endorsement, "help or hurt?" Why won't the Democrats, asked one of the show's guests, "call him a dictator?" And so the beat, however faint, goes on.

NOTES

This essay is reprinted with permission of the author from www.tomdispatch.com/post/174903, 6 March 2008.

1. Castro surprises. I wrote the above in 2008, when it seemed not only that he wasn't long for this world, but that Washington's Cold War stance toward Cuba was immutable. But here we are in 2016, on the threshold of yet another presidential election, and the Old Mole is still around, still commenting on U.S. politics. Moreover, President Obama has made a historic visit to Cuba to speak to the Cuban people and meet with Raúl Castro, who had unexpectedly teamed up with Obama to flip the script, beginning, in December 2014, the process of diplomatic normalization between Havana and Washington. In effect, Obama nationalized the Cuba question. Polls indicate that the majority of U.S. voters support normalization, even in Florida. This means that now, instead of Democrats having to travel to Florida to pledge to an increasingly small group of ideologues that they will keep things as they are (as Obama did in 2008), Republicans, still chained to a policy of isolating Havana, will have to explain to a larger electorate why they want to return to the past—why, say, Iowa shouldn't be able to sell corn in Cuba or lung cancer patients shouldn't have access to lifesaving drugs developed by the Cuban pharmaceutical industry.

Border Crossings

Renato Rosaldo

I.

Eyes glimmering, sorrow in his skin,
he told me work was hard to find.
In 1932, leaving Mexico City,
my father settled in Chicago.
One night he dreamed of Charlie Chaplin,
then schemed with a Mexican neighbor.
Next dawn, at the factory gates,
his neighbor lifted a ring of keys
and announced the job had been filled.
It dissolved the line of waiting men.
My father stepped into the job: spray-painting.

A college sophomore in Mexico, here he lacked Civics
and American History and returned to high school.
His accent melted into radio English.
He slid down-state to college,
married an Illinois woman,
and taught his youthful love
—Mexican literature.

Cruces de Fronteras

Renato Rosaldo

I.

Ojos relucientes, tristeza en la piel,
me dijo que no encontraba trabajo.
En 1932, dejando la ciudad de México,
mi padre se asentó en Chicago.
Una noche soñó con Charlie Chaplin
luego conspiró con su vecino mexicano.
La próxima madrugada llegó al portón de la fábrica,
su vecino levantó un llavero,
proclamó que ya no había plaza,
disipó la cola de hombres que esperaban.
Mi padre asumió el empleo: pintor con atomizador.

Iba a la mitad de su carrera en México, pero le faltaba civismo
e historia de Estados Unidos, tuvo que volver a la preparatoria.
Su acento se fundó en el inglés de radio.
Se deslizó hacia el sur, a la universidad,
se casó con una mujer de Illinois,
empezó a enseñar el amor de su juventud
—literatura mexicana.

II.

Years later, Dad bought me a puppy,
named him Chico,
but after a week the dog rolled over,
whimpering and vomiting.

Dad rushed him to the vet,
came back home that afternoon,
successful, collapsed on the couch,
chuckled on and on without stopping.

He began laughing tears,
his words burst breathlessly,
immaculate clinic . . . starched white nurse . . .
a form . . . patient's name, date of birth—of a dog!

III.

Rushing brown river. Men used ropes to ferry our car;
summer in Mexico, new road, no bridges.

Dad's mother, Mama Emilia, held my newborn brother, shit flowed
along her leg, water rose above her calves.
Dad said, *I thought you loved adventure,*
she answered, *Never said I was Christopher Columbus.*

Teaching summer school for Americans,
he became Mexican culture,
translated himself back into English,
told of a hero's head, spiked on the corner,
the grace of fishing with butterfly nets,
how seven reed meant a date on the Aztec calendar.

Años después, Papá me compró un perrito,
le nombró Chico,
pero a los ocho días se puso patas arriba,
gemía y vomitaba.

Papá le llevó volando al veterinario,
regresó a casa esa tarde,
exitoso, se cayó sobre el sofá
se reía más y más sin parar.

Empezó a reír lágrimas,
brotaron sus palabras sin aliento,
*clínica inmaculada . . . enfermera blanca almidonada . . .
una forma . . . nombre del paciente, fecha de nacimiento—¡de un
    perro!*

III.

Río arenoso que corre rápido. Hombres llevaron nuestro carro con
    sogas,
verano en México, una carretera nueva, sin puentes.

La madre de mi papá, Mamá Emilia, abrazaba a mi hermano, recién
    nacido,
mierda corrió por su pierna, agua subió por sus pantorrillas.
Papá dijo: *¿No dijiste que te encantaban las aventuras?*
Ella dijo: *Nunca dije que era Cristóbal Colón.*

Al enseñar en una escuela de verano para gringos
se convirtió en la cultura mexicana,
luego se tradujo otra vez al inglés,
contó de la cabeza de un héroe, clavada en el rincón,
la manera precisa de pescar con redes de mariposa,
el significado de siete juncos en el calendario azteca.

He became the department head.
Swelling importance shrank his laughter.

My brother died suddenly. Mama Emilia
fainted into my father's pain.
He teetered over the grave,
praying to trade, his life for his son's.
At home, sitting, his knees rose up and shook.

Three white colleagues circled him like sharks,
Love the culture you study,
but don't let a Mexican run the department.
They called in their Bircher buddies.

He never recovered, lost the job,
and suffered one stroke after another.
He spoke about his grandmother, Mama Meche,
his eyes sparkled, then faded.

IV.

Llegó a ser director del departamento.
Su cargo creció, se encogió su risa.

Mi hermano murió de repente. Mamá Emilia
se desmayó dentro del dolor de mi padre.
El se bamboleaba a la orilla de la sepultura,
vibró con ganas de cambiar su vida por la de su hijo.
Sentado en casa, se levantaron sus rodillas. Temblaban.

Tres colegas blancos le rodeaban como tiburones,
Ama a la cultura que estudias,
pero no dejes que un mexicano se encargue de nada.
Llamaron a sus amigos de la derecha dura.

Nunca recuperó, perdió la plaza,
y sufrió embolia tras embolia.
Hablaba de su abuela, Mamá Meche,
brillaban sus ojos, luego se amortiguaron.

FOUR

From Illustrating Problems to Offering Solutions

LATIN AMERICA AS A GLOBAL SOURCE
OF SOCIAL INNOVATION

Gabriel Hetland and Peter Evans

THROUGH MOST OF ITS FIVE hundred years of colonial and neocolonial history, Latin America's challenge was defined in terms of its ability to absorb policy prescriptions generated in Europe and the United States. Its inability to do so was considered to define the failures of its institutions and culture. From seventeenth-century Iberian mercantilism to nineteenth-century liberalism to twentieth-century American neoliberal corporate capitalism, imported ideological agendas dominated the policy agendas of most Latin American states, partly because of military and economic domination by the North but also partly because the ideas of the North were hegemonic, assumed, at least by elites, to reflect Latin America's interest in development. These agendas were always ineffectual, but the victim was given the blame for their failure, and, punctuated by dramatically exceptional rebellious episodes, Latin America largely accepted the onus of failure, leading Albert Hirschman to coin the term *fracasomania*.

This historical context makes Latin America's global role at the turn of the third millennium surprising and refreshing. The North has given up any credible claim to being the (sole or primary) source of solutions for present problems or visions of the future. Politics in the United States is crippled by the increasingly unrestrained power of finance capital and popular imaginations that cannot let go of the reactionary fantasy of returning to a mythical eighteenth-century laissez-faire paradise. Europe is convulsed with political crises and grasping to come up with any ideas, new or old, that might resolve its current predicament.

While the old sources of "modernity" struggle and become more back-ward-looking Latin America has been experimenting with ideas that have been taken up around the world. These range from surprisingly effective economic responses to the North's 2008 financial crisis to the range of new cultural production chronicled in this volume.

We examine four cases of innovation in social movement strategy and social policy that have reverberated beyond the region's boundaries and been taken up by other actors in both the Global South and the North: participatory budgeting, transitional justice and human rights, new strategies for rural mobilization, and new arguments for addressing climate change. These examples range from what might seem like simple technocratic fixes (certain versions of participatory budgeting) to what might seem like quixotic efforts to affect global politics (e.g., Bolivia's efforts to reshape climate change politics).

The extraregional travel of these ideas has not been entirely straightforward. In most cases, powerful global actors have played an important role in this process. Thus, the World Bank began promoting its own version of participatory budgeting and the most important source of global advice to countries trying to implement transitional justice is the International Center for Transitional Justice (ICTJ) in New York City.

The appropriation of Latin American ideas by global actors might seem to negate Latin American agency and suggest that old structures of Northern domination have not really been challenged. But such a mechanistic view of how social innovation occurs is particularly inappropriate for looking at global processes. The infiltration and partial subversion of dominant ideas always coexists with the apparent co-optation of potentially disruptive ideas in a delicate interplay that does not always lead to real change but is, at the same time, the only thing that does.

Likewise, cynics will note that these Latin American innovations do not have the power to reshape global policy regimes in the way that global capitalist policy paradigms reshaped the world and argue again for *plus ça change*. We would argue that this is evidence of thinking trapped in the past. To the extent that Latin America is generating a new model for the global flow of ideas, this model is less about imposing Latin American ideas on the rest of the world, even if that were possible. Instead, it is contributing to new patterns of global flows that are part of a diverse set of "counterhegemonic" currents involving a horizontal exchange of ideas and practices among relatively equal partners.

Participatory budgeting is a practice giving ordinary citizens control over local budget decisions.[1] Normally, this takes place through several rounds of public assemblies where residents, in consultation with government officials and experts, discuss and then vote on their priorities. Local government subsequently implements winning projects, at times with substantial community involvement. The most well known example of participatory budgeting (often referred to as PB) is Porto Alegre, Brazil, which implemented an ambitious participatory budget during the 1990s and early 2000s that involved tens of thousands of residents and hundreds of millions of dollars.

Following its success in Porto Alegre, PB spread in an ever-increasing manner: in the mid-1990s, to other cities in Brazil mostly run by the Workers' Party (PT) and to cities run by other Left parties in several other Latin American countries; in the late 1990s, to many more Brazilian cities, over a third run by centrist, and a few conservative, parties; and from 2000 on, to cities around the world, in all regions of Latin America, Europe, Africa, Asia, and North America. PB is now practiced in fifteen hundred cities on all continents and is nationally mandated in Peru, Venezuela, and the Dominican Republic.

The global spread of participatory budgeting can be traced to a series of events. In 1996 Porto Alegre's participatory budget was awarded a UN Habitat Prize in Istanbul. From 2001 to 2005, Porto Alegre hosted the World Social Forum four times, bringing hundreds of thousands of international activists to the city. In the late 1990s and early 2000s, the UN and EU both launched organizational initiatives promoting PB. The Workers' Party, and Porto Alegre's PT administration in particular, played the key role in the global promotion of PB in the late 1990s and early 2000s. By the early 2000s, however, a very different institution—the World Bank—became the most important actor promoting PB. Since 2002, the World Bank has spent at least $280 million (and likely much more) supporting PB and PB-related projects in at least fifteen countries.

The dizzying speed of PB's global diffusion (particularly since 2001) and the shift in the main actors promoting it—from relatively marginal radical Left parties in Latin America to the world's most important international development organizations—raises profound questions. In particular, should the travel of participatory budgeting be interpreted as an example of "counterhegemonic globalization" or the neutering of a formerly radical practice by the powers that be?

The answer is "both" and "it depends." The transformative potential of PB appears to be shaped, above all, by the local and national configurations of class and political power in which particular PB experiments are embedded. As one might expect, PB appears to be most transformative and empowering when implemented by a radical Left party that is closely linked to an autonomous and mobilized social base. But "less radical" cases of PB can have important consequences as well. To illustrate this, we briefly discuss two cases of PB that have occurred in markedly different contexts.

In 2005, Torres, a semirural municipality in the central western Venezuelan state of Lara, initiated an expansive participatory budget that gives local residents control over 100 percent of the municipality's investment budget (US$6.8 million in 2006). Thousands (and probably tens of thousands) of local residents have participated in this process, most via one of Torres's six hundred communal councils and other civic associations. Torres's participatory budget was introduced by Julio Chávez, a self-described socialist revolutionary who was elected mayor in 2004. Unlike the World Bank, Chávez sees PB not as a form of good governance but as an integral component of "twenty-first-century socialism." As mayor, Chávez (no relation to Hugo Chávez) was closely linked to Torres's powerful urban and rural social movements. This allowed Torres's participatory budget to survive fierce resistance from agrarian elites and the Fifth Republic Movement, Hugo Chávez's party (through 2007, when it was replaced by the United Socialist Party of Venezuela), which controlled Torres's municipal council during Julio Chávez's tenure and repeatedly tried (and failed) to block the mayor's agenda during his first two years in office.

In 2012, Vallejo, which gained notoriety in 2008 by becoming the largest city in California history to declare bankruptcy, became the first city in the United States to implement a citywide participatory budget. Vallejo's decision to implement PB, in a considerably more modest fashion compared to Torres (or Porto Alegre), is an indirect consequence of the city's bankruptcy, which in 2011 led voters to approve a one percent sales tax increase, providing the city with $10 million per year. At the behest of an entrepreneurial city councilor (inspired by stories of PB in Chicago and Porto Alegre), $3.2 million of this was devoted to PB. Though less than 2 percent of Vallejo's budget, this is the largest PB amount a single group of voters has decided on in the United States. Given the city's fiscal woes, dearth of civic associations, and the mayor's opposition, the fact that PB came to Vallejo at all is quite remarkable. But there are doubts about the impact and long-term sustainability of

FIGURE 4.1. Participatory Budget Assembly, Cecilio Zubillaga Parish, Torres, Lara, Venezuela, November 2009. Photo by Gabriel Hetland.

FIGURE 4.2. Participatory Diagnosis, neighborhood of La Guzmana, Carora, Torres, Lara, Venezuela, June 2008. Photo by Gabriel Hetland.

the process. An external organization, the Participatory Budgeting Project (a U.S.-based NGO founded by researchers who studied PB in Brazil and Argentina), provided support for the process in its first year. The city council approved PB for a second year but lowered the amount to $2.4 million, which may dampen spirits and lower turnout. In addition, despite a sizable and relatively diverse turnout for the final vote (in year one), the process suffered from low participation among low-income groups and people of color, particularly in the project design phase.

Do the differences between PB in Torres and Vallejo mean PB inevitably becomes "PB lite" as it travels the globe? We reject this interpretation. There is considerable variation in PB in both the North and the South, making broad generalizations relatively useless. We agree with other scholars who suggest that PB should not be evaluated by a single one-size-fits-all yardstick. Rather PB should be assessed based on how (much) it transforms particular cities *compared to what might have occurred in its absence*. Vallejo's PB may appear insignificant compared to experiences like those of Torres and Porto Alegre. But for (some of) the hundreds of citizens who volunteered their time and the thousands who voted in the process PB is seen as a potential turning point for the city, with residents expressing hope that Vallejo will come to be seen as a leader in innovation and civic participation rather than an example of fiscal irresponsibility and poor management.

HUMAN RIGHTS / TRANSITIONAL JUSTICE: LATIN AMERICA AS A FOCAL POINT FOR GLOBAL INNOVATION

In the 1970s state officials guilty of violating the human rights of their citizens were still benefiting from a legal institutional framework that was "rather new and still quite inert" (Sikkink 2011: 90).[2] Over the course of the 1980s and 1990s, what Kathryn Sikkink calls a "justice cascade" transformed global norms for the prosecution of state officials responsible for murder, torture, and disappearances up to and including heads of state. The process of change was global, but Latin America was the innovative focal point.

The story of human rights prosecutions in Argentina is the best lens for illustrating this momentous change, both because of Argentina's crucial role and because Sikkink has documented the case so well. Sikkink succinctly sums up the bottom line as follows: "Argentina helped invent the two main accountability mechanisms that are the focus of much of the debate on transitional justice: truth commissions and high level human prosecutions. . . . Argentine human rights activists were not passive recipients of a justice cascade, but pioneers and propagators of multiple new tactics and transitional justice mechanisms" (Sikkink 2011: 87, 89).

One of the most interesting and least known contributions of the Argentine human rights movement was its foundational role in the creation of the science of forensic genetics. It was the quest of the Abuelas of the Plaza de Mayo in Argentina to find a credible technology that would enable them to find their lost grandchildren that transformed forensic genetics from a nascent and dubious technique to a global tool for human rights investigations. Lindsay Smith summarizes this contribution as follows: "Forensic genetics had its genesis in human rights work in Argentina in the early 1980s, with the development of the Index of Grandpaternity, a legally recognized genetic test capable of proving genetic relatedness between a grandparent and a child in the absence of the parental generation."[3] But, while forensic genetics is an excellent example of how Latin American struggles generate innovations with global impacts, the principal contributions of Latin American human rights movements were political and institutional transformations that moved from the local to the global and back.

The Mothers and Grandmothers of the Plaza de Mayo, the Center for Legal and Social Studies (CELS), and a host of other human rights NGOs—braving the threat of repression to protest the military's human rights violations—initially sparked the process. By 1983, with the military regime at its end, there were forty thousand people marching in Buenos Aires and, once in power, Alfonsin's democratically elected government formed a "truth commission" (National Commission on the Disappearance of Persons, or CONADEP),[4] which published its pathbreaking report, *Nunca Más,* in 1984. CONADEP's fifty thousand pages of evidence provided the foundation for the conviction and sentencing to life imprisonment of the two top military leaders.

For a country to be able to send its own leaders to prison for violating the rights of its own citizens represented a sea change from the Nuremburg model of foreign victors judging vanquished leaders. The process of innovation was simultaneously highly indigenous and fully global.

The political will to bring the perpetrators to justice came from activists and human rights lawyers in Argentina. At the same time, Argentine activists and human rights lawyers did not make history by themselves. Networks of global support were crucial. While the energy of the rank-and-file activists came precisely from the fact that they were locally rooted, many of the key legal actors honed their skills and expertise while in exile. The Inter-American Commission on Human Rights (IACHR), which was just beginning to play a significant role in defending hemispheric human rights in the late 1970s, provided invaluable support in the form of a 1980 report based on research done in Argentina.

Argentina's contributions were also unexpectedly global in terms of their impact. Unlike the 1970s prosecutions in Greece and Portugal, which barely made ripples in the global panorama of human rights institutions, the Argentine process was projected around the world. The most important link may have been the South-South networks that connected Argentine activists and lawyers to South African activists who then incorporated the Latin American experience in the development of their Truth and Reconciliation process. The Latin American experience also spread to the North, both in terms of its influence on global norms and via individuals who took their experiences with them as they played roles in global institutions. For example, Luis Moreno-Ocampo, who was the assistant prosecutor in the trials of the Argentine generals in the 1980s, ended up three decades later as the chief prosecutor of the International Criminal Court (ICC). And when the South African Truth and Reconciliation model went global with the establishment of the ICTJ in New York, its research director was Pablo de Greiff, from Colombia.

Global human rights institutions today bear the indelible imprint of Latin American contributions over the course of the past three decades. Latin America still leads the world in terms of numbers of human rights prosecutions and is the only region of the world in which there has been a clear decline in average levels of repression over the course of the past quarter century, providing a global model for the efficacy of human rights advocacy. Perhaps even more important, however, is the influence of Latin America's pioneering experience on the shape of the global justice cascade that evolved in the 1990s and the first decade of the twenty-first century.

The momentum of the justice cascade in the North also reverberated back to Latin America, enabling key breakthroughs in the region. The British arrest of Augusto Pinochet in 1998, in response to a Spanish request for his extradition under the Convention against Torture, helped catalyze new progress in human rights prosecutions back in Chile. The Alien Tort Claims Act in the United States has been used to prosecute Latin American torturers who thought that they had a secure refuge in the North. South-North synergies are a defining characteristic of the justice cascade.

Despite Latin America's pioneering role in the transformation of global human rights norms and institutions, it has, of course, no way of controlling the evolution of the global structure it helped construct. There is no hegemony here. The ICC and the ICTJ are likely to take on agendas quite different from those that Latin American pioneers had in mind. Nor do these global structures have the power to supersede the core interest of hegemonic states. Officials of the Bush administration are unlikely to ever be prosecuted for their role in torture, despite the fact that the United States (uncharacteristically) ratified the Convention against Torture.

Lack of ability to dominate the long-term evolution of global norms and networks, even in an arena in which it has made such fundamental contributions, should not be taken as a "failure." To the contrary, Latin America's role in human rights should be taken as a model of how a democratized global polity might operate. Innovation would emerge in regions and/or arenas where a problem was particularly acute. Other regions would then benefit from these pioneering innovations, and they would become incorporated into global norms and institutions. From the perspective of this arena at least, what historians will remember is that Latin America moved from being a regional exemplar of the problem to being a key player in the search for a global solution.[5]

PEASANTS OF THE WORLD UNITE! THE MST AS A GLOBAL MODEL OF RURAL MOBILIZATION

The domestic accomplishments of Brazil's Movimento dos Trabalhadores Rurais sem Terra (MST; Landless Workers Movement) are impressive.[6] Since 1984, the MST has led hundreds (possibly thousands) of land occupations, resulting in the settlement of over 100,000 families in two thousand settlements taking up 3.5 million hectares of land. Within its settlements, the MST engages in extensive educational-cum-ideological work among its members. The MST has also pushed successive Brazilian governments to implement comprehensive land reform. The MST uses its triple strategy of direct action, education, and engagement with the state to pursue an overarching goal of "food sovereignty." La Vía Campesina, an international organization that the MST helped found and plays a leadership role in, defines this as follows:

In order to guarantee the independence and food sovereignty of all of the world's peoples, it is essential that food be produced through diversified, farmer-based production systems. Food sovereignty is the right of peoples to define their own agriculture and food policies, to protect and regulate domestic agricultural production and trade in order to achieve sustainable development objectives, to determine the extent to which they want to be self reliant, and to restrict the dumping of products in their markets. Food sovereignty does not negate trade, but rather, it promotes the formulation of trade policies and practices that serve the rights of peoples to safe, healthy and ecologically sustainable production. (McMichael 2005: 291)

In addition to its work in Brazil, the MST has played a crucial role in the global movement for food sovereignty. This has taken place in several ways. The MST is active in international networks linking small and medium agricultural producers in the North and South. La Vía Campesina, which was founded in 1993 by peasants' and farmers' movements from Central, South, and North America, is the largest such network, encompassing over 150 national and subnational rural social movement organizations from fifty-six countries around the world. The MST is also an influential member of the Latin American Coordination of Peasant Organizations (CLOC). Since the 1990s, La Vía Campesina and CLOC have played a key role in a number of international campaigns: for external debt forgiveness for poor nations, against the Free Trade Area of the Americas, and in the "anti-globalization" movement of the late 1990s and early 2000s, made famous by protests in Seattle, Prague, and Genoa.

In addition to being part of these formalized international networks, the MST has devoted significant resources to direct exchanges between its membership and other movements in the Global South. Significantly, the MST has established international brigades—often in collaboration with La Vía Campesina—in Haiti, Central America, South Africa, Vietnam, Palestine, and several other countries. The MST has also created numerous Friends of the MST committees in the United States, Canada, and Europe. These committees were set up as a way for Northern activists to support the MST's activities. Over time, however, the MST discovered that its organizational capacity often exceeds that of its international supporters, leading to recent discussions about how the MST can provide support *to* Northern activists.

Finally, the MST has educated rural activists from throughout Latin America and to a lesser extent the world. Since 2005, these educational initiatives have often taken place in the MST's Florestan Fernandes National

School, which offers several courses focused on Latin America and political economic theory. Examples are monthlong political theory courses for leaders of Brazilian social movements; annual five-week courses on Marxism, the Agrarian Question, and the theories of Florestan Fernandes; and a three-month course every year on political theory in Latin America. Activists from Latin America, the Caribbean, Africa, and Europe have attended these courses, with Brazil, Argentina, Paraguay, Venezuela, and Colombia sending the most students.

What has the MST's (and allied organizations') global work led to? The MST has obviously not succeeded in its long-term goal of replacing what Phillip McMichael calls the "corporate food regime." But in conjunction with other organizations, the MST has reshaped global debates about land reform and issues of food, social justice, and urban-rural relations. Given the far greater resources wielded by the MST's main adversary—global agribusiness—this is a significant feat.

TURNING THE WORLD UPSIDE DOWN: BOLIVIA'S
EFFORTS TO RESHAPE CLIMATE CHANGE POLITICS

Since the 1992 "Earth Summit" in Rio de Janeiro, which established the United Nations Framework Convention on Climate Change (UNFCCC), Latin America has played an important role in international efforts to address climate change.[7] Latin America has hosted (or will host) four of the twenty annual UNFCCC Conferences of the Parties, the most important official gatherings addressing climate change. Latin America has also played a key role in alternative efforts to address climate change, which have sprung up in response to the frustration felt by activists and political leaders (mostly from the Global South) at many Northern countries', and especially the United States's, inability and unwillingness to come up with meaningful ways to reduce global greenhouse emissions.

Since Evo Morales's 2005 election as his country's first indigenous president, Bolivia has assumed a leading (but not fully consistent) role in the effort to forge a new type of global climate change politics. This is due, in part, to the fact that, as Oxfam has noted, Bolivia is among the countries that are least responsible for global warming yet most exposed to its effects. Bolivia's actions have taken place on three fronts: discourse regarding climate change, fostering international gatherings and networks linking social movements and Southern states, and coordinated interstate action through the Group of 77 (G77), which includes 133 developing nations.

Morales has repeatedly used the global platform provided by UN General Assembly meetings and international climate change conferences to enumerate the dangers of climate change. He is especially critical of Northern powers, like the United States, which bear the greatest historical responsibility for climate change but have failed to address the issue and actively blocked global efforts to do so. In Morales's view, the North owes the South a "climate debt." In concrete terms, this would mean that countries like the United States would pay a disproportionate amount of the costs that nations like Bolivia and the Maldives (i.e., those bearing little responsibility for global warming but suffering its worst effects) face in adjusting to climate change.

Official efforts to address climate change have focused, in large part, on how markets could be used to address the issue (e.g., through the creation of carbon markets). Morales, by contrast, is highly critical of markets and, like other Latin American leaders such as the late Hugo Chávez, views capitalism and climate change as closely connected:

> Competition and the thirst for profit without limits of the capitalist system are destroying the planet. Under Capitalism we are not human beings but consumers. Under Capitalism Mother Earth does not exist, instead there are raw materials. Capitalism is the source of the asymmetries and imbalances in the world. It generates luxury, ostentation and waste for a few, while millions in the world die from hunger. In the hands of capitalism everything becomes a commodity: the water, the soil, the human genome, the ancestral cultures, justice, ethics, death . . . and life itself. Everything, absolutely everything, can be bought and sold under capitalism. And even "climate change" itself has become a business. (Morales 2008)

In response to the ineffectiveness of UN-sponsored climate change conferences, in April 2010 Bolivia hosted the People's World Conference on Climate Change and the Rights of Mother Earth, a four-day gathering bringing together 35,000 participants from 140 countries, including 56 government delegations and 9,000 participants from outside South America. The most important aspect of the conference is that it brought together social movements and governments, the two key actors needed to build an effective climate justice movement. The conference produced the "People's Agreement" on climate change, which closely resembles Bolivia's stance on the issue and which Morales and social movement leaders hand-delivered to UN Secretary General Ban Ki-moon.

According to the environmental activist Bill McKibben, averting catastrophic climate change requires leaving $20 trillion worth of fossil fuels in the ground. Pushing powerful multinational corporations, and the governments that so often do their bidding, to make this kind of economic sacrifice will obviously take more than fiery rhetoric and international gatherings, however important these may be. This is why Bolivia's effort to engineer joint action by the Group of 77 (which includes two-thirds of the world's nations) may be the most consequential aspect of its leadership on climate change.

During the 2013 Warsaw Climate Change Conference there were intense negotiations over an issue known as "Loss and Damage," which would require that developed nations compensate developing nations for damages linked to climate change. When Australia and other developed nations refused to agree to provisions on Loss and Damage, Bolivia engineered a collective walkout of all the countries belonging to the G77. This was an unprecedented example of coordinated collective action by the Global South regarding climate change. In January 2014, Bolivia assumed the leadership of the G77, and in June 2014, the organization celebrated its fiftieth anniversary at a summit held in the Bolivian city of Santa Cruz. Climate change was one of the themes discussed at the summit, and Morales has promised to use the G77 to continue pressing for greater action on this issue.

It is important to note that there is, unfortunately, a major contradiction between Bolivia's *international* leadership with respect to climate change and its *domestic* policies. Evo Morales has faced harsh, and it seems quite justified, criticism from indigenous and environmental groups within (and outside) Bolivia for his aggressive continuation of extractive policies. This has led to several major conflicts regarding extraction in the Maddidi National Park and the construction of a road through the Territorio Indígena y Parque Nacional Isiboro Sécure (TIPNIS).

LATIN AMERICA'S EMERGENCE AS A GLOBAL LEADER

Latin America continues to live in a global political economy dominated by the North. Part of the North's domination is its continued ability to promulgate and enforce policy ideas that have failed to deliver social benefits in either the North or the South. But in the areas we have focused on—social movement strategy and social policy—Latin America has been at the forefront of forging models for a new sort of global regime, one in which innovative ideas can spread and be used by governments and social movements in countries around the world, regardless of where they originate, as long as they offer solutions.

We have described a small sample of Latin America's global contributions. Explaining the historical changes in the region and in the world that have made Latin America's new role possible would be a task of much larger magnitude, but a couple of obvious observations are worth making. Within the region, the connection between innovation and democratization is undeniable. The political effervescence associated with the overthrow of authoritarian regimes unleashed a wave of political creativity from which both Latin America and the rest of the world have benefited.

Oddly enough, the North's romance with extreme forms of politically liberal corporate capitalism probably also helped open the doors for Latin American innovations in two quite different ways. First, of course, unregulated capitalism's failure as a social and economic doctrine created a global policy vacuum into which people with different ideas could step. Second, and at the same time, efforts to appropriate old emancipatory ideas like democracy and human rights provided global legitimation to those who wanted to instantiate them in progressive ways. Latin Americans took advantage of this opportunity.

We have focused on only four innovations here. Many others could have been discussed. Latin America's innovative role in exploring the potential of conditional cash transfers as an antipoverty strategy is one obvious example. And even within the small sample we have chosen, there is great diversity, making it difficult to draw general lessons. Nonetheless, we would like to suggest that there are some threads that run through the four cases and tie them together. We will underline five.

First, these innovations do not just invoke democratic values as an ideological legitimation, but have a deeply democratic character in their origins and their practices. Democracy in Latin America has historically been more notable for its persistent failures than for its occasional successes, and it remains problematic. But these examples suggest that over the course of the region's checkered political history, Latin Americans have developed an immense set of skills using democratic practices and institutions for progressive ends. Participatory budgeting may be the most obvious example, but innovative democratic practices are integral to all of our cases. Given the glaring "democratic deficit" in our current structures of global governance, the democratic current of Latin America's global contribution makes them especially valuable.

Second and relatedly, these cases show that democratic practice cannot be limited to selecting the members of the political elite that will hold power. The powerful must be held accountable. Here the case of transitional justice is exemplary, demonstrating a way for citizens to hold their political and military leaders to account, including for truly horrendous atrocities. Participatory budgeting and MST-style direct action provide different ways to reach accountability as well.

Third, all of these cases depend on building links between states and social movements. The latter are crucial, as a source of energy, creative ideas, and prefigurative experiments that show the world the types of new institutions it needs. But without the fiscal resources and administrative capacity that only states can provide, movements will be profoundly limited in what they can accomplish. Even when the state is a target and an adversary, as in the human rights case, it is the eventual ability to "capture" the state while still retaining the capacity to act independently of, and if necessary in opposition to, the state that is the measure of success.

Fourth, the relationship between different scales—the global, the national, the local—is not linear or one-way. It is interactive and synergistic. The reforms discussed above all began at the local and/or national level. Solutions to local and national problems (related to budgeting, human rights, landlessness, water scarcity, etc.) must of course be locally and/or nationally effective. But they also involve forging links across the globe. This is most obviously true in the case of climate change. But it is equally true of the struggles of the MST, Argentine human rights' activists and globally minded PB activists.

Fifth and finally, global interactions do and must involve both North and South. South-South cooperation is a powerful source of transformation. But despite the North's culpability in creating the problems facing Latin America and other regions of the South, finding allies in the North and shaping institutions based in the North are also fundamental. Effective transformations bridge the North-South divide, connecting nations and citizens of the South with potential allies in the North. There are obviously political dangers inherent in forging links with groups whose location in the North privileges them (whether they like it or not), but these examples show that the gains can outweigh the dangers. The greatest danger would be a failure to take action in the face of the pressing problems confronting Latin America and the world.

REFERENCES AND SUGGESTED READING

Ganuza, Ernesto, and Gianpaolo Baiocchi
   2012   "The Power of Ambiguity: How Participatory Budgeting Travels the Globe." *Journal of Public Deliberation* 8.2: 1–12.
McKibben, Bill
   2012   "Global Warming's Terrifying New Math." *Rolling Stone,* 19 July.
McMichael, Phillip
   2005   "Global Development and the Corporate Food Regime." In *New Directions in the Sociology of Global Development Research in Rural Sociology and Development,* vol. 11, ed. Frederick H. Buttel and Philip David McMichael, 269–303. Bingley, U.K.: Emerald Group Publishing.
Morales, Evo
   2008   "Evo Morales on Climate Change: 'Save the Planet from Capitalism.'" *Links:International Journal of Socialist Renewal,* 28 November. http://links.org.au/node/769.
Oxfam International in Bolivia
   2009   "Bolivia: Climate Change, Poverty and Adaptation." www.oxfam.org/sites/www.oxfam.org/files/bolivia-climate-change adaptation-0911.pdf.
Sikkink, Kathryn
   2011   *The Justice Cascade: How Human Rights Prosecutions Are Changing World Politics.* New York: W. W. Norton.
Smith, Lindsay
   2013   "'Genetics Is a Study in Faith': Forensic DNA, Kinship Analysis, and the Ethics of Care in Post-Conflict Latin America." *Scholar & Feminist Online* 11.3. http://sfonline.barnard.edu/life-un-ltd-feminism-bioscience-race/genetics-is-a-study-in-faith-forensic-dna-kinship-analysis-and-the-ethics-of-care-in-post-conflict-latin-america/.

NOTES

   1. This section draws on Gabriel Hetland's fieldwork in Torres and Vallejo; Ganuza and Baiocchi 2012; and Benjamin Goldfrank, "The World Bank and the Globalization of Participatory Budgeting," *Journal of Public Deliberation* 8.2 (2012).
   2. This section draws particularly on the work of Kathryn Sikkink and her collaborators, Carrie Booth Walling and Ellen Lutz. See especially Sikkink 2011.

3. Lindsay Smith, "'Genetics Is a Study in Faith': Forensic DNA, Kinship Analysis, and the Ethics of Care in Post-Conflict Latin America," *Scholar & Feminist Online* (Barnard Center for Research on Women, 2014), 5, http://sfonline. barnard.edu/life-un-ltd-feminism-bioscience-race/genetics-is-a-study-in -faith-forensic-dna-kinship-analysis-and-the-ethics-of-care-in-post-conflict-latin-america/.

4. For an English translation of the published version of the commission's report, *Nunca Más,* see www.desaparecidos.org/nuncamas/web/english/library /nevagain/nevagain_001.htm.

5. It should, of course, be noted that Latin America's global contributions to human rights did not come out of the blue at the end of the twentieth century. As Kathryn Sikkink, "Latin American Countries as Norm Protagonists of the Idea of International Human Rights," *Global Governance* 20.3 (July–September 2014): 389–404, points out, long before the military regimes of the 1970s, Latin American countries were early protagonists of human rights in the post–World War II era "drafting of the first intergovernmental declaration of rights—the American Declaration of the Rights and Duties of Man, a full eight months before the Universal Declaration of Human Rights (UDHR) was passed" (391).

6. This section draws on discussions with Rebecca Tarlau, an expert on the MST, and the following works: Phillip McMichael, "Global Development and the Corporate Food Regime," *New Directions in the Sociology of Global Development Research in Rural Sociology and Development* 11 (2005): 269–303; Saturnino M. Borras Jr., "La Vía Campesina and Its Global Campaign for Agrarian Reform," *Journal of Agrarian Change* 8.2–3 (2008): 258–89; Breno Bringel and Flávia Braga Vieira, "Educational Processes, Transnational Exchanges and the Reconfiguration of Internationalism in Brazil's MST and La Via Campesina" (paper presented at the XXI International Congress of the Latin American Studies Association, 2013, Washington DC).

7. This section draws on the following sources: http://rt.com/news/climate-change-walkout-warsaw-050/; www.un.org/News/briefings/docs/2014/140108 _G77.doc.htm; Jessica Camille Aguirre and Elizabeth Sonia Cooper, "Evo Morales, Climate Change, and the Paradoxes of a Social-Movement Presidency," *Latin American Perspectives* 37.4 (2010): 238–44.

Prologue

Manga: "Che Guevara," by Kiyoshi Konno and Chie Shimano.
(Upper left) Today, no matter where we go
(Upper right) All around the world
(Lower) We can see "him."

(Upper left) "Hi there, do you know what kind of person he is, by the way?"
(Upper right) "You know, the face on your T-shirt"
"Do you know, dude?"
"Nah"
(Middle) "Oh, then why are you wearing it?"
"Well, you see, this man . . ."
(Lower) "I don't know why but he's just so cool"

(Upper) The man's name is—
(Lower) Ernesto Rafael Guevara de la Serna

通称
チェ・ゲバラ

様々な形で彼の姿は
世界中、イコンのように
広がっている

(Upper) People call him Che Guevara
(Lower) His image has spread around the world like an icon in many ways.

PART TWO

Tongues and Feet

INTRODUCTION

WITH NOT-SO-SUBTLE REFERENCES TO THE culinary delicacy *lengua* (cow tongue) and the instruments of *fútbol* (soccer) success, "Tongues and Feet" introduces us to the making, performing, and consuming that electrifies the circuits of global Latin America. Chapters take us from Andean music concerts in Japan to lines of people waiting for Korean barbecue served from taco trucks in Los Angeles. This part helps us to situate the sensory experience of Latin American cultural life from afar, giving time, place, and specificity to what can easily seem to be timeless tradition, style, and taste.

"Tongues and Feet" puts the oft-used word *authenticity* on the front burner. Authenticity is certainly no longer (as if it ever was) a pristine ideal to be discovered but an ongoing process of re/creation. These chapters are filled with myriad examples of fusion, mixture, and appropriation. The suffix *-ization* recurs throughout as we learn about the Africanization of Latin American rhythms, the creolization of Iberian languages, and the fitnessization of dance styles. Together they show how another "-ization" that has quickened the pace of cultural mixture—globalization—has ironically placed a premium on supposedly genuine local and regional cultural forms. The greater intensity of global connections has been a boon to the market for the seemingly pristine and exotic, as many seek "authentic" cultural expressions unsullied by the hyperconnected, digital, neoliberal now, just waiting to be "discovered" in an edgy part of town or on an adventure south of the border.

While the chapters explore the making and remaking of authenticity in language, sport, dance, and food, they are not amusing cultural profiles divorced from ballots and business. We encounter here the financial and political consequences of the trade in authenticity as the authors detail the inequities that accompany cultural appropriation. From protest on the soccer pitch to the price of quinoa, the chapters take us into the places where cultural capital—a currency of upward social mobility—is created and exchanged. That market has clear winners at certain times and places, like the few who make it to the premiere leagues in Europe or the immigrant food entrepreneurs who become cable television stars after whetting the appetite of the U.S. television personality Anthony Bourdain. Yet there are countless others who do not make it big. They remain line cooks in the back of the kitchen and fans cheering for their team on television because they cannot afford the price of a game ticket.

Moving from sites of production to consumption, these chapters explore the symbolic prestige and social distinction to be gained by knowing the location of the hippest food truck or by keeping time with the newest Caribbean rhythms from afar. Yet the authors show how cultural forms lose much of their ideological content when they travel far from home. The Buena Vista Social Club comes to represent the Cuba of charismatically aged cars and colonial charm, not the Marxist revolutionary state. All the while newer envelope-pushing global sounds, like reggaetón and hip-hop, are brushed aside as lacking in skill and taste. These authors do not uniformly support or criticize these processes. Instead, their works highlight how culture is in flux in the twenty-first century, seemingly at ever-increasing speed and with the ever present expectation of reinvention.

Global Latin America has had an outsized influence worldwide. The region bequeathed to the rest of the world the study of language (philology), as Paja Faudree and Daniel Suslak show. Brenda Elsey writes that Latin Americans have perfected the English invention of soccer, "beat[ing] the industrialized North at its own game." Yet measuring the depth of Latin American impact does not capture the fullness of global Latin America. This story is not just about one- or even two-way relationships of influence and exchange. Instead, a vast array of individuals participate in the expression and re-creation of regionally recognizable cultural forms.

Global Latin America is therefore made in music studios in the United States and Japan, where some have become entranced by what Michelle Bigenho terms an "imagined Andean indigenism." It is fashioned through the reinsertion of African rhythms into salsa via a transnational music scene stretching from Dakar and Abidjan to Havana and New York City. It takes shape through each new lexical addition to Spanglish, which in 2014 earned an entry in the Royal Spanish Academy's dictionary. These are the realities of global ingenuity, and they beckon an authentic appreciation for creative re/production.

"Tongues and Feet" assembles scholars from history, anthropology, language studies, literature, and linguistics to grapple with one of most powerful and enduring metaphors of a refried global Latin American culture. The foundation of numerous national identities and a topic of scholarly inquiry, the celebration of mixture and syncretism has persisted over the long duration and in diverse places throughout Latin America. The increasingly uncertain lines between Latin America and elsewhere and the search for authenticity in a seemingly homogenizing world may ultimately reshape the premium on the blended. In any case, the global interplay between the creators and consumers of Latin America remains, at least for the moment, as lively as ever.

FIVE

Borges's Library

LATIN AMERICA, LANGUAGE, AND THE WORLD

Paja Faudree and Daniel Suslak

The universe (which others call the Library) is composed of an
indefinite and perhaps infinite number of hexagonal galleries. . . .
The Library is total and its shelves register . . . Everything . . .

JORGE LUIS BORGES, "The Library of Babel"

IN THE FAMOUS STORY BY THE Argentine author Jorge Luis Borges, the
Library of Babel contains every book ever written and destined to be written,
in every human language. The entire linguistic history of humanity is contained in that magical library—a vast hexagon that remains hidden, perhaps,
somewhere in a forgotten quarter of Buenos Aires. It is an apt metaphor for
Latin America itself: a living repository of global conversations and a catalog
of human lives and encounters. And like the relationship between the words
preserved in the Library's books and what is said beyond its mirrored walls,
Latin America's linguistic biography is always being rewritten.

To better understand the linguistic legacy of Latin America and its contribution to our shared global lexicon, we start with the corner of the library
dedicated to Latin America's pre-Conquest roots and the linguistic consequences of the colonial legacy, tracing the movement of people in and out of
this region and the words that made the journey with them. We focus on
three key communication practices, beginning with how the indigenous residents of the Americas and the European colonizers named the new things
they encountered. We then consider how they put to work both indigenous
modes of writing and European alphabetic writing to capture language and
reach out to (or exclude) new and larger audiences. Finally, we discuss how
five centuries of engagement generated distinctively Latin American varieties
of Spanish and Portuguese, fundamentally changed how indigenous Latin

American languages are spoken, and gave birth to wholly new languages, such as Haitian Kreyòl. Along the way we also highlight the importance of religion and religious institutions in shaping Latin American ideas about language.

In the second half of this chapter we turn to the area of the library where new acquisitions are kept. Here we find evidence of the growing presence of Latin American languages around the world, as their speakers travel and their cultural productions circulate ever more widely. We pay particular attention to Latin American entanglements with their Anglophone neighbors in the United States. We also pause to consider what the future holds in store for Spanish and Portuguese, as American varieties of these languages further outpace their European counterparts in numbers of speakers and political influence.

As we explore the mirrored halls of this library, we celebrate the myriad ways that Latin American languages have influenced how people speak in other corners of the globe. The collection of stories filling its shelves demonstrate how language and conflicts about language have played essential roles in shaping this region's complex history, giving voice to its politically fraught current condition and foretelling its future, which will continue to be one of porous and shifting borders, dynamism, and global engagement.

FROM INCAS AND AZTECS TO ARGENTINE NOVELISTS: A BRIEF HISTORY OF LATIN AMERICA'S LINGUISTIC LANDSCAPE

Names

The very name "Latin America" weds geography and language. The region is generally defined as consisting of those countries in the Americas whose official languages are descended from Latin. In the colonial period, those languages were Spanish and Portuguese; later, other languages—such as English and French—would complicate this picture. Even so, Latin America's coherence as a region today is largely linguistic. The Río Bravo—which north of the border becomes the Rio Grande (with a silent *e* and no accent)—is not only a political boundary but also a linguistic one, at least in the national mythologies that have sprung up on either side of it.

The dominance and prevalence of Spanish and Portuguese in the region stem from the discovery of the Americas by the Catholic kingdoms of Spain and Portugal at the end of the fifteenth century and their subsequent efforts to conquer and colonize those lands. Pope Alexander VI brokered treaties between Spain and Portugal that divided the globe in two. Portugal was awarded evangelical responsibility for a territory stretching from the eastern shores of South America to Japan, and Spain a swath of the world stretching from Florida to the Philippines. Echoes of this treaty can be heard today in the names of cities like Los Angeles and Bombay (from Portuguese *bom baim*) and in words like *arigato* in Japanese (from Portuguese *obrigado,* "thank you") and the English word *peon* (from Spanish *peon,* "footman or footsoldier"). As is well known, large swaths of the New World, from New Spain to the Amazon, were named after Old World locales and myths. But at times the politics of naming was more complex. In 1510, for example, the Spanish writer Garci Rodríguez de Montalvo—his head filled with reports from Columbus and Cortés—wrote a popular novel featuring a warrior queen named Calafia, from a mythical island in the Indies named "California." That evocative name, in turn, is thought to be the source of the name given to the long stretch of the North American Pacific coast running from the U.S. state to the tip of the Baja peninsula. Today, like countless other Latin American place-names, it has been taken up in names for public places and businesses found across the world.

Well over a thousand distinct tongues were spoken in Latin America when the first Europeans arrived on its shores, all of them radically different from the languages spoken in Europe. During the Conquest, an immense communication gulf existed between the Europeans and the American indigenous peoples. Miscommunications abounded. One such storied case involved the name Yucatán, which now refers to a single region of Mexico but initially designated a vast stretch of Spain's New World discoveries, extending from Mexico to Panama. The Spanish conquistador Hernán Cortés claimed that the name for this marvelous land was mistakenly derived from a Maya expression meaning "I don't understand"—a reply by Maya locals when newly arrived Spaniards asked what their homeland was called. Some modern scholars have taken a similar view, while others have claimed that Cortés's story was itself probably based on a bad interpretation. In either case, accounts agree that none of the multiple possible sources for the name correspond with any Maya place-name. Countless other misunderstandings of this sort are lost to history. Colonization decimated many indigenous peoples, who took their languages with them to their graves. Nevertheless, several hundred indigenous languages are spoken today. At Conquest, two of the most widely spoken were Quechua (principal language of the Inca Empire) and Nahuatl (principal language of the Aztec Empire); several million people speak modern varieties of those languages today. You can learn to speak them, too, in courses offered at universities across the globe.

Grammars, Alphabets, and Writing

Catholic priests did much to bridge the communication gap between the Old World and the New. They studied indigenous Latin American languages intensely, turning to them as objects of epistemological inquiry and tools for evangelization. They focused especially on widely spoken languages like Quechua, Nahuatl, Yucatec, and K'iche' Maya—languages that were also granted legal and administrative standing in colonial Spanish courts and government offices. This engagement by colonial authorities irrevocably changed Latin America's indigenous languages. They were soon pervaded by Spanish and Portuguese loanwords and began to undergo more profound grammatical transformations as a result of the forced imposition of new legal and religious discursive norms. At the same time, colonial legal institutions were forced to accommodate to indigenous norms as well, as when royal courts accepted as legal documents pictorial texts written in a mixture of Latin characters and Mesoamerican glyphs.

The formal study of the world's languages was, in many ways, hatched in Latin America. The creation of the first modern grammars is often attributed to the Spanish grammarian Antonio de Nebrija, whose 1486 grammar of Latin was followed by one for Castilian in 1492. He reputedly presented the latter to Spain's Queen Isabella with the fateful phrase, "Majesty, language is the perfect instrument of empire." And, indeed, language contact formed a crucial front in Spain's overseas expansion: Catholic priests were charged with learning Amerindian languages and using them as instruments of conversion and colonization. A lesser-known part of this story, however, is the fact that many of the grammars that followed were studies of indigenous languages like Nahuatl, Zapotec, and Guaraní. These works became the foundation for the modern study of languages across the globe while helping to cement the ongoing influence today of particular languages. Guaraní, for example, is one of Paraguay's official languages and continues to be spoken by a majority of its population. English and other languages have acquired a number of words from Guaraní, including *tapir, piranha,* and, most recently, the trendy berry *açaí.*

Latin America also became "Latin" America via the use of the Latin alphabet. The production of written texts—religious, legal, scholarly—was central to the colonial enterprise. But writing in the Americas has a previous history as well: several of the world's oldest and most sophisticated writing systems began developing some twenty-five hundred years ago in Mesoamerica (roughly, Mexico and Central America). Many were still widely used upon the arrival of the Spanish and for many decades after. But as colonial rule took hold in the Americas, the Spanish launched concerted efforts to gather and destroy texts written in indigenous languages, viewing them as idolatrous. Although this savage repression of indigenous religion nearly wiped out the region's ancient writing traditions, the remaining texts have come over the past century to attract widespread attention. The Mesoamerican codices that survived the purges ended up stashed in libraries in Paris, London, and elsewhere in Europe. Yuri Knorozov, the man who cracked the "Maya code," was born in Ukraine and studied ethnology and Egyptology in Moscow. His seminal work on Mayan writing, published in 1952, was based on codices that the Soviet Red Army snatched up from Berlin's national library in the aftermath of World War II. Knorozov's work also drew heavily from the writings of a sixteenth-century Spanish bishop named Diego de Landa. De Landa helped purge the Yucatan of Mayan writing, but in an ironic twist, his notes provided the key to rediscovering its lost meaning. Four and a half centuries later, Mayan communities in Mexico and Guatemala have reclaimed their symbols and now put them to use in street signs, logos, and other displays of local identity—everything from tattoos to online avatars. And the millions of tourists from around the world who visit the Mayan region every year take pieces of that ancient writing home with them, as Mayan glyphs emblazoned on T-shirts, jewelry, and other souvenirs.

Linguistic Contact and Borrowing

Contact between Iberia and the Americas transformed the linguistic character of both. Spanish became what it is today largely through engagement with Latin America. Across Europe, local vernaculars took the place of Latin as languages of authority. As the outlines of modern Spain coalesced behind the Kingdom of Castile, its royal house became the Spanish Crown. Castilian—only later known as "Spanish" in many parts of the world—became the language of that emerging nation and was carried with colonists to the Americas along with novel ideas and goods. Speakers of Amerindian languages had to invent new words for these. One strategy was to extend the meaning of already existing native words, such as using the word for "deer" to refer to horses as well. In a number of cases, speakers distinguished native things from imports by adding *castellano* to the name. For example, in the Mexican language Mazatec, the word for "bread"—a food dating from colonial days— is *ñoxtila* (Castilian tortilla); the word for "chair," a type of furniture likewise of colonial provenance, is *yaxile* (Castilian wood[en thing]).

Centuries of Moorish presence in Iberia also gifted Spanish and Portuguese with hundreds of Arabic loanwords from diverse realms of experience; from religion, *ojalá* (from *law šha' allāh*, "God willing"); from architecture, *adobe* and *alcoba* (alcove); from material culture, *almohada* (pillow); from agriculture, *café, azúcar, zanahoria, aceituna,* and *algodón* (coffee, sugar, carrot, olive, and cotton, respectively); from politics, *asesino* (assassin) and *alcalde* (mayor); from mathematics, *algebra* and *cero* (zero); and from commerce, *tarifa* (tariff). Many of these Arabic loans made their way into English, by way of contact with Spanish, and they were incorporated into indigenous Latin American languages as well. For example, the word for "coin" or "money" in many of these languages is derived from *tumn,* an Arabic loanword for "silver coin," as in the Nahuatl word *tomin* or the Mixe word *meen.*

Meanwhile, different national varieties of Spanish emerged across Latin America as they acquired distinctive rhythms and vocabulary taken in from the indigenous languages spoken all around them. This, in turn, sowed the seeds of linguistic conflict, as the divergence of Latin American Spanish from its peninsular parent led to the formation of the Real Academia Española (Royal Spanish Academy), which was charged with policing the language's boundaries and codes of contact. Early contact between Spanish and Taíno (a language widely spoken in the Caribbean before Conquest) gave Spanish the words *canoa* (canoe), *barbacoa* (barbecue), *hamaca* (hammock), and *cacique* (chief, boss), not to mention the names of two essential global food staples: *maíz* (corn) and *patata* (potato). Nahuatl heavily influenced Mexican Spanish, which absorbed names for places (Tlaxcala, Acapulco), plants (*tomate, chili*), animals (*ocelote, coyote*), cuisine (*tamales, chocolate*), and other things previously unknown to Europeans, such as *hule* (rubber) and *copal* (the crystallized sap of a New World tree used as incense). A similar process took place with Quechua words adopted into Andean Spanish, among them *llama, jerky* (as in beef jerky, from Quechua *ch'arki*), *condor, puma,* and the fashionable grain *quinoa.* Che Guevara got his famous nickname from the interjection *che* (man! dude!) used in Argentine and other varieties of South

American Spanish. One popular but contested narrative holds that it, too, is an indigenous loanword, originating in Mapudungun, the language of the Mapuche people of southern Chile and Argentina. In the territories controlled by Portugal, contact between Portuguese and indigenous languages such as Tupí was less extensive, although they nevertheless left an indelible mark on Brazilian Portuguese. Ponder that as you sit on the beaches of Ipanema ("fishless water"), drinking your *caipirinha* ("little hillbilly").

Thus Latin American words have been exported out of the region for centuries and have taken up residence in languages around the globe. The Spanish colonizers brought many Taíno and Nahuatl loanwords with them to the Philippines, where they entered into Tagalog. American English absorbed a large number of indigenous terms as well, through contact with Mexican Spanish. The list of Nahuatl loanwords in English includes staple crops such as maize, potatoes, tomatoes, and tobacco. Some of our favorite foods and drinks—such as guacamole, chocolate, and tequila—are also loans from Nahuatl. And there are other partially obscured Nahuatl gems in English such as Chiclet gum (from *tzictli*), chia pets (from *chian*), and shack—as in Radio Shack or "shacking up" (likely from *xacalli,* "hut"). Virtually all of these indigenous terms entered English indirectly, via Spanish. There is, though, at least one English word that possibly made the jump from an indigenous Latin American language directly into English via slave traders who passed through the Gulf of Mexico in the mid-sixteenth century: a sea creature with razor-sharp teeth that Mayans called *xook*. Today, English speakers call it *shark*.

Migration and the Slave Trade

The colonial era ushered in other waves of massive migration and forced movements of people into and out of Latin America. Throughout the region, European colonialism was firmly harnessed to emerging forms of global trade. Eventually this led to the development of one of the most notorious, tragic institutions in human history: the transatlantic slave trade. The introduction of maize from the New World led to explosive population growth in parts of Africa, which in turn made it possible for millions of Africans to be captured as slaves and forcibly relocated to the New World. Today, the profound and far-reaching legacies of this history are most visible in the millions of Afro-descendant Latin Americans, with populations of varying size in every Latin American country. The Caribbean islands, whose indigenous inhabitants were almost completely wiped out during the initial decades of Conquest, are now predominantly inhabited by Afro-descendant people. Brazil has a similar demographic profile: its small indigenous population, while politically and symbolically important, is dwarfed by Afro-Brazilians.

There are audible legacies of the slave trade as well. Creole languages are spoken throughout the Caribbean and coastal regions of South America. Combining elements of European, African, and Amerindian languages, these linguistic hybrids emerged directly out of the linguistic realities of slavery. Slave traders and owners tried to disrupt deliberately the transmission of African languages such as Igbo and Yoruba from one generation to the next by separating speakers of the same language. Hundreds of African loan-words—such as *marimba, merengue, mucama* (housemaid), *guineo* (banana), and *mandinga* (devil or goblin)—came to infuse not only Latin American varieties of Spanish and Portuguese, but eventually their European counterparts, too. And in Latin America's syncretic religions such as Santería and Candomblé, African languages and creolized varieties serve vital liturgical functions. In the wake of slave revolts and nineteenth-century wars of independence, a number of these creoles rose to become official languages of the new nations, such as Haitian Creole and Guyanese Creole. In the twentieth century, Jamaican Patwa—a rich blend of English, the West African language Akan, and parts of other African, European, and indigenous Caribbean languages—has had an enormous influence on global pop culture via the rise and spread of Rastafarianism and reggae music. A less well known but fascinating story is that of the Afro-Brazilian presence in Ghana. In the first half of the nineteenth century, several thousand former slaves returned to Ghana, bringing their variety of Portuguese with them. Still known today as the Tabom people (from Portuguese *ta bom*, "it's okay"), their Portuguese surnames are scattered across southern Ghana and the city of Accra. Contact between the Caribbean and West Africa is ongoing as Cuban medical brigades work with West African health officials to contain outbreaks of diseases like Ebola.

Over the past three centuries, developments in Latin America have shaped the world's linguistic landscape in other ways, too. Migrants from across the globe came to Latin America fleeing religious and political persecution or seeking economic opportunity. As a result, there are pockets of minorities across the region who speak languages that are neither indigenous nor stem directly from colonialism or the African slave trade. In the nineteenth century, for example, Tamil-speaking laborers were brought to Caribbean

French colonies, Hindi speakers to British Guyana, and Chinese laborers, both indentured and contract, to various parts of the region through the coolie trade; Chinese–New World culinary fusions—*chifa* food in Peru and *comida China-Cubana* in New York—represent a well-known legacy of this contact. From the Middle East, Lebanese descendants in Latin America include some of the region's most influential people: from Mexico's richest man, the Forbes list–topping billionaire Carlos Slim Helú, to the Colombian pop star Shakira. Diverse groups of Europeans also migrated to the region in sizable numbers, with linguistic consequences that continue today. In the 1860s and 1870s, several thousand Welsh nationalists moved to Patagonia to establish a colony there, far from the reach of the English-speaking world; Patagonian Welsh continues to be spoken in the Chubut province of Yr Ariannin (their name for "Argentina"). Communities of German speakers exist in almost every Latin American country, including Mennonites in Mexico and Paraguay and coffee plantation owners in Mexico and Guatemala. Buenos Aires became a global center for Yiddish theater in the first half of the twentieth century and today has one of the world's few remaining daily newspapers in the language.

Language and Religion

Not only a haven for religious minorities fleeing persecution, Latin America has also been the birthplace of new syncretic religions and a beacon for missionary and revival movements. Protestantism, for example, has had a deep and ongoing relationship with the region's indigenous languages—which in turn has had a significant impact on Protestant missionary work in other corners of the globe, especially that pursued by the Summer Institute of Linguistics (SIL). The field arm of the Wycliffe Bible Translators, the SIL is a recognized authority on the world's languages. In the process of attempting to translate the Bible into all living languages, the SIL has generated a vast trove of basic descriptive linguistic work that is global in scope. Yet many of the methods and approaches allowing them to accomplish this remarkable feat were forged and refined in Latin America. Its founder, a Protestant missionary named William Cameron Townsend, began his career as a Spanish-language Bible salesman in Guatemala. He soon realized that the Kaqchikel Maya speakers with whom he lived would be much better served by religious materials that they could actually understand and that "spoke to their hearts." Initially the SIL focused on Mexico and the Amazonian areas of

Peru. By the 1960s it had placed Bible translators in communities across Latin America and had begun making forays into Africa and Oceania. Their work has played a crucial role in subverting "linguistic racism" based on beliefs that indigenous languages are inherently inferior to European ones. The SIL has also been an important if controversial force of change, participating in and making possible the dramatic rise of Protestant evangelization across Latin America over the past century.

Latin America's linguistic influence on the world has been particularly tied to the evolution of the Catholic Church. Today, five centuries after the Catholic Church drew a dividing line through the Americas that granted one piece to Spain and the other to Portugal, the church has its first New World pope (see Scheper-Hughes and Scheper Hughes, this volume). He, like Borges, is Argentine. And like the renowned author, Pope Francis speaks a variety of Spanish that in many ways conforms to the standards promoted by Spain's Royal Spanish Academy—whose motto, tellingly, states its goal to "Limpia, fija y da splendor" (Clean, set, and give splendor [to]) the Spanish language. Yet his Spanish also departs from those norms, as when the pope recently said, "Dios nos premerea," drawing on *porteño* (Buenos Aires) soccer lingo, that could be glossed as "God goes out to meet us, he gets out ahead of us, he surprises us." This reflects the Catholic Church's ongoing reorientation over much of this century toward ideas and agendas anchored in Latin America.

The church was massively influenced by liberation theology; alternatively embraced and rejected by the church hierarchy, the movement originated in Latin America in the last half of the twentieth century and called for Christian teachings to be directed toward liberation from unjust social conditions. Pope Francis's recent decision concerning the assassinated priest Óscar Romero reflects the power of Latin American concerns to shape the church's direction: a Salvadoran and leading liberation theologian, Romero's leftist views previously had been the grounds for church officials in Rome to block his beatification. This shift in the balance of power within the church, like the pope's use of Argentine Spanish, is also part of broader realignments in the geopolitical order and their linguistic entailments: as some Latin American countries have moved past their former colonizers in the configuration of global power relations, New World varieties of Spanish and Portuguese have increasingly come to eclipse their peninsular counterparts in the global "marketplace of languages." This has implications for the global standing of Latin America's other languages as well. Since taking office, for example, one of Pope Francis's most remarkable decisions has been to approve a request from the Diocese of San Cristóbal de Las Casas (in Chiapas, Mexico) to officially approve the use of Mayan languages for mass, confession, and other Catholic rituals.

PAPAL *PORTEÑO* AND PRISON NAHUATL: LATIN AMERICA, LANGUAGE, AND THE WORLD TODAY

The Circulation of Things

Today, the reality of Latin America's national languages is one of global influence, and of crossing rather than remaining within national borders. This shift has been made possible by the circulation of people, ideas, and things—including a wide range of cultural goods tied to Latin American languages. These include music (Maisonnave this volume), film (Guillermoprieto this volume), *telenovelas* and other television programming (Benavides this volume), cuisine (Portnoy and Pilcher this volume), artwork, dance forms, and literature (Stavans this volume). Even languages themselves have made a splash on the global stage, as when the story of Ayapaneco—a dying indigenous language spoken in the Mexican state of Tabasco—recently became the centerpiece of an advertising campaign produced for the German telecom company Vodafone. Peruvian Quechua, famously, made it to a distant galaxy far, far away when George Lucas appropriated it for an alien argot in the original *Star Wars* movie.

Food terms like *chipotle,* which comes from Nahuatl *chili poctli,* "smoked chili pepper," and *tapioca,* from Tupí, are not only part of our shared global culinary vocabulary; they also function as symbolic gateways, inviting people to explore Latin America in a deeper way. Musical language serves a similar role. The global circulation of Latin American music and dance means that names such as *merengue, tango, cumbia, calypso, bolero, bossa nova,* and *samba* have been absorbed into languages around the world. And because the music itself is circulated and performed in Latin American languages, they, too, have a global presence, even for consumers who do not understand them. The same is true of Latin America's vibrant tradition of literary, film, and television production. Even in translation, elements of the original language are preserved, broadening the global influence of Latin American languages.

Migration

People have been moving to Latin America for centuries. Yet the region is more often portrayed not as a destination for migrants but as a mass producer of them. One of the best-known—and heavily stereotyped—vectors of Latin American linguistic influence on the world concerns this movement of Latin Americans into other countries across the globe. Latin Americans carry their languages with them on their journeys; badges of identity, they are also symbolic resources useful in establishing and maintaining connections in their destination countries. Latin American migrants have succeeded, to varying degrees, in preserving the use of their languages across multiple generations and in establishing public places for them. Pope Francis's family history exemplifies such trends. Born Jorge Mario Bergoglio in Buenos Aires in 1936, he was a child of immigrants who fled to Argentina to escape the fascism of Benito Mussolini's Italy. And like countless Latin Americans, he has "returned" to a place where he has roots that are not only cultural and historical but also linguistic. As Latin Americans have moved in large numbers to countries where they share the national language—Peruvians and Ecuadorans migrating to Spain, Brazilians to Portugal—their movement mirrors in reverse colonial-era migrations from Europe to the Americas.

The pattern has been echoed by people with ties to countries other than the Iberian colonial powers. Thus today there are large groups of Spanish-speaking Argentines, Chileans, and Venezuelans in Italy, Germany, and France; in Japan, there are sizable numbers of Peruvians and Ecuadorans. Though many do not speak the national language of the destination country, they have nevertheless been exposed to it in myriad ways through the presence of languages such as German, Italian, and Japanese in Latin America. Borges's own history echoes similar engagements with other countries and their languages. The author was raised in a bilingual Spanish-English household (one grandmother was English) and spent his formative years at schools in Switzerland and Spain.

Latin Americans in the United States

The country with the single largest number of Latin American migrants is the United States. This case exemplifies the dynamic flow of languages and ideas about them out from Latin America into the rest of the world. The history of U.S. influence in Latin America has often appeared—

notwithstanding official views to the contrary—to be little more than a new form of imperialism. But however one interprets U.S. political involvement in the region—from the Monroe Doctrine through the Cold War into the present—that history has positioned English as an invaluable linguistic resource across Latin America. While a relatively small percentage of Latin Americans speaks English as a first language, English has been of critical importance for Latin Americans moving back and forth between the region and the United States (and Canada) out of economic necessity. It has also played a crucial role in the lives of elite Latin Americans, who often pursue university education, shop, vacation, and do business in the United States. Within Latin America, English has been and continues to serve as a medium for political and economic transactions and as a gateway to Anglophone culture. Latin Americans have become adept at varying their spelling and pronunciation with great precision in order to indicate whether borrowed bits of English are meant to be understood as useful additions to local vocabulary or as evidence of American imperialism. It may be *Halloween* for a school lesson on American holidays, but it quickly becomes *Jalowín* in a sarcastic rant about the Americanization of Mexico's Day of the Dead festivities. Young people across Latin America ("fresas" in Mexico, "chetos" in Uruguay) pepper their speech with English slang in order to strike a cosmopolitan, upper-class pose. A wildly popular Mexican-Venezuelan children's television program called *La CQ* has teenage girls all over Latin America yelling, "¡Focus, chicos! ¡Focus!"

Anglo Americans do comparable symbolic work with badly mispronounced and ungrammatical Spanish. Often it gets used in clearly pejorative ways, as when a used car is sold "for pesos." Somehow a siesta sounds more decadent than an afternoon nap, a fiesta wilder than a festival. At other times, mock Spanish seems to evoke a fun-loving casual stance: "No problemo, man" (the grammatically correct version is "No hay problema"). And of course, there is a long and storied association in the American imagination between Spanish and the "Wild West." This includes places, such as the Ponderosa and Laredo; people and animals, such as buckaroo (*vaquero,* "cowboy") and mustang (*mesteño*); and institutions, such as ranch, rodeo, and hoosegow (*juzgado,* "jail").

Diverse communities of Latin American migrants have played a prominent role in American public life. Over the past century, Dominicans, Puerto Ricans, Haitians, and Cubans have all migrated to the United States in large numbers for reasons ranging from political repression and upheaval to economic necessity. Latin American migrants have a highly visible commercial presence, with restaurants and stores catering specifically to migrants and often targeting customers by country of origin; their influence is also felt through numerous cultural and religious organizations and events. Their existence has linguistic implications as well. Such businesses, institutions, organizations, and activities revolve around the use of Latin American languages. They create public spaces where using Latin American Spanish and Portuguese, Caribbean creoles, and Amerindian languages are legitimized and given value. This supports their transmission across generations and even recruits new speakers. Their use in the United States creates new spaces for linguistic mingling, where the dynamics of linguistic and cultural coexistence can be worked out in practice.

Immigrants are drawn to particular parts of the United States not only by networks of kinship but also by other forms of alliance that include sharing a language, even if not a country of origin. Thus most Portuguese-speaking immigrants to the United States moved to New England: initial migrants from Portugal, who arrived to work in the fishing and whaling industries, were later joined by migrants from Brazil, Cape Verde, and even Angola, all bringing along their own varieties of Portuguese as well as local creoles. Guatemalans and Salvadorans, for example, have tended to settle in regions with large communities of Mexicans and Mexican Americans—in a few cases, through connections made during their journey to the United States, which generally involves passing through Mexico first.

As the single largest group of Latin American immigrants to the country, the tens of millions of Mexicans and Mexican Americans living in the United States are perhaps a special case. In some locales—California, Texas, and Florida, as well as major cities like Chicago and New York—their numbers are especially large. But there are also sizable populations in nearly every state. Their relationship to the United States is conditioned not only by complex political and economic dynamics but also by geographic ones born of sharing—and fighting over—a common border. Officially the dividing line where Latin America ends, the U.S.-Mexico border is also one of the longest, most politically fraught, and most economically unequal international boundaries in the world.

Yet in the context of lived daily experience, the boundary between Mexican immigrants and the rest of the U.S. population is largely marked—and politicized—by language. Most Mexican immigrants speak Spanish, relatively few arrive speaking English, and most will conduct the bulk of their professional and personal lives in the United States in Spanish, even if they settle in the country permanently. The sheer size of the Spanish-speaking population in the United States makes this possible. Combined, Mexicans and other Spanish-speaking immigrant communities support a vast array of Spanish-dominant workplaces, businesses, service and cultural organizations, and media outlets. Their overwhelming numbers, geographic spread, public presence, and political prominence has made Spanish a de facto second language in the United States—a trend alternately lauded and attacked.

Lesser known is the extent to which many Mexican migrants are indigenous, and may speak little or no Spanish—sometimes resulting in tragic situations where individuals have been committed to mental institutions or denied legal rights. In other ways, however, indigenous Mexican languages have a demonstrable if modest public profile. The city of Los Angeles, for example, has both Zapotec and Mixtec newspapers and radio stations. And as with Latin American national languages, migration patterns between the United States and Mexico are shaped by indigenous languages: indigenous Mexicans overwhelmingly tend to migrate to areas where there are sizable groups of migrants who share their native language, as is the case with communities of indigenous Mexicans in Oxnard, Poughkeepsie, and Raleigh-Durham.

Language Debates

Debates about the presence of Latin Americans in the United States have had an outsized effect on conversations about Latin America's engagement with the world. On the one hand, in American popular culture, Latin American languages and their speakers serve as stand-ins for the quintessential Other. Their use in American films is particularly evocative: in thousands of films, spanning decades, Spanish-speaking Latin Americans and Latinos are portrayed as villains. On the other hand, the presence of Latin American languages in the United States has been a tale of increasing acceptance. Spanish has permeated English to the point, for example, that "Hasta la vista, baby!" can be uttered without translation in a Hollywood blockbuster.

Yet the increasingly public presence of Spanish on everything from voting ballots to billboards has also been the target of pointed critiques. While such arguments may be undergirded by anti-immigrant or even outright racist sentiment, they take language use as an acceptable site for expressing xenophobic views. A widely circulating Internet meme has an image of John Wayne in front of an American flag saying, "Now just why in the HELL do

I have to press '1' for English???" Language use is an arena where broader conflicts about immigration are waged, as reflected in debates about the acceptability of such phrases as "illegal immigrant" and "undocumented worker." While the choice between them may be cast as a dispute about labeling, the argument is animated by deeply conflicting political views about the relationship between Latin Americans and the United States.

Sometimes these debates move in unpredictable directions and spawn unexpected consequences. One striking example involves the way that Mexican gang members in U.S. prisons use Nahuatl as a private form of communication and demand access to materials about the language on cultural grounds. Another relevant example concerns the deportation of people who arrived in the United States as children and have spent the majority of their lives there. Because they speak fluent and "unaccented" American English— often speaking it better than they do Spanish—they have become coveted employees for American companies seeking to cut costs by locating customer call centers outside the United States.

The circulation of things Latin American has boosted the worldwide influence of Brazilian Portuguese and Latin American varieties of Spanish. Though long treated as inferior to the versions one hears in Portugal and Spain, Latin American varieties now dominate second language instruction, bowing to the reality that 90 percent of the world's Spanish speakers and 75 percent of its Portuguese speakers reside in the Americas. Each year, the Royal Spanish Academy's dictionary includes an ever larger percentage of words with New World origins. When the Academy decided to add the term *espanglish* to its 2014 dictionary, advocates of this English-Spanish hybrid were pleased. But when they found out that the Academy intended to define it as "*a form of speech used by some Hispanic groups in the United States, in which they mix deformed elements of vocabulary and grammar from both Spanish and English,*" the reaction was swift and loud. The Academy finally relented and agreed to remove the word *deformed* from the definition.

One of the most distinctive features of some varieties of Latin American Spanish is the *voseo*—the widespread use of *vos*, "you," as a formal second-person pronoun. It is a more archaic form than the *usted* form of "you" found in Caribbean and Iberian Spanish. *Vos* flourished, especially in South America, during an era of relatively little contact between the New World Spanish colonies and Europe. Something comparable happened with Brazilian Portuguese. *Vos*-filled Spanish is the style that Borges used in his writing and that Pope Francis has now brought to the Vatican. We live in an era when the centers of linguistic influence have shifted from Madrid to Mexico City and Miami, from Lisbon to Rio de Janeiro and New Bedford. If the Latin American *vos* eventually fades out of use, it will be because of the popularity of Mexican soap operas—and the *vos*-free variety of Spanish spoken in them—rather than the edicts of the Royal Spanish Academy's "language cops."

Language has shaped Latin America as a region and mediates its connections with the rest of the world. Heated debates about language—about what languages to speak and who should be speaking them—are taking place right now in Latin America, just as they are across the border in the United States and in places around the globe where Latin Americans reside. Should we raise bilingual children? How can we maintain the vitality of Latin America's hundreds of indigenous languages? Is it okay to code-switch, use borrowed words, speak Spanglish or Portuñol, use *vos* rather than *usted*? Such questions are simultaneously about language loyalties and the social landscape writ large. The Latin American "Library of Babel" is kaleidoscopic, unpredictable, conflictive, and vibrant: an archive of Latin America's history, it is also a story about the region's globalized future, told in a thousand different tongues.

SUGGESTED READING

Clements, Clancy
   2009 *The Linguistic Legacy of Spanish and Portuguese: Colonial Expansion and Language Change.* Cambridge: Cambridge University Press.
Coe, Michael D.
   2012 *Breaking the Maya Code.* 3rd ed. London: Thames & Hudson.
Romero, Simon
   2012 "An Indigenous Language with Unique Staying Power." *New York Times,* 12 March. http://nyti.ms/1Sw3Xo6.
Stavans, Ilan
   2004 *Spanglish: The Making of a New American Language.* New York: HarperCollins.
Terán, Victor, and David Shook, eds.
   2015 *Like a New Sun: New Indigenous Mexican Poetry.* Los Angeles, CA: Phoneme Media.

SIX

Love, Protest, Dance, Remix

Michelle Bigenho

FROM HIS HOME IN JAPAN, Takaatsu Kinoshita had been following Andean music since he was a young boy in the 1980s.[1] He was not alone. Several members of his family also were involved in this hobby. At the age of nineteen, he bought a one-way ticket to Bolivia. Twelve years later, he returned to Japan and began making a living as a professional, playing Andean and Latin American music. Japanese audiences have been drawn to Andean music since the 1970s when they first heard the sounds of the notched Andean flute called the *quena*. It was the instrument they heard in Simon and Garfunkel's hit rendition of "El cóndor pasa." Japanese audiences initially made few distinctions about the origins of this music, outside the frame of the "Andes" and the well-known reference to the Incas. As touring contracts were set up with different musicians from Peru, Argentina, and Bolivia, Japanese audiences became more discerning. Eventually, Bolivia became a key destination for Japanese sojourners who sought to better understand how this music is played. In turn, connections with these travelers opened doors for Bolivian musicians in Japan.

LOVE, PROTEST, DANCE, REMIX . . .

Depending on one's age, music from Latin America produces in the mind's ear and eye different sounds and images. One might see and hear Desi Arnaz playing his drums in a "Latin" act on television's *I Love Lucy*. One may hear Carmen Miranda, the Portuguese-born Brazilian-identified "bombshell," singing samba, a genre with Afro-Brazilian roots. Of course, one is perhaps more likely to remember Carmen Miranda by her movie image—the actress who wore a fruit headdress that seemed to extend endlessly to the sky. It's bananas all the way up! Her singing talents secured a ticket to Broadway and Hollywood. She even participated in World War II–era U.S. foreign policy on Latin America. Hollywood and the U.S. State Department swept her up in films aimed at Latin Americans. Assuming what would become a stereotypical Latina role, she starred in several films that showed a mishmash of cultural cues from Brazil, Mexico, Cuba, and Argentina. No wonder Brazilian and Argentine audiences rejected films like *Down Argentine Way,* in which Miranda sang not the Argentine tango but a rendition of Cuban rumba. Although Miranda's signature fruit headdress played off styles worn by Afro-descendants who live in Bahía—legacies of forced African displacements via the long history of the Portuguese Brazilian slave trade—her Hollywood representations were more Europeanized versions of Latin America. For the U.S. State Department, these films were aimed at Latin America's European-descendant elites, who tended to be white. Afro-descendants had no place in that picture.

Perhaps one remembers the mid-1990s brief macarena fad, a group dance that had publics in entire stadiums doing a routine with set steps anyone could learn. While the macarena was marketed like other Latin dance crazes—tango, rumba, mambo, and cha-cha-cha—it was originally recorded by the Spanish duo Los del Río.

Perhaps one hears the 1990s sounds of nostalgia for an old Cuba. One sees elderly Cuban musicians wandering the streets of Havana and New York City, as in the 1999 documentary *Buena Vista Social Club.* This recording initiative was preceded by the Vieja Trova Santiaguera, financed by the Spanish entrepreneur Manuel Domínguez and promoted through his world music label, Nubenegra. Such projects allowed Western audiences the pleasures of hearing an "old" Cuban music without being interrupted by the ideological disputes behind the Cuban Revolution and without hearing the sounds of contemporary Cuban hip-hop and reggaetón. Global Latin American music has always gone down multiple paths of pleasure, politics, and business.

LOVE, PROTEST, DANCE, REMIX . . .

Non–Latin American listeners have fallen in love with Latin American sounds, and in the process some people have cried foul. Some stories about how Latin American music travels the world criticize the marketing of nostalgia and exotic worlds. Powerful culture industries, usually controlled by those who are not Latin American, exploit these cultures of the Global South, mining "culturally rich" places for the profits and pleasures of non–Latin Americans. Tales of appropriation and commercial exploitation, however, do not make up the whole story of Latin American music in the world, because they fail to account for different types of listening and creative synergies. Latin American music has entered into wide global circulation through immigrant communities, recording industries, and touring musicians, but it has changed along the way. Global Latin American soundscapes can be read against histories of military dictatorships, protest songs, social inequalities, out-migration, and political exile. While Latin American immigrants have drawn on musical soundscapes from home as they craft a sense of belonging in a new place, non–Latin Americans have listened to and learned to participate in these sounds, whether that involves playing Latin American music, expressing leftist solidarity politics, or getting into a local salsa dancing scene.

Even though U.S.–Latin American connections are overwhelmingly a part of this soundscape, the sounds flow multidirectionally and circle back in some surprising ways. The present digitally saturated era makes the cultural politics of remix even more a part of the scene, democratizing some of the creative capacities of sound mixing and producing new creative effects, even if these developments have not dislodged long-standing relations of power and inequality. Taking listening seriously in global Latin American music means paying attention to how people reshape and participate in these soundscapes.

LOVE, PROTEST, DANCE, REMIX . . .

Love

"I was born into Bolivian music when I heard Simon and Garfunkel's 'El cóndor pasa,'" Ernesto Kawamoto told me at a café in Tokyo. "I also sang [Simon and Garfunkel's] other songs. But that one song! It was another kind of music! What instruments! It made me imagine something else. So I started to pursue the sound of the *quena* instrument." From another Japanese man, Kawamoto began to learn to play this Andean flute. Through his work for the magazine *Revista Latina,* Kawamoto studied Spanish as he followed tango and folklore performers in their concert tours of Japan. By then, he was dividing his time between playing music and working at his office job with the magazine. In 1982, when his boss forced him to choose between doing music and working at the magazine, he quit his job and went to Bolivia for three months. He described this trip as a transformative experience in which he met musicians in the legendary Peña Naira, a folklore nightclub in La Paz that was closely associated with the earlier performing days of those who, since the 1960s, were legends in these music traditions. "Takaatsu [Kinoshita] was the first Japanese to enter the Peña Naira. I arrived after him but during the same year. After that, many Japanese went to Bolivia. Takaatsu and I are part of that history." Kawamoto described hanging out at Peña Naira, getting to know the performers, and even substituting for some of them when they did not arrive for an evening's performance. Kawamoto set up an Andean music academy in Tokyo, and he has made a name for himself among Bolivian musicians who have toured Japan and among Japanese who are involved in Andean music.

Japanese fans of Andean music mention again and again their love for the song "El cóndor pasa." It literally opened their ears to a sound that was at the same time different and somewhat familiar—the winning formula in the world music scene. How did this specific song become the global calling card for Andean music? In the 1960s, Simon and Garfunkel shared a Paris stage with an Andean folklore ensemble that was first known as Los Incas and later as Urubamba. Simon and Garfunkel became intrigued by this band's performance of "El cóndor pasa."[2] The piece they played had been only a small part of a musical theatrical production (*zarzuela*) that was composed by the Peruvian Daniel Alomía Robles in 1913. In Peru, the early twentieth-century production's plot line was about foreign exploitation of indigenous miners in Peru's central highlands. In its heyday, this was an extremely popular theatrical production in Lima, and it was presented some three thousand times in five years. Alomía Robles's composition was like the other *indigenista* artistic expressions of the time, musical compositions that followed European patterns and aesthetics while drawing inspiration from indigenous music of the Andean countryside. Fast forward to Simon and Garfunkel's 1960s Paris encounter with Los Incas-Urubamba, an ensemble composed primarily of Argentine musicians. Paul Simon set his own lyrics to the opening melody, and thus was born one of the most controversial tunes that fueled the Andean music boom, a classic case of a first world musician supposedly "discovering" and then shaping these sounds into marketable form. Peruvians have been indignant about Simon's purported theft of the tune, and they have clamored to reclaim this composition as national heritage. Bolivian musicians' attitudes about the tune vary. Most of them are just tired of playing it for international audiences, even if it remains a mainstay of the Bolivian performance repertoire in Japan.

LOVE, PROTEST, DANCE, REMIX . . .

. . . Protest

Sometime between the 1960s and 1970s, the global circulation of Andean music fused exotic Indian worlds to leftist solidarity politics.[3] A coup in Chile played a key role in this development. In 1973, the U.S. CIA backed the overthrow of Salvador Allende, Chile's democratically elected socialist president. The coup was followed by the dictatorship of Augusto Pinochet, a regime responsible for countless human rights abuses. During the political movements leading up to the election of Allende, singers and songwriters like Violeta Parra and Víctor Jara had developed the protest style *Nueva canción*, or New Song. When Pinochet took power, Inti-Illimani and Quilapayún, bands formed in these moments of social protest, went into exile and found politically sympathetic audiences in Europe and beyond.

. . .

Inti-Illimani toured Australia in 1977. Ten years later, other Chilean exiles living in Tasmania formed the band Arauco Libre. While Chilean exiles arriving in Australia had to disrupt the Hollywood stereotypes of Latin Americans that had been established since the days of Carmen Miranda, bands like Arauco Libre created their own imaginaries too. For example, their name, Arauco Libre (Free Arauco), referenced indigenous people who had very little to do with those from whom the now well-known Andean sound had been appropriated. The band's name referenced the "Araucanians," the Spanish colonizers' term for those who were associated with the present-day Mapuche indigenous peoples in Chile and Argentina, peoples who had never come under Inca rule. In New Zealand, other Chilean exiles formed the band Kantuta (referencing the national flower of Bolivia and Peru), but this ensemble presented a broader Latin American repertoire, performing warhorses like "Guantanamera" and "La cucaracha," and eventually moving into romantic salsa.

When Chile returned to democracy in 1990, protest music in Australia held on to the indigenous associations that then entered a world music stage. Second-generation migrants in Melbourne musically developed not their parents' themes of dislocation, protest, and exile but their own concerns about seeking a Latin American identity. The band Inka Marka, formed in 1997, did so by taking a name that conjured up connections to the ancient Inca Empire.

. . .

Protest traditions have a long and continuing history in Latin American music, but they do not all cross over so easily into global contexts.[4] *Corridos,* a ballad form popular in northern Mexico and the U.S.-Mexico border region, tell tales of underdogs who stand up to power and fight back, whether those fighters are running from abusive Texas Rangers, engaged in the Mexican Revolution alongside Emiliano Zapata, or even running drugs (as sung in *narcocorridos*) because that is the only way to make ends meet. With its accordion-based polka rhythms, *corridos* do not inspire much dance movement outside the Latino community, and its forms of protest are often buried in many Spanish verses. As a genre heavily driven by lyrics and ballad storytelling, it appeals to Mexican and Mexican American audiences in the United States, but remains somewhat under the radar among U.S. Anglos. However, this rather globally uncelebrated genre took the stage in a new way when makers of the hit television show *Breaking Bad* hired the band Los Cuates de Sinaloa to compose and perform a *corrido.* The show featured a plot about Walter White (alias Heisenberg), an Anglo Albuquerque-based chemistry-teacher-turned-meth-dealer. The band's *narcocorrido* "Negro y azul" included an accompanying video that lionized this fictional dealer and depicted Heisenberg's legend as it was imagined to have traveled down into Mexico.

LOVE, PROTEST, DANCE, REMIX . . .

. . . Dance

When I was in Tokyo in 2003, the Bolivian dancer Zenobia Mamani invited me to a *cueca* class she was teaching. *Cueca* is a Bolivian genre danced by couples. In her country of origin, Mamani married a Japanese Andean folklore musician who had lived over a decade in Bolivia before returning to Japan with Mamani and their son. In a foreign country, Mamani went to work with her skills as a Bolivian dancer, drawing as her students Japanese Andean music enthusiasts who sought out dance classes in order to feel the groove of more complicated genres like the *cueca*. A year later, I met up in Bolivia with a Japanese couple from Mamani's class. They were spending a few months there, hoping to fulfill the dream of learning the many distinct *cueca* dance styles found in different parts of Bolivia: La Paz, Chuquisaca, Cochabamba, Tarija, and El Chaco.

. . .

While Andean music, like most music of the world, is meant for dancing, it is not the kind of Latin American music that draws the most non–Latin Americans to the dance floor. That honor has gone to tango and salsa. The Argentine tango arrived in Japan via 1920s Paris and then in British instruction manuals.[5] Paris was consecrating Latin American music for the world long before the "El cóndor pasa" saga. In the 1930s, the French Moulin Rouge Tango Band played in Tokyo's Florida Ballroom. And during World War II, tango continued to be played in Japan, even though most foreign music was banned there at the time. Some form of "the tango" is now part of the ballroom dance scene in many parts of the world. Its dance steps, like a series of complicated balancing exercises, have even been seen as potentially therapeutic for the elderly and those suffering from Parkinson's disease.

. . .

Many people agree that salsa music gets a lot of people dancing, but few people agree on the music's origins. Cuban? Puerto Rican? Colombian? Venezuelan? Nuyorican (New York Puerto Ricans)? The symbolic conflicts over the origins of salsa reflect political histories. To summarize very briefly, in the 1960s, the New York–based Fania Records started using "salsa" as a marketing label, but some people said that these recordings were nothing more than Cuban music dressed in new clothes.

Even if one wants to remain out of the fray in this origin war, three points are worth keeping in mind. First, U.S.-Cuban relations, beginning with the 1960 embargo, reshaped the previous musical flows between the island and the United States. Second, Nuyorican salsa formed as a vital part of 1960s and 1970s grassroots movements for Latino identities and civil rights. Third, the lack of agreement on the national origins of salsa music is in itself significant, reflecting the music's long-term historical roots in colonialism and the Caribbean-based African diaspora.

The salsa origin wars hardly kept non–Latin Americans away from dancing this music, which experienced a major crossover in the 1980s and 1990s. When I was studying for a master's degree in Lima, Peru, I remember dancing to Orquesta de la Luz, a Japanese salsa band that in 1990 had a number one album on Billboard's tropical chart. The 1989 flash-in-the-pan fame of lambada set off a renewed interest in couple-based dancing. For those who did not experience or who cannot remember this moment, lambada was a genre briefly popularized by the French Brazilian band Kaoma in albums like *World Beat* and *Tribal-Pursuit*. Video presentation of lambada showed a dance in which women in short skirts and revealing underwear gyrated their crotches against the thighs of their male partners, all while keeping the hips in constant motion. What looked great in the videos seemed impossible to replicate in the layperson's social dancing encounter. Some attempts led to dancing disasters, long before "Miley Cyrus" and "twerking" collided in the U.S. national lexicon. If awkwardness did not completely kill the trend, the law did. The Bolivian Andean band Los Kjarkas successfully sued Kaoma for the unlicensed cover of "Llorando se fue." The Hermosa brothers of Los Kjarkas had composed this tune, which had become the single song most associated with lambada.

While lambada fell flat, salsa took off as a global dance phenomenon among non–Latin Americans. If non–Latin Americans were drawn to the sounds of stoic Indians in an imagined Andean indigenism, in salsa they were drawn to imagined tropicalized sounds. Participating in this scene meant going to clubs, taking classes, and attending congresses in North America and Europe. In the crossover, salsa dancing went from being improvised to being choreographed. In marched a de-Africanized ballroom aesthetic that involved moves to be learned and a hip fetish that ignored the necessary corresponding knee and ribcage movements. Men who have taken salsa classes may feel the need to show off all their leading moves, each one studied, memorized, and pulled out to impress. On this salsa floor, one can forget too easily the very pleasurable feeling of simply getting in a good groove and staying there for a long time. In cities like Montreal, salsa roulette has taken this genre in yet another direction. In this form, several couples dance together, changing partners and completing moves according to the calls of a lead male dancer. Think here about square dancing or contra dancing, but salsified.

Nacho Gálvez initially arrived in London as yet another Chilean exile. At first, he opened a club that featured Chilean New Song, but by the 1990s, the folk protest songs were replaced by salsa. London clubs catered to either working-class immigrants or non–Latin Americans who were drawn to salsa dancing. The United Kingdom Alliance of Professional Teachers of Dancing and Kindred Arts professionalized salsa with examinations, certificates, formal competitions, a registry of steps, and even health and safety rules. Latin American immigrants in London did not take well to the idea of the English telling them how to dance their own music! When non–Latin American salsa dancers ventured out to Latin American contexts, they were dismayed to find their own "official" style was little more than a parody of "the real thing."

LOVE, PROTEST, DANCE, REMIX . . .

. . . Remix

Alberto "Beto" Pérez, a Colombian born in Cali who immigrated to the United States at the end of the 1990s, developed the carefully trademarked Zumba exercise classes that have become common at many gyms.[6] While non–Latin American salsa and tango dancers may take special pride in learning their steps and coming to a greater understanding of Latin American cultures, some might say that quite the opposite is the case for these remixed Latin rhythms that have stopped being a mode of pleasure and now have been put to the more utilitarian end of making people around the world more fit. Some people, however, have suggested that Zumba fitness and the music used in this workout have created a new fan base for Latin musicians like Daddy Yankee and Don Omar, both Puerto Rican reggaetón artists.

. . .

When the reggaetón artist "El General" traveled to Chile, officials confiscated his performance costumes. Pinochet, who was not a fan, had the singer unnamed and derobed. Will the real General please step forward? El General, the artist, would only be allowed to perform in civilian clothes and under his birth name, Edgardo Franco. El General was born in Panama but began his singing career when he went to New York in 1985. His trajectory exemplifies the transnational and multilingual aspects of the reggaetón genre whose grassroots origins are in Panamanian and Puerto Rican Spanish-language reggae, U.S. hip-hop, and Jamaican dancehall. The genre has been shaped heavily in the United States but also has roots in West Indian immigration, Jamaican patois, and Rastafarianism. Today's digital recording tools have facilitated reggaetón's remix, production, and distribution across a wide section of U.S. and Latin American creators and audiences. Unlike many other global Latin American genres that have become more Europeanized, reggaetón still embraces its black roots. Young people in Cuba are listening and dancing not to the nostalgic Buena Vista Social Club sounds that enchant foreigners but to the trans-American and trans-Caribbean sounds and languages of reggaetón.

. . .

If the Global North's approach to salsa Europeanized the dance, salsa also had its circuits of re-Africanization—processes that occurred between Cuba, New York City, and West Africa.[7] In 1931, the Cuban "Peanut Vendor Song" ("El manicero") arrived in West Africa via RCA Victor's recording by Don Aspiazu and his Havana Casino Orchestra. When Radio Dakar went on air in 1949, its programming also reflected the French colonial love for Latin American music. By the time of the Cuban Revolution, an African-based recording industry was booming, Abidjan had become a show business center, and wealthy Ivorians were sponsoring tours of their favorite artists from Cuba and New York. The African recording industry also catered to African students who had studied in Cuba and then returned to the continent with a thirst for Cuban music.

The Senegambian singer Laba Sosseh occupied a prime place in this re-Africanization process. But Sosseh always denied that he was a salsa musician. Born into a griot family in Gambia in 1943, Sosseh came to see Afro-Cuban music as a sound of liberation. He had no interest in the Cuban Revolution but took seriously the black anticolonial alliances he established with musicians from Cuba and New York City. Fania Records stars, like "Monguito" (Ramón Sardiñas Quián), played with Sosseh, finding common connections through black cultural elements that were then rerooted in Africa. When Sosseh traveled to Cuba, however, around the turn of the twenty-first century, he faced challenges because of his focus on blackness.

Such ideas that highlighted race did not go over well in a context where official policy still presented Cuba as a raceless society.

. . .

Other social and musical remixes show ties that do not fit neatly in the usual critiques of how the Global North and West exotify the Global South and East. The Chinese are investing more in Latin America, taking more vacations to the region, and hearing at home more sounds from Latin America, whether as part of the Chaoyang International Pop Music Festival, as entertainment at an Argentine-themed bar in Shanghai called Boca, or as part of the repertoire performed by the Chinese National Orchestra. In this last case, the Chinese musicians played Latin American music on traditional Chinese instruments and also paired up with a Colombian dance troupe, Sankofa, which emphasizes the African roots of Colombian music and dance.

In India, one can encounter Latin American music in the everyday gym workout. Zumba and the "Afro-Cuban Dance Routine" now sit next to other local gym class offerings like "Masala Bhangra" and "Bollywood Workout." For those who want to become dance enthusiasts, they may take salsa dancing at studios like the Hot Shoe Dance Company in Chennai, where Jeffery Gerard Vardon teaches salsa after having received classical ballet training in Russia and salsa dance training in Melbourne, Australia. In addition, Indian artists have been working Bollywood–Latin American fusions. Tanvi Shah, an Indian singer-songwriter, won a Grammy award for Spanish lyrics in a song from the film *Slumdog Millionaire*. She began listening to Latin American rhythms in her college dormitory when she studied as an undergraduate in the United States. Back in India, she now sings in Spanish and Portuguese (among many other languages) and claims to be inspired by the likes of Celia Cruz and Gloria Estefan; the first artist was well known for her stunning salsa career, notably developed outside Fidel Castro's Cuba, and the second artist is a Cuban-born U.S.-based singer-songwriter whose family fled revolutionary Cuba when she was quite young.

. . .

As many Bolivian musicians say, "The Andean music boom is over." They talk frankly about how their tours of Europe and now Japan will not last forever.

They are scrambling for new proposals, as economic necessity forces some of them to consider what they themselves label as completely fake—dressing in the stereotypical image of a native North American Indian and giving a techno New Age spin to one's music. They call this, or any other kind of musical faking, *vendiendo la pomada* (selling the pomade), which translates as something like "selling snake oil." Digital tools have made selling snake oil all the easier.

When I wanted to know more about this new generic Native American style, I was told to look up some Peruvian groups on YouTube, artists who are shown as singers or flute players, standing on boulders in the middle of rivers. The artists wear their hair long and loose, with headbands and sometimes feathers. Some of them don a stereotypical Native American buckskin suit with decorative details and fringes. Bolivians told me that artists like these sell their recordings to street musicians, who then use playback performances to promote the sale of the recordings in Europe. One person confessed that a Bolivian residing in Germany asked him to make a recording in this style; the producer asked him to alter his playing, to perform in a "flat" (*plano*) way, without the usual dynamics and inflections he would give a phrase. He in turn specifically asked that his name not be listed among the recording musicians. Another musician admitted he wanted to use his own studio to make these kinds of recordings, but he wanted to leave it to others to perform this music on the street, to actually "sell the snake oil."

The Bolivian musicians' disdain for these new styles and their embarrassment about participating in their production show the complicated positions of musicians as they face the shifting demands of a global market. Bolivians perform with pride their interpretation of Bolivian indigenous representations, but "Indian" here is not universally interchangeable. Bolivians feel silly altering their musical and sartorial aesthetics in order to look and sound like a native North American, and perhaps even more problematically, like those from their rival neighboring country, Peru. To participate in this new music economy that meets an external shift in the desired exotic, some Bolivian musicians have preferred the anonymity the recording studio allows. While Bolivian music production used to be concentrated in the hands of a few large labels, today small private recording studios are found in many Bolivian musicians' homes, sometimes even at the center of that home.[8] Although not without their own set of problems, in these studios musical and cultural remixes have become so much easier with digitally assisted moves.

Latin American musics have traveled the globe through love, protest, dance, and remix. Trafficking in nostalgia and the exotic, global Latin American music depends on frames of tropicalization and nativization. But these frames do not capture the sincerity with which many non–Latin Americans become participants in these musical worlds. In the post–protest song era, non–Latin American enthusiasts are less engaged in solidarity politics and more attuned to fitness crazes and techniques of specific dance moves, although re-Africanization circuits are exceptions, calling forth common histories of colonization, slavery, and diaspora. Moreover, for Latin Americans living outside the region, playing one's own music can still be a deeply political act, as people forge a sense of self and community in foreign and often alienating contexts.

SUGGESTED READING

Aparicio, Frances, and Cándida F. Jáquez, eds.
  2003 *Musical Migrations.* Vol. 1: *Transnationalism and Cultural Hybridity in Latin/o America.* New York: Palgrave Macmillan.
Bigenho, Michelle
  2012 *Intimate Distance: Andean Music in Japan.* Durham, NC: Duke University Press.
Clark, Walter Aaron, ed.
  2002 *From Tejano to Tango: Latin American Popular Music.* New York: Routledge.
Rivera, Raquel Z., Wayne Marshall, and Deborah Pacini Hernández, eds.
  2009 *Reggaeton.* Durham, NC: Duke University Press.
Waxer, Lise, ed.
  2002 *Situating Salsa: Global Markets and Local Meanings in Latin Popular Music.* New York: Routledge.

NOTES

1. Throughout this chapter, I draw on my own work as found in *Intimate Distance: Andean Music in Japan.* In the following section, I also draw on the work of Walter Aaron Clark, Eric Galm, Melinda Russell, Ariana Hernández-Reguant, and Geoffrey Baker.

2. In the following discussion, I draw on the work of Lynn A. Meisch, José Antonio Llórens Amico, and Anahid Kassabian.

3. In this section, I draw on the work of Fernando Rios, Jan Fairley, and Dan Bendrups.

4. In this section, I draw on the work of Richard Flores, José E. Limón, and Elija Wald.

5. In this section, I draw on the work of Marta Savigliano María del Carmen de la Peza, Madeleine E. Hackney, Svetlana Kantorovich, and Gammon M. Earhart; Louis A. Pérez; Robin Moore; Frances Aparicio and Cándida F. Jáquez; Shuhei Hosokawa; Norman Urquía; Frances Aparicio and Susana Chávez-Silverman; Jonathan Skinner; Sheenagh Pietrobruno; Joanna Bosse; and Patria Román Velázquez.

6. In this section, I draw on the work of Christopher Twickel and El General; Raquel Z. Rivera, Wayne Marshall, and Deborah Pacini Hernández; and Geoffrey Baker.

7. In the following section, I draw on the work of Ariana Hernández-Reguant and Richard Shain.

8. Here I draw on the work of Henry Stobart.

Lo Prohibido

Renato Rosaldo

ICE states its mission: *to protect national security,*
enforce immigration laws, fight crimes and terrorist activity.

In Manhattan, the phone woke me.
My daughter, Olivia, called from Oakland,
told what José, her fourth-grade student,
told her that morning. Face flushed, eyes wide,
he spoke only Spanish, el idioma
en que pudo decir lo prohibido.
On his way home from César Chávez Elementary School
in Richmond, the migra called ICE, asked,
Who in your house has no papers?
I'm a citizen, born here, the boy said.
As José arrived home,
the migra burst in,
dogs straining on leashes.
The boy's eyes fixed
on jaws, snarls, white teeth.
His family has papers,
but, in five days, José will be sent
back to Mexico, where he's never been,
the walk home from school without dogs.

SEVEN

Breaking the Machine

SOUTH AMERICAN *FÚTBOL*

Brenda Elsey

FOOTBALL WAS CREATED IN ENGLAND but perfected in South America. It would be difficult to think of another cultural practice so closely identified with the region. Football is unique in that it is formally governed, it is supremely popular, and it moves bodies across borders. Football both reflects broader trends and deviates sharply from them. Like many of the region's resources, football is an export commodity. In Argentina and Brazil, the exportation of football players has surpassed that for traditional commodities, such as beef. However, it is not a simple matter of shipping off the cheapest raw materials to developed markets. From Spain to Indonesia, clubs around the world seek South American coaching, playing, and technical talent. On the pitch, unlike in the global economy, South Americans have beaten the industrialized North at its own game.

Football diffused in the late nineteenth century as part of European imperialism. Its lag in popularity in the Caribbean, behind baseball and cricket, is a testament to distinctive colonial histories. In addition, the Caribbean, Central American, and Mexican football federations are institutionally separated from their South American counterparts in the world governing body of football, the International Federation of Association Football, or FIFA. The South American Football Confederation formed in 1916 to encompass most of the mainland. Despite these divisions, when luminaries have sought a common thread to knit together *Latin* America, they have looked to football. Football's recent surge in popularity in the Caribbean, most notably Cuba, reflects the increasingly integrated cultural identity of Latin America, motored by Spanish and Portuguese media conglomerates.

There are countless stories worth telling of how South America nurtured the global game. On the pitch, South Americans developed a style of play that emphasized artistry over force. The "beautiful game," or *jogo bonito* in

Brazil, was first a nickname for the South American style of football and later for the sport itself. Characterized by speed, grace, and creativity, this style has been interpreted by fans as a rebellion against the mechanization of leisure. This style of play helped to popularize the game in Asia, Africa, and the Middle East. European football clubs favored spatial strategies, mechanical set plays, and ultra-defensive tactics. Football publics, not only players, created styles of play. Passion for football has been fueled by this relationship between group experience and interpretation. The story of South American style is much more complicated at the level of organization and governance. Off the pitch, scholars have criticized the role of football in state propaganda, consumerism, and social inequalities.

FOOTBALL, INFORMAL EMPIRE, AND REFORM
MOVEMENTS

Bankers, engineers, dockworkers, and other brokers of British investment in South America introduced football to the region. By the 1890s, every major port city boasted a football club. Despite its rapid dissemination, British club directors found it inconceivable that "colonials" could master the game. In 1885, Montague Shearman, founder of the Amateur Athletics Association, predicted that football would become "a common pastime for all *English*-speaking nations of the globe." Children of British immigrants returned from their studies in England eager to launch clubs. The story of the patriarch of Brazilian football, Charles Miller, who returned from boarding school in Southampton and founded the São Paulo Athletic Club, is exemplary.

British managers encouraged employees in the mines and railroads to organize football games in order to develop discipline. For example, in 1903, while building the railroad in Barranquilla, the Colombian Railway Company gathered the first team that claimed to be a "national" squad. Educational institutions served as another conduit for the diffusion of football. Schoolteachers, like the "founder" of Paraguayan football, the Dutchman William Paats, sought a pedagogical tool to instill morality in their students. Middle- and upper-class reformers across the Americas, anxious about labor agitation, hoped football would encourage young men to develop healthy habits, time management, and respect for authority. Moreover, leaders hoped football could repair supposed racial deficiencies of their nations, exacerbated by the popularity of indigenous and African practices, such as capoeira in

Brazil. Thus, in football's early years, directors tied the sport to eugenics and racial hierarchies.

Waves of immigrants to South America between 1880 and 1920 cross-pollinated football fields on both sides of the Atlantic. Newcomers found that participating in football clubs eased the transition into their new homes and helped them maintain ties to one another. By 1914, half of Buenos Aires was foreign born, with the majority arriving from Spain and Italy. Immigrant football clubs built stadiums, offered literacy classes, and hosted politicians. In addition to southern Europeans, Asian and Middle Eastern immigrants shaped football in South America. Club Palestino in Chile and Esporte Clube Sírio in Brazil are a testament to this history. Chinese laborers founded clubs as well, including the popular Peruvian institution, Club Alianza Lima.

To appreciate the influence of South America on the global game, one must consider the politics of club organization, which contrast starkly with the British model. Ignoring the pleas of football patriarchs to keep politics out of sport, anarchists and socialists organized clubs as vehicles to build solidarity among workers. During times of repression, football clubs acted as makeshift headquarters of labor unions. By 1906, there were enough of these clubs in Santiago alone to form the Chilean Workers' Football Association, which fought discriminatory practices in public parks and created worker-controlled governance in clubs. Influenced by these leaders, footballers in South America structured clubs as nonprofit, amateur, and collectively owned entities. Members of these clubs gained valuable political skills, including public speaking, writing petitions, and lobbying politicians. Football clubs played a particularly important role when the state failed to provide public services.

The organization of international tournaments elevated football's importance and intensified its transnational character. This process was facilitated by innovations in communications, especially film and the telegraph. In addition, trains, ocean liners, and cars made it possible for players to travel faster and farther than ever. In the very early 1900s, only the wealthiest players represented national teams. By the 1920s, football had become a yardstick for national progress and the pressure to win proved stronger than the desire to exclude. That players from humble backgrounds could lead national squads reversed some of the shame associated with poverty. Talented football stars constructed alternative masculinities that demonstrated the strength, rather than the decadence, of the working-class male body. The football icon presented a counterpoint to the military man, the dominant model of masculinity in the region.

NUNCA se nos hubiera ocurrido que pudiera existir en Chile un club de foot-ball formado por jóvenes pertenecientes al sexo débil y bello. Si las fotografías no mienten, hé aquí dos gallardos teams formados por un grupo de beldades bastante atrayente. LAS mujeres adictas para robar á los hombres todos sus campos, hasta los de foot-ball... y, á decir verdad, que en este terreno serán invencibles, porque, ¿quién será el valiente que se atreva á luchar contra estos grupos de gracias?

Team Talca de la Escuela Normal

FIGURE 7.1. A newspaper featuring the women football players of Team Talca, Chile, in the early 1900s. Courtesy of Museo Histórico Nacional Chile.

As football became a vehicle for developing masculinity, club directors marginalized women from the sport. Women organized teams in South America as early as the 1890s. Typically, journalists expressed shock at discovering women's interest in football. In response to the formation of a woman's club in the early 1900s, one journalist remarked, "It would never have occurred to us that there could exist in Chile a football club formed by young members of the weak and beautiful sex." Fan chants of many clubs ridiculed the opposing teams for their femininity and supposed homosexuality. In this way, clubs created a hostile environment for women, as well as gay spectators. Although some clubs provided an auxiliary membership category for women, they were usually grouped with children. In looking through media, correspondence, and memoirs of the time, it is apparent that men viewed football as an escape from domestic life. Cartoonists caricatured women as angry wives waiting for their husbands to arrive from the football club or as transgressors in the stands. Humor based on violence and ridicule of women was a mainstay of sports magazines.

Despite these obstacles, women's football teams and fan clubs developed in fits and starts. Legislators in Brazil found women footballers threatening enough to prohibit them from playing between the 1940s and the 1970s. The dictatorships that came to power in South America hampered efforts to develop women's sports. Military juntas promised the restoration of traditional gender roles. Eventually, incentives to organize women's football came from abroad, particularly with the interest of FIFA in developing, and controlling, women's participation. South American women players have recently taken important positions on European and U.S. women's club teams. Without any infrastructure to speak of, Brazil has produced the most decorated football player in history, man or woman, in Marta Vieira da Silva. Like her male counterparts, Marta's style has been influential in reframing football from a disciplinary to a creative sport.

NATIONALISM, RACE, AND THE BORDERS OF FOOTBALL

The growth of international competitions led to a stronger association between football and national progress. For a long time, Europeans ignored the effervescence of football in South America. After dozens of invitations from South American associations, British clubs began tours of the region in the 1910s. Newspapers reported that curious fans came out in droves. The Brazilian Club Fluminense sponsored a tour of Oxford players in the hope that they would teach the masses correct sporting behavior. Curiously, South American associations clung to amateurism longer than the British. Whereas the British permitted professionalism in the 1870s, South American associations forbade it until the 1930s. Prolonged amateurism and the persistence of member-owned clubs created a perception of South American football as "antimodern."

South American national teams included players "of color" much earlier than their European counterparts, which had a profound effect on the global game. Black players stood out among South America's first superstars, especially in Uruguay. Many players of indigenous descent "passed" into national

FIGURE 7.2. Afro-Uruguayan star José Andrade behind a bar during the 1928 Olympics in Amsterdam. Photographer unknown, National Archives of the Netherlands.

First African Players

categories of mestizo, avoiding overt stigma. Racial integration of football did not reflect egalitarian societies. Still, there were moments when athletic excellence disrupted racist beliefs. The Afro-Uruguayan players Isabelino Gradín and Juan Delgado led their national team to victory in the first South American Cup of 1916. Like many of their generation, Delgado and Gradín could identify their ancestors connecting them with slavery. Delgado was a *candombe* drummer, a musical genre created by slaves on the sugar plantations. *Candombe* continues to be the signature sound of Uruguayan football.

The 1924 and 1928 Olympics, as well as the first World Cup of 1930, made it impossible for Europeans to ignore the excellence of South American football. Uruguay won all three competitions, with Argentina following close behind. In the 1928 Olympics in Amsterdam, the Uruguayan forward, José Leandro Andrade, known as the "black marvel," was a sensation. Reportedly the son of an Argentine woman and an escaped Brazilian slave, Andrade did not find the same opportunities as his white counterparts, who were offered professional salaries to play in France, Italy, and Spain. When not shining shoes or selling newspapers, Andrade worked as a carnival musician. Whether athletic success translated into better quality of life for Afro-Uruguayans is difficult to determine. After Isabelino Gradín's death, black clubs held fundraisers to help his family. José Andrade did not fare much better: he died in a nursing home for the poor.

The question of whether South Americans played differently than Europeans in the 1920s is a thorny one for scholars. Recently, film footage has become available, but reviewing it does not help us understand the significance for people living in that moment. When asked about style in this period, the historian Jeffrey Richey explained, "When you read South

American and European accounts of South American players in Spain, they are totally at odds. There are omnipresent complaints about the referees favoring one side or the other. Thus, the question of style is distorted by pressures of the press to defend their own." The Uruguayans, and to a lesser extent the Argentines, dominated their European competitors in a way that surprised even themselves. The European press seemed to agree that South American players brought a lightning-quick, short-pass game that befuddled their opponents.

As European clubs toured South America with greater frequency, the football fan cultures made an impression on visitors. Fans integrated other cultural forms into their game rituals. Visiting sportsmen saw fans playing national musical styles, like the tango, which became a sensation in the United States and Europe. The famed tango singer Carlos Gardel visited the Argentine football squad during both the 1928 Olympics and the 1930 World Cup. In Argentina and Uruguay, tango musicians dedicated songs to footballers, as did samba musicians in Brazil. The intimate connection between dance and football existed in the minds of players, who frequently attributed their prowess on the football field to their dancing.

The first transatlantic football transfers flowed in the opposite direction of labor migration, from South America to Europe. Italian clubs touring South America met talented players who were eager to earn a decent wage playing sports. As a result, Julio Libonatti made the first "official" transfer in 1925, from Newell's Old Boys in Argentina to Torino FC in Italy. Libonatti represented both the Italian and Argentine national teams. This was legal until the 1960s, when FIFA prohibited players from representing more than one nation. Representing Italy presented challenges for those with more distant ties to the country. Famed striker for Juventus, Raimundo Orsi, for example, could not understand Italian. Still the Argentines made an important impact on Italian football and popular culture. The Argentine forward Renato Cesarini inspired the Italian phrase, the *zona cesarini*. It refers to the waning moments of a match, when Cesarini looked to score. In politics or journalism, it is a common term for a decisive last-minute maneuver.

South American players who transferred to Spain and Italy became known as the *oriundi*. The historian John Foot has argued that the return of the diaspora fit with Benito Mussolini's agenda to expand the boundaries of Italian identity. On Mussolini's orders, four Argentines played for the Italian team that won the World Cup of 1934. Raimundo Orsi, beloved among fans, feared for his life during the tournament. According to Orsi, Mussolini threatened to "cut their throats" if they lost. Luckily, he scored in Italy's victory over Czechoslovakia in the final match. A few months later, Orsi fled with three of his fellow Argentines across the French border rather than serve in the Italian army. When things went badly, the *oriundi* were blamed for poor performances and sent packing. Similar trends occurred in Spain, which banned all foreign players from 1963 to 1973.This strategy did not pan out well for Spain, which subsequently failed to qualify for the World Cups of 1970 and 1974.

The lure of Europe forced South American associations to adopt professionalism in the 1930s and 1940s. In the Cold War period, those who thought football was being ruined by consumerism fought a pitched battle against those who thought it should be open to the free market. Clubs watched with great interest as Fidel Castro deprofessionalized Cuban baseball. In that moment, football associations throughout the region strengthened their relationships with leftist political parties and labor unions. For example, in 1945 the Brazilian Communist Party organized a fund-raising football tournament for their political candidates. In the lead-up to the 1962 World Cup in Chile, amateurs organized successful protests against the razing of working-class neighborhoods, rampant speculation, and state subsidies for professional clubs. These protests, among countless others, inspired similar actions around the world. Perhaps most prominently, exiles from South America led protests of military dictatorships during Germany's 1974 World Cup.

ON THE PITCH AND BEHIND THE CURTAIN

The status of South American football soared because of the remarkable success of the Brazilian national team, which won the 1958, 1962, and 1970 World Cups. The enduring color line in Europe helped Brazilian clubs retain their best black players. Edson Arantes do Nascimento, known as Pelé, and Manuel Francisco dos Santos, known as Garrincha, represented unprecedented success in football. Garrincha and Pelé never lost a game when they played together. Of African descent and humble backgrounds, the two are remembered differently. Whereas Garrincha spiraled into bad health and financial difficulties, Pelé embodied professionalism and ties to multinational corporations through endorsements. The Brazilians succeeded not only with talent but also because of the Brazilian Football Confederation's methodical planning. Recognizing their players' working-class backgrounds, the confederation made medical care an important part of the Brazilian strategy. Players came to training with a host of problems, from parasites to tooth decay. The focus on "total care" became a signature of the Brazilian team.

During the 1960s, Pelé, famous for his balance and ball control, became the face of football and South America. He represented athletic excellence in a black body that shaped the visual landscape of sport. A national decree mandated that Pelé remain with the Brazilian Club Santos. After retirement, he played for the New York Cosmos, drawing millions of fans to football in the United States. Whether as the character in Atari's first football video game or as the muse for an Andy Warhol piece, Pelé came to be identified in spheres outside of football as the "best ever," and it was important that the "best ever" was black.

Pelé transcended national identity to embody an image of Pan-African success. When asked about the importance of Brazil to African football, the historian Peter Alegi explained that in the midst of decolonization, visits of racially integrated teams to African countries "excited the imagination about what was possible on an international scale." Pelé and his teammates at Club Santos toured Mozambique and Nigeria in the late 1960s. Alegi said, "That football was an artistic endeavor and an expressive celebration, not just the moral package of the British, was influential in forging different playing styles and cultures across the continent." That the leaders of the Brazilian team also came from impoverished neighborhoods and difficult circumstances created solidarity with players across the Global South.

Brazilian leaders expanded the power of South American football beyond the stadiums to the international governing body, FIFA. Based in Switzerland, FIFA operated as a Eurocentric, paternalistic, and provincial organization for most of the twentieth century. During the 1960s, FIFA's reputation suffered from its president Stanley Rous's decision to support the apartheid-era South African Football Association. Jean-Marie "João" de Havelange, president of the Brazilian Football Confederation, launched the first public campaign to become the seventh president of FIFA in 1974. João Havelange mobilized South-South solidarity to woo African and Asian delegates. He toured approximately ninety countries during his campaign, frequently appearing with Pelé. Havelange successfully positioned himself as a candidate from the "developing world," despite having been educated in France and benefiting from a European identity in Brazil. He promised, and delivered, development money, technical training, and expanded berths in the World Cup.

Considering South American football's reputation for rebellion against hypermodernity and the mechanization of team structure, it is ironic that João Havelange created an intimate relationship between FIFA and sports marketing firms, sponsors, and television moguls. Havelange remade the World Cup tournament into a financial behemoth that rode on the wave of the sport's ever-increasing popularity. His efforts resulted in huge contracts with the shoe company Adidas and the soft drink company Coca-Cola to underwrite soccer's expansion. Under Havelange, the World Cup attracted the largest television audiences ever recorded. Along with lucrative contracts, however, João Havelange brought corrupt business practices to FIFA. To obstruct inquiries into his financial practices, he installed his son-in-law, Fernando Teixeira, in his former post as president of the Brazilian Football Confederation. The Brazilian military government relaxed restrictions on foreign investment, which enabled the flow of unchecked funds across borders.

João Havelange ingratiated FIFA with the military dictatorships that ruled Argentina, Brazil, Chile, Paraguay, Peru, and Uruguay in the 1970s and 1980s. Characterized by gross human rights abuses and neoliberal economic reforms, the military governments used football pitches, from grandiose national stadiums to makeshift neighborhood fields, as torture centers. Amateur club directors were public figures in unions, leftist political parties, and universities. Many lost their jobs, their passports, and, in the worst instances, their lives. Military juntas banned club elections and placed military leaders at the head of football associations. FIFA enabled dictators to mobilize the global popularity of football to their own benefit. The most striking example of this was the World Cup of 1978, organized by the Argentine Football Association under the auspices of a brutal military government.

The resistance to military rule in South America reverberated well beyond the region. For example, shortly after the 1973 coup in Chile, the Soviet Union refused to play in the stadium where the military had detained and murdered supporters of the democratically elected government. This helped Chile qualify for the 1974 World Cup in West Germany, during which the dictator Augusto Pinochet sent the national team with a letter assuring fellow participants that Chile was "restored" from socialism and ready for investors. During the tournament, solidarity activists drew attention to the atrocities occurring in Chile with teach-ins, protests outside the team's quarters, and actions inside the stadiums. During Chile's matches, protesters chanted, "Chile si, Junta no." A daring group smuggled in a banner that read "Chile Socialista" and ran onto the field, unfurling it during the game.

Chilean activists organized solidarity tournaments in Ethiopia, East Germany, France, and Italy. They refused to allow the military governments to marshal the popularity of football without a fight.

Those who have sought to protest authoritarianism, consumerism, racism, and sexism in sport have found innovative campaigns in South American football. In Brazil, Club Corinthians launched a radical experiment to democratize club governance by empowering players to vote on decisions. Players extrapolated their criticism of club governance to national military rule. Led by "Dr. Socrates," an attacking midfielder with a medical degree, Corinthians bucked the trend of apolitical athletes in the late 1970s. In 1982, Corinthians' players wore shirts that urged fans to vote, and Socrates spoke eloquently on the subject of oppression in Brazil. Examples like Corinthians were powerful. Still, many fans turned away in disgust as fan violence increased and military governments intervened in football.

As Brazil democratized, the country debated one of the most radical pieces of sport legislation in history. In the early 1990s, public criticism of the lack of accountability of projects overseen by the Confederation of Brazilian Football (CBF) grew steadily. In reaction, President Fernando Henrique Cardoso appointed Pelé as minister of sport, making him the first black cabinet member in Brazil. Pelé publicly accused the CBF president Teixeira and FIFA president Havelange of demanding personal bribes for television rights. In 1998, he introduced a law that limited the power of the CBF over players, opened access to stadiums, and required transparent accountability. Before it could be implemented, however, Teixeira and Havelange convinced a number of legislators to hack away at it. Currently the law is only a fraction of its original size and scope. If the law had remained as proposed, the 2014 World Cup in Brazil would have drained fewer public resources.

So it was in keeping with the history of football on and off the pitch that the protests in Brazil began during preparations to host the 2014 World Cup. Beginning at the 2013 Confederations Cup, protesters drew international attention. From banners that read "FIFA Go Home" to strikes over worker safety, Brazilians used the World Cup as an opportunity to protest the inequalities unresolved by a decade of Center-Left governance. Protesters also criticized the changes to the legal infrastructure demanded by FIFA. Stars who had previously voiced criticism, Pelé included, appeared as minions of the World Cup machine, even chastising protesters demanding reasonable bus fares and the construction of hospitals. Real estate speculation was rampant, reminiscent of the 1919 construction of Fluminense's stadium in Rio de Janeiro. Government reaction to the protests revealed the militarization of mega sporting events and the degree of importance given to international, rather than domestic, audiences.

GLOBALIZED TALENT

Football's labor market has globalized along with its politics. In a recent report, the International Center for Sports Study stated that the proportion of footballers who have migrated internationally is at an all-time high, approximately half of all professional players. These findings confirm an acceleration of the internationalization of football players' labor market. The English Premier League imports approximately 60 percent of its footballers. Unlike a century ago, South Americans are not exclusively headed to Europe. Many find themselves in China, one of the places with the highest wages, as well as Indonesia and the United Arab Emirates. The Argentine Robertino Pugliara, who played in Jakarta, was shocked to find that his Indonesian teammates already drank the traditional South American tea, maté.

It *is* striking that South America continues to produce the world's best football players in spite of deep economic inequalities, political turbulence, and the decay of its leagues. They are joined by an increasing number of Africans. Like their predecessors, these players tend to be goal scorers who excel at passing and ball control. Leading the current generation is the Argentine forward Lionel Messi. It is difficult to explain Messi's sublime talent to those unconverted to football fandom. The estimated cost for a club just to hire him is over $331 million. Analysts frequently fall back on the common axiom that football is popular because it is cheap and that poor people are good at it because they have little else to hope for. These simplistic explanations reproduce an unfounded assumption that poor people's talent comes from innate physicality or desperation.

If it is difficult to prove that demonstrable differences exist between South American and European players, however, it is easy to see that coaches, players, and fans *believe* it to be true. When asked why he left Argentina, the midfielder Jorge Valdano replied that he played "like a German." He continued, "The Argentinean game features agility and mobility. We all know the stock image: ultra-imaginative, ultra-creative . . . I was no Maradona. The sad truth is that, as a fan, I too would have rather watched Maradona than

Valdano." South American football was supposed to be spontaneous, creative, and genius. An influential group of British journalists attributes some of the South American success to cheating. The spectacular handball, dubbed "the hand of God," of Diego Maradona in the 1986 World Cup is one of many examples they cite. South American athletes, fans, and journalists counter that cheating is only "dirty" if you assume the system is clean. For generations that grew up under military dictatorships, this would have been both a dangerous and a daft assumption.

So how might we explain South American excellence without relying on elitist assumptions about what poor and black people are good at? In the first place, the informal spaces of football in the region have been fertile grounds for developing talent. Financial investment helps with youth camps, medical bills, and equipment. However, football can become too regimented for young bodies. In South America, football is highly social and less compartmentalized. It is played on trips to the beach and at picnics and parties. According to sports therapists, these opportunities prevent early burnout and injury. Players also develop ball control in smaller spaces. Moreover, South American excellence embodies a unique history of football publics. South American audiences value innovation, indeed demand it. When the Argentine Club Estudiantes de la Plata adopted a highly defensive style in the 1960s, Argentines called it *antifútbol*. "Anti-football" has come to mean any tactic that impedes the flow of the game, including premeditated violence.

South American publics expect their talented superstars to exhibit social consciousness, although they are frequently disappointed. In an industry worth trillions of dollars, which usually serves to reproduce and obfuscate inequality, it is striking when athletes side with political causes like human rights campaigns. Despite the decay of South American professional leagues, there is a strong grassroots structure that connects football to broader issues of social justice. For example, many of the Argentine players have joined in the efforts to find the children abducted by the military during the 1970s and 1980s. Brazilian wunderkind, Neymar Jr., was expected to show support for the protesters of the 2014 World Cup, even if he was also supposed to win the tournament for Brazil. Journalists ask footballers to comment on issues ranging from congressional elections to Middle Eastern diplomacy. They frequently comply, at times to their own detriment. This contrasts sharply with the traditions in Europe and North America.

In recent years, fan interest in football's megastars has grown exponentially and in areas without a long football tradition. An illustrative example

FIGURE 7.3. Luis Suarez, Neymar Jr., and Lionel Messi (left to right) playing for Barcelona FC. As a result of the game's globalization, the South American superstars play in Spain for a team sponsored by Qatar's air carrier. Courtesy of Reuters News Agency.

occurred in 2013 when a Japanese game show challenged Lionel Messi to try to score against a robot built to block penalty shots. The show titled the segment in English, "Man versus the Machine." Messi, who engenders sympathy because of his small stature alone, is notoriously shy and subdued. While his personality lacks the characteristic bravado of South American strikers, his playing style fits the model perfectly. Messi stared down at the ball, dribbled a few times, and took his first shot. The robot veered to its right and blocked it. Messi responded to the robot with a look of surprise. His second attempt hit the goalpost. At this point, the "man" exhibited some degree of frustration. Players of Messi's caliber are acutely aware of geometry, and he appeared to calculate the mechanics of the robot. On the third attempt, Messi scored by grounding the ball in front of the robot, causing it to bounce behind it. He looked almost as excited as in a real game. Messi scored in his next attempt and appeared satisfied with his performance. The vignette of Lionel Messi's victory over the robot created to destroy him was contrived. Nonetheless, it remains incredibly attractive. It is a good illustration of South American football's universal appeal. We are all standing in front of a machine that we have created, somewhat hapless and hoping ingenuity will help us.

Since football's diffusion, South Americans have sought out the world. In magazines, clubhouses, and stadiums, football has been a site where hierarchies of race, gender, and class are created, reproduced, and, sometimes, challenged. Many have tried to mobilize passion for the game to promote social justice and transnational solidarity. Over the course of a century, football has become intertwined with national identities. It should give us pause to wonder what the world would look like if more national identities were founded on creative brilliance, grace, and engagement with the world, win or lose. Perhaps that is South America's most beautiful contribution to the beautiful game.

REFERENCES AND SUGGESTED READING

Archetti, Eduardo
    1998 *Masculinities: Football, Polo, and the Tango in Argentina.* Oxford: Verso.
Bocketti, Gregg
    2016 *The Invention of the Beautiful Game: Football and the Making of Modern Brazil.* Gainesville: University of Florida Press.
Elsey, Brenda
    2011 *Citizens and Sportsmen: Fútbol and Politics in Twentieth-Century Chile.* Austin: University of Texas Press.
Gaffney, Christopher
    2010 *Temples of the Earthbound Gods: Stadiums in the Cultural Landscape of Rio de Janeiro and Buenos Aires.* Austin: University of Texas Press.
Goldblatt, David
    2008 *The Ball Is Round: A Global History of Soccer.* New York: Riverhead.
Kittleson, Roger
    2014 *The Country of Football: Soccer and the Making of Modern Brazil.* Berkeley: University of California.
Nadel, Joshua
    2014 *Fútbol! Why Soccer Matters in Latin America.* Gainesville: University of Florida Press.
Richey, Jeff
    n.d. "Playing at Nation: Soccer, Racial Ideology, and National Integration in Argentina." Unpublished manuscript.

EIGHT

Roy Choi, Ricardo Zárate, and Pacific Fusion Cuisine in Los Angeles

Sarah Portnoy and Jeffrey M. Pilcher

LOS ANGELES, A CITY LONG known for its cultural diversity, has become a center for one of the most important recent culinary trends, the upscale food truck phenomenon. The iconic Kogi truck, serving Korean barbecue tacos, was the creation of Chef Roy Choi, who was born in Seoul and grew up in Los Angeles. Unemployed after the financial crash of 2008 and desperate to do something exciting, he combined his Korean heritage and knowledge of Mexican street food, thereby gentrifying the working-class Mexican *lonchera* (food truck). His innovative creations took off within a year and set a national trend, as Kogi copycats began popping up in cities across the United States, including New York, Austin, and San Francisco. Meanwhile in 2009, a Peruvian-born chef named Ricardo Zárate, who had trained in London and worked at a Japanese restaurant in Los Angeles, opened a simple food stall called Mo-Chica in the Mercado La Paloma, a cooperative nonprofit market south of downtown Los Angeles. In another version of Pacific fusion, Zárate's cuisine mixes Peru's traditional *criollo* (creole) dishes with those of the country's sizable Japanese population. Word spread quickly among foodies, and the chef became a national phenomenon; in 2011, *Food & Wine Magazine* awarded him the title "Best New Chef, People's Choice."

Is it a coincidence that these two very different chefs began their rise to prominence in Los Angeles within a year of each other with Asian-Latino fusion creations? Explaining the phenomenon of Pacific fusion cuisine both in Los Angeles and globally raises two important questions: How does culinary influence move within the transnational circuits that constitute global Latin America? Why did these fusion foods take off when they did, and what does that tell us about opportunities for immigrant and ethnic entrepreneurs? Within Los Angeles, a conjuncture of space and time—ethnic

FIGURE 8.1. Kogi truck, Los Angeles. Photo by Sarah Portnoy.

enclaves of Koreans, Mexicans, and Salvadoreans living in very close proximity and the financial crash and recession of 2008, which inspired residents to search for alternatives to high-end dining—created a unique environment that encouraged Choi's and Zárate's initial success. Equally important for their success was the status of Los Angeles as a global city that was integrated into circuits of migration, transnational restaurant markets, and global culinary fashions.

Because food is ingested daily and literally becomes part of the body, cuisine is a powerful metaphor for identity, particularly in moments of cultural encounter. The culinary transformations of the "Columbian exchange," which spread through the Atlantic world after 1492, are now well known, but the parallel history of Pacific Rim fusion has gone largely unnoticed. This neglect results in part from the invisibility of Asians within national identities throughout the Americas. For example, the Latin American conception of the "cosmic race," although theoretically embracing all of humanity, was usually concerned with the *mestizaje*, or mixing, of Europeans and Native Americans. By contrast, African slaves, Asian indentured servants, and Middle Eastern immigrants have been marginalized by nationalist ideologies. Nevertheless, culinary encounters have historically helped forge relationships that crossed lines of race, class, ethnicity, and nationality through the sharing of ingredients, techniques, and dishes. Instances of culinary and cultural fusion between masters and slaves, immigrants and locals can be seen in cooking and consumption throughout the Americas, from Brazilian *feijoada* (black beans and rice) and Peruvian *chaufa* (fried rice) to Texas fajitas. Although once scorned as plebeian, these dishes acquired deep symbolic meanings that ultimately made them emblematic of regional and national identities. In a similar fashion, twenty-first-century Pacific fusion has become fashionable in Los Angeles and other cities around the world precisely because of its exotic, mixed origins and its street food image.

The gentrification of global street food has resulted from trends in both the production and the consumption of culinary culture. Scholars have tended to focus on the latter by showing how contemporary gastronomic discourse has glorified the "omnivorous" consumer, who is knowledgeable not just about French haute cuisine but about all the world's foods. Nevertheless, the pursuit of exoticism and authenticity among ethnic and working-class foods has not democratized gourmet culture; instead, elites have begun to use culinary tourism as means to acquire expert knowledge and social distinction. Through the act of curating ethnic foods, connoisseurs position themselves as culinary artists, drawing on raw materials provided by "exotic" and "authentic" immigrant cooks, who are thereby seen as incapable of fully entering American society. But although the elitism of culinary discourse is unmistakable, the careers of Roy Choi and Ricardo Zárate demonstrate the ability of immigrant and ethnic entrepreneurs to shape the contemporary gastronomic field through their labor and taste (Johnston and Bauman 2010; Ray 2011). Moreover, while both producers and consumers have helped define culinary fashions, the restaurant industry is heavily influenced by an underlying infrastructure of media and food critics, culinary education and professional training, food distributors, transnational labor markets, and the local and national regulators that govern these diverse activities. The Pacific fusion moment in Los Angeles arose at the intersection of consumer desire for a particular form of exoticism, the skilled labor and entrepreneurship of chefs such as Choi and Zárate, and a culinary infrastructure that brought together these dreams, aspirations, and tastes.

PACIFIC FUSION IN HISTORICAL PERSPECTIVE

Cultural exchange is always a two-way street; in *Cuban Counterpoint: Tobacco and Sugar* ([1940] 1995), Fernando Ortiz coined the term "transculturation" to emphasize the effects on conquistadors as well as on the conquered. During the early modern period, culinary exchanges across the Pacific Ocean came primarily through the introduction of new foods, carried both east and west by Portuguese merchants and by the Manila Galleon, which linked Spain's colonies in the Americas and the Philippines. In the nineteenth century, migration flowed largely from Asia to Latin America with the demand for labor on tropical plantations following the abolition of the African slave trade. Despite restrictions on "coolie" workers, Asian migrants became prominent in the grocery and restaurant trades, thereby contributing to Latin America's diverse *criollo* and mestizo cuisines, terms that refer to popular cultural mixing and local identity. By the end of the twentieth century, however, the global prominence of Latin American cuisines had begun to reverse this culinary flow, establishing a prominent place for Mexican and Peruvian restaurants in Asia as in other regions of the world.

Colonial trade in foodstuffs between Latin America and Asia was generally mediated by European merchants, and as a result, culinary techniques were often left behind in the exchange. Prolific and nutritious Latin American staples such as maize, sweet potatoes, cassava, and peanuts contributed to early modern population growth in Asia, while chile peppers, tropical fruits, and other American condiments also became indispensable in the cuisines of India, Southeast Asia, and parts of China (Ho 1955; Mazumdar 1999). Spanish and Mexican cooking styles had some influence in the Philippines, but on the whole, the new crops were cooked using indigenous Asian recipes (Pilcher 2012: 33–45). Meanwhile, Spanish officials had limited success in their campaign to transplant Asian spices to the Americas; only relatively common and unprofitable spices such as cinnamon, ginger, and tamarind acculturated, although they made important contributions to local cuisines (de Vos 2006). Asian travelers on the Manila Galleon did introduce some cooking techniques, including tandoor ovens along Mexico's Pacific coast, but popular attributions of many culinary influences are mistaken. Latin American rice is not a Chinese import but rather derives from a Persian "pilau" introduced to Spain by medieval Arabs. Ceviche, the process of "cooking" raw fish with citric acid, comes not from Japanese sushi—a nineteenth-century invention—but instead from the Arabic preserving method, "sebich" (Bauer 2001: 87–90).

Latin American culinary cosmopolitanism of the nineteenth century was divided along class lines; while elites looked to France for fine dining, popular cuisine was influenced by proletarian migrants from around the world. Asians were prominent among these new migrants, drawn by the economic opportunities of the California Gold Rush and the plantation labor contracts of Peru and the Caribbean. Chinese groceries and restaurants, the latter called *chifas* in Peru, at times incited nativist fears of rats and other unmentionable foods, but they were nevertheless frequented by the working classes for affordable and tasty meals of stir-fried rice, stews, and seafood (Balbi 1999; Drinot 2005). Tamales, chili con carne, and *mofongo* (mashed and fried plantains) inspired similar fears of contamination in the United States, but they too gained a following among both budget-minded workers and thrill-seeking bohemians. Tamale pushcarts, which were driven from the streets of Los Angeles in the early 1900s by Progressive-era reformers, returned in the 1970s in the form of *loncheras* providing a quick lunch for Mexican and Mexican American construction workers (Pilcher 2012: 111–13). Caribbean foods meanwhile influenced the cooking of the Harlem Renaissance, as the historian Frederick Opie (2008: 139–53) has demonstrated, thereby becoming precursors of "soul food."

Even as *lonchera* and soul food insurgencies arose in the postwar United States, a revolution of "nouvelle cuisine" was taking shape that would soon undermine the hegemony of French haute cuisine. The movement began from within, as revolutions often do, when the distinguished chef Paul Bocuse traveled to Asia and began incorporating Japanese aesthetics into his cuisine. The international youth movement of the 1960s meanwhile embraced supposedly more authentic peasant cuisines as an antidote to industrial processed foods. By the end of the century, the Catalan chef Ferran Adrià had begun experimenting with food technology to create a modernist gastronomy of flavored foams and other whimsies. Nouvelle chefs in the United States sought out regional roots for authentic American cuisines; for example, Spanish and indigenous foods inspired the "New Southwestern," which began in Los Angeles and Santa Fe in the 1980s under the leadership of John Rivera Sedlar. Meanwhile, Rick Bayless introduced traditional Mexican cuisine at his Chicago restaurant Frontera Grill and through his long-running public television show, *Mexico: One Plate at a Time*. In contrast to the English author Diana Kennedy, who began publishing ethnographically informed Mexican cookbooks in the 1970s, Bayless seeks to translate Mexican cuisine for American audiences.

But this gourmet movement was not limited to the Global North; Latin American culinary professionals sought to claim these often-indigenous cuisines for their own national projects. Mexican chefs pioneered the *nueva cocina mexicana* (nouvelle Mexican cuisine) in the 1980s, often based on more or less fanciful imaginations of "pre-Hispanic menus." The recipe called for large quantities of what anthropologists call "peasant essentialism," exploiting the supposed backwardness of working-class, often indigenous populations, but it proved wildly popular with tourists, including both the national bourgeoisie and foreigners in search of Aztec and Maya exoticism. By the turn of the twenty-first century, patriotic Mexican food critics could take delight as "authentic" taco trucks and chile sauces (*moles*) spread around the world, displacing Tex-Mex versions that had been propagated by restaurateurs and food processing companies from the United States. To achieve this goal, the Mexican government and private groups invested in a national culinary infrastructure of food media and cooking schools to counter the influence of the Michelin Guide and the "other CIA"—the Culinary Institute of America. The enormous success of this tourism development campaign became a model for other Latin American nations.

Peruvians have created the most successful rival to Mexico's gourmet movement with the less nationalist sounding *cocina novoandino* (nouvelle Andean cuisine). Peru's culinary infrastructure was delayed by the economic crises and the Shining Path civil war of the 1980s, but the country has made up for lost time, opening a total of fifty culinary schools in Lima alone, plus another thirty in the provinces. Gastón Acurio, the son of a prominent politician, is the leading figure of the *novoandino* movement; trained at Le Cordon Bleu in Paris, he returned to Peru in 1994 with his German-born pastry chef wife, Astrid Gutsche. Their collaborative restaurant, Astrid y Gastón, won popular acclaim for its innovative, signature ceviches and spawned a global franchise with outposts in Madrid, Manhattan, Miami, Bogotá, and Mexico City. The interest in Peruvian flavors has recently inspired pilgrimages by such international celebrity chefs as Ferran Adrià, Rene Redzepi, Michel Bras, and Dan Barber. The revered sushi chef Nobuyuki Matsuhisa actually developed his unique fusion style while working in Lima.

Latin America's global culinary influence has gone through two distinct periods, the early modern spread of cultivars and a contemporary fashion within the restaurant industry. The former period led to the globalization of maize, potatoes, tomatoes, and chiles, while shops today increasingly stock tomatillos, quinoa, tequila, and pisco, Peru's fiery grape brandy. Yet Latin Americans have received little credit for these gifts; early modern plants were often attributed to the European merchants, and the contemporary interest in Latin American food has come as part of a global fashion for peasant and street food. The sudden interest in quinoa, for example, has meant that many Peruvian farmers cannot even afford to eat their own staple grain, and most tequilas are bottled in the United States, with little profit for Mexican agave growers. Market and class inequalities thus determine who benefits from food fads.

Roy Choi's Kogi taco trucks illustrate both the cross-cultural influence of Latin American cuisine and the importance of culinary infrastructure for achieving success even for street food. In establishing his business, Choi drew on the resources and cultural capital of his entrepreneurial Korean family, training at the Culinary Institute of America, professional experience in leading restaurants, and media-savvy business partners. Timing was just as important, for the market crash and recession of 2008 left countless young members of the middle class desperate for new forms of status and entertainment based on cultural and media knowledge. Hip young people used their cell phones to follow the seemingly random tweets of the Kogi truck and then waited in impossibly long lines with like-minded folk. The Kogi trucks thus became a beacon for a generation that could no longer afford the fancy restaurants that had defined status in the pre-crash era but yearned for a similar form of distinction. It also represented the shifting world of social media in which food trends are not discovered by food critics but via Twitter, Instagram, and Yelp. In this way, the Kogi truck paved the way for a national trend of mobile dining tracked through social media. The "luxe-lonchera" with an edgy Asian flavor followed the cool style pioneered by the chef–writer–television personality Anthony Bourdain, who in turn published Choi's memoir-cookbook, *L.A. Son: My Life, My City, My Food* (2013), in his food-centered series.

Kogi fusion grew from Choi's childhood in the culinary and social borderlands of Los Angeles. Already by the early twentieth century, the area east of downtown, particularly Boyle Heights, was a gathering place for diverse migrants, including Mexicans, Italians, and Jews, as well as Koreans, Japanese, Chinese, and Filipinos. Choi arrived as a toddler in the early 1970s as part of the boom in Asian migration following the 1965 Immigration Reform Act. His parents struggled to make a living for many years, opening a Korean restaurant in Garden Grove that did not succeed along with a series of other unsuccessful business ventures. A latchkey child, Choi ate his way alone through Koreatown's barbecue restaurants, Jewish delis, Salvadoran *pupuserías,* and Mexican *taquerías.* Choi's taste buds were informed by these years of walking the streets of Los Angeles, where Mexican food blends seamlessly with American fare through cross-cultural marketing and intermarriage. Neon signs advertise historic institutions such as Lucy's Mexican-American Food, selling hamburgers and tacos, or Kosher Burrito, a downtown food stand opened by a Jewish man married to a Sonoran woman. In this way, a Korean boy would have easily understood Mexican food as part of the mosaic that makes up American food. If ethnic cuisines mixed easily across the neighborhoods of Los Angeles, the diverse peoples often came into conflict. In 1992, the city erupted in violence when white police officers were acquitted of brutally assaulting an African American named Rodney King. Korean business owners were a particular target of violence of the predominantly black crowd. In an interview with Anthony Bourdain on his popular television show, *Parts Unknown,* Choi described watching the riots from the roof of a building and feeling besieged for three days until police finally restored order.

Choi rebelled at first against the professional expectations of his immigrant parents but later fulfilled them in an unorthodox manner by training as a chef and acquiring the techniques of French haute cuisine. After college, he worked for a few years as a stockbroker, then attended Western State University Law School for a single semester, in 1994, all the while abusing drugs and alcohol. He found new purpose in life with a decision to become a chef, worked evenings to gain the basic skills, and eventually, in 1998, graduated from the Culinary Institute of America. He interned in Manhattan at the Michelin three-starred Le Bernardin, then passed through a string of high-profile restaurants before landing a coveted position as chef de cuisine at the Beverly Hills Hilton in 2007. His professional experience reinforced his childhood impressions from the streets of Los Angeles; although the restaurant dining rooms served an exclusive clientele, the kitchens were mixed with a predominance of Latino line cooks as a result of culinary labor market trends. Choi took advantage of his coworkers' knowledge of Mexican street food; on one memorable occasion, while working at a Palm Springs resort, he helped butcher a goat and make *birria* at a Mexicali restaurant owned by the family of one of his cooks.

The crash of 2008 provided Choi with the opportunity—and the need— to fuse the polyglot street foods of his youth with his years of professional training. Having just been laid off from a high-end restaurant, he got together with a Hilton colleague, the Filipino American Mark Manguera, who suggested the idea of a Korean barbecue taco truck. Choi began his research in the aisles of the Korean markets, while Manguera arranged the lease on a food truck. With professional credentials, they easily passed the licensing and inspections that can be so troublesome for immigrant entrepreneurs. Kogi hit the streets in late 2008, featuring a menu of short rib tacos, kimchi quesadillas, and Kogi sliders. Diverse culinary influences also fill the pages of his autobiographical cookbook with accessible street food recipes such as "Kimchi and Pork Belly Stuffed Pupusas," a sauce called "Splash" made with soy sauce, rice vinegar, and jalapeño, "Ketchup Fried Rice," and "LA Corner on the Cob."

Kogi's fusion cuisine was not just a mixture of cultures; it also reflected the cross-class encounters of the Los Angeles streets, as Choi combined a tattooed, hip-hop street cred with the professionalism of a CIA training. Such a combination became possible through a new form of culinary infrastructure leveraging the social media of Twitter. Only those who followed the Kogi truck's whereabouts online could be sure of scoring a taco, providing an exclusivity to the digitally savvy, even if they did not have a Google expense account. The trucks created a roving party atmosphere and brought people from different walks of life together. Loyal fans followed the trucks to neighborhoods they would not normally frequent and interacted with strangers, waiting in line while listening to a deejay play dance tunes. A hypermasculinity, common to both hip-hop artists and celebrity chefs, seemed to heighten the transgressive appeal for young hipsters, who were willing to wait in long lines for a late-night, short rib taco. Parked by a street corner or in an empty lot, the trucks became an itinerant equivalent of an exclusive nightclub, a new experience that was both uniquely local to L.A. and yet global in its Latin American and Asian influences.

Choi capitalized on his success to expand a budding restaurant empire, adopting new variants on the boundary-crossing theme. By 2009, four Kogi trucks were cruising the streets of Los Angeles as the Korean barbecue taco went viral across the country. A year later, Choi opened a brick-and-mortar restaurant, Chego, serving elevated street food such as Kimchi Spam bowls. Next he installed an A-frame in a former I-Hop and served modern picnic food, messy dishes meant to be eaten with the hands such as Cracklin' Beer Can Chicken and Baby Back Ribs, along with well-named cocktails that included the Venice Walk of Shame and Spittin' Distance. Quotes on the menu offered a calculated disingenuousness: "It's how I'd cook for you if this was a house party. No ridiculous pretentiousness, no hors d'oeuvres." Such informality had little appeal for Korean traditionalists, and it was striking that Kogi attracted no culinary copycats in Seoul, even as the pop musician Psy's "Gangnam Style" became a global phenomenon. Nevertheless, in the summer of 2014, Choi opened yet another restaurant, Pot, serving his take on traditional Korean dishes in the heart of L.A.'s Koreatown, a move sure to irritate many old-timers but a draw for a younger, more diverse crowd. Choi's success has elevated him beyond the level of popular chef to a television host. In August 2014, CNN announced that Choi was joining the network and would be hosting his own show titled *Street Food*.

Although Choi imagined Kogi as a democratizing force that could bring gourmet food to the masses, there were limits to how far the trucks and their customers would go across Los Angeles's social and spatial boundaries, as the sociologist Oliver Wang has recently discovered. Using Twitter's public database, Wang mapped the stops made by Kogi's four trucks from 2009 to 2011. He found the majority of stops in two regions, north from Venice to Downtown, and south, in Orange County. The space in between, dubbed "The Void" by Wang, "encompassed long-standing zones of class and racial segregation in the area, including the South Bay, Harbor, South L.A., Southeast L.A., and East L.A." (Wang 2013: 85). The few stops in this zone were exceptional, as when a truck broke down at the corner of Figueroa and Fifty-ninth. Thus, Kogi has pursued an audience of young, middle-class whites and Asian Americans.

For Roy Choi, the Kogi taco truck has become a method of "Americanizing" the cuisine of his home country. The choice is a significant one, disdaining the plainness of a sandwich, which has long been a traditional pattern of immigrant assimilation, and instead choosing to emphasize its exotic roots and spicy flavor by way of the taco, thereby appealing to consumers hungry for border-crossing novelty. The cool of the taco truck scene is nevertheless backed up by the professional infrastructure of the restaurant industry, in contrast to the ad hoc version of the traditional *lonchera*. And whereas other restaurants had relied on the fickle opinion of critics, the Kogi team leveraged new social media to define their own image and appeal to a crowd of surfers, hipsters, and digerati. Meanwhile, another immigrant chef, Ricardo Zárate, has sought recognition from foodies by elevating and transforming street and bar food into his own professionally refined cuisine.

RICARDO ZÁRATE AND PACIFIC RIM COSMOPOLITANISM

"The story of Mo Chica is the journey of my career," declared Ricardo Zárate in an interview with Sarah Portnoy on 14 February 2014. While it is a personal story about the drive of labor migration, professional training, and entrepreneurial ambition, it also reflects the networks and infrastructure of the international restaurant industry. Like Roy Choi's fusion taco truck, timing was crucial for Zárate's success in introducing Peruvian food as haute cuisine to Los Angeles. At a moment when restaurant celebrities around the world were looking to Lima as the latest thing, local food critics and knowledgeable diners embraced a Peruvian chef they could call their own. Yet consumers were not fixated on trendiness alone; Peruvian food also spoke to the modern desire for indigenous authenticity, the romance of both the ancient Inka civilization and the peoples living at the headwaters of the Amazon River. Peruvian ceviche meanwhile offered a spicy, new take on Japanese sushi, which had gained elite status with Western consumers in the 1980s. Zárate and his media interlocutors skillfully crafted this image with the goal of establishing the Peruvian national cuisine as a global leader in culinary tourism.

Zárate started cooking as a teenager in the family kitchen in Lima, learning from his mother and grandmother the *criollo* dishes that were as cosmopolitan in their own way as the street foods of Los Angeles. He was born in 1973 under the military dictatorship, and the hyperinflation of the 1980s hit middle-class families hard, including his own. Nevertheless, they could still afford dishes such as *chanfaina,* a Spanish Andean stew of organ meat and potatoes, and *lomo saltado,* a Chinese-inspired, stir-fried pork. Although in interviews Zárate has expressed disappointment at the time with his education at the Instituto de las Américas in Lima, where the curriculum emphasized restaurant management rather than classical cooking, his later experiences opening three Los Angeles restaurants in succession required as much skill in management as in cooking.

Circuits of labor migration provided Zárate with opportunities for professional training and advancement abroad that were unavailable at the time in Peru. In the early 1990s, he moved to London and found work as a dishwasher at a Benihana chain restaurant. His coworkers soon recognized his ambitions, and within six months, he had perfected the theatrical, knife-juggling skills of the hibachi chef. After two years, he moved on again, working in a succession of jobs and learning whatever he could in each new kitchen. Following a stint under Chef Mark Gregory at One Aldwych, he became executive chef at the contemporary Japanese restaurant, Zuma. Finally, after twelve years in London, Zárate realized that while he had honed his professional skills, he was unable to raise the investment backing needed to open a Peruvian restaurant. Therefore, he decided to move to Los

Angeles and in 2007 found work in a Venice sushi shop while planning his venture.

Zárate was right about the opportunities in Los Angeles for a gentrified version of Peruvian street food. In 2009, while still working evenings in Venice, he opened Mo-Chica as a food stall in the Warehouse district Mercado La Paloma. The menu included *criollo* dishes such as *papas a la Huancaina* (potato salad), the *chifa* standby *lomo saltado,* Peruvian fried chicken, and an excellent, frothy Pisco sour. The stand was such a success that he quit his job and within a few years had put together the financing for a move to a trendier, downtown location. The restaurant opened in 2012 to a packed crowd in a newly revitalized area of Los Angeles. By that point, he had already opened his second restaurant, Picca, in Beverly Hills, a far more upscale establishment that attracted a different clientele. Zárate maintained his street food motif even in this neighborhood, calling the restaurant a cantina, with the connotation of a lowbrow watering hole but also implying a traditional gathering place serving street fare, such as *anticucho corazón* (beef heart) and *anticucho culito* (crispy chicken tail). In 2013, he opened a third restaurant, Paiche, in Marina del Rey, as a Peruvian version of an *izakaya,* essentially a gentrified Japanese cantina. As an example of this Pacific fusion, Zárate serves ceviche cut in small pieces, sashimi style. Each of his restaurants represented a different concept, demonstrating the flexibility of Peruvian cuisine.

Zárate's culinary artistry was carefully calculated to appeal to fashionable diners and particularly to critics. The *Los Angeles Times* restaurant reviewer Jonathan Gold described him as a "chef's chef" and his cuisine as "artfully deconstructed versions of Peruvian dishes like papas a la huancaina, which is presented as a bacon-wrapped terrine of neat potato slices lightly drizzled with the traditional sauce of cheese and amarillo chile." The market stall became not only a foodie destination but also part of a global trend for Pacific fusion. Once he had moved Mo-Chica beyond its food court origins, Zárate arranged for a fashionable postindustrial décor, including an expansive mural resembling street graffiti and Peruvian figurines designed by local celebrity chefs, all accompanied by pulsating salsa music. Thus, the opening of Paiche, named after an endangered Amazonian fish, in 2013 in a distant outpost near the ocean, Marina del Rey, was much hyped and anticipated by the growing number of food bloggers following Zárate's rise to stardom; everyone from the *LA Times* food writers to Eater.com blogged about opening night. In 2013, *Esquire* magazine named Paiche one of the best new restaurants of 2013. Yet things did not continue so smoothly for Zárate. A year later, after the hype had died down, the *Los Angeles Magazine* critic Patrick Kuh gave the restaurant one star only in an extensive review and mused that Zárate might be overreaching with his expanding empire. Unfortunately, Kuh's predictions turned out to be correct. In 2014, Zárate was forced out of his own hospitality group, Zarate Restaurants, by his investors. By October 2014, he was removed from all three restaurants, and soon after both Paiche and Mo-Chica closed. Was Zárate ousted because he tried to grow too quickly and lost his original focus on serving high-end, innovative Peruvian cuisine? In October 2014, *Los Angeles Magazine* published an article titled, "What the Heck Happened with Ricardo Zarate?" The rumor was that he was too busy expanding his Peruvian restaurant empire and not spending enough time in the kitchen of his restaurants anymore. He was also working on a cookbook, *The Fire of Peru: Recipes and Stories from my Peruvian Kitchen,* published in 2015. As of late 2015, he was back in the kitchen with a successful but greatly scaled-down pop-up restaurant in Santa Monica and was looking for locations for new restaurants.

From his initial move to Los Angeles, Zárate's business planning had always been premised on the notion of leveraging Peruvian cuisine as a culinary brand. He took a risk at the original Mo-Chica by purchasing sushi-quality seafood, which alone cost more than the entire check at nearby food court stalls, but it paid off with the quick success of his ceviche lunches. He explained, "Nobody understood what I was trying to do with Peruvian cuisine and no one thought I could make the food be competitive with other cuisines." Such stereotypes were crucial for building the investment capital needed to open a high-end restaurant. Zárate had opened the Mercado La Paloma stall with only $30,000; formal restaurants, by contrast, often require millions in financing. Investors told him his food was incredible, but what he was doing was very risky since Peruvian cuisine was not well known and he was trying to do something new.

As a self-proclaimed ambassador for Peruvian cuisine, Zárate recognized the high stakes in the competition between national cuisines within the global culinary industry, not just for restaurateurs, but also for agricultural exports, everything from fruits and vegetables to tequila and pisco. The association with Japanese fusion was also a savvy one for branding Peruvian food, given the upscale connotations of sushi and sashimi. Zárate admitted that he had not grown up eating at Japanese restaurants in Lima because of persistent discrimination against the Japanese as late as the late 1970s and 1980s, an ironic twist given the election of Alberto Fujimori to the presidency in 1990.

While hoping that Peruvian cuisine would follow the success of Japanese restaurants, Zárate also expressed concern that growing popularity could have a negative side effect. He fears that rapid expansion could lead Peruvian cuisine, like Mexican, to be seen as inexpensive, Americanized, and lowbrow. Instead, he hopes that Peruvian chefs will continue to use only the finest ingredients and set the bar high to enhance the global reputation of their national cuisine.

MAKING LATIN AMERICAN FOOD GLOBAL

Latin American foods have spread around the world with remarkable speed in the twenty-first century. Although Tex-Mex first gained a foothold in Europe and Australia in the 1960s and 1970s, Mexican chefs did not begin to replace Americanized taco shells and burritos with regional cooking until around 2000. Peruvian cuisine was scarcely noticed until the early 1990s and has now become almost ubiquitous. In September 2013, London's Lima Restaurant received a Michelin star, a first for Latin American cuisine, while several other Peruvian restaurants have received critical acclaim across the United States and Europe. With their growing presence, even in Asian and African tourist destinations, Mexican and Peruvian foods have come to represent a form of global modernity. This presence is all the more ironic because Latin American foods originally became popular as "authentic" counterparts to the standardized products of the industrial food system. As "undiscovered" regional cuisines become more scarce, bohemian trend-setters such as Anthony Bourdain more avidly pursue—or invent—them.

While the fashion for fusion cuisine has put Latin America in a global spotlight, few have tried to explain these cultural influences, beyond seeing them as a supposedly natural product of a cultural melting pot. Choi has described his cuisine by saying simply, "This is what Los Angeles tastes like." Yet as the anthropologist Richard Wilk (2006: 112) has observed, the "melting pot" does not just happen; creole cuisine is the product of labor and creativity. There may be diverse motivations for culinary mixing, using food for status, convenience, and comfort. Sidney Mintz (1985: 186) even defines a category of food as drugs, which would surely include chile peppers along with sugar and caffeinated stimulants. Fusion cuisine can impart status in many forms, as Choi and Zárate demonstrate, whether through techniques such as those of French haute cuisine or through the association with

Japanese sushi. Convenience foods are now more typically associated with supermarkets and fast-food restaurants, but the availability of ingredients and the ease of preparation can also be a motivation for culinary mixing. Comfort foods may derive from familial and lowbrow connections, including the use of a taco filled with Korean barbecue.

Ethnic entrepreneurialism and class relations were also important in determining the economic success of fusion cuisines. Street foods and enclave restaurants have always been an avenue for entrepreneurs with little capital to invest, since businesses could support a family through sweat equity. Scholars generally attribute immigrant entrepreneurship to racism and the restriction of entry into professional occupations. By contrast, Ricardo Zárate and Roy Choi achieved professional status as chefs following entrepreneurial career paths. Zárate arrived in the United States with cultural capital from his culinary training in Peru and London, while Choi defied his immigrant-restaurateur parents' expectations that he attend law school and opted instead for the Culinary Institute of America. Without trying to generalize from these two exceptional cases, it seems possible that such nontraditional career paths will become increasingly attractive as a result of the downgrading of the professions under neoliberal capitalism. Certainly the contemporary restaurant world makes such movements possible in new ways, at least for those with sufficient cultural and economic capital. Yet although Choi has suggested that Kogi-style trucks may improve the image of traditional *loncheras,* Oliver Wang and other critics have not been so optimistic that working-class Latino *loncheras* can achieve the crossover appeal of the gentrified "taco" truck.

The tremendous success of Roy Choi and Ricardo Zárate pays tribute as much to the importance of culinary infrastructure as to individual artistry or consumer desire. Whatever a chef's vision, it cannot be realized without additional markets for supplying ingredients and labor. Professional training through culinary education also emerges as a vital path for aspiring professionals. Indeed, the spread of cooking schools in Peru, Korea, and elsewhere demonstrates the perceived importance of culinary tourism. Yet the restaurant industry maintains a highly racialized, two-tiered labor market, in which few migrant workers have the cultural and economic capital to rise beyond the ranks of the line cook. The media plays an equally crucial role in crafting the expectations of culinary tourists, and the Kogi team's ability to harness innovative forms of media were fundamental. While Choi and Zárate developed their Pacific fusion cuisines with very different goals, the former searching for a uniquely American blend and the latter preserving his Peruvian national identity, Western expectations for Asian and Latin American foods largely dictated the presentation of their dishes as exotic fare. Yet despite these limitations, tacos and ceviche have achieved a remarkable global presence in a few short decades, and they are just the appetizers. Latin American cuisine holds even greater riches for diners of the world to discover.

REFERENCES AND SUGGESTED READING

About Kogi.
    n.d.   http://kogibbq.com/about-kogi/.
Balbi, Mariella
    1999   *Los chifas en el Perú: Historia y recetas.* Lima: Universidad San Martín de Porres.
Bauer, Arnold J.
    2001   *Good, Power, History: Latin America's Material Culture.* Cambridge: Cambridge University Press.
Choi, Roy
    2013   *L.A. Son: My Life, My City, My Food.* New York: HarperCollins.
de Vos, Paula
    2006   "The Science of Spices: Empiricism and Economic Botany in the Early Spanish Empire." *Journal of World History* 17 (December): 399–47.
Drinot, Paulo
    2005   "Food, Race, and Working-Class Identity: Restaurantes Populares and Populism in 1930s Peru." *The Americas* 62.2: 245–70.
Ho, Ping-Ti
    1955   "The Introduction of American Food Plants into China." *American Anthropologist* 57.2: 191–201.
Johnston, Josée, and Shyon Baumann
    2010   *Foodies: Democracy and Distinction in the Gourmet Foodscape.* New York: Routledge.
Mazumdar, Sucheta
    1999   "The Impact of New World Food Crops on the Diet and Economy of China and India, 1600–1900." In *Food in Global History,* edited by Raymond Grew, 58–78. Boulder, CO: Westview Press.
Mintz, Sidney W.
    1985   *Sweetness and Power: The Place of Sugar in Modern History.* New York: Viking Press.
Modern Peruvian Cuisine
    n.d.   www.chefzarate.com/.
Opie, Fredrick Douglass
    2008   *Hogs and Hominy: Soul Food from Africa to America.* New York: Columbia University Press.

Ortiz, Fernando

[1940]   *Cuban Counterpoint: Tobacco and Sugar.* Translated by Harriet de Onís.
1995   Durham, NC: Duke University Press.

Pilcher, Jeffrey M.

2012   *Planet Taco: A Global History of Mexican Food.* New York: Oxford University Press.

Ray, Krishnendu

2011   "Dreams of Pakistani Grill and Vada Pao in Manhattan: Re-Inscribing the Immigrant Body in Metropolitan Discussions of Taste." *Food, Culture, and Society* 14.2: 243–73.

Valle, Victor, and Rodolfo Torres

2000   *Latino Metropolis.* Minneapolis: University of Minnesota Press.

Wang, Oliver

2013   "Learning from Los Kogi Angeles: A Taco Truck and Its City." In *Eating Asia America: A Food Studies Reader,* edited by Robert Ji-Song Ku, Martin F. Manalansan IV, and Anita Mannur, 78–97. New York: New York University Press.

Wilk, Richard R.

2006   *Home Cooking in the Global Village: Caribbean Food from Buccaneers to Ecotourists.* London: Berg.

PART THREE

Science, Technology, and Health

INTRODUCTION

EXPERT KNOWLEDGE—WHAT RENATO Rosaldo terms "know-how" in this section's poem, "Perfecto Flores"—is not a commodity traded on global exchanges. The chapters in "Science, Technology, and Health" suggest that someday this might change. The development of know-how and its transfer across international borders is an old and, in the case of Latin America, gripping story. Current patterns reflect the shifting global political landscape and Latin America's prominent role within it.

In this part one historian, two natural scientists, and two social scientists bring an expectant if critical eye to the roles of Latin American experts in science, technology, and health in meeting growing global challenges. Observers tend to describe the scale of twenty-first-century challenges as "unprecedented," requiring, not surprisingly, "unparalleled" solutions. Among the more immediate "known unknowns" are climate change, food insecurity, resource scarcity, and antibiotic shortages and resistance. Extraordinary cooperation and collaboration across borders—especially between so-called developed and developing nations—will be fundamental to the success of initiatives that address these challenges. More than a handful of Latin American countries sit at the crossroads in that dualistic worldview of development, and they will serve significant roles, beyond just mediating between parties, in pioneering ways forward.

Highlighting the environmental costs of food production or the inequities and ironies embedded in the global war on drugs, readers encounter here three case studies that highlight the messy complexities of solution making. These authors do not paint simplistic, two-dimensional portraits of success.

They complicate the very premise of solutions, exposing the consequences and new challenges that accompany innovation: the by-products of "steps forward." The different disciplinary backgrounds of the authors—spanning the natural and social sciences and humanities—reflects the diversity of training and thinking necessary for such conversations.

While principally focused on contemporary stories, these chapters counter long-enduring myths about the relationship between know-how and Latin American people and places. One of those myths characterizes Latin America as blessed with bountiful, exotic natural richness that can only be studied and put to good use by foreigners, on whom it is thus dependent and therefore deferential. Picture Charles Darwin peering into the eyes of a giant tortoise on the Galápagos, or imagine Alexander von Humboldt and Aimé Bonpland shuddering from shocks as they study the bioelectricity of electric eels on the Orinoco River. Here we see that those are stale if quaint versions of who makes innovation happen in the region.

The authors in this part are not revising narratives to be geopolitically correct. Instead, they are bringing to light genuine individual and institutional agency throughout the region. Brazil—the new colossus on the twenty-first-century block—occupies a continent-sized role in this story. For instance, in just over three decades, federal initiatives and innovative agronomic science transformed the nation from a net food importer to one of the world's most promising breadbaskets. The local environmental conditions for this advance—a highly acidic, low-fertility expanse in the country's interior—make that transformation all the more remarkable. Brazilian soybeans, now serious competition for more established U.S. counterparts, help feed the cattle that emerging middle classes are increasingly consuming worldwide. In their chapter, the biologists Christopher Neill and Marcia Macedo outline the agronomic and institutional inner workings that led to this advance.

Countries gain soft and hard power by capitalizing on the development of knowledge within their borders by exporting it beyond them. The sociologists Wendy Wolford and Ryan Nehring explore power and knowledge via the transfer of expertise eastward from Brazil to Mozambique. Their study plumbs the limitations and possibilities of expertise beyond surface-level "cultural differences," instead emphasizing the rooted social and economic structures that distinguish one place from another. Specialists of the Global South will find particular interest in this story of Brazil's expanding reach and a case of attempted development through South-South cooperation. Scholars working in many corners of global Latin America will also gain much, as shifting geopolitical alliances and trade configurations—"pivots" to the east and west, toward the Pacific Rim and toward Africa—make such cases even more relevant.

These chapters do not brush aside the social intersections and implications of new advances in science, technology, and health. A key thread running through them, especially in Paul Gootenberg's chapter on global drug culture, encourages us to rethink notions of who belongs at the table in conversations about globally significant policies and challenges. Gootenberg draws our attention to the progenitors of curative substances from Mexico to the Andes who helped preserve herbal cures—some now considered "miracle drugs"— over centuries in the face of persecution and criminalization. Members of those same indigenous populations have assumed important roles in debates about global climate change, with some residents of the Amazon helping draw attention to the local realities of deforestation. As they broaden the definition of expert, chapters like Gootenberg's should inspire policy makers toward greater inclusion in both addressing global problems and forging broadly relevant solutions.

"Science, Technology, and Health" provides a glimpse at innovation in global Latin America and will tempt readers to seek further examples. They may encounter the biologists at the University of Buenos Aires who sequenced the genome of quinoa and found its nutritional density and resistance to salty soils crucial traits in the twenty-first-century fight against food insecurity. They may find references to *bacillus megaterium uyuni,* a bacterium scientists encountered in Bolivia's salt flats that can be used in the production of polymers that generate "natural" plastic. A broad view of these discoveries and innovations suggests that in the years ahead expertise will serve as a valuable exchange good helping to fuel new geopolitical alignments with Latin America at the center. While unequal North-South relationships of yesterday may morph into South-South inequalities of tomorrow, these chapters showcase how centuries-old and decades-new Latin American know-how is making a global impact.

NINE

The Rise of Brazil's Globally Connected Amazon Soybean Agriculture

Christopher Neill and Marcia N. Macedo

TRACTOR-TRAILER TRUCKS LINE up along a red and muddy earthen road. Large vinyl tarpaulins secured by ropes cover the open-topped hoppers of each one. Truck drivers hang out and prepare simple meals using stoves and kitchen utensils contained in a compact box built into the side of the truck cab. It's early March, still the middle of a lush and highly predictable rainy season. The trucks wait for their turn and then enter a large modern compound with a football field–sized building where they are loaded with recently harvested and dried soybeans and weighed.

From the gate of this modern farm facility in the state of Mato Grosso in Brazil's southeastern Amazon, these trucks will drive 75 kilometers to the nearest paved road. From there, most will travel another 1,500 to 2,000 kilometers, mostly on two-lane highways, to the Atlantic Ocean port of Santos near the city of São Paulo or Paranaguá in the state of Paraná in southeastern Brazil. There, they maneuver onto tilting, truck-sized ramps that disgorge their contents into a giant hopper, from which the protein-rich cargo will be loaded onto giant oceangoing ships and sold around the world. Although the exact pathways soybeans take to the global market differ slightly, this scene is repeated across a 2,500-kilometer-wide continental-scale swath of the Amazon stretching from Rondônia in the southwest through Mato Grosso and Pará in the east.

The rise of the soybean agro-industry in Mato Grosso is a recent and fast-changing phenomenon. Mato Grosso occupies 900,000 square kilometers at the agricultural frontier of Brazil's southern Amazon (fig. 9.1). As late as the 1980s, Mato Grosso's agricultural landscape consisted of large-scale cattle ranching on land cleared from either native savanna/grassland (Cerrado) in the south or the perennially green and higher-stature closed-canopy Amazon

FIGURE 9.1. *Opposite page:* (A) Aerial view of Mato Grosso soybean field showing Amazon forest in the background and uncultivated but degraded riparian vegetation in the foreground. (B) Trucks waiting to be loaded with soybeans to be transported to port. *Above:* (C) Soybean field after harvest. Fields have little plant cover during the dry season, and the next year's crop is planted in the stubble of the previous crop using minimum tillage. (D) Rain over a Mato Grosso soybean field. Reductions in rainfall are projected because of regional decreases in forest cover, but their magnitude and timing are still uncertain. Image A by Paulo Brando, others by Christopher Neill.

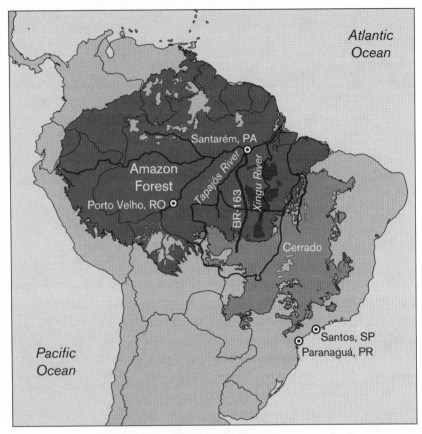

FIGURE 9.2. Map indicating the location of Mato Grosso state, Brazil (outline). Mato Grosso encompasses both Amazon forest (green) and Cerrado savanna (orange) vegetation. Map by Paul Lefebvre.

forest in the north (fig. 9.2). The region has a tropical monsoonal climate with a roughly six-month rainy season and total annual rainfall that ranges from about 1,700 to slightly more than 2,000 millimeters. In less than thirty years Brazil has transformed itself from a food importer to one of the world's great agricultural powerhouses and grain exporters—the only tropical nation to break into that elite group. The area of soybean cropland in Mato Grosso increased from less than 2.0 million hectares in 1990 to 7.5 million hectares in the 2012–13 cropping season. Over the same time, soybean production rose from less than 2 million metric tons per year to more than 24 million metric tons per year. Compared to changes in agricultural production in the temperate north, that's an astounding rate of change. Between 2008 and

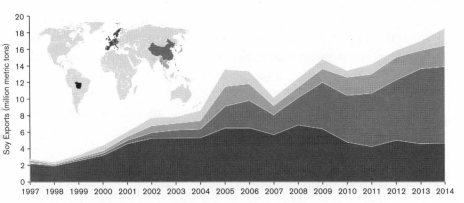

FIGURE 9.3. Destination of Mato Grosso's international soybean exports, 1997–2013. Export statistics are from the Brazilian Agency for Agriculture, Livestock and Food Supply (MAPA).

2012, Brazilian national soybean production grew a total of 9 percent while U.S. production grew less than 0.5 percent. Mato Grosso now leads Brazil in both soybean and beef production, responsible for 31 percent of the nation's soybean production and more than 13 percent of its cattle herd in 2009.

The ultimate destination of Brazil's Amazon soybeans has also changed dramatically. As recently as 1997, Mato Grosso exported less than 2 million metric tons of soybeans, and more than three-fourths of that went to the European Union. By 2012, Mato Grosso exported more than 10 million metric tons, nearly 7 million metric tons of that to China (fig. 9.3). This shift positioned Brazil, in 2014, to vie with the United States for the title of the planet's largest soybean exporter. But while Brazil gains income by selling Amazon soybeans in the international market, purchasing countries now effectively export the substantial impacts and environmental costs of growing soybeans in the Amazon back to Brazil. Brazil also exports soybean production knowledge and technology—and because most of the earth's potential new farmland lies within tropical latitudes, Brazil's influence over global agricultural expansion and production will continue to grow in coming decades.

Within Brazil, the rise of soybeans in Mato Grosso shifted the trajectory of Amazon deforestation. From 1996 to 2005, the frontier states of Mato Grosso, Rondônia, and Pará accounted for 85 percent of all Amazon deforestation. This clearing converted an average of 16,600 square kilometers of forest to agricultural uses each year (by comparison the area of Belgium is 30,528 square kilometers), but the underlying forces that drove agricultural expansion shifted dramatically in that period. During the 1970s and 1980s, government investments in road infrastructure and subsidies for Amazon land distribution often rewarded deforesters with formal land titles. Cattle pasture was the overwhelmingly predominant use of cleared lands in the Amazon and Cerrado at that time. By the early 1990s, many of the policies that stimulated deforestation were removed and global markets for commodities such as soybeans started to exert an increasing influence on the Amazon economy. The focus of Amazon deforestation began to shift to Mato Grosso and by the early 2000s, the state accounted for 40 percent of all deforestation in the Brazilian Amazon. Twenty-six percent of forests cleared in Mato Grosso from 2001 to 2005 were converted directly into soybean croplands, and cropland expansion in Mato Grosso far outpaced that of other Amazon states.

TRANSFORMATION OF TROPICAL AGRICULTURE

There are many roots of Mato Grosso's transformation from extensive cattle farming to intensive production of grains for global markets. Some of these roots are global, but others have their origins inside Brazil. Three largely Brazil-grown advances were agronomic: (1) overcoming the high acidity and low fertility of native soils, (2) designing varieties of soybeans adapted to hot temperatures and low latitudes, and (3) developing soil management practices for tropical soils that maintain soil structure and good infiltration capacity.

Agronomists have long recognized potentially severe limitations for continuous crop production on most of the natural *terra firme* (nonfloodplain) soils of the lowland American tropics. One of those limitations is acidity. This derives partly from the naturally acidic granite bedrock that underlies most of the Brazilian Shield of Mato Grosso. The region also has generally low topographic relief and has been covered with naturally acid-producing forest and savanna vegetation that has existed in a relatively high-rainfall environment for hundreds of thousands of years. Without major tectonic uplift or other geologic processes that can deposit new soils or expose soils to more alkaline rocks, these features produced deep, old, and highly weathered soils that are high in iron and aluminum clay minerals but low in pH (a measure of acidity; low pH indicates greater acidity).

This combination of high aluminum and low pH is toxic to soybeans and many other crops. Many of the soils in the soybean-growing regions of Mato

Grosso are classified as "Latossolos" that can be tens of meters deep, contain anywhere from 20 percent to more than 70 percent clay, and have a pH of less than four. In contrast, soils in much of the soybean-growing regions of the United States have a much smaller proportion of clay and a much more crop-friendly pH closer to six. The same wet conditions and ancient soils that created low soil pH also caused very low levels of soil phosphorus, an essential crop nutrient. This is because almost all of the phosphorus contained in the original bedrock has been dissolved and leached away. Natural inputs of phosphorus to the Amazon region are so low that even very small inputs, derived from the fallout of dust transported across the Atlantic Ocean from the Saharan region of North Africa, are suspected of playing an important role—over millennial time scales—in maintaining the phosphorus fertility of *terra firme* Amazon rain forests.

The recognition that amendments of lime and phosphorus and potassium fertilizer could overcome low pH and low phosphorus fertility was a key breakthrough that allowed soybean cropland expansion—and simultaneously created large demands for imported fertilizer—in Mato Grosso. This advance originated almost completely within Brazil, and was largely the outcome of the founding in 1973 of the Brazilian agricultural research agency, Empresa Brasileira de Pesquisa Agropecuária (Embrapa), and the formation in 1975 of the soybean-specific Embrapa Soybean. Embrapa operates under Brazil's federal Ministry of Agriculture, Livestock and Food Supply (MAPA). It has remained a major innovator of agricultural technology in Brazil and in 2013 had an annual budget of approximately $1 billion Brazilian reais, with 2,400 researchers (of whom more than three-fourths have PhDs) among its approximately 9,600 employees.

Embrapa contributed other major agro-technical advances that improved production and made it profitable to grow Amazon soybeans for global markets. One was the development of soybean varieties that tolerate both the short tropical days and the warm tropical climate that occur below 20° latitude. Soybeans have their biological origin in China and up until the 1980s were grown almost exclusively as a temperate crop, primarily in North America, Europe, and the states of Paraná, Santa Catarina, and Rio Grande do Sul in southeastern Brazil. Improved cultivars first allowed soybean cultivation to spread to the higher elevation and slightly cooler portions of the Cerrado region of Mato Grosso in the 1980s. Second- and third-generation cultivars followed in the 1990s and 2000s, totaling more than three hundred varieties tailored to different conditions, which allowed the more recent expansion to hotter regions of the forested north. Embrapa's cultivars now account for more than 50 percent of the national seed market. During this period, productivity on soybean farms in Brazil tripled from barely 1,000 kilograms per hectare to more than 3,000.

The physical properties of many Amazonian Latossolos are also favorable for crop production, once the low pH and phosphorus fertility are corrected with amendments. Many have good drainage and physical condition, or tilth, despite their clay content, which is typically higher than that of the soils that cover most major temperate grain-producing regions. This is because clay particles aggregate into larger, more sandlike particles that allow water to infiltrate freely while still holding enough water to maintain soil moisture. But this aggregation can be disrupted by tillage, especially when soil is either very wet or very dry—both of which are common under tropical conditions. In Mato Grosso, this problem was greatly reduced by Embrapa's development and widespread promotion of zero-tillage technology, in which seeds are drilled directly into the stubble of the previous crop with minimal soil disturbance. This requires specialized planting machinery but has proved very effective at avoiding disruption of soil aggregates. Except for the initial tillage required to prepare soybean fields following conversion from other land uses (Cerrado, forest, or pasture), today no-tillage practices are the norm across Mato Grosso. The area of cropland under zero tillage in Brazil's Cerrado and Amazon regions exploded from near zero in 1990 to more than 25 million hectares in 2009.

The high fertilizer requirements for Mato Grosso soybean cropping also required the development of a supporting fertilizer supply chain, particularly for phosphorus and potassium. Today this supply chain is heavily weighted toward imports. Brazil contains only about 2 percent of the world's phosphorus reserves and accounts for about 4 percent of global annual production of the phosphorus rocks that are the precursors to phosphorus-containing fertilizers. Soybean expansion in Mato Grosso was the most important reason that Brazilian use of phosphate minerals increased from just over one million metric tons in 1990 to 4.3 million metric tons in 2013. Sixty percent of that demand is supplied within Brazil, and 40 percent, or 1.7 million metric tons, was imported from the United States (21 percent), Morocco (25 percent), Russia (14 percent), Israel (10 percent), China (13 percent), or other countries (17 percent). For potassium, Brazil relies even more heavily on imports; only 8 percent of potassium fertilizer demand is supplied by domestic production. Brazil's main sources of potassium are Canada (27 percent), Belarus (22 percent), the

European Union (20 percent), the Russian Federation (15 percent), and Israel (12 percent); other countries account for 4 percent. Brazil's internal capacity to produce both phosphate and potassium fertilizers is now expanding rapidly.

Transporting harvested soybeans from the relatively remote interior of Mato Grosso to the coast remains a major infrastructural challenge. Almost all of Mato Grosso's soybeans travel by truck between 900 and 1,300 miles to Atlantic ports. A much smaller amount travels west to Porto Velho, where it is loaded onto barges that will travel down the Madeira River to ports in Itacoatiara or Santarém—site of a new deepwater port built by Cargill at the confluence of the Amazon and Tapajós Rivers—where soybeans can be loaded onto oceangoing ships. An even smaller amount travels directly north by road from Mato Grosso to Santarém on the controversial BR-163, the still partially unpaved "soybean highway" that cuts a swath through remaining Amazon rain forest (see fig. 9.2).

In 2012, it cost about US$50 to ship a metric ton of soybeans to Shanghai, China, from Santos, Brazil's largest soybean port in the state of São Paulo. It costs more than twice that to get the soybeans to Santos from Mato Grosso by truck over Brazil's road network, 86 percent of which is still unpaved. But because dried soybean grain is nonperishable and can be shipped in large trailer trucks, this transport cost is still a very small proportion (about one percent) of the total cost of Mato Grosso soybean production. Truck transport costs remain an important constraint on Brazil's soybean exports and are one link in the export chain where soybean exports from the U.S. Midwest have a price advantage. In 2012, it cost $87 to ship a ton of soybeans from Davenport, Iowa, to Shanghai, China, on the Mississippi River via the Port of New Orleans, compared to $161 for the same ton shipped from Sorriso, Mato Grosso, to the Port of Santos. This will soon change because contracts were signed in 2014 to finish paving the BR-163 roadway, which will lower the cost of trucking Mato Grosso soybeans north to the port at Santarém.

GLOBALIZATION OF AMAZON SOYBEANS

In 2012, two-thirds of Mato Grosso's soybean exports traveled to one nation—China. Much smaller amounts went to Spain, the Netherlands, Thailand, Norway, and Taiwan. Eighty-three percent of soybeans shipped through Santos went to China. Brazil now competes with the United States to be the world's largest soybean exporter: both nations shipped 37 million metric tons of soybeans in 2013. Brazilian and U.S. soybean exports dwarf the 10 million metric tons shipped by third-place Argentina. Brazil's Amazon states, mostly Mato Grosso with much smaller contributions from Rondônia and Pará, now produce 31 percent of Brazil's soybeans and account for 35 percent of Brazil's soybean exports. Soybeans now rank third, behind iron ore and crude oil, as Brazil's most valuable export commodity.

Chinese soybean imports grew explosively from almost nothing in 1990 to more than 70 million metric tons in 2014. This trade drives the expansion of Brazil's Amazon soybean production and is closely linked with the rise of a large—and increasingly meat-eating—Asian middle class. According to the U.N. Food and Agriculture Organization, per capita meat consumption in industrialized countries increased from 62 kilograms in 1965 to 88 in 1998 and is projected to grow to 100 by 2030. Over the same period, per capita meat consumption in China increased from 9 to 38 kilograms and is expected to reach 59 kilograms by 2030. Roughly 70 percent of this consumption is pork, 20 percent is chicken, and a small (but growing) fraction is beef. For comparison, between 1980 and 2010, meat consumption in the United States increased from 22 million to 32 million metric tons, while meat consumption in China rose from 10 million to 70 million metric tons. The U.S. Department of Agriculture estimates that while demands for soybeans from the rest of the world will remain relatively flat through 2025, Chinese imports will continue to grow to 110 million metric tons. Much of that demand is and will continue to be supplied by Mato Grosso and Brazil's Amazon region.

Several other factors also contributed to the increased demand for Mato Grosso soybeans in the 2000s. Demand increased when "mad cow" disease (bovine spongiform encephalitis, BSE) appeared in Europe's cattle herd in 2000. In reaction to BSE, Europe banned meat and bone meal ingredients in all livestock feeds, creating a greater demand for protein-rich soybeans on the global market. In 2001, an outbreak of foot and mouth disease (FMD), a serious and highly infectious viral disease of domestic cattle and other hoofed animals, occurred in Britain and required the slaughter of many animals. Threats of FMD also occurred in several other countries at about the same time. In 2003, Brazil successfully eradicated FMD from the southern Amazon—a 1.5-million-square-kilometer area that included Mato Grosso—enabling beef exports outside the Amazon and spurring the expansion of Mato Grosso's cattle herd. The threat of FMD in Brazil concurrently contributed to modernization of the cattle industry in Mato Grosso, including more extensive vaccination, tracking animals through the production and commodity supply chains, use of improved genetic lines of cattle, artificial insemination, and improved pasture management that allowed greater cattle production per hectare of land. Amazon slaughterhouses now export a growing proportion of their products from the region, and in June 2015 the USDA's Animal and Plant Health Inspection Service amended its rules to allow import to the United States of chilled or frozen beef from several Brazilian regions, including Mato Grosso.

Increasing the supply of soybeans to meet this growing demand required capital investments of an unprecedented scale, but during a decade of financial crisis in the 1980s the Brazilian government had little capacity to provide new lines of credit for the agricultural sector. Starting in the mid-1990s, however, private bank financing increased sharply and the overall availability of credit expanded rapidly. During this period, a number of innovations enabled new sources of finance, including the development of the "Soja Verde" program for finance and production of soybeans in the Cerrado during the 1980s, as well as the granting of private land titles. Once these mechanisms were in place, trading on the international markets began to play a key role in providing capital to producers, who in turn guaranteed a certain level of food supply and security. These mechanisms greatly increased the credit available to the agricultural sector by giving producers in the region access to international credit lines. It also provided a way for producers to hedge their bets through contracts in international commodities exchanges.

NEW PATHWAYS TO ENVIRONMENTAL GOVERNANCE

The explosive growth of soybean cropland area in Mato Grosso during the late 1990s and into the 2000s drew global attention as total Amazon deforestation rose steadily to a high of 27,772 square kilometers in 2004. A September 2003 article ran in the *New York Times* under the headline, "Relentless Foe of the Amazon Jungle: Soybeans." Within Brazil, articles began appearing in regional newspapers with headlines like "Holocausto Verde" (Green Holocaust). In 2006, Greenpeace launched a major protest campaign called "Eating Up the Amazon" that highlighted Brazil's 2004 Amazon deforestation rate of 3 square kilometers an hour or, as Greenpeace put it, "a football pitch every eight seconds." It targeted three major U.S. companies that exported Amazon soybeans to Europe (Archer Daniels Midland, Bunge, and Cargill) and focused attention on the new Cargill soybean terminal being built in Santarém.

The protest campaign got results. In July 2006, the Associação Brasileira das Indústrias de Óleos Vegetais (ABIOVE) and the Associação Nacional dos Exportadores de Cereais (ANEC) and their respective member companies pledged not to trade or finance soybeans produced within the Amazon biome on lands deforested after that date. This unique initiative, known as the "Soy Moratorium," sought to reconcile Amazon environmental preservation with economic development. Major international conservation organizations, including Conservation International, the World Wildlife Fund, Greenpeace, and The Nature Conservancy, are parties to the moratorium, which was renewed indefinitely in May 2016. Each of these groups has offices within Brazil. Brazilian conservation organizations also played an important role in supporting the moratorium and in creating mechanisms that enable market pressures to promote better agricultural practices. For example, the Instituto de Pesquisa Ambiental da Amazônia conducts scientific research and promotes stronger environmental enforcement, and Aliança da Terra created the Registry of Social-Environmental Responsibility, which enrolls farm property owners and works with them to incorporate more socially and environmentally responsible production practices. In addition, compliance with the moratorium was monitored by the Brazilian Space Agency (INPE) via annual satellite mapping of deforestation. The moratorium also resulted in the establishment of a formal land registry for rural properties, known as the Cadastro Ambiental Rural (CAR), which improved transparency and enforcement of illegal deforestation in Mato Grosso. In 2012, the Brazilian federal government expanded the CAR by making it a national policy and establishing SICAR, a georeferenced, online registry of properties that uses satellite-derived spatial data to track native vegetation in private properties.

The moratorium had a dramatic effect on Amazon deforestation rates. From 2006 to 2010, deforestation in the entire Amazon declined from 14,286 to 4,571 square kilometers per year. New clearing in Mato Grosso declined even more, to an estimated 850 square kilometers by 2010—just 11 percent of its historical average of 7,600 square kilometers from 1996 to 2005. The moratorium's main effect was to push deforestation onto land cleared before 2006, which meant converting mainly existing, low-productivity pastures—a process that Mato Grosso's cattle sector carried out without a drop in production. The effectiveness of the moratorium also changed the tenor of international media coverage about Amazon soybeans by reducing talk of soybeans as destroyers of the Amazon, increasing news reports of Brazil's success

FIGURE 9.4. Soybean croplands in Mato Grosso, Brazil. The double-cropped area in the state expanded substantially from 2001 (upper) to 2013 (lower). Map by Paul Lefebvre, based on data from Spera et al. 2014.

in curbing deforestation, and even raising the possibility of reducing deforestation to zero. As the soy moratorium drew close to its scheduled end in 2014, the Brazilian soy industry voted to extend it for another eighteen months into early 2016. Part of the political pressure for its continuation was a 28 percent upturn in deforestation from 2012 to 2013, as well as concerns that relaxation of legal requirements for forest and savanna protection and reforestation (resulting from modifications to Brazil's Forest Code passed in 2012) would spur accelerated clearing. The new Forest Code grants amnesty to landowners who deforested illegally before 2008 and reduces the area that landowners are required to reforest from 500,000 to 210,000 square kilometers. The new law also allows legal deforestation of an additional 400,000 square kilometers of the Cerrado, an area almost the size of California.

It is unclear how long the containment of deforestation rates in Mato Grosso and other Amazon frontier states can last. Planned new infrastructure, including the completion of the BR-163 and construction of several large hydroelectric dams, will greatly reduce transport costs and likely increase pressure to expand the amount of land under soybean cultivation in the corridor to Santarém. As soybeans replace cattle pastures, there is growing concern that they may push cattle ranching farther into the forest frontier, as those who sold their ranchlands at a profit in regions of recent cropland expansion invest in new lands farther from roads. These indirect land use changes are very hard to quantify and fall largely outside the influence of the soybean moratorium.

Even as the soybean moratorium moved soybean cropping to Mato Grosso's previously deforested lands, a second wave of intensification began sweeping the state in about 2000, as producers shifted to planting a second late-season crop following the main soybean harvest. In this farming system, soybeans and a second crop (most commonly corn but also cotton) is planted and harvested within the same six-month rainy season. While in 2001 only 500,000 hectares of Mato Grosso's 3.3 million hectares of mechanized cropland were double-cropped, by 2013 almost half (2.8 million) of the state's 5.8 million hectares of mechanized cropland were double-cropped (figs. 9.4a, 9.4b). Corn accounted for 94 percent of all double-cropping in 2013. The expansion of double-cropping slowed after 2008, which may have been related to falling corn prices on the international market, limitations on the capital to purchase specialized equipment required for corn planting and harvest, and limits in the infrastructure needed to store large amounts of harvested grain.

The rapid expansion and intensification of agriculture in Mato Grosso poses major environmental costs that lie at the heart of the debate over the future of Brazil's Amazon forest. Because the native forests and savannas of Mato Grosso contain a very rich assemblage of plant and animal species compared to other tropical regions, Mato Grosso's agricultural transformation has undoubtedly had large consequences for biological diversity. The Amazon forests at the epicenter of soybean expansion in Mato Grosso contain as many as one hundred tree species per hectare. Although this is less than half the species richness found in the central and western Amazon, it is high compared to temperate forests and likely an underestimate, given that many locations in Mato Grosso are poorly inventoried. The ecological forces that control tree diversity across the Amazon are not well understood, and the underrepresentation of many southern Amazon sites makes it likely that rare species remain undetected in these regions.

The greatest impact of land transformation on vertebrate animals may be on the fish of the southern Amazon. The number of fish species in the Amazon likely rivals the number of fish species in all other basins of the world combined. Its riverine headwaters—including the headwaters of the Xingu and Tapajós basins, which dominate northern Mato Grosso—are thought to be areas of particularly high endemic fish species diversity. This diversity arises from some of the same factors that shape the region's soils, including the ancient river drainage networks that separate headwater river systems. Current estimates are that about 40 percent of Amazon fish species have yet to be discovered and described in the scientific literature.

Among the largest impacts of agricultural expansion on fish and aquatic biodiversity may be the loss of streamside forest vegetation, which leads to warmer water temperatures in stream channels. In Mato Grosso, the loss of forests bordering streams raises streamwater temperatures between 2 and 4 degrees Celsius. The biological effects—and hence implications for global fish diversity—of this change are poorly known but are likely important because tropical aquatic organisms evolved in relatively stable thermal regimes compared to those in temperate regions, which experience greater seasonal variation in temperature.

The Cerrado is particularly vulnerable to the effects of agricultural expansion. Despite its high levels of endemism, about 66 percent of the Cerrado is now altered by cropland or managed pasture and less than 7 percent of the remaining area is legally protected—in stark contrast to the Amazon biome to the north. The Cerrado contains more than 12,000 plant species, as many as 800 fish species, and 777 bird species and contains more endangered species of plants and animals than the Amazon. Much like the Amazonian regions of Mato Grosso, most of the Cerrado is poorly inventoried, and species distributions are not well known except in a few relatively small reserves.

The potential regional and global impacts of agricultural expansion in Mato Grosso extend well beyond local losses in biodiversity. First, the use of nitrogen fertilizers is the largest single human-caused source of emissions of nitrous oxide—a powerful greenhouse gas with three hundred times the heat-trapping capacity of carbon dioxide. While emissions of nitrous oxide from single-cropped soybeans appear to be very low, the consequences of expanding double-cropping are not known. Second, the shift to intensive crop production systems could have widespread and detrimental effects on water quality. Experience with intensive crop agriculture around the globe shows that the consequences of nutrient runoff from intensive croplands can be severe. For example, runoff of nitrogen and phosphorus from extensive farmland has created large "dead zones" of oxygen-depleted estuarine water at the mouths of the Mississippi, Yangtze, and other rivers. The ultimate effect of Mato Grosso's intensive crop production on the surface waters of the Xingu and Tapajós Rivers remains unknown. Some recent work suggests that nutrient and sediment losses from single-cropped soybeans in parts of Mato Grosso are very low. This likely occurs because weathered tropical soils bind strongly to phosphorus and because soybeans require minimal inputs of nitrogen fertilizer (soybeans are members of the legume family and capable of fixing nitrogen directly from the atmosphere). Furthermore, the flat, weathered soils of Mato Grosso appear to have relatively high rates of water infiltration and infrequent occurrence of lateral flows that generate erosion. Double-cropping of corn or cotton may change this pattern dramatically because both crops require relatively high rates of nitrogen fertilizer addition, which appears more capable of moving through soils and into groundwaters and streams compared to phosphorus. In this case, the patterns observed during the relatively brief period of soybean single-cropping may not be an appropriate indication of future impact.

The high use of pesticides in Mato Grosso's cropping systems poses another potentially large impact on water quality and human health. Soybean farming accounts for about a quarter of all pesticides used in Brazil. In Mato Grosso, soybean farms routinely use pesticides with about forty different active ingredients. The largest single class of pesticides is glyphosate-based broad-spectrum herbicides used to kill weeds before planting and to speed drying of soybean plants before grain harvest. Herbicide use is greater than that of insecticides and fungicides combined. Glyphosate has a half-life of about sixty days in soils and a few days in water. It adheres strongly to soil and does not bioaccumulate in food chains. Large farms now use fewer of the pesticides most toxic to humans than do smaller farms, and the overall use of most highly toxic compounds has declined since 2002. There have been some reports of pesticide impacts within the Xingu Indigenous Park downstream of large soybean growing areas in the basin's headwaters, but there have been no comprehensive scientific studies of pesticide impacts in Mato Grosso.

While soybean cropping poses environmental problems, gains in productivity and a strong connection to global markets also present opportunities—as illustrated by the Soy Moratorium—to shape production systems and agricultural frontier landscapes in ways that conserve some existing natural land and reduce environmental risks. Some mechanisms currently exist for reducing the biodiversity consequences of agricultural land conversion. One of the strongest such mechanisms is the Brazilian Forest Code, which mandates the conservation of large blocks of forests, protection of forest buffer zones along streams, and restoration of illegally deforested areas on private farms. A hotly contested revision to the Forest Code in 2012 maintained a provision instituted in 1996 that Amazon property owners maintain 80 percent of the total area as intact forest, but it reduced the requirement for restoration to 50 percent of the farm area for lands deforested (illegally) before 2008 and reduced the width of required stream forest buffer zones on small properties. This reduced the total forest area to be restored by 41 percent, compared to the previous (pre-2012) Forest Code, and rendered it more difficult to reshape forest connectivity and habitat conservation at landscape scales.

As many as 18 billion metric tons of carbon—a number equivalent to more than half the world's annual carbon dioxide emissions—could ultimately be emitted from the approximately 88 million hectares of private property in Brazil that could be deforested legally under the new Forest Code. Several mechanisms might reduce this total, but they are largely untested. One is the introduction of an environmental reserve quota—a tradable legal title to areas with intact vegetation that exceed Forest Code requirements—that could be traded to compensate for a forest area debt on another property. Exchange of these quotas could be a cost-effective way to increase Forest Code compliance while protecting areas that might otherwise be deforested. Brazil has also created a low carbon agriculture program that subsidizes loans to producers who lower carbon emissions associated with agricultural production activities. The future tradeoffs between the costs and benefits of different agricultural and regional land management options are far from certain.

By buying soybeans from Mato Grosso, China and other nations effectively capture resources from the Amazon and export some of their environmental impacts to this developing region. By one estimate, 30 percent of Brazil's carbon emissions from deforestation were "exported" between 2000 and 2010. Twenty-nine percent of these emissions came from soybean production and 71 percent from cattle ranching. Higher values for cattle ranching were due to more active clearing for pastures, which occurred primarily in Amazon forests with higher biomass (hence higher carbon stocks). The amount of water "embodied" in soybean exports to China increased from 10 to 38 cubic kilometers between 2001–5 and 2006–10. This represented about 23 percent of all the rainwater required to grow the crop locally. Total carbon emissions caused by soybean production during the same period fell from about 92 million to 78 million tons, mainly because the total deforestation rate declined.

Currently, large amounts of fertilizer are imported to Mato Grosso, but only part of that fertilizer leaves in the harvested grain crop. This leaves behind large amount of nutrients in soils where they contribute to soil fertility but may eventually cause nutrient impacts to freshwaters. Those impacts may be relatively minor for phosphorus based on the high ability of soils to bind free phosphorus. They are less known and likely increasing rapidly for nitrogen. The total global land area over which any of these impacts could occur may explode again if Brazil successfully exports its soybean-growing expertise to the still largely uncultivated savannas of eastern and southern Africa.

The largest potential environmental impact of converting Mato Grosso's forests and savannas to soybeans is likely the threat to the Amazon climate system, which maintains the regular wet season rainfall that makes Amazon dryland cropping systems possible. Because soybean plants have less total area of leaf surfaces and occupy land for only part of the year, soybean croplands return much less water to the atmosphere than the native forest or woody savannas they replaced. In small watersheds in Mato Grosso soybean regions, this causes a three- to fourfold increase in river flow in streams draining soybean fields, compared to those draining evergreen Amazon forests. These measurements do not, however, account for potential reductions in rainfall that could occur if less water is recirculated to the atmosphere through native vegetation. Current models indicate that in the Xingu River basin decreased rainfall caused by loss of forest cover has approximately compensated for higher discharge caused by lower evapotranspiration. So the lack of obvious net changes in the Xingu River flow may mask existing changes to the basin's overall water dynamics. Those same models project a 16 to 26 percent reduction in soybean crop production due to changing rainfall regimes by 2040 to 2050. Double-cropping may be the first victim of these climate shifts because the growing season lengths for combined soybean and corn crops require nearly the full annual period of regular rains.

In October, talk in the farm offices and farm towns of central Mato Grosso often centers on the appearance of the all-important first rains that will determine the timing of the new cropping season's soybean planting dates. All of the investments—in soil management, crop varieties, roads, and international fertilizer supply chains that made the rise of this remarkable Amazon farming system possible—for the moment seem secondary. The same question now confronts climate scientists. New evidence suggests that the first effects of deforestation-induced climate changes will be an extension of the dry season, but by how much and how soon are still unanswered questions. For now a farming system carved from the earth's greatest expanses of rain forest and savanna still depends—to a very real degree—on how much of those forests and woodlands remains standing. Exactly how long this remarkable agricultural boom can continue almost certainly rests on the answer to that question.

ACKNOWLEDGMENTS

This work was supported by grants from the National Science Foundation (NSF DEB 1257391, NSF ICER 1342943, NSF IOS 1457662). We thank Paul Lefebvre for producing the figures, Stephanie Spera for data on double-cropping in Mato Grosso, and KathiJo Jankowski for comments on earlier drafts.

REFERENCES AND SUGGESTED READING

Anonymous
    2010   "The Miracle of the Cerrado." *Economist,* 26 August.
Lathuillière, M. J., M. S. Johnson, G. L. Galford, and E. G. Couto

2014   "Environmental Footprints Show China and Europe's Evolving Resource Appropriation for Soybean Production in Mato Grosso, Brazil." *Environmental Research Letters* 9.7, doi 10.1088/1748–9326/9/7/074001.

Macedo, M. N., R. S. DeFries, D. C. Morton, C. M. Stickler, G. L. Galford, and Y. E. Shimabukuro

2012   "Decoupling of Deforestation and Soy Production in the Southern Amazon during the Late 2000s." *Proceedings of the National Academy of Sciences* 109.4: 1341–46.

Nepstad, D. C., C. M. Stickler, and O. T. Almeida

2006   "Globalization of the Amazon Soy and Beef Industries: Opportunities for Conservation." *Conservation Biology* 20.6: 1595–1603.

Spera, S., A. S. Cohen, L. K. VanWey, J. F. Mustard, B. F. Rudorff, J. Risso, and M. Adami

2014   "Recent Cropping Frequency, Expansion, and Abandonment in Mato Grosso, Brazil,Had Selective Land Characteristics." *Environmental Research Letters* 9.6, doi 10.1088/1748–9326/9/6/064010.

TEN

Constructing Parallels

BRAZILIAN EXPERTS IN MOZAMBIQUE

Wendy Wolford and Ryan Nehring

THERE IS MUCH TALK TODAY of South-South development that involves emerging economies, such as Brazil, Russia, India, China, and South Africa (often referred to as the BRICS), helping nations in the Global South to achieve higher standards of human and economic well-being. Organizations like the World Bank believe that South-South development will be a partnership, in contrast to traditional forms of North-South development, which have tended to replicate colonial relations and elite political interests. South-South connections purportedly take place between equals and do not officially impose conditions or obligations because they are fed by collaboration, solidarity, and similarity.

One of the key players in emerging South-South development discourses and partnerships is Brazil. Since the election of Luiz Inácio Lula da Silva to the presidency in 2002, the Brazilian government has created foreign assistance projects around the world, particularly in Latin America and sub-Saharan Africa.[1] In this chapter, we focus on Brazil-Africa relations as they are unfolding in the arena of rural development in one country, Mozambique.

There have long been diplomatic connections between Brazil and Portuguese Africa, including Mozambique, but they have not been part of an overarching program of political and economic development. This changed when Lula took office. Over the course of his two terms as president, Lula made more visits to Africa than all of his predecessors combined. In 2010, when he left the executive office, Lula had the distinction of having made more visits to African nations than any other sitting president in world history. During the same period, Brazil's foreign ministry, Itamaraty, opened twenty new embassies on the continent and dramatically increased development assistance spending and projects. South-South development in Africa represents a means for Brazil to acquire more geopolitical influence in the region, a goal that many African leaders support. As then-president of Cape Verde, Pedro Pires, said at a meeting in 2010, "Brazil is a country that is respected and listened to, and its president is a great defender of Africa's interests. It should have a permanent seat on the United Nations Security Council."

In many ways, it is logical for Brazil to be taking up the reins of South-South development. The country had remarkable success in the first decade of the new millennium combating poverty, hunger, malnutrition, and illiteracy. One of the key factors behind this success has been the growth and spread of the country's agro-industrial sector. From 1975 to 2010, Brazil went from being a net food importer to one of the top producers and exporters in the world of key commodities such as corn, wheat, soy, sugar, and cotton. Agricultural exports from the agro-industrial sector accounted for a third of all exports in 2010 and more than a fifth of GDP, which has helped to open fiscal space for public welfare programs like the popular Bolsa Família cash transfer scheme, which provides monthly payments to poor families, conditional on children attending school and getting vaccinated.

As Brazil invests in development abroad, a key component of the country's work builds on its successes in agricultural production and productivity, particularly in sub-Saharan Africa. In 2006, Lula inaugurated the African headquarters of the Brazilian Agricultural Research Corporation (Embrapa), in Accra, Ghana, and by 2015, nine more Embrapa training, research, and development centers had been established throughout the continent. According to the state-owned agency, its scientists are "exporters of knowledge" who promote agricultural development through germplasm exchanges, capacity training workshops, technology development and transfer, and market intensification. Brazil is well recognized as having built one of the most successful large-scale agro-industries over the past forty years and is "paying its agricultural success forward," according to one USAID report.

The secrets of Brazil's success with agricultural production are particularly desirable internationally in the wake of multiple food crises such as the doubling of global food prices in 2007–8 and again in 2011. Representatives of the United Nations suggested in 2008 that food production needed to double in the next thirty years. This has spurred a massive hunt for new land and technologies around the globe. For investors of various kinds, from state-owned enterprises in the Middle East and Asia to private investors, corporations, and large retirement funds like TIAA-CREF, land has become one of the most attractive asset classes, with expectations that it will provide returns of over 20 percent in the event of ongoing consumption increases and price shocks.

Between 2008 and 2013 alone, conservative estimates suggest that the amount of land changing hands annually increased fifteen- to twenty-fold over the annual average for the preceding forty years. This rush to acquire land is referred to by many as the global land grab, and it is predicated on inequalities that manifest as "high-yield gaps" where local production yields per hectare do not yet meet the levels achieved by the most productive farmers globally. It is believed that creating large-scale, modernized farms using industrial techniques on this underproducing land will reap high yields in both commodity crops and financial profits. This is where Brazilian agricultural development projects have focused their efforts: on providing the scientific and technological basis for improving farm productivity in sub-Saharan Africa. In the words of an Embrapa soil scientist, the aim is to create "intelligent farms in any part of the world."

Mozambique is one of several former Portuguese colonies in Africa where, as in Brazil, Portuguese is spoken. It is the single largest recipient of Brazilian assistance and home to the controversial agricultural development project ProSAVANA. ProSAVANA illustrates the ways in which South-South development initiatives play out in the context of significant inequalities between various actors within the so-called South. We show how development experts, government officials, scientists, and agrarian elites use the notion of "parallels," or similarities, to justify development projects between Brazil and Mozambique. However, we suggest that a comparison of land-labor relations in the two countries illustrates the salience of difference rather than similarity.

We outline the history of agricultural development in Brazil, in particular, the development of the program ProCerrado, on which ProSAVANA is based. We suggest that ProSAVANA is unfolding very differently than ProCerrado in Brazil because of differences in the way that land, labor, and capital are used and exchanged in the two countries. Privately owned land and command over wage labor and capital continue to be necessary for market exchange and capitalist development, but they are not always freely available as commodities. We examine the different ways in which these factors have been produced and put to work in the Brazilian Cerrado and the Mozambican savannah, learning from interviews we conducted with Embrapa personnel and officials from the Brazilian Cooperation Agency in

Brazil, as well as Embrapa staff working abroad in Mozambique between March 2013 and August 2014.

BRAZIL AND MOZAMBIQUE:
CONNECTED AT THE HIP

Millions of years ago, Brazil and Africa were joined in a single landmass.

WORLD BANK, *Bridging the Atlantic, Brazil and Sub-Saharan Africa*

ProCerrado, the basis for ProSAVANA, was a trilateral development program pioneered in the 1970s by the United States, Japan, and Brazil as a way to bring agricultural modernization and market development to Brazil's internal frontier, the vast grasslands of the Cerrado in the center-west of the country. The term *cerrado* literally means "closed" in Portuguese, symbolizing the imaginary of the region as empty, forbidding, and barren before the 1970s. The transformation of the region was a product of state-led, large-scale modernization fueled by agricultural expertise from the United States. The military government in Brazil in power during the 1970s provided incentives to farmers from the south of the country who could industrialize their production rapidly with existing knowledge of mechanized farming at scale.

Agricultural expertise in farming at scale came from extension agents with the U.S. Agency for International Development (USAID) who worked to promote agricultural development in Brazil through transfers of technology such as mechanized farming and genetic research as well as training and scientific education. USAID contributed approximately U.S.$40 million to support the work of Pedro Sanchez, who won the World Food Prize in 2002 for research on soil fertility conducted in Brazil during the 1970s and 1980s.[2] Sanchez was a soil scientist at North Carolina State University, where he led the campaign to "turn the acidic, tropical soils of the Cerrado region of Brazil into 75 million acres of productive farmland."

To mediate the transfer of agricultural expertise and facilitate colonization of the Cerrado frontier, the Brazilian military government created Embrapa in 1973. Throughout the 1970s, a majority of the organization's personnel were trained at U.S. universities in agricultural and veterinary sciences. These highly specialized Embrapa agronomists then worked with farmers throughout Brazil, particularly "modern" producers from the south, who were offered generous credit terms to buy cheap land and finance investment in the region. A former executive director of Embrapa said in a personal interview that "land in [the state of] Bahia was so cheap that you could buy a hectare with a pack of cigarettes, so farmers from the south realized they could sell [their family farms] and move north to own four or five times the land."

Over the next twenty years, the dramatic rise and success of soybean production prompted enthusiastic comparisons between the Cerrado and the U.S. Midwest. A poetic 1999 article in the *Economist* described the Cerrado as "a limitless green prairie carpeted with swelling crops." "The monotony of the landscape," it continued, "is broken only by the artifacts of modern agribusiness: a crop-dusting plane swoops low over the prairie to release its chemical cloud, while the occasional farmhouses have giant harvesting machines lined up in the yard outside. It could be the mid-western United States. In fact, it is the very heart of tropical South America, its central watershed, in the Brazilian state of Mato Grosso."[3]

The way in which science, agriculture, industry, and the state were brought together in the Cerrado encouraged large-scale export production standardized for global markets. With technological and financial support from USAID, scientific knowledge from Embrapa privileged large-scale, highly capitalized farmers who were amenable to modern technology and production methods. While there are ongoing concerns about the sustainability of the region (Altair Sales Barbosa, a leading archaeologist who works in the region, has gone so far as to say that the entire Cerrado biome has now become "extinct"), the ability to farm the grassland frontier has propelled Brazilian agribusiness into global leadership. Innovations developed through research at Embrapa helped Brazil become the agricultural commodity giant it is today. Increasingly, the success of the Cerrado has prompted many to ask whether the Brazilian miracle can be exported to Africa to address rising global food insecurity.

The answer is ProSAVANA. This twenty-year program funded by the Brazilian Cooperation Agency (ABC) and the Japanese International Cooperation Agency (JICA) is intended for the northern Nacala Corridor in Mozambique where the most favorable high-yield gaps are deemed to exist. If planted to commodity crops with modern methods and inputs by large-scale farmers, this region is envisioned to become the breadbasket of southern Africa. When we interviewed the director of ProSAVANA in Mozambique's capital, Maputo, he pointed enthusiastically west to Zambia and Malawi and east through the second-deepest ocean port on the eastern coast of Africa straight to the highly lucrative markets of East Asia. Although the project only officially started in 2013, a year later researchers from Brazil were conducting field trials of new varieties for selected crops, namely, corn, soy, rice, wheat, and sugar. Together, the Brazilians and Japanese are building new laboratories for further research, importing agricultural machinery, and planning model exposition farms.

ProSAVANA intends to strengthen the capabilities of innovation and extension systems in strategic areas (explicitly the Nacala Corridor) to improve rural development and food security and increase exportable surpluses. According to Embrapa, 14.2 million hectares of arable land have been identified as suitable for full mechanization, and it is estimated that only 30 percent of arable land appropriate for agriculture is being utilized. The soil has good natural characteristics, with limestone and phosphate already available based on land surveys and soil analyses that have been conducted. Extension agents from Embrapa and the Mozambican Institute for Agricultural Research (IIAM) have identified twelve districts in the northern provinces of Nampula and Niassa for the early phase of the work, which began in 2011.

Brazil's actions through ProSAVANA are considered by the World Bank to be paradigmatic of the potential of South-South development. Brazilian diplomats pride themselves on doing development differently than North-South Official Development Assistance (ODA): Brazil's development work in Africa is not aid; Brazilian public investments in Africa go through ABC, under the Ministry of Foreign Relations. Program officers are not in the business of "donations"; rather, Brazil-Africa cooperation is a partnership for transferring knowledge. As the head of one Brazil-Mozambique project told us, the Brazilians do not want to cultivate dependency, so they don't provide "unnecessary" assistance: "If I hold a one-week training session, I can't buy people cookies or even bottles of water. They have to provide that."

And support for this mode of collaboration rather than ODA is clear in media reports, official documents, and the expressions of the people who represent the Brazilian and Mozambican governments. Officially, the logic behind Brazil's assistance to Mozambican agriculture turns on the notion of similarity—or what the Brazilians call "parallels"—both in printed documents and in conversation. From media reports, material written by participating organizations, and interviews with key project personnel, three main similarities between Mozambique and Brazil are being invoked.

The first parallel is ecological. In this sense, the concept of parallels derives from Cartesian logic that elides socioecological difference through latitudinal

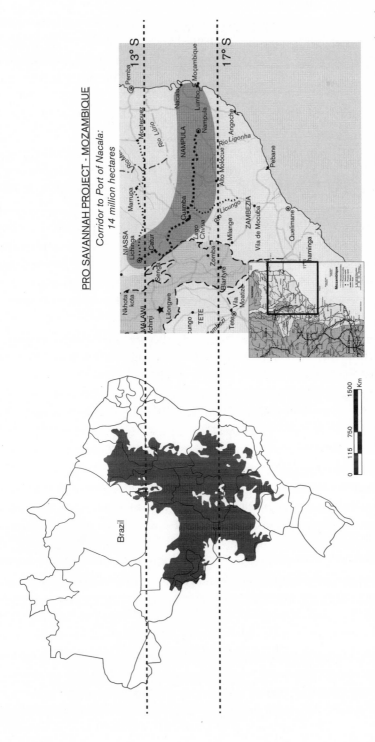

FIGURE 10.1. Structuring projects in Africa. Source: Embrapa, cited in World Bank 2011: 55. Bottom image, Brazilian Cooperation Agency (ABC), Japan International Cooperation Agency (JICA), the Brazilian Agricultural Research Corporation (Embrapa) and the Ministry of Agriculture of the Republic of Mozambique.

categories such as the tropics, savannas, and corridors. Embrapa is carrying out a satellite monitoring project, aptly named *paralelos* (parallels), to generate an ecological and geographic database through GIS that maps out Mozambique's natural features with specific details on the Nacala Corridor. The Brazilians invoke parallels because the region of the country's greatest agricultural success sits at roughly the same latitude as this part of Mozambique, the region considered to sustain the largest high-yield gap.

Historically, Brazilian foreign policy and territoriality was premised on the notion of "living borders," which emphasized engagement with neighboring countries and rhetorically favored cooperation over separation. The World Bank has taken this notion to an extreme, invoking the supercontinent of Pangaea (300 million–200 million years ago) to suggest that living borders once existed (in geologic time) between Brazil and Africa. Because of this prehistoric proximity and latitudinal equivalence, Brazil and Mozambique are thought to share ecological characteristics such as tropical climate and landscape, which supports the idea that the transfer of expertise and technology is a "natural" partnership.

The second set of similarities being invoked between Brazil and Mozambique derive from their common colonial heritage. This idea of "lusotropicalism," or seeing Africa as an extension of Portuguese soil, is a key piece of the argument that "future Brazils" can exist in former Portuguese colonies. The shared experience of Portuguese colonization would perhaps be meaningless given the extreme difference in the experiences of Brazil and Mozambique and the lack of real institutional coherence or convergence as a result. However, the two countries do share a common language, and many people interviewed in Mozambique suggested that this similarity was the key Brazilian advantage in their country. Most of the other development workers, one woman from USAID said, speak English, so when Brazilians speak Portuguese, it's "like they're not coming in from the outside in the same way."

The third similarity between Brazil and Mozambique goes beyond colonization to their common roots in indigenous Africa. That these roots came to Brazil through four centuries of slavery is not usually dwelled on; rather, official discourse—particularly that provided by former president Lula—invokes cultural similarities between Brazil and Africa that can only be explained by their shared blood. "The Brazilian people," Lula said at the inauguration of Embrapa's African headquarters in 2006, "owe their color, their happiness, their dances, and a large part of their culture to our African brothers." The suggestion that slavery has created a bond between the two regions rather than a barrier derives from a peculiarly Brazilian rendering of slave relations in which master and slave were bound together by ties of affection and care rather than discipline and punishment.

CRITIQUING DESCARTES:
FROM PARALLELS TO PRIVATIZATION

The notion of parallels is seductive, but the term "South-South" highlights the dangers of Cartesian logic that ascribes similar characteristics to groups of countries on the same latitudinal coordinates and fails to do justice to considerable political, economic, and social differences. It is difficult to put Mozambique and Brazil in the same category of the South given that Brazil is the seventh largest economy in the world with a per capita income of over twenty times that of Mozambique. Not only is Brazil an "emerging" economy quite distinct from most others in the Global South, the project Brazil is implementing in Mozambique is really a trilateral agreement between Brazil and the North: the United States and Japan.[4] Even the notion that Portuguese ancestry unites Brazil and Mozambique is problematic given that Portugal's influence over Brazil largely ended in the early nineteenth century, with Portugal the weaker of the two when Brazil declared independence in 1822. In contrast, Portugal exerted the most influence in Mozambique during the mid- to late twentieth century, when Portugal was under the dictatorship of Antonio de Oliveira Salazar. Salazar implemented a authoritarian form of nationalistic corporatism in Mozambique that operated through a small elite for the purposes of indirect colonization and resource extraction.

To understand what is happening in Mozambique beyond the rhetoric of parallels, then, requires that we analyze the making of so-called modern agriculture in both countries. To do this, we focus on the three factors of production necessary for market-based modern agriculture: land, labor, and capital. In what follows, we discuss the nature of land, labor, and capital in Mozambique by situating them historically in comparison to Brazil. Doing so highlights the importance of difference rather than similarity.

Creating Land

The first difference between Brazil and Mozambique is in the relationship between people and the land. Land is perhaps the most important element of rural society. The way in which it is accessed, used, owned, cared for, and lived on is fundamentally important for everything from the wealth of nations to household livelihoods. From the enclosures of the English commons starting in the seventeenth century to Hernando de Soto's "other path" of land titling programs and the formalization of "dead" capital, the concept and project of development has meant the transformation of life on the land.

In Mozambique all land is state-owned and has been since independence in 1975. Post-independence Mozambique was governed by a single socialist party, Frelimo (Frente de Libertação de Moçambique), which abolished colonial plantations and established collective farms. The rise of a counterrevolutionary party, Renamo (Resistência Nacional Moçambicana), pushed the county into a devastating civil war during which many of the collectives were abandoned, along with any systematic effort to modernize agriculture. It was not until the Rome Peace Accords in 1992 that the conflict ended and land issues became a priority of the new democratic government. Two key pieces of legislation were passed in 1997, the national Land Policy and Land Law, that codified land as state-owned while also recognizing traditional land tenure systems through land use rights (officially called DUATs). The DUAT system gives individuals and communities the right to certify their occupancy and use of the land; the most common use right is for traditional communities that work the land collectively or in very small household and individual plots that range from one to five hectares. A five-hectare plot, we were told by an astonished Brazilian, is a large farm in Mozambique. Today, Mozambique is still largely an agrarian society, with a vast majority of its population peasants, migrant laborers, commercial farmers, and traditional elites.

The issue with land use in Mozambique is that officially there is no formal land market; land cannot be bought or sold because it all belongs to the state. Corporations and foreigners can apply for use rights, though the latter can only access leases for up to 50 years, renewable for another 49 (making it the traditional 99-year lease so familiar to students of colonial history). To say that landownership in Brazil is largely private and that in Mozambique it is largely state-owned is to gloss over a long and important history with many caveats and particularities—but it is basically accurate.

Without going into the complexities of uncertain tenure, jurisdictional overlap, and corruption, there are two issues with the state ownership of land for ProSAVANA. First, large-scale agricultural programs in Mozambique are only likely to be profitable if land can be freely bought and sold. This is why outside interests like the U.S. Millennium Challenge Corporation (MCC) are investing in "land administration" in Mozambique. Although it is an aid organization, the MCC only invests in projects that demonstrate a very high economic rate of return (EROR). The corporation believes that investing in a land management system will generate a high EROR because the value of land will increase dramatically once it can be bought, sold, and turned to large-scale commodity production. The MCC went ahead with its project even though there is no legal market for land in Mozambique because improving the management system would shore up the "informal land market," allowing individuals to lease their land to commercial interests and render a very high return.

Second, if land needs to be acquired at scale and *can* be acquired because of a growing informal land market, then it will likely be well-capitalized foreigners who purchase large properties. Accordingly, the Mozambican government has set aside approximately 14 million hectares for foreign investors who will engage in large-scale agricultural production. This area is precisely where ProSAVANA is to be rolled out, as representatives of both the Brazilian and Mozambican governments say that the land is empty—"If you run into one person in 25 miles, that's a lot," one official told us—but this characterization has generated considerable protest, as community groups argue that the land is empty only because they have been dispossessed.

Creating Labor

The second important difference between Brazil and Mozambique is the issue of labor and, specifically, who will work the land being developed under ProSAVANA. One of the much-admired effects of the privatization of land is the release of laborers who were formerly subsistence farmers but who will subsequently work for a wage. From the putting-out system in seventeenth-century Europe to industrial agriculture, the proletarianization of agricultural labor has historically been considered essential for rural and urban development alike. In Mozambique today, almost 80 percent of the population lives in rural areas, and more than half of the rural population lives below the absolute poverty line. Education levels are extremely low, hunger and malnutrition levels are high, and very few people have experience with large-scale, technologically intensive farming methods. A Brazilian official told us that "Africans are 40 percent illiterate" and that "any project must have a component of education if they are going to realize the potential of their natural resources." Both Brazil and Mozambique are investing in farmer education and training, but it is not considered fast or deep enough, so labor will be generated for ProSAVANA in much the same way land will be—from abroad.

The idea that we heard several times from key figures in the Mozambican government is that farmers will be imported to work in the ProSAVANA region. Farmers will (and have already) come from South Africa and Zimbabwe as well as from Brazil. As the minister of agriculture in Mozambique said, the country has reached out to Brazilians in particular because "Brazilian farmers have gained experience that is very welcome. We want to repeat in Mozambique what they did thirty years ago in the Cerrado." Official delegations of farmers have traveled through northern Mozambique to visit farmland and it is reported that 6 million hectares have been set aside specifically for Brazilian farmers, an offer deemed very tempting across the Atlantic: as the Amapá state representative for the Brazilian Association of Cotton Producers Association (ABRAPA), Carlos Ernesto Augustin, stated, "The price of the land there is too good to ignore." He added, "The risks inherent in buying Brazilian land as a producer were enormous because of high [land] costs and stiff environmental regulations." Embrapa project managers and Mozambican officials welcome the introduction of Brazilian farmers because, although they pay little for the land, they will bring technology, or know-how, to production on the land. In this scenario, small-scale farmers from Mozambique will be incorporated into ProSAVANA as out-growers— farmers who grow crops on their own land under contract to the large farmers or distributors and processors.

Creating Capital

The third key difference between Mozambique and Brazil is access to capital. In Brazil, agro-industrial development was financed by a relatively strong midwife state that had already fostered significant industrialization beginning in the 1930s. Bolstered by military authority, the Brazilian state in the 1970s was able to centralize development programs into key poles of activity selected for efficiency rather than political expediency. In Mozambique, on the other hand, the state is seen as too weak to shepherd this delicate development process. A century of colonial resource extraction followed by two decades of civil war and political infighting among a small elite have left the state extremely weak financially and politically. In 2010, over 50 percent of the country's income came from international aid, and another large percentage came from the sale of natural resources, including coal, natural gas, and now perhaps land.

According to one of the program directors at the ABC in Brasília, triangulating development projects bypasses some of Brazil's funding regulations and expands donor opportunities. This is the case with ProSAVANA: Japan provided an investment of US$38 million to fund early research and the drawing up of a master plan. According to Mozambique's minister of agriculture, José Pacheco, the hope of this plan is that "there will be a consignment of specific resources for development of the Nacala Corridor" in order to encourage the private sector to finance the public mission of development.

In a 2013 speech to investors, then–vice president for Africa at the World Bank, Obiageli (Oby) Ezekwesili, argued that investors should "rediscover Africa" because the rate of return on investments was high and governments were creating a friendly environment for investment. As the World Bank says, "Over the past decade, Africa has become a continent of opportunities." Brazilians are keen on developing these relationships to establish a new market for their manufactured goods and technologies. In 2009, Lula said optimistically, "I want to sell much more to those who have never bought from us in a continent that will have 700 million habitants in twenty-five years."

The private sector is the best option, because, according to USAID, progress has to be *fast*. Practitioners are exhorted to have deliverables, by going after what Jeffrey Sachs in the Millennium Development Goals calls "low hanging fruit" like combating malaria by handing out mosquito nets. In the case of ProSAVANA, according to USAID, "we need to seize the moment. . . . Mozambique's leaders are anxious to see quick results." And the only sector able to deliver urgently needed results quickly is the private sector: "Building public extension services that can reach smallholders requires long-term efforts to address capacity and governance issues—but harnessing private sector dynamism to transfer improved seeds and production methods to smallholders and provide them with inputs and access to markets can move this process more quickly."

So, ultimately, Brazilian expertise in Africa is funded by the public sector but is paving the way for private investment. Brazilian firms have set up a "Nacala fund" based in Luxembourg to attract private foreign capital, and in the wake of growing global concerns about resource scarcity, food prices, peak oil, and climate change, hundreds of millions of dollars (roughly U.S.$2 billion) are expected. By its own estimates, the Nacala fund aims to give its investors a 12 percent initial rate of return based on the projections of ProSAVANA "to achieve scale, productivity, and attractive profitability." And even Embrapa hopes to make a return on its investment. In 2003, its funding was cut and a new law was passed that incentivizes the agency to supplement its budget from private sources, so Embrapa personnel are very clear that the agency needs to be able to increase its influence by working abroad. Having lost its historical dominance over the domestic market share in seeds, Embrapa is keen to expand public-private partnerships and strengthen private sources of revenue abroad. In 2012, a special commission proposed the creation of a new private subsidiary to be called Embrapa Tecnologias (Embrapatec) that will act as the agency's marketing and intellectual property branch. According to the commission's author, Senator Delcídio do Amaral, "[Embrapatec] will serve as an arm of Embrapa abroad." "We have fantastic potential on other continents, including Africa," he continued, "where the company [Embrapa] plays a fundamental role in combating hunger." While it is still uncertain whether this initiative will become reality, it does reveal the political and economic motivations behind the mobilization of Embrapa's science and scientists abroad. New initiatives such as the expansion of intellectual property rights as well as Embrapa's role as a key stakeholder in Brazil's foreign policy have seen the budget grow. The agency now has well over five thousand public-private agreements, and its budget has more than doubled in the past ten years.

CONCLUSION: SCIENCE AND TECHNOLOGY IN NEW ENCLOSURES

So, far from South-South collaboration, one could be forgiven for seeing in ProSAVANA the triangle trade of old. The largest farmers' organization in Mozambique, União Nacional de Camponeses (UNAC), put it bluntly, "ProSAVANA can be summed up in this simple equation: Mozambique supplies the land, Brazil does the farming, and Japan takes the food. It is a vast project being coordinated by the governments of the three countries that involves billions of dollars and millions of hectares of land. It may amount to the biggest farmland grab in Africa." Brazil's director of South-South development countered this statement, describing local resistance to the Brazilian presence as "a small portion of the civil society in the region that doesn't have the discipline to work with the government or stakeholders." Development through ProSAVANA presupposes a transformation of life on the land whereby "empty" land becomes high yielding and "wasteful" or unproductive peasants become disciplined out-growers, commodity producers, or urban migrants.

The diversity of development projects under the banner of South-South development demands further investigation of the important differences in land, labor, and capital within the broad category of the Global South. Brazilian agricultural development efforts in Mozambique constitute a diverse set of institutions and projects—from the establishment of seed banks and germplasm exchanges to funding the public procurement of "family farm" produce. This promotion of "family farm" policies in conjunction with technological, logistical, and financial support for agribusiness in Mozambique has been described as Brazil exporting its own dual model of a family farm sector producing for the domestic market alongside export-oriented industrial agriculture. However, such a dichotomy fails to adequately capture the differences and inequalities between Mozambique and Brazil highlighted above. Furthermore, the case of the megaproject ProSAVANA demonstrates where the vast majority of resources are being spent, both by the Brazilian government and by multinationals, in furthering the development of an agribusiness sector in Mozambique.

As we write this, in early 2015, it is unclear how ProSAVANA will unfold, but it is clear that the nature of its unfolding will be shaped by the particular incorporation of land, labor, and capital as well as by the discourses and demands of the current conjuncture, a conjuncture dominated by widespread fears of food and fuel security manifested in the rush for land. These fears motivate the combination of elite actors behind the design and implementation of ProSAVANA in such a way that the project is portrayed as both the building of a productive breadbasket and the profitable transfer of technology. Brazil-Mozambique cooperation rests symbolically and rhetorically on the invocation of equality and similarity, and indeed the two places share a number of ecological, historical, and cultural characteristics. But development will look very different in the two places because of the very great differences in the way that land, labor, and capital are being brought into the process. This should come as no surprise: the commodification of land, labor, and capital is a process shaped by the relations between social classes in particular contexts at particular times, and the nature of that process has tremendous implications for the nature of development. What is surprising is that given the importance of place-specific land-labor-capital relations, development projects are still constructed in ways that assume their irrelevance.

REFERENCES AND SUGGESTED READING

Borras, S. M., J. C. Franco, S. Gómez, C. Kay, and M. Spoor
    2012   "Land Grabbing in Latin America and the Caribbean." *Journal of Peasant Studies* 39.3–4: 845–72.

Dávila, Jerry
    2010   *Hotel Trópico: Brazil and the Challenge of African Decolonization, 1950–1980.* Durham, NC: Duke University Press.

Economist
    1999   "Growth in the Prairies." 10 April, p. 30.

Leite, I. C., B. Suyama, L. T. Waisbich, M. Pomery, J. Constantine, L. Navas-Alemán, A. Shankland, and M. Younis
    2014   *Brazil's Engagement in International Development Cooperation: The State of the Debate.* Evidence Report 59. Sussex: IDS.

O'Laughlin, B.
    1996   "Through a Divided Glass: Dualism, Class and the Agrarian Question in Mozambique." *Journal of Peasant Studies* 23.4: 1–39.

Urioste, M.
    2012   "Concentration and 'Foreignisation' of Land in Bolivia." *Canadian Journal of Development Studies* 33.4: 439–57.

Wolford, W.
    2015   "From Pangaea to Partnership: The Many Fields of Rural Development in Mozambique." *Sociology of Development* 1.2: 210–32.

World Bank
    2011   *Bridging the Atlantic, Brazil and Sub-Saharan Africa: South-South Partnering for Growth.* Washington, DC: World Bank.

NOTES

The authors thank the scientists, politicians, and activists in Brazil and Mozambique who agreed to be interviewed for this piece. We received very helpful comments from colleagues in the Contested Global Landscapes theme project at Cornell, as well as from two anonymous reviewers for the *Canadian Journal of Development Studies,* where the piece originally appeared. Funding for this chapter came from the National Science Foundation (Directorate for Social, Behavioural and Economic Sciences / Division of Social and Economic Sciences, Award No. 1331265) and the Institute for the Social Sciences at Cornell University. Finally, the authors thank Matthew Gutmann and Jeffrey Lesser for their support. All mistakes are our own.

1. Brazilian investors and agro-industrial capitalists are also involved in acquiring land and productive capacity in Latin America, a trend referred to as "foreignization," or land grabbing, in the region (Borras et al. 2012; Urioste 2012). Because Brazil's involvement in Latin America is distinct from its efforts in Africa, we focus only on the latter in this chapter.

2. The research is carried out today by a nonprofit organization, Fundação Bahia (Bahia Foundation), supported by seed companies, and input and agricultural chemical firms.

3. "Growth in the Prairies," *Economist,* 10 April 1999, 30.

4. Thanks to Sara Pritchard for pointing out that what appeared to be a South-South collaboration was really a North-South collaboration in many ways.

Perfecto Flores

Renato Rosaldo

Back in Fowler, where it all began,
he caresses a naked woman's moist contours,
allows a scorpion, a niño de tierra,
to witness their union blessed by breaking day.
Let my lust for Leonora be undiminished, he prays.

He drives a dilapidated Chevy Capri,
labor camp to labor camp, grapes shriveling in the sun,
shadows of birds bobbing on waves of heat.
*Let me walk the valley of the shadow
beauty and grace by my side,* he prays.

He carries a red tool box for the chance odd job.
The other men call a job well done a Perfecto Flores.
To barter for the loyalty of Estrella, thirteen years old,
he offers know-how, claw hammer and crescent wrench,
tools for literacy, V like the split of a hammerhead.

At dusk he walks from the fields,
puffs of dust drag behind him,
row after row, sun upon sun,
He stands unblinking, refuses to be short-changed.
May the boss drown in a vat of molten cash, he says.

ELEVEN

A Long Strange Trip

LATIN AMERICA'S CONTRIBUTION TO WORLD DRUG CULTURE

Paul Gootenberg

PERHAPS IT'S RISKY, EVEN FOOLHARDY, for a historian to suggest that drugs are one of Latin America's enduring contributions to world culture. Today, "drugs" mostly conjures up cocaine, meth, addiction, corruption, traffickers, DEA drug wars, and the unfathomably brutal bloodletting along the northern borders of Mexico. It also suggests the unfortunate tendency of (North) Americans to blame their intemperate desires for consuming drugs on evil foreigners, the Pablo Escobars and Chapo Guzmáns, or wily "cartels" (a term that makes specialists cringe). It also serves to sweep under the rug the complicity of our institutions and badly conceived drug laws and policies—namely, global drug prohibition—in igniting the kinds of mayhem that have afflicted places like Colombia, Peru, and Mexico in recent decades. So, here, I'd like to step back and suggest as a corrective a few less sensationalistic, less ahistorical, less U.S.-centric points: the richer, longer cornucopia of mind-altering goods the Americas have offered the world; some of the changing historical entanglements of these drugs with global culture; and, most recently, promising new shifts, coming from the Global "South," on how to rethink our bellicose current posture on illicit drugs. This long trip through hemispheric drugs is rich in historical ironies.

PSYCHEDELIC CIVILIZATIONS

Thousands of years ago, prehistoric Americans invented what the ethnobotanist Winston LaBarre termed the "American drug complex," the world's widest and wildest menu of psychotropic drugs. Four-fifths of known mind-altering plants come from what is today Latin America, mostly from hot spots in Mesoamerica and western Amazonia.[1] They include well-known soft stimulants like coca leaf, mate, tobacco (the most all- and pan-American of intoxicants), and cacao, the active ingredient in chocolate. There were also scores of Native American ritual hallucinogenic plant-drugs such as peyote buttons (mescaline), "magic mushrooms" (usually psilocybin), *ololiuhqui* (Mexican blue morning-glory seed), *salvia divinorum*, ayahuasca (yajé or caapi), yopo and virolá snuffs, san pedro cactus (a South American mescaline), and the countless datura, brugmansia, and other nightshade species brewed by medicine men in the rain forests of today's Colombia and Ecuador. Some peoples tapped toxins of brilliantly colored poison frogs for sacred ceremonies, ecstasy, and healing. This cornucopia was partly ecological accident: mind-bending alkaloids, which make us high, evolved as built-in plant insecticides against the voracious bugs on year-round tropics foliage. The rapid rise of American agriculture kept indigenous peoples, who likely trekked in mushroom cults from Siberia, foraging and discovering the New World's wild diversity of plants. Alcohol was known—maize-based chicha beer, agave pulque (the octli "wine" of the Aztecs)—but its low potency was unlikely to drown out knowledge of entheogenic drugs as occurred in ancient Europe and the Middle East.

When three thousand years ago state-led agrarian civilizations and empires arose in the Americas, Olmecs, Mayas, Mexicas (aka the Aztecs), and a kaleidoscope of pre-Incan states in the Andes, earlier drug cultures became subsumed and regulated by priestly castes. They amplified and remade in still unexplored ways shamanistic practices, visions, and beliefs as their sacred "Plants of the Gods." The Aztec priesthood, for example, instituted the "Divine flesh" Teonanácatl and *ololiuhqui* (which contains LSD-like lysergic acids) in specific flower gods, Xochipilli, used for official divination and sacrificial rites and to steel their dominant military castes. The transcendent intellectualism of the Mayan nobility was energized by cacao, mushrooms, and trance states induced by a narcotic water lily (Dobkin del Rios 2009). Serious archaeology also suggests that the drug-motif obelisks of Chavín—the mother of Andean civilizations—relate to priestly control over remote Amazonian psychedelics. On the Pacific, the militarist power of the Moche state—mostly remembered today for the culture's stunningly erotic pottery—also channeled the cosmic powers of drug plants.

In a way, then, today's global fascination with the cosmological complexities and visionary aesthetics of ancient American peoples like the Mayans and Aztecs is, unwittingly, a fascination with their exotic drugs. And on the margins of these civilizations, countless small mobile peoples conserved a world of religious and curative practices around drugs, such as northern Mexico's Huichol with their still central peyote cult. As intoxicants had medicinal values, even the early and often sickly Spaniards (who disdained most things native) showed an interest in superior herbal cures. The untapped diversity and intimate knowledge of plants has in our times drawn modern pharmaceutical giants into formal "bio-prospecting" contracts with rain forest tribes in Central America and the Amazon in search of the latest miracle drugs.

The original American drug cornucopia has passed through many acts and phases of suppression and rediscovery by the outer world. During colonial times (in a preview of today's drug prohibitions) Catholic Spanish authorities piously extirpated as pagan devil worship the most hallucinogenic of plants. They survived at jungle or desert margins or moved deeply underground, sometimes for centuries, in Mexican Indian communities. Mexican sources cryptically spoke of pre-Conquest *tzitzinthlápatl* plants as a form of indigenous myth or madness. Early in the twentieth century, peyote spread north of the border, until then completely unknown, as a restoration cult among U.S. and Canadian Native Americans, now legally protected as religious practices of the Native American Church. In the 1940s and 1950s, anthropologists, bohemians like Allen Ginsberg, eminent ethnobotanists like Harvard's Richard Evans Schultes, and other seekers scoured Mexico and Amazonia for lost drug traces. In the more culturally open and indigenous-friendly 1960s, surviving drug practices began to come out in the open. In Mexico, the Mazatec shaman María Sabina, who knew a lot about psilocybin mushrooms, became a kind of global celebrity. Her remote village in the mountains of southern Oaxaca state, Huautla de Jiménez, turned into a kind of hippie tourist mecca. These psychedelic discoveries contributed in no small way to scientific study of such drugs and to the flowering of "drug cultures" among middle-class youth in the United States and Europe. One UCLA-trained anthropologist, Carlos Castañeda, earned a small fortune (and much professional chagrin) with his new-agey Don Juan book series, a how-to vision quest inspired by his encounters with a Yaqui *curandero* from Sonora. They likely sold more copies in English than all the García Márquez novels combined, in fact, some 28 million worldwide. New Agers, led by gurus like Timothy Leary and later Terrance McKenna, admired not only the intricate chemical knowledge of Indians, but the subtle craft and values of the guide, who could safely manage powerful mind drugs through time-honored social rituals. Even today, the Native American drugs keep coming: the *salvia* craze a few years ago, which briefly panicked American parents, or as the *New York Times* recently reported, the new high-class New York fashion of introspective ayahuasca soirees, imbibing the juice of the Amazonian "vine of the soul" (widely popular as well with New Age Brazilians), which contains the nauseating and often disturbing DMT compound.

PSYCHOACTIVE COLONIALISM

The conquest and colonial exploitation of the Americas closely dovetailed with what the world historian of drugs David Courtwright (2001) dubs the "Psychoactive Revolution" of the seventeenth century. The influx of such novel "drug-foods" (a kindred concept of the food anthropologist Sidney Mintz) transformed European consciousness, capitalism, and culture. Mainly from Latin America, they stimulated the rise of global markets, bourgeois mentalities, and even some revolutionary political ideas. Select native intoxicants underwent complex transformations into major European trade goods and addictive Europeanized customs.[2] Tobacco leaf, that strange and pernicious fount of alkaloids, became one of the first true world commodities beyond precious coins, soon traded as far away as Africa and Asia. Its evolution from an indigenous medicine, hallucinogen, and meditative rite into the shockingly novel European habit of smoking (and snuffing) has long fascinated historians. Spain branded its top quality tobacco in Havana factories, though English rivals managed to smuggle strains to found the broad market and well-taxed Virginia tobacco industry. In reigning Galenic medicine, smoking was the "dry inebriant," a recognition of nicotine's drug qualities, and a fine way to dry out alcohol-drenched European people. Yet tobacco, both among aristocrats and the middle class, retained a subversive even indigenous spiritual edginess, a new history reveals, fostered by *converso* (Jewish) merchants and plebeian sailors plying it across the Atlantic for Spain (Norton 2008).

In contrast, coffee, like later cannabis, was a transplant to the Americas, native to East Africa, molded by Islam, but seeded by the enterprising Dutch in the seventeenth century into a colonial good (hence, its stubborn nicknames like mocha and java). However, by the mid-eighteenth century the epicenter of the coffee boom gravitated to the Caribbean, as an odd assortment of European powers (even the Danes) seized potentially fertile tobacco and coffee islands. By 1750, the French raised most of the world's coffee crop in their infamously brutal and lucrative slave colony of Saint-Domingue (Haiti). As historians love to recount, coffee drinking, the great "soberer," jolted Europe into a modern bourgeois age. The institution of the coffee shop proved the key civilizing alternative to the raucous low-class beer tavern. Thousands dotted London and Paris by the eighteenth century. Coffee shops inculcated rising "Protestant" values: sobriety, intellectuality and communication, tolerance of foreigners, the public sphere, and a capitalist business ethos (Schivelbusch 1992). Coffee shops birthed gazettes and newspapers, and in one port, Lloyds of London transformed from a place to talk shipping news into the pioneer global insurance broker. Michelet famously attributed the outbreak of the 1789 French Revolution to rationalist plotters in the cafés of Paris, a stunning irony, for if true, such revolutionists were willfully dependent on slave-grown caffeine from the hellish French plantations of Haiti. The Rights of Man soon also bequeathed the monumental slave revolt known as the Haitian Revolution, whose fury against planters, in another irony, finally shifted coffee's bonanza south to nineteenth-century Brazil.

Other colonial stimulants played out quite differently. Mexican cacao, shed of prior Mayan and Aztec cosmology, became creolized by the seventeenth century into the warmed and sweetened-up Spanish Catholic chocolate beverage. If anything, historians stress its luxuriant, aristocratic, anti-Protestant roles, at least until the nineteenth century, when strict Protestants in Holland, England, Switzerland (and somewhat later, Hershey, PA) industrialized chocolate into cocoa powder and a sugar-laden solid candy for the masses. Spain also mined the medicinal drugs of the Americas, such as cinchona or Peru Bark, antimalarial quinine later whisked out by botanical spies and remade on a plantation scale to secure the insalubrious tropical realms of the British Empire. A vestige of this White Man's burden is the bitter tonic we call "quinine water." Also notable is coca, the "Sacred Leaf of the Incas." With its subversively alive Andean meanings, Spain could only tolerate its use as a salve to the Indians forced to harshly labor in the altiplano silver mines of Potosí, making coca into part of a pan-Andean commodity circuit, rather than an export good, and into a degrading Indian vice. However, indirectly, this means that "cocaine" (coca's most notorious alkaloid) helped stimulate the expansion of the early modern European world economy, fueled, as any economic historian knows, by the rich bounty of Peruvian silver.

Latin America's independence in the 1820s ushered in a long if murky century of nascent national drug cultures. The divide widened between coveted legal world stimulants, national-identity drugs, and the first signs of submerging drug cultures. By 1900, coffee's exponential growth became practically synonymous with the free trade liberation of Latin America, a good remaking the new national economies and states of Brazil and Colombia and the mini-nations of Central America.[3] Brazil's rise as a world caffeine "superpower"—by 1905, some 20 million bags a year, five times the rest of all world producers combined—was intimately linked to the rise of the mass-market all-American "cup of Joe," a new people's standardized coffee culture advanced by patriotism (British tea boycotts), frontier roasters and grocers, Civil War caffeine rations, and industrial "coffee breaks." By 1900, Americans gulped down half the world's coffee, a share that rose to its peak in the 1960s. In Brazil, slaves and then legions of immigrants, such as indentured Japanese, opened the vast hilly plantation hinterlands linked to São Paulo's port of Santos. Brazilian supply was so ample that by 1906 the country announced an OPEC-like monopoly price policy with the crop, "valorization," a revenue stability that was to help the country successfully transform into an industrial giant later in the century. In contrast, quality highland Arabica Colombian and Central American coffees mostly flowed to pickier and better-heeled European drinkers (Topik, Marichal, and Zephyr 2006). The smiling, well-kempt, fair-skinned "peasant" Juan Valdéz personified Colombian origins—at least until eclipsed by scary mug shots of Pablo Escobar in the 1980s. Latin America's contribution to global coffee culture proved decisive—a role eroding only in recent decades with the diversifying rise of high-end Yuppie Coffee (the coffee anthropologist Bill Roseberry's moniker) and the unprecedented post-1989 spread of coffee farming across the tropical peasant belts of Asia and Africa.

In contrast to coffee's lasting imprint is the curious case of coca. Denigrated by the Spaniards, the Andean stimulant's prestige soared with scientific fascination after 1850, including the 1860 German isolation of cocaine. This actually led—from 1860 to 1910 at least—to a legal boom of the dried leaf and coca syrups to Europe and the United States. The coca craze, a stimulant to combat elite and female nerve fatigue, began with French Vin Mariani, a classy and sexy Incan-inflected red wine coca beverage. Its innovative celebrity endorsement campaigns made Vin Mariani a sensation across Europe by the 1870s. Less known is that American Coca-Cola actually began life as a frank yet dry imitation of Vin Mariani, concocted by the Atlanta pharmacist John Pemberton in 1887 as an invigorating and sexually healthy "soft" drink, and which conceals to this day a close but covert link between Andean coca and American mass culture (Gootenberg 2008). By 1910, however, the brief age of coca was cut short by exaggerated associations with the new drug menace, cocaine. Coca-Cola went on to become the American taste of the twentieth century, shorn of its Andean and French origins. Energy drinks remain an American obsession, including many now tapping import extracts of Amazonian guaraná fruit, the basis of exciting Brazilian national brand sodas like Guaraná Antartica.

This was also an age of regional identity and national drugs, exemplified by tequila and yerba mate. Tequila is one of dozens of age-old Mexican fermented agave cactus "mescals," whose Jaliscan roots whitened and elevated it into a national insignia of Mexicanidad. At first a hard drug associated with cheap Mexican drunks, then tipsy postwar tourists, Tequila has morphed since the 1980s into the ultimate high-end export, with a registered Mexican domain à la French champagne and artisanal $200 bottles that hint at a druglike commune with ancient and earthy agave Mayahuel spirits. At the other end of the Americas is yerba mate, a Guaraní xanthine-rich tea that Jesuits traded from colonial Paraguay across the greater Río de la Plata. By the late twentieth century, the popular gaucho ritual of mate from shared drinking gourds consolidated as the identifying Argentine national habit, and with an equivalent devotion in neighboring republics. However, in highly circuitous ways, mate is only now becoming a world drug. Druze laborers in Buenos Aires carried it back to the Middle East, dispersing it again after Lebanon's modern civil wars. And a diaspora from Argentina's anti-Semitic despots of the 1970s, small Israeli-Argentine entrepreneurs, are now spreading their scaled-up mate drinks worldwide, popping up in hipster Brooklyn cafés and the shelves of Whole Foods.

But in contrast to these successful legitimated drugs, regional and ethnic drug complexes were emerging that after 1900 become targets of growing class and racial taboo. Chinese minorities, as in the United States, were despised most everywhere and brought the respectability and legality of opium down with them. Cannabis, another import to the Americas, surfaced in a number of ways across the long nineteenth century. African slaves or sailors brought cannabis to Brazil (*maconha*) and to Colombia's Caribbean coast (*marimba*); in British colonies like Jamaica and Trinidad it arrived as *ganja,* a work and spiritual aid of indentured East Indian workers, the so-called ganja complex. A remarkable story is Mexico, a place that gringos reflexively imagine as weed's ancient Eden. A new history by Isaac Campos (2012) not only shows how new it was, gradually bred by rural folk into "mari*h*uana" out of colonial Spanish hemp fields, its use as a drug noticeable by the mid-nineteenth century. By 1900, it was strongly associated with the feared "degenerative" underclasses—convicts, lunatics, conscripts, and, naturally, Indians—and orientalized as a spur to random violence and madness. Indeed, such mind associations, Campos subtly argues, may have indeed made Mexican weed a manic, hard, sometimes murderous drug. The hygienic and puritanical modernizers who arose out of the Mexican Revolution were thus in the 1920s among the first in the hemisphere to ban it. Campos even suggests that this Mexico backstory, not just the usual anti-Mexican racism, was the inspiration for the "Reefer Madness" panic used to push through our own marijuana prohibition in the late 1930s.

Now that American social mores are fast turning positive about cannabis (and, according to federal statistics, we are evolving into a pot nation) perhaps it's time to stop denigrating its hemispheric roots. During the 1960s, after crackdowns at home, proximate areas south of the border became the chief purveyors of quality marijuana and of marijuana culture—branded, as old-timers may recall, as Acapulco Gold, Oaxaqueño (a word that nicely rolled off the boomer tongue), Panama Red, and Colombian and Jamaican Golds. We can only speculate about one big historical riddle: the cultural transformation of manic reefer into our mellow weed. By the 1970s, long faded jazz-era referents to the drug ("tea"), or its European hashish mystique, were supplanted by colorful images of spiritual and resistant Bob Marley-style African-roots Rastafarians, or with a laidback borderlands culture—the stoners now called "Pachuco" or "Pacheco" by Mexicans—so infamously portrayed by those slapstick Southern Californians Cheech & Chong. A striking transitional figure here was Tucson-born Lalo Guerrero, the "Father of Chicano Music" (honored as such with a 1996 National Humanities Medal), whose all but forgotten bilingual 1949 "Marihuana Boogie," right off the zoot suit era, put a decidedly upbeat spin on the killer weed. How Jerry Garcia, of the essay title, the Ur-druggie of West Coast music, lost these Latin roots (along with his *apellido*'s accent) is the mystery of marijuana's assimilation north with a hippy ethos. The 1960s makeover of a drug of dubious origins into a peaceful, dreadlocked people's herb is perhaps another Latin American addition to drug culture.

DRUG WARS AND DRUG PEACE?

After 1910, the United States began a century-long crusade to banish unwanted drugs, not just at home, but across the Americas, perceived from the start as a contaminating source of drugs. Among the many explanations, I like the drug historian David Musto's notion of "the American disease"—a kind of bipolar "love-hate" relationship with drugs that tells why we relish and consume them with unrivaled passion, yet expect our leaders to violate our cherished freedoms to puritanically punish users and periodically prohibit drugs (Musto 1973). We also like to mix our racial contempt with banned drugs, against distinctive user groups at home (Catholics in Prohibition, African Americans with early cocaine) or against entire browner continents as imagined global pushers. When international bans against narcotics and cocaine began after 1910, which was a new and progressive historical concept, U.S. authorities tried to convince our neighbors too. There was some push-back: Peruvians ignored us for decades to protect their tiny cocaine industry; Bolivian delegates at the League of Nations defended, in ironically racist terms, their Indians laboring needs for benign national coca leaf; Lázaro Cárdenas experimented with a social program of medical treatment for Mexican opiate addicts. However, deep-seated elite (and, in some cases, popular) fears and prejudices, for example, about marijuana and opium in Mexico, led after World War II to widespread compliance and complicity with U.S. prohibition and our aggressive drug interdiction ideals, sometimes offset by some foot-dragging of drug-enriched politicos. The Cold War helped too in this consensus, by magnifying U.S. strategic influence and by persuading Latin American governments and militaries that illicit drugs were basically a problem of subversion and national security. By the 1970s, the U.S. drug war was going hot in Latin America, in Operation Intercept, Operation Condor, and so many more to come. By then, Latin America was the closest and biggest source of drug trafficking, pot, some opiates, and a billowing stream of cocaine into a post-1960s drug-thirsty North America.

The rest, you might say, is history, though it still needs to be rigorously researched and written. The Latin American bonanza with illicit drugs, peaking in the 1980s–1990s age of Colombian cocaine, was surely one of history's largest and most notorious illicit trades. We call them "cartels" as if to cover the glaring fact that trafficking organizations are highly competitive capitalistic networks and that drugs are very hot commodities. The sensationalism of illicit drugs now overshadows and even erases our sense of Latin

America's longer established role in the commerce of acceptable stimulant goods. The Organization of American States (OAS) estimates the hemispheric revenues in illegal drugs today at $150 billion yearly, though precious little (less than one percent) of that ever reaches the impoverished peasant growers at the far end of the profit chain. And despite the hype about drugs, coffee still employs many more people across the Americas, in a trail from highland campesinos to Starbucks baristas at the mall. Still, the spiral of militarized and institutionalized drug wars set off by Richard Nixon in 1970, ratcheted up and extended across the Andes by Ronald Reagan during the mid-1980s crack scare, has, in most expert opinion, utterly failed to stem U.S. drug use. At most, it may have changed our drug mix and geographies over the decades, and not as intended. It mostly led to a swelling flood of cheaper drugs flowing invisibly across our borders as traffickers and growers constantly outwit prohibitions with greater cropping, shifting routes and grow plots, and ever more able and ingenious smuggling organizations. Despite billions thrown at the problem, there have been few if any policy successes— "Plan Colombia" after 2005, perhaps, at quite a cost to U.S. taxpayers and to the Colombian people.

There's plenty of grassroots "agency" at work here, an always trendy term with academics, but it's a stretch even for me to turn this decades-long drug exporting boom into a shining Latin American achievement. Yes, places like Medellín and Sinaloa displayed an extraordinary burst of entrepreneurial verve and creativity in a Catholic culture that at least traditionally is regarded by outsiders as low in business acumen. Drugs were a predominantly "Latin" trade, still in local hands, manned by ambitious, often rustic, yet modernizing newcomers. Money-laundered profits have refashioned the architectural facade and shopping malls of many Latin American cities, Miami included. Some rural towns or declining peasant districts may have survived on drug remittances and not a few national exchange rates have stayed afloat with recycled dollars. Some might celebrate a cultural explosion with drugs: "narcocorrido" musical combos (Wald 2001), sensually violent hit *telenovelas,* urbane "narco" crime novels, the cross-border influence on popular culture in *Miami Vice,* remakes of *Scarface,* Netflixed *Narcos* and the cartel-accented black humor of *Weeds* and *Breaking Bad.* One could even suggest, in a strict Utilitarian calculus, that the thousands of drug-fueled parties and orgies in Hollywood, Wall Street, discos, suburban dens, blighted ghettos, and, increasingly, Brazilian clubs and favelas (or vaguer drug-inspired personal insight, creativity, or health gains) have spread more human happiness than was offset by the misery of drug-related arrest, addiction, madness, user degradation, or prohibition violence.

However, these claims are dubious if not trivial compared to the untold destruction and scale of human suffering this permanent state of hemisphere war has wrought over the past four decades: the millions of Colombians displaced by hard-line drug eradication strategies, tens of thousands of Mexicans brutally tortured and murdered by cartel warfare and military repression since 2007 alone, the thousands of desperate Honduran kids fleeing drug gang violence now on our doorstep, environmental degradation of the marvelously biodiverse Andean tropics, destabilizing insurgencies, massive corruption, and, in a host of nations, a grave undermining of human rights, legitimacy, citizen security and trust, and perhaps even democratic futures. Not to mention our own costly post-1980 police-state roundup, in the name of a "drug-free America," of millions of mostly poor disenfranchised black and Latino youth, making us disgracefully, as Michelle Alexander tells us, the most incarcerating democracy in the history of the world.

But here's the paradox I'd like to end on: perhaps the notable new contribution of Latin America to global drugs has been to finally break their political silence and diversify the global debate about drugs. Until recently, Latin American oligarchs, fearing the undermining of values by illicit drugs, generally followed the hard-line U.S. doctrines. In fact, they served as a pillar of the inter-American drug war waged since the 1970s, though these guardian elites quietly griped that the real problem is the voracious U.S. demand for drugs. However, in 2008 a handful of eminent Latin American leaders in the Latin American Commission on Drugs and Democracy (followed by a deeper and broader official 2013 OAS report) began to call on world leaders to fundamentally rethink the ways we control drugs (OAS 2013). Left and right, Latin American nations have entered this debate, Bolivia, Colombia, Uruguay, Brazil, Ecuador, Guatemala, among them. Our most devoted allies—the Colombian political and military caste that waged a decades-long fight against traffickers, guerrillas, and peasants on our behalf—now loudly voice concerns for sustainable policies in their recovery from drug war. Following deep-seated legalist traditions, South American supreme courts keep declaring drug possession laws unlawful infringements of liberty. Drugs like cannabis are quietly decriminalized as a drain on police resources across the hemisphere or in Uruguay's case, and soon Jamaica, fully legalized by the democratic process (as in our own states of Colorado and Washington). Drug sentencing is moving from punitive models, for example, in Ecuador, which with a decidedly Catholic flair has made the pardon of personal drug sin into a policy of national reconciliation. Bolivian peasant unions and nationalist politicians like Evo Morales have since 2006 successfully defied the DEA (which pulled out of the country) and the UN regime to uphold the cultural value of traditional coca leaf and to experiment with peaceful local policies to stop its processing into cocaine. The reasons for these shifts are no doubt complex but surely relate to how Latin Americans—witnessing from the front lines the disastrous violence and havoc in Mexico, and the latest wave of trafficking wars unfolding across a vulnerable Central America—have borne the destabilizing cost of the stubborn U.S. crusade to rid itself of drugs. Washington, with its historically Puritan "just say no" religion, is out of touch with these dilemmas and perhaps with a more flexible Latin culture itself. The debate also reflects the growing sovereignty of Latin American states, defying the United States on a key issue in ways unthinkable before or during the Cold War.

Europeans have a growing social democratic "harm reduction" version of drug reform, and in the United States we have our own brand of libertarian dissent to drug prohibition, at last catching fire around pot decriminalization and unjust racial sentencing. Some Latin American nations like Mexico and Peru, and often the popular classes, remain wary about drugs. But the drug reform movement in Latin America, should it continue, offers a possibly distinctive approach, focused on reducing the damage inflicted in plying and transiting drug commodities to the outside world, especially in much-needed programs of violence prevention. At the very least, it is shaking a pillar of a long hemispheric drug war. Moreover, the number of Latin American states joining this debate could have an impact on the larger UN drugs system, recently contested out loud in meetings around the 2016 UNGASS reform of world drug conventions. Perhaps North Americans—who seem incapable on their own of ending their overseas drug wars and prohibitionist institutions—will be prodded along by outspoken Latin American reformers. It's a new twist in the long saga of Latin American drugs, with their many contributions to world culture, their ironic worldly entanglements, and the changing meanings of drugs themselves.

Are there any lessons from this millennium of tangled drug histories? I think so. Mind drugs went from being the spiritual glue of close-knit communities to tools of priestly, militarist, and merchant power to expansive and addictive colonial and capitalist world goods and (under the duress of modern global prohibitions) to the savagely illicit, lean and mean commodities of today's world order. As we inch ourselves to drug reform, we might well ponder the historical error of commodifying the special powers of drugs. We might seek creative solutions beyond simply repackaging cannabis and other untamed drugs legally along the lines of Big Tobacco or Big Pharma. Ways that take us back, however imperfectly, to the peaceful and less commercial garden.

REFERENCES AND SUGGESTED READING

Campos, Isaac
    2012 *Home Grown: Marijuana and the Origins of Mexico's War on Drugs.* Chapel Hill: University of North Carolina Press.
Courtwright, David T.
    2001 *Forces of Habit: Drugs and the Making of the Modern World.* Cambridge, MA: Harvard University Press.
Dobkin del Rios, Marlene
    2009 *The Psychedelic Journey of Marlene Dobkin del Rios: 45 Years with Shamans, Ayahuasqueros, and Ethnobotanists.* Rochester, VT: Park Street Press.
Gootenberg, Paul
    2008 *Andean Cocaine: The Making of a Global Drug.* Chapel Hill: University of North Carolina Press.
Organization of American States (OAS) (Secretary-General José Miguel Insulza)
    2013 *The Drug Problem in the Americas.* Washington, DC: OAS.
Musto, David
    1973 *The American Disease: Origins of Narcotic Control.* New York: Oxford University Press.
Norton, Marcy
    2008 *Sacred Gifts, Profane Pleasures: A History of Tobacco and Chocolate in the Atlantic World.* Ithaca, NY: Cornell University Press.
Schivelbusch, Wolfgang
    1992 *Tastes of Paradise: A Social History of Spices, Stimulants, and Intoxicants.* New York: Vintage Books.
Schultes, Richard Evans, and Albert Hoffman
    1992 *Plants of the Gods: Their Sacred, Healing, and Hallucinogenic Powers.* Rochester, VT: Healing Arts Press.
Topik, Steven, Carlos Marichal, and Frank Zephyr, eds.
    2006 *From Silver to Cocaine: Latin American Commodity Chains and the Building of the World Economy, 1500–2000.* Durham, NC: Duke University Press.

Wald, Elijah
2001 *Narcocorridos: A Journey into the Music of Drugs, Guns, and Guerrillas.*
New York: Rayo.

NOTES

1. Winston LaBarre, "Old and New World Narcotics: A Statistical Question and Ethnological Reply," *Economic Botany* 24 (1970): 73–80. This pre-Columbian section is based largely on Dobkin del Rios, *Psychedelic Journey* (2009); and Schultes and Hoffman, *Plants of the Gods* (1992).

2. This discussion of colonialism and drugs draws liberally from Courtwright, *Forces of Habit* (2001); Schivelbusch, *Tastes of Paradise* (1992); and Norton, *Sacred Gifts, Profane Pleasures* (2008).

3. Stimulant and export commodities of the age are examined in Topik, Marichal, and Frank, *From Silver to Cocaine* (2006); and Gootenberg, *Andean Cocaine* (2008), chaps. 1 and 2.

PART FOUR

Communities

INTRODUCTION

BY DEFAULT OR DESIGN, GEOGRAPHY often determines how we draw lines between "us" and "them." Social groups cohere around spatial constructions like the *barrio* (neighborhood), *pueblo* (village), and *nación* (nation). *Global Latin America* challenges this familiar link between geography and community by suggesting the region is simultaneously unbounded by space (i.e., global) and spatially specific (i.e., "Latin American"). In an age when distance seems to matter less than ever before, global Latin Americans are helping to develop alternative forms of coming together as groups, whether through neighborhoods, regions, or societies. In part 4, five authors profile diverse individuals and a range of influences helping to make and remake communities.

If communities are not static, fixed, predetermined entities, then who helps to create them? Key participants are those involved in social movements, who, not surprisingly, have central roles in many of this part's chapters. In assuming the representation of groups of individuals, activists often help to define the contours and composition of communities. Such is the case of the famous indigenous leader Rigoberta Menchú Tum, who gave voice to the victims of genocide in the midst of Cold War–fueled civil war in Guatemala (1960–96). Menchú's role as a charismatic and moving spokesperson for Latin American indigenous rights helped to propel a now-global indigenous people's movement that aims to forge new networks of communal belonging across vast stretches of space.

While familiar perhaps to some readers, Menchú's case stands out as an exception among the narratives collected here. The past three decades of globalization and digital revolution have made the ability to communicate and transmit media more rapid and diffuse than ever before. These changes have reshaped social movements, which have become less centralized, at times even relatively leaderless. The category "community leader" seems to have receded as the power to participate in—and sometimes ignite—social and political change has shrunk to a handheld device. The seeming insignificance of physical space in this global digital age means that certain manifestations of communities can exist in digital space with members whose lives span the globe.

Readers will encounter a case of community linked through such digital sinews in Denise Brennan's chapter on sex work in the Caribbean and South America. Channeling voices from her fieldwork with sex worker activists, Brennan urges government agencies and human rights activists to pay attention to the often-muddled distinction between human trafficking and sex work. Brennan emphasizes that many of the transpeople, women, and men who have built a sprawling network of support over the past two decades do not see themselves as trafficked persons. They identify themselves as workers and heads of families and have successfully lobbied for rights and protection from national governments; a few have run successfully for public office. This collective—what Brennan terms "transnational kin"—has pioneered models of aboveground and underground solidarity influencing movements elsewhere in the Global North and South.

Brennan's piece intersects on multiple fronts with Florence Babb's chapter, which tracks the footsteps and preconceptions of U.S. tourists as they visit Latin America and return to their homes. Babb shows how a form of community can take shape through intimate vacation encounters between locals and tourists. While such encounters are fraught with exotic expectations and asymmetrical relationships of power, we learn that many on both sides describe the formation of genuine affective ties. Such relationships sometimes become alternative or parallel families stretching thousands of miles, with long gaps between visits punctuated by continued communication and financial support. Some readers may find similarities in the immigrant families who have long maintained intimate and practical ties despite vast distances between places in Latin America and home or destination lands elsewhere. However, Babb and Brennan show us how "experiential tourism" is generating novel types of transnational and transactional relationships that in turn affect conventional forms of family structure and gender roles.

Helping to situate the idea of global Latin America in historical context, the Brazilian anthropologist Ruben Oliven takes the scale of analysis from the more localized frames of social movements and families to the nation as a whole. Benedict Anderson, an influential international studies scholar, described the nation as an "imagined community" bound by the "deep, horizontal comradeship" of its members, most of whom will never meet their comrades in person. In a far-reaching few pages, Oliven outlines how Brazilian elites have imagined the national community at influential moments over five centuries—a process fundamentally informed by questions and international conversations about ethnic and racial identity. Linking long-term historical commentary to the current century, Oliven discusses the rise of millions into Brazil's middle class and initiatives for affirmative action to address racial disparities. As with the chapters by Babb and Brennan, Oliven tells the stories of populations throughout the western hemisphere that are pioneering new forms of solidarity across borders in the service of struggles for recognition and equity within them.

Readers will find a cohesive tone and thematic similarity in the chapters assembled in this part. Three of the authors are trained anthropologists (Brennan, Babb, and Oliven) who tell stories of peoples and cultures and support their claims with a mix of field observations and scholarly literature. Lines from Renato Rosaldo and Rigoberta Menchú complement the anthropologists' chapters with firsthand perspectives. Taken together, these authors invite us to think about communities as they were, are, and will be. From families stretching thousands of miles to networks of global activists, individuals from Latin American and the Caribbean continue to write new chapters in the global history of communities.

Introduction to Rigoberta Menchú Tum

NO ONE COULD MISS THE significance of Rigoberta Menchú Tum on the Nobel stage in Oslo, Norway, in 1992. She was the first woman and the first nonwhite person from Latin America to receive the Nobel Peace Prize. She delivered the speech exactly five hundred years after Columbus arrived in the Caribbean in 1492, beginning a series of encounters that would annihilate millions of natives over the following five centuries. Menchú's Nobel Prize was a tribute to centuries of struggles against oppression by indigenous populations in Latin America, including the very contemporary victims of the Guatemalan civil war (1960–96) that was then ongoing. Among the thousands murdered in that conflict were Menchú's own mother, father, and brother. Menchú escaped death and was exiled to Mexico. Her powerful 1984 testimonial, *I, Rigoberta Menchú: An Indian Woman in Guatemala,* made her a global voice for human rights.

In her Nobel speech in Oslo, Menchú embraced the symbolism of the award as an honor to indigenous people and sought to make the honor an instrument for global action. She appealed for peace, reconciliation, and justice and decried discrimination and racism. She urged the United Nations to hasten its participation in the Guatemalan peace process and to broaden its attention to human rights abuses elsewhere. She argued for the recognition of indigenous land rights and for resources to improve the most basic measures of human well-being, such as infant mortality, literacy, and nutrition.

Though delivered nearly twenty-five years before the publication of *Global Latin America,* the speech remains as alive as ever. Trials for reconciliation and justice from the Guatemalan conflict continue before international tribunals. A global indigenous people's movement propelled by grassroots activism and international organizations like the United Nations proclaimed two official Decades of the World's Indigenous Peoples (1993–2004 and 2005–14) and the Declaration on the Rights of Indigenous Peoples (2007). This movement that Menchú helped spark now represents more than 350 million indigenous persons across ninety countries and increasingly overlaps with other social movements like climate change activism and environmentalism more broadly.

Rigoberta Menchú's legacy endures through her famous 1984 testimonial book and ongoing leadership in human rights campaigns. Recognized by the Nobel committee in 1992 "for her work for social justice and ethno-cultural reconciliation based on respect for the rights of indigenous peoples," Menchú exemplifies the reach and leadership of global Latin Americans.

By Andrew Britt

TWELVE

Nobel Lecture

Rigoberta Menchú Tum

Your Majesties, the King and Queen of Norway,
The Honorable Members of the Nobel Peace Committee,
Your Excellency, the Prime Minister,
Your Excellencies, Members of the Government and the Diplomatic Corps,
Dear Guatemalan countrymen and women,
Ladies and Gentlemen,

I feel a deep emotion and pride for the honor of having been awarded the Nobel Peace Prize for 1992. A deep personal feeling and pride for my country and its very ancient culture. For the values of the community and the people to which I belong, for the love of my country, of Mother Nature. Whoever understands this respects life and encourages the struggle that aims at such objectives.

I consider this Prize, not as a reward to me personally, but rather as one of the greatest conquests in the struggle for peace, for Human Rights and for the rights of the indigenous people, who, for 500 years, have been split, fragmented, as well as the victims of genocides, repression and discrimination.

Please allow me to convey to you all, what this Prize means to me.

In my opinion, the Nobel Peace Prize calls upon us to act in accordance with what it represents, and the great significance it has worldwide. In addition to being a priceless treasure, it is an instrument with which to fight for peace, for justice, for the rights of those who suffer the abysmal economical, social, cultural and political inequalities, typical of the order of the world in which we live, and where the transformation into a new world based on the values of the human being, is the expectation of the majority of those who live on this planet.

This Nobel Prize represents a standard bearer that encourages us to continue denouncing the violation of Human Rights, committed against the people in Guatemala, in America and in the world, and to perform a positive role in respect of the pressing task in my country, which is to achieve peace with social justice.

The Nobel Prize is a symbol of peace, and of the efforts to build up a real democracy. It will stimulate the civil sectors so that through a solid national unity, these may contribute to the process of negotiations that seek peace, reflecting the general feeling—although at times not possible to express because of fear—of Guatemalan society: to establish political and legal grounds that will give irreversible impulses to a solution to what initiated the internal armed conflict.

There is no doubt whatsoever that it constitutes a sign of hope in the struggle of the indigenous people in the entire Continent.

It is also a tribute to the Central American people who are still searching for their stability, for the structuring of their future, and the path for their development and integration, based on civil democracy and mutual respect.

The importance of this Nobel Prize has been demonstrated by all the congratulations received from everywhere, from Heads of Government—practically all the American Presidents—to the organizations of the indigenous people and of Human Rights, from all over the world. In fact, what they see in this Nobel Peace Prize is not only a reward and a recognition of a single person, but a starting point for the hard struggle towards the achievement of that revindication which is yet to be fulfilled.

As a contrast, and paradoxically, it was actually in my own country where I met, on the part of some people, the strongest objections, reserve and indifference, for the award of the Nobel Peace Prize to this Quiché Indian. Perhaps because in Latin America, it is precisely in Guatemala where the discrimination towards the indigenous, towards women, and the repression of the longing for justice and peace, are more deeply rooted in certain social and political sectors.

Under present circumstances, in this disordered and complex world, the decision of the Norwegian Nobel Peace Prize Committee to award this honorable distinction to me, reflects the awareness of the fact that, in this way, courage and strength is given to the struggle of peace, reconciliation and justice; to the struggle against racism, cultural discrimination, and hence contributes to the achievement of harmonious co-existence between our people.

With deep pain, on one side, but with satisfaction on the other, I have to inform you that the Nobel Peace Prize 1992 will have to remain temporarily in Mexico City, in watchful waiting for peace in Guatemala. Because there are no political conditions in my country that would indicate or make me foresee a prompt and just solution. The satisfaction and gratitude are due to the fact that Mexico, our brother neighbor country, that has been so dedicated and interested, that has made such great efforts in respect of the negotiations that are being conducted to achieve peace, that has received and admitted so many refugees and exiled Guatemalans, has given us a place in the Museo del Templo Mayor (the cradle of the ancient Aztecs) so that the Nobel Prize may remain there, until peaceful and safe conditions are established in Guatemala to place it here, in the land of the Quetzal.

When evaluating the overall significance of the award of the Peace Prize, I would like to say some words on behalf of all those whose voice cannot be heard or who have been repressed for having spoken their opinions, of all those who have been marginalized, who have been discriminated, who live in poverty, in need, of all those who are the victims of repression and violation of human rights. Those who, nevertheless, have endured through centuries, who have not lost their conscience, determination, and hope.

Please allow me, ladies and gentlemen, to say some words about my country and the civilization of the Mayas. The Maya people developed and spread geographically through some 300,000 square km; they occupied parts of the South of Mexico, Belize, Guatemala, as well as Honduras and El Salvador; they developed a very rich civilization in the area of political organization, as well as in social and economic fields; they were great scientists in the fields of mathematics, astronomy, agriculture, architecture and engineering; they were great artists in the fields of sculpture, painting, weaving and carving.

The Mayas discovered the zero value in mathematics, at about the same time that it was discovered in India and later passed on to the Arabs. Their astronomic forecasts based on mathematical calculations and scientific observations were amazing, and still are. They prepared a calendar more accurate than the Gregorian, and in the field of medicine they performed intracranial surgical operations.

One of the Maya books, which escaped destruction by the conquistadores, known as The Codex of Dresden, contains the results of an investigation on eclipses as well as a table of 69 dates, in which solar eclipses occur in a lapse of 33 years.

Today, it is important to emphasize the deep respect that the Maya civilization had towards life and nature in general.

Who can predict what other great scientific conquests and developments these people could have achieved, if they had not been conquered by blood and fire, and subjected to an ethnocide that affected nearly 50 million people in the course of 500 years.

I would describe the meaning of this Nobel Peace Prize, in the first place as a tribute to the Indian people who have been sacrificed and have disappeared because they aimed at a more dignified and just life with fraternity and understanding among human beings. To those who are no longer alive to keep up the hope for a change in the situation in respect of poverty and marginalization of the Indians, of those who have been banished, of the helpless in Guatemala as well as in the entire American Continent.

This growing concern is comforting, even though it comes 500 years later, to the suffering, the discrimination, the oppression and the exploitation that our peoples have been exposed to, but who, thanks to their own cosmovision— and concept of life, have managed to withstand and finally see some promising prospects. How those roots, that were to be eradicated, now begin to grow with strength, hope and visions of the future!

It also represents a sign of the growing international interest for, and understanding of the original Rights of the People, of the future of more than 60 million Indians that live in our Americas, and their outcry because of the 500 years of oppression that they have endured. For the genocide beyond comparison that they have had to suffer throughout this epoch, and from which other countries and the elite of the Americas have profited and taken advantage.

Let there be freedom for the Indians, wherever they may be in the American Continent or elsewhere in the world, because while they are alive, a glow of hope will be alive as well as a true concept of life.

The expressions of great happiness by the Indian Organizations in the entire Continent and the worldwide congratulations received for the award of the Nobel Peace Prize, clearly indicate the great importance of this decision. It is the recognition of the European debt to the American indigenous people; it is an appeal to the conscience of Humanity so that those conditions of marginalization that condemned them to colonialism and exploitation may be eradicated; it is a cry for life, peace, justice, equality and fraternity between human beings.

The peculiarities of the vision of the Indian people are expressed according to the way in which they are related to each other. First, between human beings, through communication. Second, with the earth, as with our mother, because she gives us our lives and is not mere merchandise. Third, with nature, because we are an integral part of it, and not its owners.

To us Mother Earth is not only a source of economic riches that give us the maize, which is our life, but she also provides so many other things that the privileged ones of today strive for. The Earth is the root and the source of our culture. She keeps our memories, she receives our ancestors and she, therefore, demands that we honor her and return to her, with tenderness and respect, those goods that she gives us. We have to take care of her so that our children and grandchildren may continue to benefit from her. If the world does not learn now to show respect to nature, what kind of future will the new generations have?

From these basic features derive behavior, rights and obligations in the American Continent, for the indigenous people as well as for the non-indigenous, whether they be racially mixed, blacks, whites or Asian. The whole society has an obligation to show mutual respect, to learn from each other and to share material and scientific achievements, in the most convenient way. The indigenous peoples never had, and still do not have, the place that they should have occupied in the progress and benefits of science and technology, although they represented an important basis for this development.

If the indigenous civilization and the European civilizations could have made exchanges in a peaceful and harmonious manner, without destruction, exploitation, discrimination and poverty, they could, no doubt, have achieved greater and more valuable conquests for Humanity.

Let us not forget that when the Europeans came to America, there were flourishing and strong civilizations there. One cannot talk about a "discovery of America," because one discovers that which one does not know about, or that which is hidden. But America and its native civilizations had discovered themselves long before the fall of the Roman Empire and Medieval Europe. The significance of its cultures forms part of the heritage of humanity and continues to astonish the learned.

I think it is necessary that the indigenous peoples, of which I am a member, should contribute their science and knowledge to human development, because we have enormous potential and we could combine our very ancient heritage with the achievements of European civilization as well as with civilizations in other parts of the world.

But this contribution, that to our understanding is a recovery of the natural and cultural heritage, must take place based on a rational and consensual basis in respect of the right to make use of knowledge and natural resources, with guarantees for equality between Government and society.

We the indigenous are willing to combine tradition with modernism, but not at any cost. We will not tolerate or permit that our future be planned as possible guardians of ethno-touristic projects on a continental level.

At a time when the commemoration of the Fifth Centenary of the arrival of Columbus in America has repercussions all over the world, the revival of hope for the oppressed indigenous peoples demands that we reassert our existence to the world and the value of our cultural identity. It demands that we endeavor to actively participate in the decisions that concern our destiny, in the building-up of our countries/nations. Should we, in spite of all, not be taken into consideration, there are factors that guarantee our future: struggle and endurance; courage; the decision to maintain our traditions that have been exposed to so many perils and sufferings; solidarity towards our struggle on the part of numerous countries, governments, organizations and citizens of the world.

That is why I dream of the day when the relationship between the indigenous peoples and other peoples is strengthened; when they can combine their potentialities and their capabilities and contribute to make life on this planet less unequal, a better distribution of the scientific and cultural treasures accumulated by Humanity, flourishing in peace and justice.

Today, in the 47th period of sessions of the General Assembly, the United Nations (UN) will proclaim 1993 as the "International Year of the World's Indigenous People," in the presence of well-known chiefs of the organizations of the Indian people and of the coordination of the Continental Movement of Indigenous, Blacks and Popular Resistance. They will all formally participate in the opening of the working sessions in order to make 1993 a year of specific actions to truly place the indigenous peoples within their national contexts and to make them part of mutual international agreements.

The achievement of the "International Year of the World's Indigenous People" and the progress represented by the preparation of the project for the Universal Declaration are the result of the participation of numerous Indian brothers, nongovernmental organizations and the successful efforts of the experts in the Working group, in addition to the comprehensiveness shown by many countries in the United Nations.

We hope that the formulation of the project in respect of the Declaration on the Rights of the indigenous People will examine and go deeply into the existing difficulty reality that we, the Indo-Americans, experience.

Our people will have a year dedicated to the problems that afflict them and, in this respect, are now getting ready to carry out different activities with the purpose of presenting proposals and putting pressure on action plans. All this will be conducted in the most reasonable way and with the most convincing and justified arguments for the elimination of racism, oppression, discrimination and the exploitation of those who have been dragged into poverty and oblivion. Also for "the condemned of the earth," the award of the Nobel Peace Prize represents a recognition, an encouragement and an objective for the future.

I wish that a conscious sense of peace and a feeling of human solidarity would develop in all peoples, which would open new relationships of respect and equality for the next millennium, to be ruled by fraternity and not by cruel conflicts.

Opinion is being formed everywhere today, that in spite of wars and violence, calls upon the entire human race to protect its historical values and to form unity in diversity. And this calls upon us all to reflect upon the incorporation of important elements of change and transformation in all aspects of life on earth, in the search for specific and definite solutions to the deep ethical crisis that afflicts Humanity.

This will, no doubt, have decisive influence on the structure of the future.

There is a possibility that some centers of political and economic power, some statesmen and intellectuals, have not yet managed to see the advantages of the active participation of the indigenous peoples in all the fields of human activity. However, the movement initiated by different political and intellectual "Amerindians" will finally convince them that, from an objective point of view, we are a constituent part of the historical alternatives that are being discussed at the international level.

Ladies and gentlemen, allow me to say some candid words about my country.

The attention that this Nobel Peace Prize has focused on Guatemala, should imply that the violation of the human rights is no longer ignored internationally. It will also honor all those who died in the struggle for social equality and justice in my country.

It is known throughout the world that the Guatemalan people, as a result of their struggle, succeeded in achieving, in October 1944, a period of democracy where institutionality and human rights were the main philosophies. At that time, Guatemala was an exception in the American Continent, because of its struggle for complete national sovereignty. However, in 1954, a conspiracy that associated the traditional national power centers, inheritors of colonialism, with powerful foreign interests, overthrew the democratic regime as a result of an armed invasion, thereby re-imposing the old system of oppression which has characterized the history of my country.

The economic, social and political subjection that derived from the Cold War, was what initiated the internal armed conflict. The repression against the organizations of the people, the democratic parties and the intellectuals, started in Guatemala long before the war started. Let us not forget that.

In the attempt to crush rebellion, dictatorships have committed the greatest atrocities. They have leveled villages, and murdered thousands of peasants particularly Indians, hundreds of trade union workers and students, outstanding intellectuals and politicians, priests and nuns. Through this systematic persecution in the name of the safety of the nation, one million peasants, were removed by force from their lands; 100,000 had to seek refuge in the neighboring countries. In Guatemala, there are today almost 100,000 orphans and more than 40,000 widows. The practice of "disappeared" politicians was invented in Guatemala, as a government policy.

As you know, I am myself a survivor of a massacred family.

The country collapsed into a crisis never seen before and the changes in the world forced and encouraged the military forces to permit a political opening that consisted in the preparation of a new Constitution, in an expansion of the political field, and in the transfer of the government to civil sectors. We have had this new regime for eight years and in certain fields there have been some openings of importance.

However, in spite of these openings, repression and violation of human rights persists in the middle of an economic crisis, that is becoming more and more acute, to the extent that 84% of the population is today considered as poor, and some 60% are considered as very poor. Impunity and terror continue to prevent people from freely expressing their needs and vital demands. The internal armed conflict still exists.

The political life in my country has lately centered around the search for a political solution to the global crisis and the armed conflict that has existed in Guatemala since 1962. This process was initiated by the Agreement signed in this City of Oslo, between the Comisión Nacional de Reconciliación with government mandate and the Unidad Revolucionaria Nacional Guatemalteca (URNG) as a necessary step to introduce to Guatemala the spirit of the Agreement of Esquipulas.

As a result of this Agreement and conversations between the URNG and different sectors of Guatemalan society, direct negotiations were initiated under the government of President Serrano, between the government and the guerrillas, as a result of which three agreements have already been signed. However, the subject of Human Rights has taken a long time, because this subject constitutes the core of the Guatemalan problems, and around this core important differences have arisen. Nevertheless, there has been considerable progress.

The process of negotiations aims at reaching agreements in order to establish the basis for a real democracy in Guatemala and for an end to the war. As far as I understand, with the goodwill of the parties concerned and the active participation of the civil sectors, adapting to a great national unity, the phase of purposes and intentions could be left behind so that Guatemala could be pulled out of the crossroads that seem to have become eternal.

Dialogues and political negotiations are, no doubt, adequate means to solve these problems, in order to respond in a specific way to the vital and urgent needs for life and for the implementation of democracy for the Guatemalan people. However, I am convinced that if the diverse social sectors which integrate Guatemalan society find bases of unity, respecting their natural differences, they would together find a solution to those problems and therefore resolve the causes which initiated the war which prevails in Guatemala.

Other civil sectors as well as the international community must demand that the negotiations between the Government and the URNG surpass the period in which they are finding themselves in discussing Human Rights and move ahead as soon as possible to a verifiable agreement with the United Nations. It is necessary to point out, here in Oslo, that the issue of Human Rights in Guatemala constitutes, at present, the most urgent problem that has to be solved. My statement is neither incidental nor unjustified.

As has been ascertained by international institutions, such as The United Nations Commission on Human Rights, The Interamerican Commission of Human Rights and many other humanitarian organizations, Guatemala is one of the countries in America with the largest number of violations of these rights, and the largest number of cases of impunity where security forces are generally involved. It is imperative that the repression and persecution of the people and the Indians be stopped. The compulsory mobilization and integration of young people into the Patrols of Civil Self Defense, which principally affects the Indian people, must also be stopped.

Democracy in Guatemala must be built-up as soon as possible. It is necessary that Human Rights agreements be fully complied with, i.e., an end to racism; guaranteed freedom to organize and to move within all sectors of the country. In short, it is imperative to open all fields to the multi-ethnic civil society with all its rights, to demilitarize the country and establish the basis for its development, so that it can be pulled out of today's underdevelopment and poverty.

Among the most bitter dramas that a great percentage of the population has to endure, is the forced exodus. Which means, to be forced by military units and persecution to abandon their villages, their Mother Earth, where their ancestors rest, their environment, the nature that gave them life and the growth of their communities, all of which constituted a coherent system of social organization and functional democracy.

The case of the displaced and of refugees in Guatemala is heartbreaking; some of them are condemned to live in exile in other countries, but the great majority live in exile in their own country. They are forced to wander from place to place, to live in ravines and inhospitable places, some not recognized as Guatemalan citizens, but all of them are condemned to poverty and hunger. There cannot be a true democracy as long as this problem is not satisfactorily solved and these people are reinstated on their lands and in their villages.

In the new Guatemalan society, there must be a fundamental reorganization in the matter of land ownership, to allow for the development of the agricultural potential, as well as for the return of the land to the legitimate owners. This process of reorganization must be carried out with the greatest respect for nature, in order to protect her and return to her, her strength and capability to generate life.

No less characteristic of a democracy is social justice. This demands a solution to the frightening statistics on infant mortality, of malnutrition, lack of education, analphabetism, wages insufficient to sustain life. These problems have a growing and painful impact on the Guatemalan population and imply no prospects and no hope.

Among the features that characterize society today, is that of the role of women, although female emancipation has not, in fact, been fully achieved so far by any country in the world.

The historical development in Guatemala reflects now the need and the irreversibility of the active contribution of women to the configuration of the new Guatemalan social order, of which, I humbly believe, the Indian women already are a clear testimony. This Nobel Peace Prize is a recognition to those who have been, and still are in most parts of the world, the most exploited of the exploited; the most discriminated of the discriminated, the most marginalized of the marginalized, but still those who produce life and riches.

Democracy, development and modernization of a country are impossible and incongruous without the solution of these problems.

In Guatemala, it is just as important to recognize the Identity and the Rights of the Indigenous Peoples, that have been ignored and despised not only during the colonial period, but also during the Republic. It is not possible to conceive a democratic Guatemala, free and independent, without the indigenous identity shaping its character into all aspects of national existence.

It will undoubtedly be something new, a completely new experience, with features that, at the moment, we cannot describe. But it will authentically respond to history and the characteristics of the real Guatemalan nationality. The true profile that has been distorted for such a long time.

This urgency of this vital need, are the issues that urge me, at this moment, from this rostrum, to urge national opinion and the international community, to show a more active interest in Guatemala.

Taking into consideration that in connection with my role as a Nobel Prize Winner, in the process of negotiations for peace in Guatemala many possibilities have been handled, but now I think that this role is more likely to be the role of a promotor of peace, of national unity, for the protection of the rights of the indigenous peoples. In such a way, that I may take initiatives in accordance with the needs, and thereby prevent the Peace Prize from becoming a piece of paper that has been pigeonholed.

I call upon all the social and ethnic sectors that constitute the people of Guatemala to participate actively in the efforts to find a peaceful solution to the armed conflict, to build-up a sound unity between the "ladinos," the blacks and the Indians, all of whom must create within their diverse groups, a "Guatemality."

Along these same lines, I invite the international community to contribute with specific actions so that the parties involved may overcome the differences that at this stage keep negotiations in a wait-and-see state, so that they will succeed, first of all, in signing an agreement on Human Rights. And then, to re-initiate the rounds of negotiation and identify those issues on which to compromise, to allow for the Peace Agreement to be signed and immediately ratified, because I have no doubt that this will bring about great relief in the prevailing situation in Guatemala.

My opinion is also that the UN should have a more direct participation, which would go further than playing the role of observer, and could help substantially to move the process ahead.

Ladies and gentlemen, the fact that I have given preference to the American Continent, and in particular to my country, does not mean that I do not have an important place in my mind and in my heart for the concern of other peoples of the world and their constant struggle in the defense of peace, of the right to a life and all its inalienable rights. The majority of us who are gathered here today, constitute an example of the above, and along these lines I would humbly extend to you my gratitude.

Many things have changed in these last years. There have been great changes of worldwide character. The East-West confrontation has ceased to exist and the Cold War has come to an end. These changes, the exact forms of which cannot yet be predicted, have left gaps that the people of the world have known how to make use of in order to come forward, struggle and win national terrain and international recognition.

Today, we must fight for a better world, without poverty, without racism, with peace in the Middle East and in Southeast Asia, to where I address a plea for the liberation of Mrs. Aung San Suu Kyi, winner of the Nobel Peace Prize 1991; for a just and peaceful solution, in the Balkans; for the end of the apartheid in South Africa; for the stability in Nicaragua, that the Peace Agreement in El Salvador be observed; for the re-establishment of democracy in Haiti; for the complete sovereignty of Panama; because all of these constitute the highest aims for justice in the international situation.

A world at peace that could provide consistency, interrelations and concordance in respect of the economic, social and cultural structures of the societies would indeed have deep roots and a robust influence.

We have in our mind the deepest felt demands of the entire human race, when we strive for peaceful co-existence and the preservation of the environment. The struggle we fight purifies and shapes the future.

Our history is a living history, that has throbbed, withstood and survived many centuries of sacrifice. Now it comes forward again with strength. The seeds, dormant for such a long time, break out today with some uncertainty, although they germinate in a world that is at present characterized by confusion and uncertainty.

There is no doubt that this process will be long and complex, but it is no Utopia and we, the Indians, we have new confidence in its implementation.

The peoples of Guatemala will mobilize and will be aware of their strength in building up a worthy future. They are preparing themselves to sow the future, to free themselves from atavisms, to rediscover their heritage. To build a country with a genuine national identity. To start a new life.

By combining all the shades and nuances of the "ladinos," the "garífunas" and Indians in the Guatemalan ethnic mosaic, we must interlace a number of colors without introducing contradictions, without becoming grotesque nor antagonistic, but we must give them brightness and a superior quality, just the way our weavers weave a typical huipil blouse, brilliantly composed, a gift to Humanity.

Thank you very much.

THIRTEEN

Sex Worker Activism and Labor

Denise Brennan

"We're bad, but we could be worse."
"Lost women are the most wanted."
"Before the show, tune your instrument."

These cheeky sayings are emblazoned on T-shirts, hats, thongs, and other clothing under the label DASPU. DASPU, a sex worker–run Brazilian fashion house, stands for "Das putas" (Of the whores). It also riffs on the Brazilian luxury brand DASLU (which threatened—and eventually dropped—a lawsuit). Chic stores like Paris's Galeries Lafayette have sold DASPU's fashion, media from around the world have covered their runway shows staged in Brazil's streets, and celebrated European designers have designed pieces for their collection. But DASPU is not just a clothing company; it has been in the vanguard of a larger global sex worker rights movement that demands justice for low-wage workers, transgender people, and communities of color.

Politically organized, vocal, and creative, sex worker rights activists in Latin America and the Caribbean have fought for—and won—gains that are a model for activists (sex worker and otherwise) worldwide. Colombia's Supreme Court recognized sex workers' agreements with clients as binding contracts. Argentine sex workers successfully lobbied for regularizing their work to receive benefits such as social security. And in Brazil Gabriele Leite, the founder of DASPU and the nongovernmental organization (NGO) Davida, ran for Congress. These political and economic wins stand out against the backdrop of dangers that sex workers the world over face daily: criminalization, violence, rape, incarceration, and discrimination.

Sex workers in Latin America and the Caribbean of course are no exception.

Sex workers have fought back. They often are expert and courageous activists who risk arrest, violence, and stigma every time they speak out. "Isabel," for example, went into hiding after testifying against police abuse in the Brazilian city of Niterói. After her testimony, she was kidnapped by four men who cut her with a razor and threatened her with pictures they had taken of her son. While she was in hiding, she was not on her own. The sex worker rights community is particularly skillful at leveraging social media and raised funds on her behalf while bringing international media attention to ongoing police brutality in Brazil.

With social media linking activists across the Global North and South, worker actions in Latin America and the Caribbean have at times outpaced and inspired actions in the North. In fact, sex worker rights activists in the United States cite DASPU and Gabriela Leite's run for Congress as among the global sex worker community's most inspiring examples of worker solidarity. Sex workers' demands and strategies find common ground with global fights for racial, gender, sexual, migrant, and poor people's justice. As a result, sex worker rights activists in Latin America and the Caribbean have led the way for movement builders in other parts of the world. This chapter shines a light on the ways the region's sex workers navigate the vulnerabilities inherent in sexual economies—such as police violence and states' and NGOs' attempts to "rescue" them in the name of ending trafficking—while they also model cutting-edge activism on the global stage.

QUASI-LEGAL: SAFETY FROM ARREST OR "RESCUE"

Sex work is not illegal in most Latin American countries, but a number of related activities are criminalized. Workers in the sex sector, consequently, live with chronic fear of arrest. Every day they risk losing everything. As the host of major international events, Brazil has undertaken a number of highly publicized campaigns to "clean up" its streets. On the eve of the UNRio+20 Conference in 2012, a wave of arrests and shuttering of brothels—including the famed Centauros, a pricey brothel that Justin Bieber later visited in 2013—shook sex workers' communities. When police raids again began in full force before the World Cup, sex workers were ready. On 16 April 2014, hundreds of sex workers in Niterói took to the streets to protest the chronic

FIGURE 13.1. Sex workers in Niterói, Rio de Janeiro, protest police harassment and illegal arrest of their colleagues in front of city hall on April 16, 2014. Their signs read: "We want to work," "Prostitution isn't a Crime," "We don't want to go to Bangu [maximum security prison]." Photo by Laura Murray, used with permission.

arrests of their colleagues with signs saying, "Prostitution is not a crime" and "We want to work." A little more than a month later, the police raided an apartment building where women worked, breaking down the doors, stealing their money, and condemning the apartments. More than one hundred sex workers were arrested. Several reported being raped during the raid—including "Isabel."

Sex workers immediately organized. They spoke out at public hearings and posted protest signs on the building. Sporting DASPU T-shirts designed as soccer jerseys for the clothing line's 2014 World Cup collection, they played a semi-naked game of soccer—as protest—outside the steps of Niterói's main municipal building. The T-shirts read, "There Will Be Sex"—a play on the protest phrase "Não Vai Ter Copa" (There Will Be No World Cup), thus connecting their demands with those of broader movements of poor communities. They also wore another protest T-shirt, "FIFA Standard Zone," which both referred to "prostitution zones" (red-light districts) and echoed popular opposition to the $11 billion the Brazilian government spent building according to FIFA standards. If stadiums were to going to be world class, why weren't ordinary Brazilians' housing, health clinics, and schools up to the same standards? Rejecting the structural violence and state surveillance and control experienced by the poor daily, sex workers placed their demands alongside those of other marginalized citizens. A member of Davida explains that their protests not only harnessed the outrage over the cost of the World Cup but also affirmed their right to work: "There is nothing illegal about adult women working during the World Cup with foreign tourists."

Like their Brazilian counterparts, sex workers throughout Latin America and the Caribbean are seasoned change agents. They have fought for their rights through grassroots actions as well as through formal political power. Paraguayan sex workers, for example, have issued statements to the international press against an ordinance that prohibits them from working in the streets. Argentine sex workers launched a Banksy-style graffiti project in Buenos Aires that features provocatively dressed women on one wall with their hands stretching around the corner to push a stroller. The visually arresting campaign hammers home their message that sex workers are not criminals—but mothers trying to put food on the table. Members of PLAPERTS (Plataforma Latinoamericana de Personas que Ejercen el Trabajo Sexual) in Quito, Ecuador, issued a rights manifesto that ends with the following call to arms: Sex Work is Work! Whores vote! We are Citizens with Rights! In Belem, Brazil, sex workers cleverly draw media attention to their rights campaigns through a "Panties Race" and an "Orgasm Workshop" on June 2, International Sex Workers Rights Day. And Gabriela Leite is not the only sex worker who has tried to effect change by running for political office. Maria Aparecida Vieira lost a bid for Congress in Brazil, while Jaqueline Montero won a seat on the city council in Haina, Dominican Republic.

Sex worker–led campaigns for worker justice are all the more remarkable in the midst of governments' implementation of antitrafficking programs, which most often have taken the form of anti–sex work crackdowns. Understood as an extreme form of labor exploitation, trafficking into forced labor is nothing new. But since 2000 all governments have had to contend with the role of the United States as what the legal scholar Janie Chuang describes as "global sheriff." Through its annual report card (the Trafficking In Persons—TIP—Report) on countries' efforts to fight trafficking, the United States imposes nonhumanitarian economic sanctions on countries that receive a bad grade in this widely criticized report. As governments have scrambled to implement antitrafficking efforts, sex workers the world over have been rebranded as trafficked persons, even while they insist otherwise. Around the same time that the United States launched its TIP Report, the George W. Bush administration also began requiring organizations that receive U.S. government funds through

PEPFAR (President's Emergency Plan for AIDS Relief) to explicitly oppose prostitution.

Brazilian sex workers mobilized and joined forces with public health experts. They stunned the international development community by refusing to sign the "anti-prostitution pledge." Brazil's then left-leaning government walked away from $40 million in U.S. HIV/AIDS funding. In so doing, they kept intact programs that international public health experts have lauded for stemming the tide of HIV in vulnerable communities. These HIV-prevention programs' success can be attributed in part to sex workers' expertise and peer-to-peer outreach—the very same harm-reduction programs the Bush administration sought to disband. In an article in *The Nation,* Brazil's national AIDS commissioner acknowledged sex workers' central role in combating HIV: "Sex workers are part of implementing our AIDS policy and deciding how to promote it. They are our partners. How could we ask prostitutes to take a position against themselves?"

Gabriela Leite, then coordinator of the Brazilian Network of Prostitutes, played a high-profile role in the PEPFAR negotiations. Brazil's snubbing of the U.S. money and Leite's involvement attracted a great deal of media attention. In an interview with the *Wall Street Journal,* Leite explained that she had assured USAID that the money allocated to eight sex workers' organizations would be used only for AIDS education and prevention. But when she and the other sex worker organizations refused to sign the anti-prostitution pledge, the deal fell apart. Brazil's public health officials and sex worker educators earned the respect of their counterparts throughout the world. This moment in the history of fighting HIV/AIDS is still referenced in public health, antitrafficking, and sex worker networks as a resounding win for sex worker–led harm-reduction programs.

With antitrafficking campaigns under way throughout Latin America, sex workers ironically have become less safe. In this current antitrafficking era, sex workers have been routinely targeted, becoming what the Global Alliance Against Traffic in Women describes as "collateral damage" in the global fight against trafficking. When policy makers, law enforcement, and the media conflate "sex work" with "trafficking," all sex workers—regardless of their working conditions—risk being classified as "trafficked." So too do migrant workers who may not be in situations of extreme abuse. This was the case with Dominican women working in Argentina in the early 2000s when officials in the Dominican embassy in Buenos Aires were accused of running a prostitution ring. As both governments raced to redeem their standing in the U.S. TIP Report, Dominican women who experienced a range of exploitation—some of which did not appear to meet the standard of trafficking—were hastily sent back to the island as "trafficked persons."

Sex workers also have been abused and arrested in antitrafficking raids designed to "rescue" them. Those who choose work in the sex sector make clear that their labor is not coerced, but these attempts to "rescue" them are. Such *coercive rescues* can lead to police violence, rape, extortion, indefinite detention, and deportation. Increased surveillance drives workers to keep a low profile, thus compromising their ability to vet clients ahead of time and to access health services.

PIONEERING PUBLIC HEALTH CAMPAIGNS AND EMPOWERING LEADERS

Sex workers in Latin America and the Caribbean long have been organized. Local organizations throughout small towns and big cities bring sex workers together. Attending the first national meeting for sex worker rights in the Dominican Republic in 1995, for example, I witnessed what was then unfurling throughout Latin America and the Caribbean: women, men, and transgender people in the sex sector were building a movement. Sex worker rights activists throughout the region were exchanging best practices and building worker power through national-level meetings. Soon after, in 1997, workers joined forces as RedTraSex (Red de Mujeres Trabajadoras Sexuales de Latinoamérica y El Caribe) for the first regional meeting. An especially active regional organization, RedTraSex has member organizations in sixteen countries, sends representatives to international conferences, and works on a host of campaigns to increase worker empowerment. In an interview with the International Organization for Migration, Elena Reynaga, RedTraSex's executive secretary, countered those who try to speak for them: "Sex workers are not part of the problem, we are part of the solution."

With scarce funding, low literacy rates, and corrupt—and often abusive—local police, Latin American and Caribbean sex workers have had to find a way to keep their colleagues safe and knowledgeable about their rights. Consequently, since the early 1990s, sex worker organizations have been perfecting low-cost and effective peer-to-peer outreach to "hard to reach" populations. Sex workers in Latin America were among some of the first peer educators to use graphic novels and to stage plays in boardinghouses, bars, brothels, and the street—standard fare in public health campaigns today.

Knowledge exchange, empowerment building, and other forms of assistance sex workers offer one another can be highly orchestrated as well as informal. Since being able to negotiate condom use and payment would reduce the likelihood of violence and unsafe sex with foreign tourists during the World Cup, the sex workers' association in Minas Gerais, Brazil, offered free English classes to sex workers in the area. Sex workers took peer education to new heights. They also negotiated a deal with Brazil's state bank, Caixa Economica, for individual sex workers to process clients' credit card payments through mobile devices. On a more informal level sex workers look out for one another every day. They fill in where the state leaves off. Sex workers share clothes, food, and babysitting. They bail one another out of jail—taking up a collection to pay bribes necessary for their friends' release. They also tip off one another about clients known to be violent. And they quickly get out the word about police raids by sending text alerts or simply knocking on women's doors. In small towns this kind of informal alert system can be as effective as more sophisticated—and capitalized—safety programs.

While politicians, policy makers, health officials, and the media lavish a great deal of attention on monitoring, restricting, and moralizing about sex workers' every move, sex workers often are left out of discussions about them. International organizations—like the International Labour Organization (ILO) and UNAIDS—have recently urged that sex workers have a seat at the table in a host of policy settings. Yet they more often than not remain excluded. While other vulnerable groups who have been invited—and funded—to attend the annual International AIDS Conference (IAC), for example, sex workers continually and conspicuously have been left out. When they have called attention to such exclusions they have faced infantilizing treatment, threats, and sanctions. During the 2008 IAC in Mexico City, for example, a local sex workers' organization, Brigada Callejera, protested their mayor's "zero tolerance" policy, which had led to mass arrests of sex workers and health educators who distributed condoms in the streets. The IAC threatened to bar the organization from future conferences, which ignited an outcry from sex worker rights organizations around the world. Lighting up the Twittersphere, sex workers' leading role as experts was clear in their hashtags: #sexworkers are the experts in our community; Nothing about Us without US, decriminalize #sexwork to #endHIV; #SexWorkers speak with experience, don't silence us, don't speak on our behalf; and #stigma kills.

While sex worker communities fight for their rights, they also are trying to earn a living. Workers may seek to develop relationships that are long term alongside one-time paid encounters. These long-term relationships can bring all kinds of material goods and cash into the household. Many sex workers try to develop at least one ongoing local transactional relationship since these clients/lovers can help pay the rent or children's school fees when money is tight.

Not all clients are local. Parts of Latin America and the Caribbean have become destinations for international tourists seeking paid sexual encounters. Diversifying clientele among locals and foreign tourists can secure against economic crises that cut into local clients' purchasing power or the vagaries of low tourist seasons. Not quite lovers, not quite clients, the foreigners involved in these relationships are not easily pigeonholed. The term "sex tourist," for example, implies some kind of fixed category that involves planning and intentionality. And the term "sex tourism" fails to capture the wide range of contexts in which travelers engage in transactional sexual encounters. "Sex tourism" can be planned (and even prepaid) but also an on-the-fly decision. Ecotourism, roots tourism, and "gay tourism" also bring foreign tourists to Latin America and the Caribbean. Tourists in these kinds of exchanges may imagine a shared "solidarity" through racial/ethnic or sexual identity. Thus (assumed) sameness—or difference—can be what tourists seek and locals perform. The sex sector involves a range of transactions between a range of actors whose gender, sexual, racial, ethnic, and class identities—and nationality and access to visas to travel—shape desire, power, and control. It can be wildly lucrative, or barely allow workers to get by. Different settings afford different degrees of worker control. One commonality across this broad labor sector, however, is the role of performance.

All kinds of assumptions are in play when individuals travel to pay for sexual encounters—when they could just as well purchase sexual experiences at home. With a host of websites perpetuating stereotypes of Latin American and Caribbean sex workers as "hot" and "fiery," foreign tourists may imagine places in Latin America as offering hypersexual and, often, racialized bodies. It is not uncommon for foreign tourists to associate greater sexual proficiency with a person's skin color as well as with tropical climates. One white German tourist who had been paying for sex every night of his vacation told me knowingly at a bar on a Dominican beach, "With German women it's over quickly. But Dominican women have fiery blood." He attributed Dominicans' "natural" skill at lovemaking in part to the climate: "When the sun is shining it gives you more hormones."

Workers, of course, capitalize on these exoticizing and eroticizing stereotypes, for example, by dancing expertly to Latin rhythms that European and North American tourists often fumble through. As they advertise their sexual availability, they also assert their command of certain cultural practices that can befuddle foreign visitors. They try to grasp the upper hand in cultural—and sexual—matters on their home turf. A group of Dominican women sex workers howled when I asked how they thought foreign male tourists saw them: "hot," "sexy," and "Dominicana." For these women, their *dominicanidad* (Dominicanness) not only was sexually charged, but also economically valuable. They cashed in by employing a variety of strategies, such as trying to move into a foreign tourist's hotel room, thus securing payment for each night of the vacation. They also develop ongoing transnational relationships—often by feigning love—to inspire clients to send Western Union money wire transfers once they return home and to return for repeat vacations (with gifts for them and their children). And, in cases when men seek women who adhere to traditional gender roles, women work to appear less demanding and more compliant than tourists' wives and girlfriends' back home while simultaneously cultivating the relationships to yield regular money wires and visits.

Thus sex workers not only perform desire for their clients but also sometimes perform emotion. To do so, they must imagine how clients imagine them. In the case of clients from other countries, the imaginings become more layered—often informed by racialized and classed desires. All the while workers must appear to not be working. This is the central seduction. For those clients who want the relationships to slip into emotional terrain—but without obligations—workers (men, women, and transgender people) may strategically use language of love and emotion. Called "romance tourism" or the "girlfriend (or boyfriend) experience," these kinds of fuzzy relationships fall within a register that disturbs easy and clear categorizations. Clients (local and foreign) and sex workers throughout Latin America and the Caribbean have described their relationships in a variety of terms that produce a variety of outcomes: material gain, pleasure, love, children, marriage, migration, divorce, and disappointment. Love and desire, of course, cannot be measured. Actions, however, can reveal degrees of commitment. Sex workers coach one another on techniques to limit time—and labor—with clients. Those who can afford to decline clients refuse to work with anyone who may be drunk, rude, or dirty or who do not agree to their terms (fee, condom use, and place for the encounter). And clients, of course, can stop returning—and sending gifts and money—at any time.

Despite clients' control over payment and gift giving, sex workers *work* at building them into their sexual and affective networks. With a thin or nonexistent social safety net in most of Latin America and the Caribbean, these relationships can supply forms of security that the state does not. In his research with male sex workers in Brazil, the anthropologist Gregory Mitchell met foreign male lovers/clients who were talked about as "uncles" and "godfathers." Young male Brazilian sex workers (some of whom were married to women and did not identify as gay) built these new queer kin networks by drawing on traditional notions of Brazilian kinship. As "godfather gringos" attend baptisms and other family-oriented events, transactional sexual relationships that often remain offstage become visibilized. Queer sex tourism and the transnational kin it produces allow new notions of family to be very much on stage and in so doing reconfigures and subverts traditional understandings of masculinity, gender roles, and family structure.

This twist on traditional kinship has consequences not only for sex workers but also for clients. They too put *work* into building and maintaining these relationships. They willingly enter territory far from the bedroom; after all, they could pay for sex at home. Even though it can be work to maintain these long-distance relationships, the payoff may extend beyond immediate pleasures. For the foreign lovers, there may be the benefits of a sense of belonging that comes with feeling a part of two spaces—and two families. While Latin American and Caribbean partners are not incorporated in their foreign lovers' lives back home, the foreign partners can enjoy all the affective joys that accompany "being family."

However long clients' generosity lasts is up to them. They can—and do—turn off the spigot on a whim. For this reason, aging sex workers try to secure investments—in jewelry, their homes, and their children's education. Obligating a client by asking him to be a godfather is one more way to secure a stream of money for one's child. Sex workers, thus, might build long-term safety nets out of a combination of local and foreign clients with whom their relationships may involve emotion and care.

CONCLUSION: ONGOING STRUGGLES

Every day sex workers in Latin America and the Caribbean undertake creative strategies to stay safe, make a living, and possibly craft long-term mobility strategies. They do so while also demanding their rights and a seat at policy-setting tables. They have called for policies that decriminalize sex work and disentangle sex work from trafficking. Their activism and knowledge—whether on the runway, in the streets, or at international conferences—have launched pioneering harm-reduction programs, reduced HIV infections, and inspired other movement builders around the world. They often pay dearly for speaking out. In the film *A Kiss for Gabriela* Gabriela Leite explains why such risks are worth it: "You don't make any movement hiding under the table."

REFERENCES AND SUGGESTED READING

Agustín, Lara María
    2007 *Sex at the Margins: Migration, Labour Markets and the Rescue Industry.* New York: Palgrave Macmillan.
Asociación de Trabajadora Autónomas "22 de Junio" de El Oro en Fundación Quimera
    2002 *Trabajadoras del sexo, Memorias Vivas.* Machala, Equador: Mama Cash.
Brennan, Denise
    2004 *What's Love Got to Do with It? Transnational Desires and Sex Tourism in the Dominican Republic.* Durham, NC: Duke University Press.
    2014a *Life Interrupted: Trafficking into Forced Labor in the United States.* Durham, NC: Duke University Press.
    2014b "Trafficking, Scandal, and Abuse of Migrant Workers in Argentina and the United States." *Annals of the American Academy of Political and Social Science* 653 (May): 107–23.
Global Alliance Against Traffic in Women
    2007 *Collateral Damage: The Impact of Anti-Trafficking Measures on Human Rights around the World.* Bangkok: GAATW.
MODEMU (Movimiento de Mujeres Unidas)
    2001 *Rien mis labrios, llora mi alma.* Santo Domingo, Dominican Republic: MODEMU.
Murray, Laura
    2013 *A Kiss for Gabriela.* Documentary. www.akissforgabriela.com/.
Open Society Foundations
    2013 "10 Reasons to Decriminalize Sex Work." New York. www.opensociety-foundations.org/sites/default/files/decriminalize-sexwork-20120713.pdf.

Family Adjustments

Renato Rosaldo

My father shrinks toward his soul,
chats with his grandmother, Mama Meche.

She watches me from a fading photograph
taken in New Orleans in 1881
before she reached Vera Cruz.
She stares sternly, her lower lip protrudes.
Day after day she studies the newspaper,
*Estos papeles no traen nada.**
The English she no longer speaks
still speaks through her.

My father tells me Mama Meche
holds some at the door,
admits others to the living room,
dines with a select few.
If they overstay, she dissolves their laughter.
She tells him, *Place a broom behind the door,
don't move, it'll sweep them away.*
My father chuckles in boyish wickedness.

He dozes. I ask what he's thinking about.
He says he's writing a short story

* These papers have nothing in them. In Spanish a sheet of paper is a *papel,* but a newspaper is a *periódico.*

Ajustes Familiares

Renato Rosaldo

Poco a poco mi padre se encoge alma adentro,
sonríe, platica
con su abuelita, Mama Meche.

Ella me mira desde una foto que se marchita,
tomada en Nueva Orleans
antes de su llegada a Veracruz en 1881.
Ella no parpadea, le sale el labio inferior.
Día tras día estudia el periódico
y dice: *Estos papeles no traen nada.*
El inglés que ya no habla
habla a través de ella.

Papá me cuenta y recuenta que Mama Meche
detiene a algunas visitas en la puerta,
recibe a otras en la sala,
come con pocos.
Si se dilatan, se desvanece la risa.
Ella le hace una seña, *Coloca la escoba detrás de la puerta,*
no te muevas, les barrerá fuera.
El se ríe entre dientes, se hincha con maldad de chamaco.

Cabecea. Le pregunto de que piensa.
Dice que escribe un cuento sobre su abuelita.

about his grandmother. My mother says
he's said that since college.

In my dream a sea captain, trading lumber,
Mama Meche's father, wears savage hair,
a blue and white shirt, red bandanna.
Sit down, he barks at me. *Eyes front,*
stretch, breathe. Then he heals me
with a wooden beam, a smack mid-back,
to loosen, he says, *the grip of family,*
holding it together is not your job.

Mi madre dice que ha dicho eso
desde que asistió a la universidad.

En un sueño un capitán de barco mercante de madera,
padre de ella, con el pelo salvaje,
camisa azul y blanca, bandana colorada.
Siéntate, me dice gruñendo. *Ojos de frente,*
estírate, respira. Y luego me sana
con un palazo a media espalda,
para aflojar, me dice, *el peso de los deberes familiares.*
No te toca sostenerlo todo.

FOURTEEN

Latin American Travel

THE OTHER SIDE OF TOURISM ENCOUNTERS

Florence E. Babb

TRAVEL POSTERS FROM THE EARLY twentieth century often featured images that called on northerners to imagine the wealth of cultural experience that beckoned from Latin America and the Caribbean. Exotic locales and beautiful women were often the sensual enticements to leave the chilly North and venture to more inviting and seductive destinations. One poster for travel to Mexico showed a voluptuous, smiling woman wearing a "peasant" blouse and long braids (and otherwise rather Anglo features) holding out a bounty of tropical fruit against a lush backdrop. And a poster advertising travel to prerevolutionary Cuba showed an exuberant woman leaping, maracas in hand, with the clever text, "So near and yet so foreign." Thus we see that calling on notions of cultural difference and promises of pleasurable experience are nothing new to the Latin American tourism industry, and today we find updated versions of familiar narratives and images designed to attract another generation of travelers.

I have looked at the tourism experience in Latin American nations rebuilding following periods of conflict, revolution, and economic hardship, considering both sides of the tourism encounter in Cuba, Mexico, Nicaragua, and Peru (Babb 2011). What were travelers' encounters with local hosts and service providers? And how did local resourceful hosts satisfy travelers' desires for a brush with different cultures? What is it that travelers took away with them from these diverse tourism encounters? I have found that in addition to the material cultural souvenirs, textiles, baskets, rum, and cigars, they take home the trophies won through their embrace with the Other—trophies of their different, exotic, and even at times dangerous experiences. Frequently, a trove of photographs provides the indisputable evidence of fascinating places visited and people met, food and music enjoyed, and so on.

FIGURE 14.1. Items for sale in a Havana tourist market. Photo by Florence E. Babb.

These are accompanied by travel narratives, and if the traveler has been daring enough to leave the fold of other tourists and make more meaningful connections with those locals encountered, this may prove particularly rich material for bragging rights. Among a certain kind of travelers, such brushes with local culture may include intimate and amorous relations or daring entanglements with adventurous individuals one would not meet back home.

Of course, many others might return from a period of travel with a new understanding of the place visited, a better appreciation for its peoples and cultures, and a sense of the value of foreign experience in bringing together humanity from distant shores. At its best, travel may contribute to our global consciousness and openness to learning other ways of being in the world. If I emphasize in this chapter the frequent misunderstandings that travelers take away from their experiences in Latin America, it is to make a case for recognizing and overcoming our own misperceptions, which are commonly based on the widely held assumptions we have about Latin America and the Caribbean.

As we consider what travelers to Latin America past and present anticipate and desire in heading South, we will see that their assumptions may lead to somewhat problematic travel accounts and a likelihood of reinforcing stereotyped notions of difference between "us" and "them," North and South.

Such misperceptions can reinforce the durable inequalities between our regions in the hemisphere. Before concluding, I comment on some auspicious signs that people-to-people tourism can serve to challenge the dusty notions of cultural difference and the "natural" order of things. Some of what I offer here would find parallels in travel to other world regions, but I highlight the specific sorts of experiences that emerge from tourism in Latin America and the Caribbean, especially among travelers from the United States.

WHAT DO TRAVELERS TO LATIN AMERICA ANTICIPATE THEY WILL FIND?

While we could go back to nineteenth-century U.S. travel to Latin America, let us begin in the early decades of the twentieth century, a time when historians of travel and tourism have shown that those with the resources to travel became more curious about their near neighbors in Mexico and the Caribbean. The tropical holiday became a status symbol for those intrepid enough to set out for places that were still little known in the United States. In the 1930s, a young tourism industry in Mexico attracted travelers who were seeking a rich natural environment, heritage-steeped archaeological sites, and famed cities to explore (Berger and Wood 2010). After World War II, travel to the Caribbean also became popular, as privileged white Americans overcame their fears of the health hazards they might encounter and expressed the desire to experience the salubrious warm climates and exotic cultures they would discover on the islands. Their adoption of "tropical white" dress gave way to a willingness to expose themselves to the sun, and become perhaps a little more like their darker-skinned hosts. Recent historical accounts suggest that this was a time of considerable reimagining, though not acceptance, of cultural and racial difference in the Americas. Nonetheless, these sojourns were, not surprisingly, fodder for travelers' stereotyped ideas of the friendly if somewhat indolent natives who provided hospitality to them (Cocks 2013).

Mass tourism came on the scene later, with the advent of increased air travel, and was booming by the 1970s, when middle-class American families began to view going on vacation as a well-deserved entitlement. Cancún was developed as a destination for those wishing to soak up the sun at an all-inclusive resort, from which they hardly needed to venture during their hedonistic holiday. On the other end of the tourism spectrum, backpacker travel emerged around the same time as a sort of rite of passage for students and young adults who wished to break free of parents and see the world. Many turned to parts of Latin America as affordable and reasonably close, yet suitably exotic destinations. I myself was among those in the seventies who eagerly set off for Mexico to learn a little Spanish and gain experience from the freewheeling journey.

While backpackers traveled on the cheap and often identified as alternative travelers rather than as tourists, they betrayed their family privilege as they eagerly consumed Mexican culture, consolidating their own power in the process. Falling between the leisure travelers and the more adventurous youth were many others who filled the niches beginning to define tourism's vast offerings: cultural and historical tourism, ecotourism, and adventure-sport tourism were just a few of the categories that emerged by the late twentieth century. By the year 2000, tourism was arguably the world's leading industry, and travelers could choose among any number of options, from high-end and exclusive to travel on a shoestring budget. There were tourism providers ready to respond to nearly any taste and any sized pocketbook.

"Visiting Latin America is like going back in time"

Notably, travelers to Latin America frequently imagine that they will be visiting not only another place but also another time. Part of the appeal of travel for them is a kind of nostalgia for a time they have not known or recall only remotely. Of course, a visit to an archaeological site like Machu Picchu in Peru, or to a colonial city like Granada in Nicaragua, transports travelers to the time when these sites of contemporary memory-making were constructed—just as historical tourism in the United States, for example, to Williamsburg, counts on visitors coming away with some deeper knowledge of the heritage site. But what about travel to vibrant cities like Havana (an increasing possibility now for U.S. citizens) or to rural communities in the Andes? Why is it that these travel destinations, which are full of life and every bit a part of today's world, are so often viewed as locked in time, even as "living history" museums, for those who are attracted to them? Much has been made of Havana's crumbling ruins, the faded glory of its beautiful architecture, as well as its more recent and spectacular makeover of the historic colonial sector—where most tourists flock.

Many know about and wish to see Havana's mid-twentieth-century cars, Buicks and Chevys that can be hired as taxis at elevated prices to get around the city. And city tours are rarely complete without a visit to one of the

FIGURE 14.2. Dancer performing at the Tropicana nightclub in Havana. Photo by Florence E. Babb.

Hemingway bars, where the writer consumed his famed daiquiris and moji-tos during the 1940s and 1950s. All of this conspires to transport the traveler to another time, even if Havana's present is very much a product of its past and not simply a residue of it. Cuba's post-Soviet economic crisis of the 1990s has marked the present period just as much as the prerevolutionary licen-tiousness of the Tropicana nightclub, though it is the latter that more tourists wish to discover on a trip to Havana.

A very different class of travelers opts for what has been called experiential tourism in the high Andean communities like Vicos, Peru, yet they too are attracted by the notion that they will get to know a place that "time forgot" and that is unmarred by modern cultural and economic development. That agricultural community, which has been of keen interest to social scientists since the time when it was a hacienda, has recently launched a small tourism project to draw visitors, many of them young and idealistic, who want to experience the "authenticity" of Andean traditional life close up over the course of several days. Arriving in small groups, they are shown the com-munity's Casa de los Abuelos (literally, "grandparents' house"), a one-room history museum of photographs and other documents of several centuries of Vicos's past, highlighting the period from the 1950s when Cornell University launched a decade-long project in applied anthropology.

Today's residents have continued to seek "progress" for the community, in part by re-creating the past for its visitors. Guests stay in lodges built next

FIGURE 14.3. Selling to tourists boarding a train to Machu Picchu. Photo by Florence E. Babb.

door to their hosts and are invited to join the families in preparing and eating meals, working on the land, and participating in other activities, such as a baptism or a wedding (as I did during a recent visit there). Hosts make a point of talking to their guests about the enduring traditions that give meaning to their lives, performing rituals with coca leaves or speaking reverently about the mountain gods. If their own modest houses now have electricity allowing them to enjoy TVs, radios, and other modern conveniences, this is not mentioned in their narratives of traditional lifeways. Indeed, a promotional brochure for experiential tourism in Vicos states that "to get acquainted with places where people once lived in ancient civilizations and to share a few days of their daily lives, all this will help you understand this part of the world's richness, which one never imagined existed far away from the cities" (Babb 2011: 87). It is no wonder then if travelers come away with a sense that they have participated in cultures that have been preserved in time.

We might ask which came first, tourists' expectations of finding lands locked in time or their hosts' desire to offer some confirmation that this is in fact what they have to offer. The commodification of cultural difference and even cultural identity—it is often iconic peasants or market women in colorful settings who serve to sell a destination—is a phenomenon that is widespread today. There is in fact a mutual complicity in such performances and consumption of age-old tradition in places that may actually be very much on the move as local residents strive to better their lives with the amenities they see around them in the wider society, in the media, and so on. If local hosts play to the romantic desires of their visitors for "authentic experience," it may be out of cultural pride *or* out of a need to earn a livelihood in order to send their children to school so that they may be prepared for employment outside the community (and sometimes both).

What fuels this route to economic development, however, may well be the sort of "imperialist nostalgia" that the anthropologist Renato Rosaldo finds in the encounters of northerners with their cultural counterparts in the Global South. There is often a fine line between the respect for tradition that visitors may share with their hosts and a kind of thinking that can serve to consolidate and legitimize differences of power. Thus the danger of tourists taking home a sense that they have truly come to know a more "primitive" or "simpler" way of life that they may indulge in for the duration of their visit and then happily return to their more state-of-the-art, Internet- and cell phone–dependent lives.

"Latin America is a continent where conflict and instability are the norm"

The historians Dina Berger and Andrew Wood write about U.S. soldiers in the mid-nineteenth century who were fighting in the U.S.-Mexican war who found time to explore central Mexico's wondrous places as the first tourists to that country. Even in the midst of conflict, these soldiers wished to see the land they were struggling over and wrote of it in rapturous tones. Since then, when visiting Latin American colonial cities during peacetime, tourists have been eager to visit sites of battle, whether to hear stories of the Liberal and Conservative Party struggles in nineteenth-century Nicaragua or of Emiliano Zapata's and Pancho Villa's successes in the Mexican Revolution. These two countries have in fact attracted "tourists of revolution" in more recent decades, with solidarity activists heading to Nicaragua after the Sandinista Revolution triumphed in 1979 and to Chiapas in southern Mexico following the Zapatista uprising in 1994. Cuba, of course, has had its share of revolutionary tourists from the second half of the twentieth century, drawing those who forgo the beach for a visit to the Museum of the Revolution or the Federation of Cuban Women.

In Peru, in contrast, the violent war of the 1980s between the military and the Shining Path movement kept tourists away until the late 1990s, when efforts were made to bring them back with assurances that the nation had been pacified. Advertising that had earlier used Andean people to draw visitors were later featuring "safe" archaeological sites so tourists could steer clear of reminders of the recent Andean conflict. Now that more time has passed, some tourists are venturing into "memory" museums where they can learn about this hidden history of bloody war.

Whether tourists in Latin America shun sites of conflict or occasionally seek them out, they frequently come away from their travel experience with a view of a continent that has only recently seen violence abate. Tourism promoters are aware of the double-edged sword of drawing travelers with promises of their safety and comfort at the same time that they know it is often recent drama subdued that captures potential visitors' imaginations. We have only to read the *New York Times* Travel Section to know the rather formulaic narrative of former hot spots now putting out the welcome mat for tourism. Readers know that if they are among the first to arrive in such formerly forbidden areas, they will beat the rush and find fewer tourists competing for space in hotels and restaurants. And for their part, local tourism operators will say that in the aftermath of conflict they are grateful that it kept their destination safe from overdevelopment; they now can reap the benefits. Thus, once again we may discover a certain complicity between hosts and guests in the tourism encounter whereby both buy into the instability as naturalized and want to be among those who can take advantage of the peaceful interludes.

Mexican soldier-tourists, revolutionary tourists, and history buffs keen on seeing sites of conflict all may return from their Latin American sojourns with stories of past conflict, memories of violence that were shared with them, and a sense of the fragility of the nations they visited. To some extent, this may reflect the very real political conflicts these nations have endured, but tourists often appear to find confirmation of their expectations of peoples and cultures that are fundamentally, even inherently, volatile. Tourism is sometimes touted as a strategy for building peace and economic security, yet it is founded on a premise that tourists can readily perceive: instability and conflict are a default setting for much of the region.

"Latin Americans are friendly and easygoing, but they lack the drive for development"

Related to the view that Latin American nations are inherently unstable is the view that Latin Americans themselves are a friendly and agreeable people but not driven toward the measures of development that are often taken for granted in the United States or Europe. This view may stem from the history of colonialism in the region and the unfortunate conclusion that if Latin America remained underdeveloped so long it was owing to the failings of the region's own peoples. Consider the familiar caricature of Latin Americans' easygoing attitudes, sometimes negatively represented by Americans' use of the term *mañana*. The notion is that Latin Americans are in no hurry, whether to race through a meal or to carry out a business proposition. While tourists might enjoy a slowed pace during a holiday, they bristle at the thought of a people who are not intent on embracing "progress" and becoming more "developed"—that is, becoming the way those in the United States pride themselves on being.

Thus, tourists come to expect friendly service when they travel to Latin America and the Caribbean, but if the hospitality falls short in their estimation, they may suggest that a venue is not up to the expected standards of accommodating tourists' needs. In Cuba, for example, while service is generally friendly, I have seen tourists complain that the socialist-oriented economy has not taught workers to be efficient and to aim to please. Of course, now that all are waiting for the floodgates to open for U.S. travel to Cuba, we may find that there will soon be a nostalgia for the days before mass tourism made a trip to the island nation indistinguishable from travel elsewhere in the region. In the Caribbean generally, tourism scholars have discussed what is "behind the smile" that is expected of all service providers. While tourists may believe that a genuine desire to satisfy the needs of their visitors is behind the smile, the story is always more complex. Clearly, the economic motivation to hold on to needed employment is a strong force in presenting a friendly tone at tourist venues, yet interviews with workers reveal greater ambivalence about the nature of the work required and the behaviors of some tourists whose expectations about local service providers may rest on stereotyped ideas about them.

The Antiguan-born writer Jamaica Kincaid, in her extended essay titled *A Small Place,* dissects the tourism encounter from the vantage point of a local observer. She is most trenchant in her view of the ignorant traveler who sees only lush environment and joyful people rather than inadequate resources, dependence on foreign food sources, insufficient schools and hospitals. Her words rebuke the traveler who would naively think that Antiguans simply enjoy serving or that they do not at times mock the pale white bodies that become bright pink in the tropical sun, and the strange manners of these individuals. If there is resentment, it is because the visitor has all the power in the relationship, brief though it may be, and the local host generally anticipates no such opportunity to see the world as a leisure traveler. *A Small Place* is not easy reading for anyone who has traveled to the Caribbean, but it may be better than any tour guide as preparation for your next trip there.

On the flip side of that poetic and acerbic narrative of the local experience of tourism, we may look for tourists' accounts of their experience and what they take away from visits to Latin America. Travel writing is abundant and ranges from eloquent and passionate accounts one may find in bookstores to bloggers' candid assessments of places visited. Ethnographers like me have gathered stories from travelers that often reveal embedded notions of the differences between travelers' homes and the places visited. It is not uncommon to hear positive reviews from travelers who were glad to leave behind their own commodified cultures of advanced capitalism; their experiences with travel may be idealized accounts of places they believe to be free of such unfettered avarice. If they were to read the words of Jamaica Kincaid, would they come to other conclusions? Addressing her imagined tourist reader, she writes, "Do you know why people like me are shy about being capitalists? Well, it's because we, for as long as we have known you, *were* capital, like bales of cotton and sacks of sugar, and you were the commanding, cruel capitalists, and the memory of this is so strong, the experience so recent, that we can't quite bring ourselves to embrace this idea that you think so much of." This indictment of colonialism and its legacy of durable inequalities under capitalism underlie Kincaid's searing critique of those who would charge that the small Caribbean nation lacks ambition or a desire for development.

It bears mentioning here that even given the persistent economic inequalities in Latin America and the Caribbean and the precariousness of many lives there, we should not overlook the very notable development under way in a number of nations. Mexico and Peru, for example, have shown dramatic growth in recent years, and Brazil is among the nations identified by the acronym BRIC (Brazil, Russia, India, and China), considered to be major players in the reconfigured global economy.

"Sensual pleasure is on prominent display in Latin America"

If tourists judge Latin America wanting in ambition or entrepreneurial spirit, they often find the region to have an excess of sensuality and seduction. This has not escaped the attention of tourism scholars, whose book titles so frequently invoke this quality, even if ironically: *Negotiating Paradise, Peddling Paradise, Pleasure Island, Caribbean Pleasure Industry,* and *Take Me to My Paradise* are a few of these titles.[1] Certainly the Caribbean has received a great deal of such attention, though Brazil and parts of Central America have also captured a share of both the scholarly and popular imagination. Why would this be? Surely tropical climate and rich natural environment are a part of it, along with an understandably languid pace as the blazing sun beats down. But recent decades have also brought sex tourism to the region, as travelers have made their way to destinations where commercialized sex has become a means of livelihood for many who lack alternatives or find them so poorly paid that they cannot support the needs of their families.

Prerevolutionary Havana was known as a playground for the U.S. military and the Mafia, with gambling and prostitution aplenty. Largely eliminated by the revolutionary government after 1959, sex work returned in the 1990s when Cuba's economy plummeted and the nation's people looked to black market activity (*jineterismo*) of one kind and another. In Nicaragua and Cuba during the last couple of decades many women and some men have been selling sexual favors to both nationals and tourists, some of whom come explicitly for the opportunity to find sex and sometimes romance on the market. Both short- and longer-term relationships have formed between tourists and locals in this way, and whether money or other gifts are offered, there is often the appearance if not the reality of affection between the parties. In diverse ways we see intimate alliances throughout the Caribbean and Latin America, many involving male tourists and female locals, others involving gay male tourists and local men who at least *perform* as gay sex workers, and still other cases in which women tourists come for amorous adventures with men, offering them cash or other gifts and entertainment they could not otherwise afford.

While Latin American nations have made efforts to curtail sex tourism, especially when it involves minors, they have sometimes also turned a blind eye to the practice, which does after all bring revenues. For the tourists themselves, there is at least short-term gratification and the sense that the region offers more open-minded acceptance of sexual indulgence. Or, in the case of

FIGURE 14.4. Tourists in Lima, Peru. Photo by Florence E. Babb.

longer-term relationships, after the holiday there may be repeat visits to reconnect as well as remittances of funds to help support the local paramour. In rare cases, local women or men may be granted visas to leave their countries and marry their tourist-suitors. The power dynamic underlying such arrangements can produce distinctly unequal terms in the relationship, and the tourist may embrace the notion that he or she is "rescuing" the vulnerable local individual from desperate life circumstances. This then becomes part of the tourism narrative as much as it is part of the romance narrative for those involved.

Researchers debate whether local sex workers *should* be viewed as vulnerable victims of tourism's commodification of culture and identity. Some argue that there is little consent when economic conditions influence Latin Americans to market their bodies and sexual services; when racial difference enters the picture, there may be the added weight of race as well as gender inequality to consider. This view is countered by others, who place more importance on the right of sex workers to earn a livelihood however they choose and on their degree of autonomy in establishing both economically driven and amorous relationships. There is much agreement, however, that tourists and their partners frequently come together with very different stakes and that power differences define the terms of these intimate relations.

If you go. . .

In January 2015, the *New York Times* Travel Section issued its "52 Places to Go in 2015" (New York Times 2015). In the lineup, the Latin American and Caribbean region was well represented, with nine sites offered. The listing of recommended destinations and the banners eagerly describing why to go there were revealing:

#2 Cuba—As relations warm, a Caribbean island is within reach.

#5 Elqui Valley, Chile—Stargaze, while you can, in northern Chile.

#8 Bolivia—Finally stable and opening up to the world.

#11 Medellín, Colombia—Urban renewal with innovative architecture and design.

#12 St. Vincent and the Grenadines—A new airport and dive center await.

#18 The North Coast of Peru—A desert coast begs to be explored.

#27 Campeche, Mexico—A less-touristed ancient Maya city.

#34 St. Kitts—Upscale in the Caribbean, but sustainable.

#37 San José del Cabo, Mexico—The mellower Cabo bounces back in style.

This sampling suggests that Latin America may have something for everyone, whether history buffs, laid-back leisure tourists, nature lovers, or those seeking to be the first to get to places recently off-limits to tourism. Places are branded as the new and the different, the just-restored, the off-the-beaten-track, or the environmentally conscious, and travelers find their niche among an increasingly wide array of offerings.

In this chapter I have emphasized ways in which some preconceived wisdom about Latin America has shaped many tourists' experiences and the stories they bring home with them. I have given examples of the pitfalls of binary thinking about us and them, traditional and modern, and how this can result in the tourism narratives that are so often repeated. Frequently, the memories brought home serve to perpetuate stereotypes and reinforce notions of indelible difference. But we can change the script, and indeed there are diverse travelers who enjoy and benefit from a wealth of new travel experiences and return from their journeys the wiser for it. At its best, travel to Latin America leads to the global circulation of ideas and understandings and a new awareness of just what has separated us and what brings us together across the Americas. What tourists believe at the outset is "unique" about Latin America may be challenged when they delve deeply into the region; when this occurs, travelers are likely to be rewarded by discovering far more than they would ever have imagined.

REFERENCES AND SUGGESTED READING

Babb, Florence E.
    2011 *The Tourism Encounter: Fashioning Latin American Nations and Histories.* Stanford, CA: Stanford University Press.
Berger, Dina, and Andrew Grant Wood
    2010 *Holiday in Mexico: Critical Reflections on Tourism and Tourist Encounters.* Durham, NC: Duke University Press.
Bowman, Kirk S.
    2013 *Peddling Paradise: The Politics of Tourism in Latin America.* Boulder, CO: Lynne Rienner.
Cocks, Catherine
    2013 *Tropical Whites: The Rise of the Tourist South in the Americas.* Philadelphia: University of Pennsylvania Press.
Cohen, Colleen Ballerino
    2010 *Take Me to My Paradise: Tourism and Nationalism in the British Virgin Islands.* New Brunswick: Rutgers University Press.
Kincaid, Jamaica
    1988 *A Small Place.* New York: Farrar, Straus and Giroux.
Little, Walter E.
    2004 *Mayas in the Marketplace: Tourism, Globalization, and Cultural Identity.* Austin: University of Texas Press.
Merrill, Dennis
    2009 *Negotiating Paradise: U.S. Tourism and Empire in Twentieth-Century Latin America.* Chapel Hill: University of North Carolina Press.
New York Times
    2015 "52 Places to Go in 2015." *New York Times,* January 11.
Padilla, Mark
    2007 *Caribbean Pleasure Industry: Tourism, Sexuality, and AIDS in the Dominican Republic.* Chicago: University of Chicago Press.
Schwartz, Rosalie
    1997 *Pleasure Island: Tourism and Temptation in Cuba.* Lincoln: University of Nebraska Press.

NOTE

1. Dennis Merrill, *Negotiating Paradise;* Kirk S. Bowman, *Peddling Paradise;* Rosalie Schartz, *Pleasure Island;* Mark Padilla, *Caribbean Pleasure Industry;* and Colleen Ballerino Cohen, *Take Me to My Paradise.*

FIFTEEN

Brazil Circles the Globe

Ruben George Oliven

AROUND THE WORLD IN FIVE CENTURIES

Portuguese and Spanish exploration at the end of the fifteenth century led to the building of the world's two largest empires. While the contemporary word *globalization* might not be appropriate for that historical moment, early European expansion produced an undeniably global economy of people, goods, and culture. Europeans bought slaves in Africa, took them to the Americas, and brought minerals and agricultural commodities back to Europe in a cycle that revolved through and around the Atlantic. Brazil possessed precious stones and gold and produced sugar and other agricultural commodities that circled throughout the world system, often returning to Brazil in a changed form. For the past five hundred years Brazil's economy, population, racial composition, and culture have been constantly interacting with the rest of the globe.

From a region sparsely populated by natives, Brazil has become home to vast contingents of people from different continents and a central player in global Latin America. In 1500, the Portuguese arrived in a land with between four million and five million natives. Contact with Europeans meant the near-extermination of this population to a point that in the 1950s several anthropologists feared it would disappear. This trend has changed, gradually, and indigenous populations are growing as they regain their traditional lands. Since it was colonized, Brazil was shaped by the contribution of people of different origins who had arrived from around the globe. Slaves were brought from Africa. Immigrants came from Europe and Asia and included, among others, Portuguese, Spaniards, Germans, Italians, Ukrainians, Lebanese, European and Middle Eastern Jews, and Japanese. Today many

FIGURE 15.1. Positivist temple in Porto Alegre, Brazil. Source: Wikimedia Commons. This file is licensed under the Creative Commons Attribution 2.0 Generic license. https://commons.wikimedia.org/wiki/File.Templo_positivista.jpg.

Brazilians of immigrant descent live outside of the country: in Europe, North America, and Asia.

The circulation of ideas to and from Brazil became especially important following two major political moments: the country's independence from Portugal in 1822 (when Brazil declared itself an empire) and the military's proclamation of the republic in 1889. The republican leaders were strongly influenced by positivism, developed by the nineteenth-century philosopher Auguste Comte. Though developed in France, positivism found its greatest success in Brazil, where it became an almost official ideology until 1930. The Brazilian flag has as its motto the phrase "Order and Progress," demonstrating the centrality of Comte's beliefs in the country's symbolism. Even today Brazil is filled with positivist architecture and temples in cities like Rio de Janeiro and Porto Alegre.

Positivism was conceived in evolutionary and linear stages that conformed to the philosophy's emphasis, according to Comte's formula, "love as a principle, order as a foundation, and progress as a goal." He believed that positivism was the way of achieving the republican ideals of better social conditions and the advancement of the nation. From the point of view of Brazil's elites, positivism was an ideology that foreshadowed modernity and justified authoritarian means of attaining it. The positivist soldier Field Marshal Cândido Rondon, for example, dedicated his life to the indigenous cause and urged that indigenous peoples be respected and not eliminated, even though eventually they needed, in his view, to be integrated into what he defined as "civilization." Positivism thus became a way for Brazil to modernize itself in relation to Europe and for Indians to "civilize" themselves in relation to Brazil. Rondon had a deep impact on global ideas about nature and indigenous people, especially after Theodore Roosevelt joined him in the exploration of the Amazon region of the "River of Doubt" in 1913 and 1914. Indeed, Roosevelt frequently circulated Rondon's ideas in speeches before such internationally important organizations as the National Geographic Society in Washington, DC, and the Royal Geographical Society in London.

Another important nineteenth-century French belief that circulated to and from Brazil was spiritism, which presents itself at once as a science, a philosophy, and a religion. According to its founder, Allan Kardec, spiritism was based on the relationship between the material world and the invisible world, the latter being inhabited by spirits. Like positivism, spiritism has an evolutionary approach where spirits progress and travel to higher spheres, and it too was more influential in Brazil than in France. Spiritist centers can be found in most Brazilian cities, and several have hospitals founded by physicians committed to the ideology. Indeed, many middle-class intellectuals and politicians are spiritists. Yet spiritism did not have a one-way trajectory. Rather, Brazilians have migrated to France to open centers as the doctrine traveled from Europe to Latin America and then back to the Old Continent.

Spiritual and social evolution, modernity and progress, these have all been concerns of Brazilian intellectuals as they have moved around the world and asked a series of questions: Can Brazil become a modern and developed country? Can civilization be built in the tropics? Are the Brazilian people ready for the country's challenges? Should Brazil develop its own culture or try to emulate that of more advanced nations? These queries have always been present in Brazilian intellectual life since all deal with the role of elites and politicians, the relation between popular and erudite culture, and the place of Africa, Asia, the Middle East, and Europe in Brazil.

Contemplating Brazil and discussing the viability of a civilization in the tropics originated when Brazil became a republic in 1889. At this crucial moment, intellectuals perceived two obstacles to their civilizing project—

race and climate. Many in the educated elite were profoundly pessimistic and prejudiced, believing the Brazilian population (because of the interaction of race and the geographic environment) was apathetic and indolent. The country's intellectual life was seen as infected with a subjective and morbid lyricism and as philosophically and scientifically impoverished.

By the 1920s this pessimism diminished as members of the elite started to appropriate cultural expressions originally restricted to certain groups and to transform them into symbols of national identity. For example, Umbanda, a Brazilian popular religion that synthesizes African, Catholic, and spiritist influences, was created in Rio de Janeiro at the beginning of the last century. While many Afro-Brazilian religions were repressed by the police and frequently had to disguise their *orixás* (a manifestation of divine spirit) as Catholic saints, they were gradually appropriated by Europeanized middle-class intellectuals. Today Afro-Brazilian religions are part of what is considered Brazilian culture, both in Brazil and abroad. Indeed, many U.S. African Americans have come to see Brazil as a kind of ethnic/spiritual home, with much of the focus on the city of Cachoeira (in the state of Bahia) and its annual festival Nossa Senhora da Boa Morte, or Our Lady of the Good Death. This is an example of how middle-class people gradually appropriated a syncretic cultural expression that originated among slaves and their descendants and then helped it travel around the globe. This process also happened historically, for example, when U.S. Confederates moved to Brazil after the Civil War to redeem their "Lost Cause" in a country that would not abolish slavery until 1888, becoming the last nation in the hemisphere to do so. More recently, the Brazilian musical genre samba, developed mainly by descendants of slaves, has become a world music phenomenon.

The symbols of Brazilian national culture also traveled in opposite ways. Carnival and soccer, for example, originated in Europe and were first adopted by the Brazilian upper classes and then gradually became popular activities and symbols of national identity. When Brazilians debate their national identity they often claim that Brazil manages to digest what comes from abroad and adapt it to its reality. One of the most important documents of Brazilian modernism, Oswald de Andrade's 1928 *Cannibalist Manifesto*, outlined precisely this vision of national distinctiveness. Andrade claimed the manifesto had been composed in the "Year of 374 of the Devouring of Bishop Sardinha," a reference to the Catholic cleric Pero Fernandes Sardinha who was shipwrecked off the coast of Brazil and eaten by the Indians in 1554.

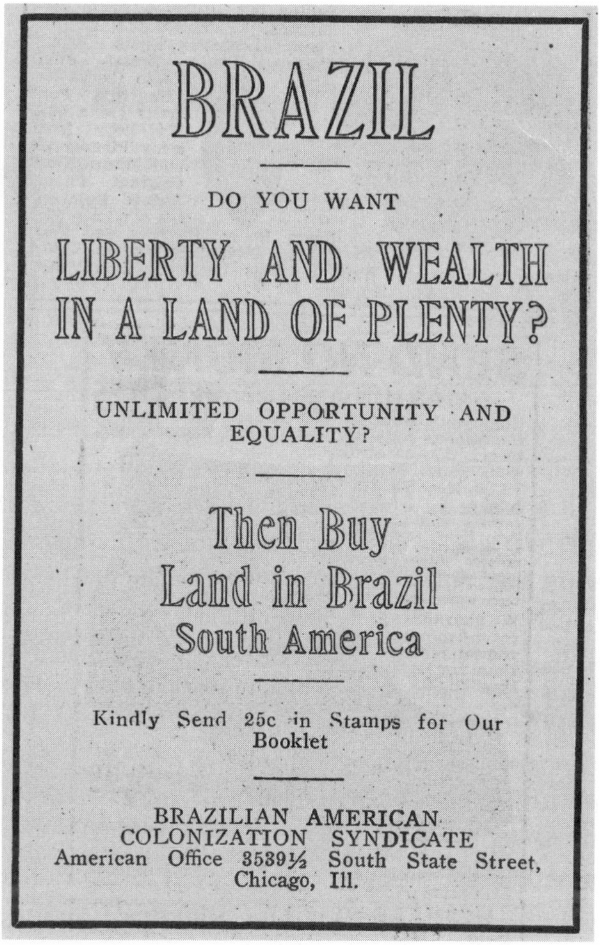

FIGURE 15.2. Brazilian American Colonization Society advertisement published in *Crisis* (March 1921). Courtesy of the Carter Woodson Papers, Manuscript, Archives, and Rare Books Library, Emory University.

REFLECTIONS ON RACE

Many Brazilians believe that certain ideas and cultural practices appropriated from abroad are "out of place," particularly in regard to political philosophies. For instance, although the Brazilian economy was based on the widespread exploitation of slave labor for three centuries, part of the imperial political elite for most of the nineteenth century adhered to the liberal ideas created in and applied to Europe. The Brazilian intellectual Roberto

Schwarz has argued that this liberal ideology was "out of place" in Brazil: what prevailed in the country was not the idea of human rights but rather the oppression of slaves and paternalistic favor toward whites who did not own land.

The concept "ideas out of place" makes less sense when we remember that Brazilian ideas moved around the globe as much as foreign ideas moved to Brazil. In other words, nothing is ever "in place" since everything leaves one place and enters another as it is adapted to the interests of different groups and changing circumstances. Cultural borrowing is a constant, and, as historians and anthropologists have shown, cultural dynamics imply a process whereby ideas and practices that originate in one space end up migrating to others. One of the creative aspects of Brazil has been precisely the capacity to appropriate what comes from outside, reelaborate it, and give it Brazilian characteristics, transforming it into something different and new. Perhaps more than any other societal feature, Brazil's "way" of race relations has made its way around the globe, influencing ideas about race and Brazilians.

Brazil imported approximately four million slaves, ten times as many as the United States. In the United States slavery was concentrated in the South, while in Brazil it was nationwide. Following Puerto Rico and Cuba, Brazil finally abolished slavery in 1888, largely in response to pressure from Britain. Around the time of Abolition, Brazil imported many nineteenth-century ideas about race from Europe and the United States. Despite its commitment to slavery in the nineteenth century, Brazil became in the twentieth century a model for supposedly positive race relations, especially in the Americas where African slavery had been the norm. The famed African American intellectual W. E. B. DuBois criticized U.S. race relations in the first half of the last century and encouraged blacks to migrate to Brazil in his newspaper *Crisis*. After World War II and in the wake of the Holocaust, Brazil drew the attention of the United Nations Educational, Scientific, and Cultural Organization (UNESCO), which commissioned a study of Brazilian race relations. Some UNESCO administrators and others throughout the world saw Brazil as a racial democracy, and this image has continued into the twenty-first century, causing particular controversy in 2001 when the Spike Lee–directed PBS film, *A Huey P. Newton Story,* was shown in Brazil. Some Afro-Brazilian activists were shocked to discover that Newton, a leader of the Black Panthers, believed Brazil was a racial paradise.

Another aspect of Brazilian race relations that has made a global impact is miscegenation. Since the sixteenth century the Portuguese court had encouraged the mostly single male colonists to mix with native and African women. Over centuries, such relationships produced a mixed population and a society with fewer qualms about interracial intercourse than the other dominant slave society of the Americas, the United States. As eugenics came to the fore in the late nineteenth century, Europeans and North Americans led the way in criticizing racial mixture and codifying racial hierarchies. Some Brazilian intellectuals responded to these ideas by attempting to "whiten" the national population through immigration from Europe. Yet at the height of scientific racism in the 1930s, the sociologist Gilberto Freyre proposed a new racial vision that promoted Brazil as a tropical civilization with unique characteristics, such as *mestiçagem* (racial mixture) and "racial democracy." Freyre was strongly influenced by Franz Boas, the founding father of American anthropology, under whom he did his graduate studies at Columbia University. Boas helped to debunk the then-prevailing importance of race as an explanation for differences between societies. Instead, he emphasized culture as the main explanatory factor.

In Freyre's vision, Brazil's racial mixture was not a problem to be "whitened" but an advantage in relation to other nations. He praised the wisdom of the Portuguese, who had built what he called a "tropical civilization" in Brazil. Freyre argued that racial mixture was perfectly adapted to Brazil's environment, making it difficult to define race in the binary way (white/black) that it was in the United States. Freyre thus became the founder of what is known as "the myth of Brazilian racial democracy," which became an official ideology of the country for decades. This mid-twentieth-century ideology permeates not only aspects of sociological thinking but also Brazilian popular thought. Indeed, numerous important North American and European social scientists argued that Brazilian racial democracy should be exported to the rest of the world, although today "racial democracy" is seen as a myth, not a reality.

BRAZIL: COUNTRY OF THE PRESENT?

"Giant by its very nature," as Brazil's national anthem declares, or "country of continental dimensions," as a frequent expression states, Brazil sees itself and is seen by others as undeniably *grande*—vast, impressive, and important. In terms of size, Brazil is the fifth largest country in the world, being surpassed only by Russia, Canada, China, and the United States. It is the largest country in the southern hemisphere and the second largest contiguous country in the Americas. With over 200 million inhabitants, it is also the fifth most populated country in the world, surpassed by China, India, United States, and Indonesia. In terms of GDP, Brazil ranks seventh after the United States, China, Japan, Germany, France, and the United Kingdom. Nevertheless, if we look at income distribution, in 2012 Brazil was ranked 81st, a much worse result.

Globalization has strongly diversified Brazil's interaction with the rest of the world, in economic exchanges, international relations, and cultural expressions such as religion, music, cinema, television, and sports. For centuries, the country was an exporter of agricultural products, mainly sugar and coffee, and an importer of all sorts of manufactured goods. Agricultural export commodities are still a very important economic activity, responsible for 23 percent of Brazil's GDP. China, for instance, has become a major importer of Brazilian goods like soybeans. But Brazil is no longer a rural society, and industry and services are now key sectors of its economy. The country has become a major industrial exporter of sophisticated manufactured goods. Many Brazilian companies have become international, competing on the world market by selling airplanes abroad, producing steel in different countries, growing oranges in the United States for juice, and exploring for and selling oil via Petrobrás, the Brazilian state-run oil company and one of the largest in the world. Of course, exchanges between different countries are unequal and depend on their positions in the global political-economic system, but Brazil has entered a new level of global influence and interaction.

Things are also changing in terms of demography. Brazil has become an urban society, with approximately 85 percent of its inhabitants living in cities. Its age pyramid has changed dramatically. Some decades ago the country's population was predominantly young, with 50 percent of inhabitants under the age of eighteen. With urbanization and birth control, population growth has decreased dramatically and life expectancy is increasing rapidly. In the future, the aging of the Brazilian population will pose a challenge for newer generations who will have to support the older ones.

Migrations flows have shifted, sometimes reversing. If historically Brazil received a vast number of immigrants from abroad, Brazilians are increasingly emigrating, with currently more than three million living elsewhere in search of better economic conditions. Brazilian migrants go mainly to the United States, Europe, and Japan, reversing the historical directions of international migration. But as Brazil becomes a major economic power, it is also receiving newcomers, often from poorer countries like Haiti, Bolivia, Senegal, and Ghana, among others.

Emigrants carry their culture with them. Brazilians thus not only preserve what they believe is typically Brazilian, but they also tend to develop and market "Brazilian culture" for the rest of the population. This can be seen in Brazilian restaurants and musical shows around the world and in huge Carnival parades in places like London and San Francisco. In many North American and European cities capoeira, initially created by Brazilian slaves as a dance, has become very popular and is taught by Brazilian masters. Indeed capoeira and "Brazilian jujitsu" have become widespread in the United States and are today hipster hobbies in the United States, Europe, and Japan.

In the past Brazil was often seen as constantly adopting ideas and modes of expression from the northern hemisphere and of course continues to receive outside influences in the sphere of cinema and music. Among these are television and musical products manufactured by multinational corporations and Hollywood cinema with its position of world hegemony. Yet for some time Brazil has also been an exporter of cultural and spiritual goods. For example, Brazilian music has had a global presence since the 1920s and 1930s when samba singers toured France and when Carmen Miranda was Hollywood's best-paid female singer and actress. Bossa nova, which interacted strongly with American music, was from its outset in the 1960s a music genre that had worldwide fans. Yet when Brazil started to produce its own rock and roll in the 1970s many critics attacked it as not being "Brazilian music." Today, however, there are Brazilian rock bands that compose songs in English and are successful in the United States and Europe. When the members of the Brazilian metal band Sepultura went to a Xavante indigenous village in Mato Grosso in search of their cultural origins, the resulting disc *Roots* became one of the biggest-selling albums in Europe in just fifteen days, surpassing Michael Jackson and Madonna in Britain, and selling more than 500,000 copies in only two months. On the one hand, the "roots" were native to Brazil, but on the other, English was the lingua franca used in order to compete in a globalized market.

Defining Brazilian cultural expressions has become much more complicated than it used to be. During the populist phase of Brazil's history (1945–64), what came from outside was often seen as foreign and therefore impure and dangerous. Thus, Coca-Cola and Hollywood films were usually cited as examples of North American cultural imperialism, while samba and Cinema Novo (New Cinema), of which the films directed by Glauber Rocha are the best known, were regarded as authentically national. Yet Cinema Novo, even while its topics were focused on Brazil, was internationally known, and the genre's films were exported far and wide and won prizes abroad.

Today the situation is more complex: the Coca-Cola logo can be found on the jerseys of Brazilian soccer teams, and the English rock star Sting, sponsored by the same soft-drink corporation, professes to defend the natives of Brazil. The film *A grande arte,* in spite of being directed by a Brazilian and filmed in Brazil, has English dialogue. Other films star television actors and compete for Oscars, their producers hiring professional lobbyists to help them win awards. Today, most Brazilian films are produced with an eye toward the international market.

Films like *Cidade de Deus* (City of God) and *Tropa de Elite* (Elite Squad) have made it internationally. They show an image of Brazil that is at the same time violent and romantic, mixing the poverty of the favelas with the beauty of Rio de Janeiro as seen from its hills. On the other side of the equator Brazilian actors like Sônia Braga and Rodrigo Santoro are incorporated into Hollywood films and have become "Latino" outside Brazil.

Although it started its life with a polemical agreement with Time-Life, Inc., Globo, Brazil's largest television network, has for some time been producing the majority of the programs it shows. It also exports its soap operas and series to countries like Portugal, France, and China, helping to make it a mass-media multinational. When Globo exports soap operas it is not only selling a commodity, but a way of life, dealing with images of the body and of sexuality. If in the past foreign travelers who came to Brazil imagined that there was no sin beneath the equator, modern Brazil has increasingly branded itself in the global arena as a country with breathtaking nature, carnival, music, beaches, beautiful bodies scantily dressed, and relaxed ways of behaving with regard to everything from sexuality to sports. In this sense the country is marketing itself as having a national identity that can be exported worldwide. Brazilian commodities and cultural products are usually associated with a "Brazilian way of life."

Religion is another area in which the transnationalization of Brazilian symbolic goods has occurred in a remarkable way. Brazil has always been a country of deeply rooted religiosity, traditionally Catholic, albeit with very particular and popular forms of that religion. Although Brazil still is the largest Catholic country in the world, the panorama is quickly changing with the growth of Afro-Brazilian religions and pentecostalism. What is most impressive is the migration of Afro-Brazilian religions into Uruguay and

Argentina, countries that generally see themselves as "European," secular, and with little African influence.

Pentecostalism has grown at an impressive speed and is now the second-largest religion in Brazil. It is not only a religious enterprise but also a political and economic one. Many pastors have been elected to Congress, where they form a group that votes together whenever a religious issue is at stake (abortion, religious education, etc.). The Universal Church of the Kingdom of God, established in Brazil in 1977, has churches in 116 other countries, including in North America and the European Union, mobilizing millions of faithful followers and large sums of money. Its founder is the owner of Rede Record, Brazil's second-largest television network.

Although Brazil did not create soccer, it has managed to establish itself as a country well known for the practice of that sport, winning the World Cup five times. Brazil is supposed to have a special style of playing soccer, famous for its improvisation and almost choreographic performances. For years Brazil has been an exporter of soccer players who play mainly for European teams. Brazil hosted the soccer World Cup in 2014 and will host the Summer Olympics in Rio de Janeiro in 2016. Having these two major international sports events in Brazil means tens of thousands of visitors and provides evidence that Brazil is capable of organizing mega events that entail international tourism, an area where Brazil often falls short.

In foreign relations Brazil has been involved in the United Nations mission in Haiti, in training Namibia's navy, and in other activities like the conflict over Iranian nuclear arms. Recently, a Brazilian diplomat was elected chair of the World Trade Organization, a forum in which Brazil has been acting to ensure that there is fair competition as regards its exports. For years, Brazil has been trying to obtain a permanent seat at the United Nations Security Council in an effort to establish itself as a diplomatic actor that is recognized according to its economic and political importance.

NEW MIDDLES

In order to be a global player, Brazil still has to face many challenges, including the issue of social justice. Historically, Brazil has lagged behind most countries in terms of income distribution. In 1989, its Gini index—which measures a country's degree of inequality in terms of income (ranging from 0 to 1, with 1 indicating high inequality)—was one of the world's highest at

0.634. According to the World Bank, that year the 20 percent of richest Brazilians concentrated 67.5 percent of all income, whereas the 20 percent of Brazil's poorest had only 2.1 percent. For a long while, the monthly minimum wage in Brazil remained below US$100, directing the economy toward a relatively small and wealthy consumer base.

In 1994, the federal government launched the Real Plan, which introduced a new currency and succeeded in curbing inflation, eliminating one of the most negative impacts on the popular classes. In January 2003, the Partido dos Trabalhadores (PT), or Workers' Party, acceded to the Brazilian presidency, where it should remain until (at least) 2018. The new administration benefited from the previously achieved economic stability and a favorable international scenario. One of the new government's actions was to distribute income by effectively raising the minimum wage, which in December 2015 was around US$200 per month.

Another initiative was a series of social programs based on conditional cash transfers. Among them is Bolsa Família, a financial aid program that encourages poor families to keep their children in school and awards financial bonuses to low-income people. This action led to a fast and steep decline in Brazil's income inequality; the country's Gini coefficient fell to 0.566 in 2005, and this had a powerful impact on the economy. All of a sudden a large portion of the so-called Class D (which the Brazilian government classifies as families with a monthly income between 768 and 1,065 reais [or about US$220 to 305 at an exchange rate of BR$3.5 to US$1]) migrated to Class C (comprising families with a monthly income between 1,065 and 4,591 reais [US$305 to $1,311]). It is estimated that, within six years, twenty million Brazilians migrated from Class D to Class C. A study based on data from the Brazilian Institute of Geography and Statistics showed that in 2008, for the first time in history, the total income of the 91 million people in Class C was greater than the sum total of Classes A and B (i.e., those with income above 4,591 reais [US$1,311]). Nowadays, Class C households account for 46 percent of the total national income, versus 44 percent of Classes A and B, which have traditionally prevailed in the Brazilian economy.

This substantial movement of people from Class D to Class C had a ripple effect, causing consumption to increase significantly. While the popular classes have always been consumers, chiefly of basic food products, clothes, and other essential items, now they began purchasing goods not traditionally purchased by the poor, such as new refrigerators, stoves, television sets, and so forth. This growth in popular consumption is reflected in many sectors, chiefly in durable goods (appliances, electronics, and furniture), which has grown twice as fast as the overall market at 30 percent per year since 2005. The new members of Class C are copiously buying furniture and appliances, suggesting that a considerable sector of the population now has access to goods that were previously restricted to the middle class. The government predicts that in the future Brazil will be mainly a middle-class country.

PATHS OF INCLUSION

Traditionally social scientists and the population in general believed that Brazilian nonwhites were worse off because they were part of the poorer sectors of the population. Recent data and interpretations show that in fact they are doubly discriminated against: for being poor and for being black. If for a long time Brazil saw itself and was seen as a *mestiço* nation where racial democracy prevailed, today there is a growing awareness that this is not so. In fact, many people now speak about what is called "cordial racism," which begins with the cultural difficulty of acknowledging that Brazil has prejudice, discrimination, and racial inequality. This is clear in official statistics that show that blacks are worse off on any social indicator, including education, income, literacy, infantile mortality, and life expectancy.

Social movements have gradually led Brazilian official institutions to implement inclusion policies. This often happens through affirmative action policies, mainly at public institutions, with regard to recruitment for civil service jobs and vacancies in public universities. One of the places where a newer and much more diverse population has seen dramatic growth is in college education. As the Brazilian middle class grows, more parents want their children to go to college, which they see as a road to upward social mobility. Such access, however, continues to be difficult. Private universities charge fees that are hard to fit into poorer families' budgets. The best research universities are the free public ones usually operated by the federal government, but the only way to enter is via a very competitive entrance exam called *vestibular,* which includes mathematics, physics, chemistry, biology, literature, history, composition, and foreign languages. Since public schools in Brazil often have low levels of graduation proficiency, students from richer families who can afford private schools have better chances of succeeding on this exam. Wealthier students also take special, yearlong private test-prep courses.

Traditionally the *vestibular* was seen as a universal and transparent way of selecting university students, based on merit and without patronage. Yet the result was that poorer students had to pay for private universities and that very few people of African descent entered public universities. In practice the white middle and upper classes were able to appropriate federal tax money in order to study for free at the best universities. Public universities thus became another among numerous places largely reserved for the Brazilian white elite.

At the beginning of this century, several public universities began affirmative action programs that benefit public school students and those who declare themselves of African descent. This move elicited strong reactions in favor and against such policies. Those opposed argued that this model was copied from the United States even though affirmative action policies were in fact challenged (and quotas were dismantled) by the North American courts. Opponents also argued that in Brazil it was not possible to define who was white and who was not and that by adopting affirmative action policies the country was introducing race and racism where it did not exist before. They further claimed that selection would no longer be based on merit but on color and social class and that students selected through affirmative action would lower the standard of teaching and learning. Brazilian social scientists were divided, writing manifestos in favor of and against affirmative action in public universities. Ultimately Congress approved a law reserving 50 percent of all federal university places for students coming from public schools and half of those for students who declare themselves as being of African descent. The law was contested in the Supreme Court, but the justices decided unanimously that the policies were constitutional.

THE GOOD, THE BAD, AND THE URGENT

Things are gradually changing in Brazil. In recent years important social justice policies were implemented and had an enormous impact on the country. Brazil is finally acknowledging the racial question and taking steps toward reducing the color gap. There are of course many challenges ahead. Public education, public health, and crucial economic sectors, particularly infrastructure, are in need of great investment.

The mass protests that swept Brazil in June 2013 show that the population decided to take to the streets to voice their demands. The protests initially arose as a movement against bus fare increases but rapidly evolved into demand for better health, better education, and an end to corruption. The movement suggests that a portion of the population represented by young people—members of a group with access to more consumer goods than their parents had—now want something more. These young people do not trust the formal organizations of a representative democracy: government, political parties, and mainstream media. There is of course a link between those protests and the Occupy movement and Arab Spring that had occurred in other countries, and like them, the Brazilian protests became inspirational in other parts of the world. With the instant communication provided by social media there is a reciprocal influence of what is happening in different places of the globe.

Brazil has become highly diversified, with the increasing emergence of fresh social players who build new identities and demand recognition and specific rights. As Brazil becomes less unequal and more educated, myriad young people are making claims and voicing their demands. If Brazil is to become even more global, its leaders and citizens have to make it widely inclusive, not a nation where global ideas of rights or employment are only for those in the dominant classes.

REFERENCES AND SUGGESTED READING

Fry, Peter
  2000 "Politics, Nationality, and the Meanings of 'Race' in Brazil." *Daedalus* 129.2: 83–118.
Lesser, Jeffrey
  1999 *Negotiating National Identity: Immigrants, Minorities, and the Struggle for Ethnicity in Brazil.* Durham, NC: Duke University Press.
Oliven, Ruben George, and Rosana Pinheiro-Machado
  2012 "From 'Country of the Future' to Emergent Country: Popular Consumption in Brazil." In *Consumer Culture in Latin America,* ed. John Sinclair and Anna Cristina Pertierra, 53–65. London: Palgrave Macmillan.
Schwarcz, Lilia Moritz
  1999 *The Spectacle of the Races: Scientists, Institutions and the Race Question in Brazil, 1870–1930.* New York: Hill and Wang.
Schwarz, Roberto
  1977 *Ao vencedor as batatas.* São Paulo: Duas Cidades.

PART FIVE

Art Moves the World

INTRODUCTION

DONNED BY THE PORTUGUESE BRAZILIAN performer Carmen Miranda from the 1930s to the 1950s, the tutti-frutti hat symbolized the supposedly exotic, beautiful, and quaint lands of Latin America. Miranda may well have been the first "Latin American" performer to move audiences on big screens and Broadway stages in the United States, but the tutti-frutti hat fails today more than ever to capture the freshness of creative production within and about the region. With chapters from two journalists, an anthropologist, and a cultural critic, "Art Moves the World" lifts up narratives of what may well be a new export boom for the region. Exploring the different dynamics between globally plugged-in producers and consumers, these chapters showcase artists from Latin America as much more than merely players on a global stage.

From stories of nineteenth-century novels to twenty-first-century *telenovelas,* these chapters offer glimpses into the making of global Latin America through art. The essayist and scholar Ilan Stavans examines how Latin American literature became globally recognized and revered. Despite precedents in the nineteenth and early twentieth century, Stavans locates the move from the local and national to the global in the *boom* generation of the 1960s. Jorge Luis Borges and Gabriel García Márquez—two of the towering luminaries of that era—innovated postmodernist and magical realist forms that have influenced generations of lettered thinkers since. In another chapter, the film megastar Gael García Bernal articulates the ambivalences of being an artist and performer from Latin America on a global stage. Over coffee with the critically acclaimed journalist Alma Guillermoprieto, García Bernal questions why national or regional labels so often accompany—and seem to qualify—the names of artists and performers from the region. Together these chapters reveal how art serves as a vehicle for the negotiation of identities and geographies of belonging in global Latin America.

Traversing and sometimes transgressing borders throughout global Latin America, this part offers stories of what is gained in translation when art upsets the familiar. The anthropologist O. Hugo Benavides shows how *telenovelas* disturb racial, gender, and North-South hierarchies. These soap-style productions have drawn loyal audiences from the Middle East and China to the United Kingdom, Russia, and West Central Africa. Though set in the drama of everyday life, these television shows reflect the geopolitical times a-changing, especially the ascendency of some Latin American countries and the increase in connections between peoples of the Global South. Other narratives reveal performers breaking the rules of artistic canons and identities in one stroke.

The journalist Fabiano Maisonnave narrates the career of Lisa Ono, the Brazilian musician and daughter of Japanese immigrants who owned a night-club in São Paulo. At ten years old, Ono returned with her family to Japan, where her parents opened another venue. Here the young Ono began playing and transforming sounds from her São Paulo youth. Following Ono's fasci-nating trajectory, the chapter ends up teaching us how a supposedly national music staple like "Brazilian" bossa nova can be transformed into a "Japanese" trend in Chinese popular culture.

The subversive capacity of art to upset the normative is never guaranteed, however. The proliferation of images and sounds through the channels of global Latin America can reinforce simplistic and disparaging misconcep-tions. Take perceptions of violence and inequality, for instance. Some coun-tries in Latin America have occupied top spots in indices of both, even though recent development projects and social programs have created new rungs of social mobility for some. Stories of inequality and violence remain prominent in films produced in and about the region, exemplified by Fernando Meirelles's and Kátia Lund's *City of God* (2002).

In 2015, the Netflix crime drama tracing the rise and fall of Pablo Escobar, *Narcos,* had both a transnational reach and a star and director who first achieved international notoriety for stories of violent collisions between police, drug traffickers, and the public in Rio de Janeiro neighborhoods. While these sorts of representations can marshal increased attention to the harsh realities of everyday life in Latin America, their increasing acclaim should also give us pause. The line between dramatization, on one side, and simplification and exploitation, on the other, can be murky despite even the best intentions.

In the second decade of the twenty-first century, many take global connectivity for granted, and some are asking whether ever denser and speedier connections are the panacea once promised. Artists within the circuits of global Latin American are, not surprisingly, weighing in on such questions. One best-selling example is the electric ambivalence about the "reflective age" that animates Canada-based Arcade Fire's album *Reflektor* (2013). The album draws heavily on rhythmic styles and spiritual symbols from the Caribbean, especially Haiti (the native country of one of the band member's parents), and the music video for the song "Afterlife" mashes together scenes from *Black Orpheus* (1959), a film set in Rio de Janeiro's Carnaval and made by the French director Marcel Camus. Whether born in the region or not, artists like Arcade Fire continue to shape global Latin America through the burgeoning marketplace for creative images, words, and sounds that cast global reflections.

SIXTEEN

The Latin American Novel as International Merchandise

Ilan Stavans

Al fin me encuentro
con mi destino sudamericano.

—JORGE LUIS BORGES, "Poema conjetural" (1943)

A SEISMIC CHANGE TOOK PLACE IN Latin American culture in the 1960s: under the banner of a movement known as *El Boom,* grouped under the aesthetics of what came to be known—and often contested—as magical realism (*lo real maravilloso*), the region's literary tradition, obscure and even provincial until then, suddenly went global by means of quick, accomplished translations of steamy, exotic, politically engaged novels.

Led by authors from an assortment of countries, from Colombia's Gabriel García Márquez to Peru's Mario Vargas Llosa, along with Argentina's Julio Cortázar, Mexico's Carlos Fuentes, Brazil's Jorge Amado, and Chile's José Donoso, the effect of this movement was deep and far-reaching. It created a shared continental history and identity, or at least the mirage of one. It placed urgent topics affecting its population, such as military repression, sexual subjugation, and economic hopelessness, in the eyes of the world. And it fostered an atmosphere of cultural transaction that made movies, theater, music, and folklore from the region bankable everywhere. In short, El Boom made Latin America marketable in Europe, Asia, the Middle East, Africa, and the United States, let alone within its own confines, making its people contemporaries for the rest of the world.

To understand this radical transformation, it is crucial to have a picture of Latin American culture before the 1960s. After the rampant wars of independence of the nineteenth century, the lineup of newly autonomous countries, from Argentina to Mexico, sought to define their national selves by stressing indigenous myths. What they understood by "indigenous" was, obviously, open to debate. In Argentina, the country's identity coalesced around gaucho lore, with the men on horseback prominently represented by the literature of Hilario Ascasubi, Benito Lynch, Hilario del Campo, Ricardo Güiraldes, and, especially, José Hernández's epic poem *The Gaucho Martín Fierro* (1872). In the country, then as now, there is a debate on the difference between *gaucho* and *gauchesco* literature. The former is a by-product of the gauchos themselves, rural cowboys with an idiosyncratic viewpoint, whereas the latter is an appropriation by city dwellers of the gaucho style. Hernández's poem, in spite of its national status, is gauchesco in that he was not a gaucho himself, meaning his celebration of the bucolic life of gauchos is derivative, an imitation and not an authentic depiction.

Similarly, in Mexico, national identity was built around the idealized view of the mestizo, as showcased in the works of José Rosas Moreno, Ignacio Manuel Altamirano, and, prominently, José Joaquín Fernández de Lizardi's novel *The Itching Parrot* (1816). The mestizo is a half-breed, part aboriginal and part European. The war of independence pushed along the concept that Mexico's identity was defined by this half-breed, and by the beginning of the twentieth century, José Vasconcelos was able to build the essentialist philosophy—in his book *The Cosmic Race* (1925)—that *mestizaje* would ultimately define not only Mexican civilization, but the entire world population.

These efforts were, for the most part, local. What was manufactured at home stayed at home because Latin America did not register as an engine of cultural exports. Indeed, up until World War I, the region's literature was made for internal consumption. Given the enormous geographic spread and the limited means of book production, literary distribution was penurious across the continent, which meant that national literatures were defined by the local and almost entirely self-contained. The generation of writers who broke this pattern, the first to be read outside the confines of their own countries, were the *modernistas*. Between 1885 and 1915, this cadre of authors from various countries built a distinct regional literature with its own ethos. Rubén Darío and José Martí were read, in newspapers and magazines and to a lesser degree in books, not only as Nicaraguan or Cuban but also, surprisingly, as Latin Americans.

Their effect reached only so far, though. A continental audience coalesced around the *modernistas,* and, to a lesser extent, they were embraced in Spain after being celebrated by intellectuals such as Miguel de Unamuno and Juan Ramón Jiménez, who applauded the fact that voices from the former colonies were finally finding their place. Yet, that almost no reaction took place elsewhere in Europe and in the United States—in spite of Martí's exile in Florida and New York—emphasizes their limited scope. This generation was not ready for global stardom. It would take time for them to be seen even as precursors.

The missing tool that kept them at bay was translation. While they struggled against trite Spanish models dating back to the Counter-Reformation and the salvos of the Spanish Empire as it lost control of the Americas throughout the nineteenth century, the *modernistas* were infatuated with French and American literatures. They translated their favorite authors into Spanish themselves, or at least actively reflected on their sensibility and overall impact: Darío championed the work of the French writers Paul Verlaine and Victor Hugo, José María Heredia translated William Cullen Bryant, and Martí praised Whitman. Yet the *modernistas* themselves would not reach other languages (French, English, German, Italian), at least not consistently, for decades.

By the 1940s, Latin American pop culture revolved around *ranchera* movies made in Mexico, with stars like Jorge Negrete, Dolores del Río, Pedro Infante, and María Félix. Their audience reached the entire Spanish-speaking world, from Buenos Aires to Los Angeles, as well as the Iberian Peninsula. Simultaneously, radio serials and incipient *telenovelas,* produced in Mexico, Peru, and Argentina, became promoters of a transcontinental identity. These lowbrow works were fervently consumed by all social classes. The bridge was the Spanish language and a shared sense of history.

Finally, something dramatic took place on the global stage in the 1950s, allowing writers from various parts of Latin America to be seen as spokespersons of their worlds. By becoming commodities, they transformed themselves into international celebrities. After World War II, the European novel, arguably the most popular of all literary genres at the time, appeared to have reached a dead end. The atrocities committed on European battlefields made the continent seem exhausted, self-possessed, and unimaginative. Figures like Marcel Proust, Franz Kafka, and James Joyce published works that felt suffocating. All of a sudden, fiction no longer seemed to invite the public to escape, to dream alternative universes, but to feel entrapped. It was then that the so-called Third World emerged as a fertile landscape. From Africa to the Caribbean, from Asia to Latin America, new kinds of novels offered vistas to alternative realities.

This is the vortex from which El Boom emerged. It cannot truly be described as a generation, for its members were born in the span of more than two decades, between 1914 and 1936. To some extent, it should not be described as an exclusively autochthonous phenomenon because it was in Barcelona, in the offices of the literary agent Carmen Balcells, where the concerted enterprise took shape. After all, it was Balcells who, shrewdly recognizing the artistic talent of about half a dozen writers, orchestrated the release of their books through Spanish publishers eager to find new audiences across the Atlantic.

In more ways than one, El Boom was as much an outburst of talent as it was an editorial phenomenon. Indeed, the name itself is an English-language loanword that loosely emulates the transnational bonanza of companies like Exxon and United Fruit that had made a fortune in Latin America in the first half of the twentieth century. Never having found markets that would make book distribution viable in Latin America countries, Spain finally realized a way to make the books of *los boomistas* available to a middle class eager to define itself within, and beyond, national borders.

Balcells is a provocative focal point for reflecting on a question El Boom posed, albeit indirectly: What are the confines of Latin America? Might there truly be such a thing as a transcontinental identity, the elusive dream of Simón Bolívar in the nineteenth century? This malleable, often abused term "Latin America" is used to refer to any nation that doesn't live in English (the United States, Canada, etc.), and, depending on the circumstance, it might include Brazil as well as the Francophone Caribbean. Yet El Boom almost exclusively came from the Spanish-speaking world. Even Jorge Amado, the Brazilian author of *Dona Flor and Her Two Husbands* (1976), said he didn't quite fit in it. In fact, only when El Boom became a marketing tool abroad did he and other Brazilian figures such as João Guimarães Rosa, João Ubaldo Ribeiro, and Nelida Piñon become included in the list. Their books were also said to have exotic elements that made them part of the same aesthetic. But this approach came as an afterthought.

The writers of El Boom, most of them coming from an urban middle- and upper-middle class, were left-leaning in their politics. A generation before, the Latin American intelligentsia had been pushed to define its views in reaction to the Spanish-American War of 1898 and the emergence of the United States as a global power. Figures like Darío and Martí openly expressed themselves against empire, first targeting Spain, then the United States. To a large extent, their successors took the same mantle. They fought for self-determination and against foreign intervention. Those views became a staple of their times through manifestos, interviews, and media appearances.

The politics of El Boom were the outgrowth of free-market policies between Europe and Latin America, put in place in the 1960s in order to expand markets, including in the cultural realm. Many countries in the region at the time were under dictatorial regimes, a model that would remain in place, more or less consistently, until the 1980s. These regimes often embraced censorship, forbidding the publication of a book considered to be testy. Still, censorship was also a publicity mechanism: that which was forbidden became instantly alluring. It is crucial to keep in mind that in the 1960s, mass media began to define all aspects of culture. Separating the national from the international became increasingly difficult. A book applauded in one country became a quick commodity in the rest of Latin America because of the increasingly easy flow of information.

Even if El Boom was a commercial, aesthetic, and ideological phenomenon, it took time for its effects to be felt globally. In retrospect, it was not until the 1980s, when a series of neoliberal policies allowed for a free flow of merchandise and when the region was involved in creating a unified identity from sports to music that was easy to export, that the brunt of El Boom was truly felt. By then its members, middle-aged, were turned into celebrities. Their views, often the first to be heard abroad, carried enormous weight.

A number of *boomistas* found themselves in Paris in the 1950s. At the time, the metropolis was seen as a meeting place for intellectuals. There, in Spain, and through travel to different points of Latin America, they became acquainted with each other and deliberately embarked, aesthetically as well as ideologically, on a common mission to renew the region's literature. The first novel to become a global phenomenon was Cortázar's *Hopscotch* (1963), which dealt with an exile, Horacio Oliveira, stranded in Paris. An experimental work inspired by Eastern religions that asks the reader to take an active role in shaping the narrative arc of the story, it came about just as the beatniks were gaining attention in the United States. Originally published in Buenos Aires, it was quickly embraced by a young generation of readers. At the time Cortázar was a dilettante with almost no interest in politics. Yet his novel was seen as a rejection of the populist politics of Peronism in Argentina, which often ridiculed Europeanized ideas. In spite of its hefty size, *Hopscotch* sold thousands of copies within weeks of its release.

In quick succession, a series of groundbreaking works by Carlos Fuentes, Mario Vargas Llosa, Augusto Roa Bastos, Guillermo Cabrera Infante, José Donoso, and others appeared in bookstores. They received prizes and accolades. However, in terms of explosive success *Hopscotch* was followed by— and, in terms of sales, superseded by—Gabriel García Márquez's *One Hundred Years of Solitude* (1967), a generational tale with biblical undertones about a Colombian coastal town. The novel covers the life of the Buendías, an outsized, idiosyncratic family with a penchant for excess and for whom memory is simultaneously a reservoir of wealth and a factory of nightmares. García Márquez was a relatively unknown journalist in exile in Europe because of his confrontation with Colombia's dictatorial regime. His book, also published in Buenos Aires, became an instant best seller, the author's profile featured on the covers of magazines across the continent.

It is important to remember that while fiction—and the novel as a genre—was enormously popular, Latin America also expressed itself to the world through poetry. The internationalization of the region is perhaps due to a single poet, Pablo Neruda, whose appeal never appears to be diminished. Even before he turned twenty, Neftalí Reyes, as he was called before he opted for his pen name, wrote a type of poetry that the masses quickly embraced. Among his first books was *Twenty Love Poems and a Song of Despair* (1924). It contains verses as famous as those of Catullus, Dante, and Verlaine. As he evolved, Neruda became ideologically engaged, using poetry as a conduit for change. He sought to give voice to the voiceless: the sailor, the housewife, the postman. And he fought to give Latin America a global identity as a continent in touch with its roots.

Other poets have played a similar role, although none has achieved Neruda's degree of acceptance. These include César Vallejo from Peru, also a Communist sympathizer, and Octavio Paz from Mexico, an *hombre de letras* whose presence enabled a dialogue between the region and cultures from around the globe. Vallejo died in Paris while the Spanish Civil War was taking place. Paz lived into his eighties, receiving the Nobel Prize in 1990. Neither of them belonged to El Boom, yet their work redefined Latin America, making it less parochial.

The term "magical realism" is a mistranslation of Alejo Carpentier's *lo real maravilloso,* which is how he described, in the prologue to *The Kingdom of This World* (1949), what he saw during a visit to Haiti, where this novel is set. At the time, surrealism was the fashion in French circles. In Carpentier's view, Haitian life was more primal than surrealism in its combination of the rough, unaffected by civilization, and its unconscious language. The result was an unadulterated dialogue between dreams and awareness, between reality and magic. Upon the success of *One Hundred Years of Solitude* that combination became, in the opinion of critics in Europe and the United States, the sine qua non of Latin American culture.

There is a forerunner to El Boom whose oeuvre opened the road to globalization: Jorge Luis Borges. Born at the end of the nineteenth century, Borges

was involved in several artistic movements that pushed Latin American literature beyond its borders, among them *Ultraísmo*. Up until the late 1950s,
Borges was the property of a small group of devoted readers. His poems, stories, and essays had begun to be translated, mostly into French. Yet he was still
a local author. Several *boomistas* discovered him in the pages of the magazine
Sur, but in 1961, Borges was the recipient of the International Publisher's
Prize, together with Samuel Beckett, which resulted in the immediate rendering of his work into various European languages. It is precisely at that moment,
just as El Boom was about to be launched, that Borge's *Ficciones* (1944) started
to become ubiquitous in Western Civilization, a canonical voice defining not
only Latin American literature but postmodern letters in general.

Almost by osmosis, the term "magical realism" became attached to Borges,
whose impact has been manifold. In spite of his blindness, he represents tire-
less reading. He also personifies the drive toward remembering everything,
toward fostering a memory without boundaries. One of his quintessential
stories is "Funes, the Memorious," about a Uruguayan whose capacity of total
recall turns him into a monster. Another crucial piece is "The Aleph," lucidly
describing a magical object, found in a Buenos Aires basement, capable of
containing the entire universe all at once. The implication is that Argentina,
and no longer Europe, is where art is to be found. Among Borges's most celebrated tales is "Pierre Menard, Author of the *Quixote,*" in which he conjures
a French symbolist author committed to a single mission: rewriting—though
not copying—portions of Cervantes's *Don Quixote*. It is extraordinarily
influential in that it suggests, among other things, that reading and not writing is what literature is about, and that originality is not about newness.

Such is Borges's impact that it is impossible to conceive of writers like John
Barth, Italo Calvino, and Danilo Kiš without him. Yet he was not the only
precursor to El Boom. Another important voice whose influence reaches
beyond Latin America is Juan Rulfo, author of *The Plain in Flames* (1953).
Unlike Borges, who was a cosmopolitan, Rulfo came from a poor family in
the Mexican state of Jalisco, which was devastated by the Revolution of 1910.
His stories are about deprivation, about the pride of people without the basic
necessities in life. Through his fiction (Rulfo also wrote the novel *Pedro
Páramo* [1955]), he reached Chinese, Brazilian, and African readers, showcas-
ing an aspect of Latin America—its rural life, bared to the bone in terms of
possessions—that allowed for another form of universalism: suffering.

For El Boom and its precursors to have a global reach, one chief factor
needs to be understood: translation. García Márquez often said that for a

Colombian writer to be applauded in Bogotá, he first needed to be read in New York. Indeed, it was thanks to translation that, as Octavio Paz once put it, "Latin Americans were invited to the banquet of Western civilization." The torchbearer among translators into English, one whose work defined the field, was Gregory Rabassa, an American of Portuguese descent.* Soon after it appeared in Buenos Aires, Harper & Row offered him *One Hundred Years of Solitude*. Working closely with García Márquez, his rendition of the novel was enthusiastically received by American readers. The author himself even said the translation was superior to the original. Rabassa also translated Cortázar's *Hopscotch,* among other works from El Boom.

American publishers, eager to see these novels become commercially successful, put Rabassa and others to work on other Latin American works. Unlike the translators of Cervantes's *Don Quixote,* who until the 1950s were British, all those involved in working with the fashionable Latin American writers were from the United States, including Edith Grossman, Suzanne Jill Levine, and Alfred Mac Adam, among others. In some cases, it was they who brought the novels to the attention of publishers. In any case, thanks to these renditions, El Boom became a global good. The writers were frequently invited to lecture at universities and to write op-ed pieces for newspapers like the *New York Times.* The film rights of their novels were acquired by Hollywood and other media institutions, and Cortázar's short story "Blow Up" was turned into an epoch-making movie (1966) by the Italian director Michelangelo Antonioni. Likewise, Vargas Llosa's novel *Aunt Julia and the Scriptwriter* was adapted for film (1990), set in New Orleans with Peter Falk. Anthony Quinn and Francis Ford Coppola tried without success to acquire the rights for *One Hundred Years of Solitude.* In the end, García Márquez did sell *Love in the Time of Cholera* (1985), which was filmed with the Spanish actor Javier Bardem.

The impact of translation must be seen under another lens. When an author knows his work will automatically be translated into other languages—and, on occasion, it will appear in one of those other languages before it does in the Spanish original—suddenly his target reader is part of a

---

* Rabassa is a Catalan surname. Rabassa's paternal grandparents were Catalan and Cuban (also of Catalan descent), and his father grew up in Cuba. His maternal grandparents were from the United States (surname Macfarland) and England, and his mother grew up in New York City. Rabassa learned Portuguese (and most of his Spanish) in high school. See Rabassa's memoirs, *If This Be Treason: Translation and Its Dyscontents* (New York: New Directions, 2005), 29, 33.

larger community of nations. In other words, translation pushed authors to think of themselves in less parochial, more ambitious terms, as citizens of the entire world. This means that literature no longer sits easily in national literary traditions but, instead, is an item for large-scale supply.

In analyzing the career of *boomistas* like García Márquez and Vargas Llosa, it is possible to state, with precision, the moment they went global. In the case of the former, this transition took place in 1982, following the publication of *Chronicle of a Death Foretold*. From that moment on, García Márquez's work no longer seemed destined exclusively for a Spanish-language public. In the case of the latter, it happened with *The War of the End of the World* (1981), when Vargas Llosa went beyond Peru to find his subject matter in nineteenth-century Brazil, in the uprising of a group of fanatics that tests the question of Brazilianness. These stratagems made the Latin American novel international merchandise.

For a while there was a group of Latin American women authors whose style depended on refashioning the aesthetics of El Boom. They include Isabel Allende, author of *The House of the Spirits* (1982), a family saga that resembles that of the Buendías, and Laura Esquivel, whose novel *Like Water for Chocolate* (1989) used a kitchen on the U.S.-Mexico border to mix ingredients as steamy as sex and magic. Why women joined the fray rather late is the result of a variety of factors, including the rise and consolidation of feminism in metropolitan centers like Buenos Aires, Mexico City, Santiago, and Bogotá in the 1970s, as well as the readiness of the literary markets to satisfy an international hunger for a more nuanced, multifaceted depiction of gender relations in the region. There were also late additions, such as Manuel Puig, the Argentine author of *Kiss of the Spider Woman* (1976), and, from Puerto Rico, Rosario Ferré, who later in life would switch from Spanish to English in novels like *The House on the Lagoon* (1995), thus inserting herself in another identity parameter: Latinos in the United States. All of these works encourage an understanding of 1960s literary works through the prism of gender. While almost all of the members of El Boom were men, we must remember that women did not enter the labor pool in full force in Latin America, even in the cultural realm, until the 1970s.

A younger crop of authors has emerged in Latin America, one whose profile is heavily defined by El Boom. Members of the next generation—Horacio Castellanos Moya, Andrés Neuman, Ignacio Padilla, Edmundo Paz Solán, Juan Villoro, and Jorge Volpi, among others—have struggled to distance themselves from a type of literature that, in their view, simplifies the region rather than making it complex. In a refutation of magical realism, they have built their oeuvre as hyperrealist, emphasizing drugs, music, video games, and excess in the urban milieu where their novels are set. Many have set their plots as far from Latin America as possible, say, Europe during World War II, as in Volpi's *In Search of Klingsor* (1999).

Arguably the most interesting—as well as the most polemical—post-Boom author whose work has redefined Latin American literature is Roberto Bolaño, who died in 2003, at the age of fifty. Although he was born in Chile, he lived in Mexico and Spain and digested Argentine literature to such a degree that his oeuvre is truly international, not only from a marketing perspective, but also in its content. He is best known for the novel *The Savage Detectives* (1996), which is set in Mexico and uses a Mexican Spanish that is utterly authentic. In fact, the book might be described as the best Mexican novel of the end of the twentieth century, a bizarre change of gears in that it announced that the local no longer belongs to the locals.

Bolaño wrote stories like "The Insufferable Gaucho" (2003) that do the same with Argentine literature, offering an utterly original rereading of Borges and Cortázar. And in his novella *By Night in Chile* (2000), he upsets Chilean letters by suggesting that the Pinochet elite created an aesthetics that even the Left wholeheartedly embraced. These and other strategies made Bolaño an enfant terrible. They also turned him into an instant success in Europe and the United States, where his books, in translation, became the subject of festivals and the staple of creative writing programs. Throughout his oeuvre, Bolaño, in explicit and subtle ways, makes a critique of El Boom: he accuses the movement of turning Latin America into a factory of kitsch, complete with clairvoyant prostitutes, forgotten colonels, and epidemics of insomnia. His argument is that in seeking internationalization the members of that generation sold their soul to the devil. Yet Bolaño loves the devil: he would have done the same.

When García Márquez was awarded the Nobel Prize in 1982, it seemed El Boom was at the center of international cultural affairs. Then, when his onetime-friend Vargas Llosa also was awarded it in 2010, the impression was that this generation had redefined the world in incisive ways, making Latin America fashionable. But success has its disadvantages. In the twenty-first century, the region is no longer seen as awkward and underdeveloped. Instead, Latin America is perceived as finding a delicate balance between its multiple, at times disparate qualities. In the drive to become international, the feeling persists that it is in the process of losing its integrity and that it is becoming like the rest of the world as it stresses its uniqueness as a tourist attraction. That is the drawback of internationalization.

KEY DATES

1963: Publication of *Rayuela,* by Julio Cortázar.

1967: *Cien años de soledad,* by Gabriel García Márquez. Translated into English by Gregory Rabassa in 1970.

1982: Gabriel García Márquez wins the Nobel Prize for Literature.

1986: Jorge Luis Borges dies in Geneva, Switzerland.

1990: Octavio Paz wins the Nobel Prize in Literature.

2010: Mario Vargas Llosa wins the Nobel Prize in Literature.

REFERENCES AND SUGGESTED READING

Stavans, Ilan
    2010   *A Critic's Journey.* Ann Arbor: University of Michigan Press.
    2010   *Gabriel García Márquez: The Early Years.* New York: Palgrave.
Stavans, Ilan, ed.
    1997   *The Oxford Book of Latin American Essays.* New York: Oxford University Press.
    2012   *The FSG Book of Twentieth-Century Latin American Poetry.* New York: Farrar, Straus and Giroux.

SEVENTEEN

Traveling Melodrama

TELENOVELAS AND EXPORTING SOUTHERN MORALITIES; OR, HOW CAN SOMETHING SO BAD STILL BE SO GOOD?

O. Hugo Benavides

THE JOKE THAT TRAVERSED the Arab world for a while in the late 1990s went something like this: The man returns home after a long day at work. The wife responds to him in classical Arabic, to which he says, what, you are speaking Mexican now? This joke referred to the fact that Mexican *telenovelas* had become the rage in Egypt and throughout the Arab world. For the producers, the distribution to each Arab country presented a linguistic nightmare that they solved quite efficiently. All the *telenovelas* (including non-Mexican ones) were dubbed in classical Arabic. This immediately brought a whole range of issues to the forefront, which highlights Latin America's contribution to globalization. They also allow us to rethink the role of media in different parts of the world, like that of the Arab-speaking world, and the manner in which culture and commodification are intricately intertwined in the contemporary production of global markets, and vice versa. In their global trajectory *telenovelas* have also, albeit unconsciously and unwittingly, successfully connected myriad global (South) communities that, although geographically dispersed and linguistically diverse, identify with the simplistic realities expressed through the Latin American melodrama.

Latin American *telenovelas* are very different from North American ones, particularly because they have shorter production runs (normally between six and eight months) and the best ones air during prime time. Perhaps it is these characteristics that contributed to them becoming a global commodity over the past four decades. The telenovelas discussed here, *Los ricos tambien lloran* (The Rich Also Cry), *Yo soy Betty, la fea* (literally, "I Am Betty, the Ugly") and *Xica* (Xica), among many others, have been successfully exported throughout the world, becoming indiscriminate ambassadors of Latin

American culture. These rags-to-riches soap operas have, not surprisingly, further contributed to enhance Latin melodramatic elements of romance and sex, drug culture, and complex family dynamics the world over. They have globalized, and glamorized, Latin American notions of what it means to love, succeed, and be powerful.

Telenovelas have a very recent history in the Americas, yet from their impact it would seem that they have been always part of Latin American culture. They did not make their appearance in South America until the early 1960s, when television entered the Latin American market. This market explosion, however, was prefigured in *radio-novelas* (radio soap operas) and *folletines* (pamphletlike novels) from several decades before, the latter coming into existence as early as the turn of the century in the 1900s. Thus *telenovelas* inherited the structure of the melodrama from both of these visual and aural media and fused them into one incredibly powerful medium of Latin American popular cultural representation. Since the 1960s *telenovelas* have had an important impact on people's daily life, as they dramatically portray such controversial issues as illegitimate children, misplaced identity, the burden of social conventions, amorous rejection, and the ever productive notion of forbidden desires, sexual and otherwise.

It is a testament to the *telenovela*'s success that many of the plot lines are reused or that a telenovela will be rebroadcast in different countries after being adapted to local dialects and cultures. This transnational element is only heightened by the incredible export success of telenovelas throughout the Americas (including the United States) and the world. And such global interaction has led some to argue that melodrama might be the most successful, popular, and culturally authentic revolution affecting the continent since the 1960s.

Of course, it is this productive tension between the local context and *telenovelas* that marks the difference between local/national contexts and the global/transnational processes. In the meanwhile these local-global tensions also help emphasize a connection between Third World nations that continues to find forms of expression in these Latin American melodramatic productions. Therefore the transnational success of these national ventures pushes us to ask: What are the local and global cultural expressions that allow these over-the-top melodramas to be readily understood in such contrasting national contexts? How do these traveling melodramas reassert their identity as Latin American productions while still having a dramatic impact on their newfound audiences? Or perhaps even more succinctly, how can something so bad be so good?

This chapter, most significantly, refers to the basic elements that *telenovelas* represent, and how they create a community of viewers worldwide, particularly in the Third World. The chapter also assesses the cultural elements in these telenovelas, which respond to both modern forms of capital and globalization and thus contribute to create different ideas about what it means to be Latin American.

TELENOVELAS AND GLOBAL CONSUMPTION

A telling element in the *telenovela*'s success is the role that guilty pleasure plays in the melodrama's powerful representation. For starters, *telenovelas* are stereotypically represented as reflecting only part of the local audience's social makeup: women and poor and working-class people. However, from the very beginning the actual economic successes of the *telenovelas* as well as the lasting cultural impact of many of them reflect quite a contrary social picture.

There are no doubts that everybody, men and women, as well as the poor and rich, are willing consumers of *telenovelas* and positively respond to the seductive images presented to them on the screen. The fact that *telenovelas* are represented as low-class entertainment with little cultural content only heightens the viewer's guilty pleasure of feeling they are enjoying something they should not be, and in that manner crossing illicitly into social mores that have been historically denied to them.

Telenovelas, in this manner, allow viewers to inhabit the closed social landscape of wealth, power, and status that has been systematically outside of the majority of the populations' reach. Yet the seductive manner in which these struggles are represented only reify these closed circuits of status and hierarchy that are exactly what both incite and repel the majority of viewers and clinch the *telenovelas*' popular success. This is also why large historical events have been successfully represented through *telenovelas* (including the Mexican Revolution, post–world war European migration to the Americas, etc.). In many regards many of these epic productions have allowed each nation in the Americas to use it to reflect upon their own historical, social, and cultural formation.

To this effect, desire, sexual attraction, and an obsessive attachment to the Other are part of *telenovelas*' central object or theme. Love, particularly a kind of forbidden, transgressive love, will always be at the heart of the *telenovela*'s main plot. This particular sentiment has traditionally been expressed in a heterosexual guise represented by the conflict between a younger (darker) woman in love with a more successful (white) man. However, this heterosexual, racial, and class facade has proved instrumental in allowing a host of other emotional and social characteristics to be successfully translated on the television screen. The stock characters of subservient maids, employees, or even slaves, and themes of racial and national divides, including perverse sexual desires, have been incorporated into what would seem, at least on the outset, as a simplified version of Latin American society.

Yet it is this emphasis on the popular cultural aspects, as opposed to aristocratic stories about the rich and famous, that may be the *telenovelas'* democratic revenge, reflected in the simple fact of having rich people competing to represent and act out the life of poor people on screen. "We the poor," *telenovelas* seem to say, "may not have your supposedly unique depth of feeling, and yet we are still capable of living fuller lives, and even offer a new mode of entertainment." *Telenovelas'* main concern is about how those hurt and abused by the powerful still manage to survive and find some solace in their daily life. Of course, all can identify with that simplistic plot, all the while knowing from lived reality that there is nothing simplistic about the human experience. It is this double standard of what you see is not what you get, however, that also marks another element of global consumption.

LOS RICOS TAMBIÉN LLORAN, OR AS THEY SAY IN RUSSIA, *BOGATY TOSZCHE PLACHUT*

Another example of this global impact of *telenovelas* is the success that *Los ricos también lloran* (The Rich Also Cry) garnered all over the world. This Mexican *telenovela* originally aired in post-perestroika Russia in 1992. *Bogaty Toszche Plachut* (the title in Russian) was an incredible success and a hit for the nation's Commonwealth Channel. It was a particular success for the Russian producer Ostankino, which gambled on buying the rights of this 1979 production. His hopes had been that the upwardly mobile story of a poor woman marrying into wealth would translate to the changing landscape of the collapsing Soviet Union and relate to the emergence of the new Russian national identity and marketplace (Helguera 2008). The producer's hope was confirmed beyond expectations. The translated *telenovela* broke all Russian television viewing records, with over 200 million households glued to the last episode. The day after the *telenovela*'s final episode was declared a national day of mourning by the government since it seemed that a national purpose, way of being, had ended, and the community had to regain its sense of self.

The fact that *telenovelas* focus on love, forbidden and impossible, is what allows their economical emotional structure and powerful facades to find such easy global translation. When Russians fell in love with Veronica Castro's downtrodden character there is no doubt they were mirroring their own sense of desolation. Just like the female protagonist played by Castro, Russians knew that their current status didn't reflect who they really were. They, the Russians, were the real owners of the house (just like Castro's character) and the rightful inheritors of one of the world's greatest civilizations. Both of them, character and nation, might be downtrodden, but they still have enormous hope, fueled by desire, that is not the end of the story. And it is precisely the national day of mourning after the last episode that provides an insight into the power of Latin American melodramas globally.

Yet before the final episode there is a lot that might happen. Because it is through love that that ancient charm (both personally and nationally) can be reignited. In this particular *telenovela* it is the love that grows between the poor woman and the rich man that allows her to reclaim her rightful place in society and, in the eyes of all, a rightful place that belongs to her by birth but that has been viciously denied her. Meanwhile, not only does she achieve her sense of self through the correct placement of her social body, but the man also achieves wholeness and a shared organic happiness that otherwise wouldn't be his.

This simple forbidden love affair of contrasting bodies serves to enshrine the desire of/for the Other. This transgressive desire as a motor for self-fulfillment also manages to critique a pervasive market economy that entitles the privileged, exposing the hollowness of elite behavior but also reinforcing the revenge of the commoner. The poor may be desirous of the rich Other, but similarly the rich cannot be complete without the consent of the oppressed. In this fashion, it is not about making as much money as you possibly can, as the traditional logic of capital would have it, but rather accruing as much emotional worth and love as you humanly are able.

True love, the *telenovela* seems to say, is not the one expressed for the Other but for the Other in oneself. The title of the *telenovela* already expresses this haunting specter of the market: "The rich also cry." It already predicts not so much that the struggle against the odds stacked against you is futile but rather that joining those odds will not truly liberate you from life's conundrum. Only by coming to terms with your origins will you have a sense of self, which only then can be expressed in a form of external love.

At the same time these sentiments are fueling constant desires that have as their ultimate purpose to continue desiring, endlessly. There is no doubt that desire is exactly what *telenovelas* do best. They provide an endless mirror image to reflect our endless selves as they are redefined by a new form of capital that no longer destroys difference but rather looks to engage and be fulfilled by it. In this manner, Veronica Castro's dark, small, voluptuous body is no longer to be simply conquered but rather inhabited from the inside out, and used to ponder the national shortcomings that the Russian nation must confront. Perhaps this is what the day of national mourning was really about, not the simple ending of a dated Mexican telenovela, but of understanding that new forms of acquiring wealth and capital are now in place. In that manner it is the end of a historic period that allows all, including Russian burly men, to out themselves as being extremely class conscious and avid consumers, even of *telenovelas*.

UGLY BETTY: THE COLOMBIAN UGLY DUCKLING

The 1976 Brazilian soap opera *Escrava Isaura* (Isaura, the Slave) is arguably one of the earliest *telenovelas* to have met with worldwide success. It was aired in over eighty countries, the first *telenovela* to be broadcast in the then–Soviet Union and the only one to ever be shown on British television. The melodramatic story about a light-skinned runaway slave who is able to pass as a white woman was met with thunderous support from different international audiences. The main actress, Lucélia Santos, was invited by leading male political leaders from all over the world, including Fidel Castro himself, to visit their countries. The racial undertones of the *telenovela* also opened the content of melodramas to a greater number of social and political themes. This is what a Brazilian journalist realized while visiting Tibet when his driver was constantly referred to as Andrés because his relatively darker skin reminded his fellow countrymen of the Andrés character in *Escrava Isaura,* which was a huge success there.

This worldwide impact perhaps has only been surpassed by the 1999 Colombian telenovela, *Yo soy Betty, la fea* (I Am Ugly Betty), which was successful beyond the Colombian producers' initial plan to such a degree that several months of programming were added to the schedule. The *telenovela* aired throughout the Americas and in over twenty countries around the world. Meanwhile, another twenty national production companies bought the rights to the program and produced their own versions of the *telenovela*. The U.S. version of the program, *Ugly Betty,* was also a ratings success, with a great female cast of stars that included Salma Hayek, Vanessa Williams, and America Ferrara (who played Betty). Obvious cultural and national translations were made, but the central plot line was maintained: an ugly duckling (geeky young woman) who is beautiful on the inside and smart on the outside struggles to find her true self/place against foes fueled by superficial values. In many ways this captured the translatable beauty of *telenovelas:* their simple and straightforward messages can easily be adapted to different cultural settings without altering their central ideas and focus.

This *telenovela,* significantly, does an interesting job of critiquing traditional models of success while rearticulating alternative models that are still solidly placed within the confines of modern desires of financial success. To this degree, the old "mafioso" family way of doing business is no longer profitable. It is at this point that the melodramatic solution, offered by a darker, awkward, "ugly" female Colombian body, proves incredibly and irresistibly seductive. Betty, as initially played by Ana María Orozco, offers what the cultural critic Stuart Hall (1997) called a "similarly different" path to success. She is the perfect antiheroine (and antihero) foil to the powerful patriarchs of the market, the taller, whiter, and stronger elite body types of the traditional owners and managers of the company.

Betty's character seduces us all. She is the "true" spirit of an egalitarian ethos, and fair play, as it is referred to obsessively in the soccer world. Betty encourages us to root for the underdog in a world market that never allows the weaker player to win. Therefore, as global spectators, we are rooting for Betty because in our hearts we know that, like us, she is not who everybody else thinks she is. On the contrary, she is the true heroine of the story, and as such the purveyor of the authentic ideals of love, family, friendship, and community. This is where her friends, nicknamed *las feas* (the ugly ones) in the *telenovela,* become important as well. We, like them, are completely loyal to Betty, wanting the true essence of beauty and kindness to win over the traditional corrupt values of the marketplace. The *telenovela* inverts our daily knowledge of reality and cohesively presents a visual representation primed for global consumption. In this melodramatic representation the truly good and beautiful are not only recognized, but actually beat the superficial monsters of the market at their own corrupt game.

Of course, all of us, from Bogotá to Dakar, know that is only a *telenovela* and not reality; it is not even reality television. Yet the hope is still so pervasive and powerful that one's fantasy is that what is true for an hour on television could actually be true for a bit longer in our own countries. What is being sold, in a way, is another market dream, one encased in a particular Latin American guise. Our hope for authenticity and emotional truth is so powerful that it is commodified, sold, and exported to the world in this melodramatic form.

It is also revealing in this regard that it is Colombia, the Latin American nation, that is most able to translate and commodify this hope in such a manner as successful as Betty. What country more than Colombia and Mexico has strived to counterbalance the inequality of the global market through the drug trade, presenting a much different way of achieving financial success through transnational cartels? In this particular way it is the victims, "the ugly ones," calling the shots and making the profit, while the rest of the "legal" world is unable to curtail the drug trade for its own profit and its own necessities. In this way, for some the drug trade represents a financial democratization of the world order.

Telenovelas are a retelling of the story of the world from the vantage point of Latin America, and not necessarily one shared by the developed world. At the heart of this concern is a profound ethical and aesthetic question about the present, globally speaking. How do we make sense of a global divide between North and South that continues to build on centuries-long colonial practices of exploitation and exclusion? This present moment of global inequality can be characterized by the exploitative process of resource extraction and also by the intellectual depravity that pushes Western intellectuals to define as normal inhumane exchanges and relationships of all kind. And this is precisely what the storyline of *Yo soy Betty, la fea,* does so well, all the while entertaining us. It allows people the world over to ponder, perhaps unconsciously, their complicity in a global market that exploits the majority of the world, perhaps including themselves.

But of course the market (i.e., all of us) is not so easily duped. After all, the *telenovela* is responding to these values that allow hope to be commodified, because Betty is looking more cosmopolitan, whiter, and stronger by the end than when she started out.

XICA: THE POWER OF BEING HUMAN

Just as all *telenovelas* have forbidden love as their melodramatic theme, their plots are about the balance of power, enabling star-struck lovers to achieve positions of power that had been originally denied to them. It doesn't matter, in this regard, that one of the protagonists (normally a male) might be elite; it only confirms that he is still part of an old corrupt system. His power comes from a false sense of security, from the old market system that places value on appearance and superficial realities. Then, through the true love of another (and oneself), for someone socially inferior, someone who comes from a place "different" from his own, he is able to reclaim a true sense of power, of self and Other, and reconnect to the national community. Both *Los ricos tambien lloran* and *Yo soy Betty, la fea,* grapple with this central issue. In both instances the main female character manages to turn the tables on the upper class and what is commonly deemed civilized society. What happens by the end of both *telenovelas* is that these supposedly worthless characters are transformed into the most valuable people on the shows. This is done not by means of characters going through dramatic conversions; it is those around them who change. It is the heartless and superficial elite who are slowly awakened to the true value of life and ultimately redefine the notion of social and emotional power from the inside out.

This power paradigm is most explicit in *Xica,* the 1996 Brazilian *telenovela* set on Portuguese slave plantations of South America in the 1700s, one that readily delved into the core question of the value of a human being. The issue was posed not only in terms of the actual commodified financial and sexualized value of enslaved African bodies, but of white bodies that were willing to traffic human beings in order to reinstate their (supposed) racialized superiority. It is partly the apt adaptation of these questions in a "sexy" Brazilian melodramatic form that contributed to the huge success of this *telenovela* the world over. The main actors, Taís Araújo and Victor Wagner, were hailed as national heroes when they visited New York City. It was also the deep ideological questioning and sexy theme that made the mainstream North American magazine *Vanity Fair* in 2000 refer to *Xica* as "half 'Roots,' half soft porn."

This central question of power is obviously more explicit in a slave setting, where, it would seem, the plantation owner is the only one in control. But in *Xica* we slowly learn it is the white plantation owners who are horribly corrupted by their monstrous desires to control and dominate the African

FIGURE 17.1 The actress Taís Araújo, who received the Ordem do Rio Branco, poses for photographers with then Brazilian President Luiz Inácio Lula da Silva and First Lady Marisa Letícia. Source: Wikimedia Commons. This file is licensed under the Creative Commons Attribution 2.0 Generic license. https://commons.wikimedia.org/wiki /File:Ta%C3%ADs_Ara%C3%BAjo_Ordem_de_Rio_Branco.jpg.

Other. In this exploitative act white people lose all ability and power to control themselves. This white anxiety and lack of control is made even more poignant by the fact that it is Xica, the African slave, who is able to seduce the Comendador, the richest white political officer of the region. She not only gains her freedom but also ends up being the owner of the richest diamond mines in the region. To this day, some Brazilian towns in the region are named Diamantina (Small Diamond) and Ouro Prêto (Black Gold). Ultimately, Xica navigates from living as a slave/nonhuman unable to even walk inside a church to becoming the mother of a priest in that same church that once denied her self-worth and humanity.

That Xica da Silva is an actual historical subject and that the telenovela more or less follows this former slave's road to freedom only heightens the melodramatic tensions of power. It is not surprising that such a seductive subject as Xica would be enticing to developed parts of the world that are grudgingly coming to terms with their part in the colonial histories of the Americas, Africa, and Asia—and also as part of a globalization process that continues to be invested in new forms of capitalism that now must incorporate, reproduce, and engage difference rather than deny it.

CONCLUSION

What is it about this melodramatic form that has been able to excite people's imagination the world over? What are *telenovelas* able to offer in the most pragmatic fashion that did not exist before or that communities didn't have on their own? Perhaps it is equally important to consider how these melodramatic ventures have been able to fly under the censorship and radar of intellectuals and cultural elites and in this manner reconnect supposedly uneducated communities throughout the world.

Telenovelas have managed to address fault lines created by centuries of colonialism. It is quite a contrast, maybe even a surprise, that what once were the destinations for slaves and the sources of raw materials are now able to represent themselves in such a manner for global consumption. After five centuries of exploitative conditions *telenovelas* present themselves as a wonderful vehicle for both the representation and the release of the native Other.

On one side they give voice (albeit in a disguised fashion) to the "natives" that supposedly have none. On the other they temper the anxieties of imperial Others who wonder if the elites went too far—without ever admitting to themselves that they know they did. To this degree *telenovelas* exemplify one of James Baldwin's prophetic lines, written long ago, in the mid-1900s: "The world is no longer white, and it will never be white again." *Telenovelas* are living evidence of this insight and of the white world's anxiety to want to laugh about or at least pretend to enjoy the changing landscape of difference. Meanwhile, the world is being transfigured, one *telenovela* at a time, in the process creating new groups of Global South communities who yearn to express new forms of self-representation, historical release, and domination.

REFERENCES AND SUGGESTED READING

Baldwin, James
  1950   *Notes of a Native Son.* Boston: Beacon Press.
Hall, Stuart
  1997   "The Local and the Global: Globalization and Ethnicity." In *Culture, Globalization and the System: Contemporary Conditions for the Representation of Identity,* ed. A. King, 19–39. Minneapolis: University of Minnesota Press.

Helguera, Pablo

2008 "The Global Pandemic of the Telenovela: Mexico's Biggest Export to the World Is an Endless, Gushing Fount of Insane Television." June 2. www.vice.com/read/global-pandemic-telenovela-151-v15n6.

Vanity Fair

2000 "Channel This." August.

Invisibility

Renato Rosaldo

We celebrate their days,
eat hot dogs, love baseball,
but they say we were born to weed,
clean houses, carry crates in the grey of dawn
while they sleep. Awake, they look at us without seeing.

We see ourselves clearly, know ourselves
precisely, without parades and picnics.
To survive, we must.

Day after day I see doors shut,
stumble over slurs, and bump into men
who nod yes, yes, but aren't listening.

Los Invisibles

Renato Rosaldo

Celebramos sus días,
comemos hotdogs, nos entusiasma el béisbol,
pero ellos dicen que nacimos para desyerbar,
limpiar casas, cargar bultos en el gris de la madrugada
mientras ellos duermen. Despiertos, miran sin vernos.

Nos vemos a nosotros claramente, nos conocemos
precisamente, sin fiestas y desfiles.
Para sobrevivir, nos urge.

Día tras día oigo las puertas cerrándose,
me tropiezo con el menosprecio, doy con los hombres
que dicen con la cabeza, que si, que si, pero no escuchan.

EIGHTEEN

———

The Girl from Shinjuku

HOW A JAPANESE BRAZILIAN DIVA KEEPS BOSSA NOVA ALIVE IN CHINA

Fabiano Maisonnave

I HEARD BOSSA NOVA AS SOON as I moved to China as a correspondent for a Brazilian newspaper in April 2010. I was getting my hair cut in Beijing when the salon was flooded with the sound of "Corcovado" (Quiet Nights of Quiet Stars), a bossa nova classic composed by Antônio Carlos "Tom" Jobim and recorded by artists like Frank Sinatra. Other bossa nova tunes followed, some of which I had never heard, and all sung in Portuguese by the same unidentifiable female voice. Intrigued by the songs playing from a laptop, I asked the shop owner about the artist. "It's Japanese music," he responded. "Her name is Lisa Ono."

Lisa who? Do you really mean to tell me that the song written in homage to Brazil's greatest symbol, Christ the Redeemer, is now Japanese?

I asked the young man to write the singer's name on a piece of paper. Then, after reading articles and speaking with my local sources, I began to understand the myth, and reality, of Lisa Ono. It was a delightful discovery. Since the 1990s, Lisa Ono—all but unknown in Brazil outside musical circles—has led the largest global resurgence of bossa nova since its inception more than fifty years ago. This revitalization stands in sharp contrast to the 1960s when Brazilian musicians brought bossa bova to the world. In China, for instance, the syncopated rhythm never came from Rio. Rather, the inspiration for Chinese bossa nova comes from neighboring Tokyo, the city where bossa nova most thrives today.

In my three years in Asia, I wrote a few newspaper articles on bossa nova. Soon enough I got to know Lisa Ono. In one of our early conversations in a Tokyo café filled with the music of Jobim, she told me—only half-joking—that "bossa nova is more Japanese than Brazilian."

Allow me to explain . . .

316

Bossa nova's history is intertwined with the biography of Lisa Ono. The daughter of Japanese immigrants to Brazil, Ono was born in São Paulo in 1962 just as the musical genre was becoming popular in Rio de Janeiro, where it had been created by the singer-guitarist João Gilberto in 1958. In that year he released his 78 rpm classic that included the still famous "Chega de saudade" (No More Blues), composed and produced by Jobim, with lyrics by the poet Vinicius de Moraes. The syncopated and versatile rhythm of the guitar, together with Gilberto's smooth voice, quickly overtook Brazilian radio and influenced a generation of carioca musicians who, hip to the jazz being produced in the United States, sought to modernize Brazilian music.

The hype around the new musical style seduced Toshiro Ono, an unknown Japanese immigrant who had recently arrived in Brazil. Understanding very few of the lyrics, Toshiro listened to the radio and followed the release of songs now considered classics, including "Samba de avião" (Song of the Jet), "Insensatez" (How Insensitive), "Vou te contar" (Wave), and "Garota de Ipanema" (The Girl from Ipanema), one of the most-recorded songs in the world—second only, perhaps, to the Beatles' classic "Yesterday." Toshiro Ono did not hear this music while lying on Ipanema beach. Rather, like the majority of Japanese immigrants to Brazil, Toshiro lived in São Paulo, a city 220 miles and a world away from Rio de Janeiro. São Paulo, Brazil's largest economic and industrial center, is ashen and has no coastline. It is said to consume culture but not produce much itself when compared to Rio. Vinicius de Moraes, the greatest bossa nova lyricist, even nicknamed São Paulo "the tomb of samba."

Before moving to São Paulo, there was little in Toshiro Ono's life connected to music. The son of an army general, Toshiro was born in Japanese-occupied Taiwan in 1924. In 1940, Toshiro's father sent him to a monastery in Pyongyang, capital of present-day North Korea. At fifteen, Toshiro's grueling daily routine included a 3 A.M. wake-up call and a sponge bath in subzero temperatures. Returning to Japan after World War II, Toshiro Ono worked for eleven years as an interpreter for the U.S. soldiers who occupied the country. The experience introduced him to foreign music and gave him the opportunity to live among strangers.

In the late 1950s, Ono decided to try his luck in Brazil, decades after Japanese immigrants had first arrived. While most of the newcomers headed for rural areas, by the fifties many immigrants and their Brazilian-born children had relocated to São Paulo and other cities. Japanese Brazilians became small-business owners, opening laundromats and bodegas, all the while gaining fame for their rates of saving and investment in education.

Ono was not one of these mythical Japanese immigrants. Breaking from his compatriots, he opened a club in the center of São Paulo, bringing Brazilian musicians—famous and less so—to his stage. One of his most important contacts was with the guitarist Baden Powell, a well-known proponent of bossa nova and coauthor of many songs with Vinicius de Moraes, who wrote the lyrics to "The Girl from Ipanema" and countless other classics. Toshiro Ono worked with Powell in 1970, while the artist was in Japan recording a live album. The environment in which Lisa Ono would flourish was in the making.

BRAZIL-U.S.A.-JAPAN

Bossa nova reached Japan thanks to its huge splash on the American music scene. Its songs telling of a "love-sea-flower" trilogy spread throughout the 1960s, attracting an audience and artists from Frank Sinatra to Elvis Presley. The so-called bossa nova invasion came to New York City's Carnegie Hall on 21 November 1962, when young artists including Sérgio Mendes, João Gilberto, and Tom Jobin all performed. Suddenly partnerships between Brazilians and Americans became the artistic and commercial rage. In 1963 a version of "The Girl from Ipanema" recorded by João Gilberto, saxophonist Stan Getz, and budding singer Astrud Gilberto sold two million copies. The list of American artists who experimented with bossa nova included just about every big name of the "classic era" of American jazz: Nat "King" Cole, Johnny Mathis, Ella Fitzgerald, Sarah Vaughan, Oscar Peterson, Al Jarreau, and Mel Tormé. Elvis Presley recorded "Bossa Nova Baby" in 1963, despite the song's fast pace and mariachi-clad musicians having little to do with João Gilberto's rhythm. Even so, the genre spread like wildfire. "Just about everyone on the face of the earth, barring Mother Theresa of Calcutta, seems to have recorded Bossa Nova at least once," writes the Brazilian journalist Ruy Castro. The American-Brazilian musical alliance reached its height in 1966, when Frank Sinatra invited Tom Jobim to record with him. The result, *Francis Albert Sinatra & Antonio Carlos Jobim,* was nominated for Album of the Year, losing the Grammy to the Beatles' *Sgt. Pepper's Lonely Hearts Club Band.*

Yet more than awards were lost in the mid-sixties. Brazil's 1964 military coup created fractures in the arts scene, as the "zen" lyrics about love and the sea were increasingly seen as too soft and apolitical for the zeitgeist. By the end of the troubled 1960s, bossa nova was on the back burner.

Deemphasizing the bossa nova beat in Brazil had an opposite global reaction. Those overtly or subtly looking for artistic freedom came to the United States, and Sérgio Mendes, along with his trumpeter, Herb Alpert, became superstars in ways they never would in Brazil. With its roots transplanted in the United States, bossa nova began to spread throughout the world. The soft sound came to Japan with the saxophonist Sadao Watanabe, a former student at Berklee College of Music in Boston, where he played with Brazilian musicians. Once back in his native country, Watanabe recorded *Jazz & Bossa* in 1967, thriving in a musical environment that had been established by Brazilian musicians such as Maysa, the first Brazilian woman singer to tour Japan in 1960. In an interview with a local TV station, she explained, "the kind of samba that . . . has absolutely nothing to do with Carnaval." In 1964, the bossa nova muse Nara Leão visited Japan, sponsored by the clothing manufacturer Rhodia. Around that time, the Los Angeles–based organist Walter Wanderley came to the island nation. Yet the most successful was Sérgio Mendes, who made many appearances in Japan from 1966 to 1968 from his U.S. base.

This was the global bossa nova environment that led the restless Toshiro Ono to return to Japan in 1972 with his ten-year-old Brazilian daughter, Lisa. With the music business experience he had acquired in São Paulo, Ono recognized a niche for Brazilian music in Japan and opened a restaurant-club. Named Saci-Pererê in homage to the boy with a magical cape popular in Brazilian folklore, the club soon became a success. Brazilian musicians flowed through the club's doors, and Saci-Pererê is still open as this book went to press. This longevity is a tribute to the local in the global, since it was the club, more than Sergio Mendes or Sadao Watanabe, that created an ever-growing bossa nova audience by connecting Japanese musicians with Brazilian colleagues who spent time in Tokyo. Saci-Pererê was also an ideal environment for an adolescent interested in music. With her father's encouragement, Lisa Ono took up the guitar, bossa nova's instrument par excellence. She hung out with musicians playing in the club, including Brazilian stars like João Donato and the bossa nova master Baden Powell.

Lisa Ono realized early on that she had to make a hard choice about language. She told me that her career could have kicked off earlier if she had agreed to sing in Japanese instead of Portuguese. That, however, was not her style. Rather, in 1989 Ono recorded her debut *Catupiry* in a studio in Rio de Janeiro. The album, whose name is a reference to a beloved type of Brazilian cheese, featured nine songs in Portuguese and three more in English. Her soft voice was well suited to bossa nova and her Brazilianness and close relationships with Brazilian musicians worked in Ono's favor. Starting in 1990 she released one recording every year, varying her collaborations with Brazilians in recording and production, as well as in the studio.

In 1994, Ono caught her big break when she recorded "Estrada Branca" with Tom Jobim in Rio de Janeiro. "It was wonderful. We rehearsed at his house, on his Yamaha acoustic piano. It was like the sound of birds," Ono recalled in a 2010 interview. Five years later, Ono recorded her biggest commercial success, *Dream*, released in Japan but also in the Chinese markets of Hong Kong and Taiwan. Produced by the Brazilian Oscar Castro-Neves, *Dream* was the beginning of what Ono calls her "musical journey." For the first time, the songs were bossa nova versions of English-language classics like "Tea for Two" (with some verses in Portuguese) and "Moonlight Serenade." In the years that followed, Ono's career grew more and more internationally focused. She released albums with global influence from Hawaii (*Bossa Hula Nova*, 2001) and Italy (*Questa Bossa Mia*, 2002) to Spain (*Romance Latino*, vols. 1–3).

Lisa Ono never forgot Brazil, even as she brought bossa nova to the world. In 2007 she headlined a major open-air show in Tokyo in honor of Tom Jobim and accompanied by Jobim's son and grandson, Paulo and Daniel Jobim. She spearheaded a phenomenon that may not have topped the Japanese charts right away but solidified bossa nova as one of the country's prominent musical niches with its own audience, artists, and industry.

JAPAN-CHINA

After its birth in Brazil and emigration to the United States, bossa nova found its heart in Japan. By 1990 Japan was the main market for established Brazilian artists like Roberto Menescal, Nara Leão, Leila Pinheiro, and Joyce. Every Brazilian bossa nova artist traveled to Japan; most of them made the trip more than once. Even the reclusive João Gilberto made the long trip to Asia to perform in 2003.

Bossa nova's momentum in Japan proliferated. No other country has a more extensive catalog of releases and rereleases. Old and rare albums in Brazil, such as the music of Chico Feitosa and the Tamba Trio, can be found in Japan in reedited versions. Some Brazilian artists released new albums in Japan that never even reached the Brazilian market. This dynamic fueled the notion that bossa nova is better suited to the supposedly reserved demeanor of the Japanese than to the ostensibly more raucous Carnaval culture of Brazil. "Bossa nova is just like Japan: very soft and gentle," said Jobim at a 1987 concert there. Paulo Caldas's documentary, *Bossa Nova—Rising Sun,* reinforces the idea that Japan and bossa nova are perfect companions: "Bossa nova complements the Japanese summer, bringing with it a cool breeze. But in the winter as well, bossa nova brings a compassionate warmth to the air and hearts of the Japanese people," remarks the bossa nova guitarist Michinari Usada, in Portuguese.

For the music producer Itoh Ryosuke, creator of a Japanese version of the classic "Barquinho" (My Little Boat), Japan's adoration of bossa nova lies in the sea: "Japan is an archipelago, a country surrounded by water, and the Japanese love the sea. The sea is always in the lyrics of a bossa nova tune!" The singer and composer Roberto Menescal suggested that the phonemic proximity between Japanese and Portuguese allows for Japan's harmonious union with bossa nova. And, according to Kepel Kimura, who has specialized in the release and rerelease of Brazilian CDs for the past twenty years, even the Japanese lifestyle lends itself to bossa nova: "The Japanese live in tiny apartments, and we can't play loud music. We play the guitar softly."

It is intriguing that bossa nova gained popularity in Japan at the same time that Japanese Brazilians began migrating en masse from Brazil to Japan. Called the "*dekassegui* movement" (literally, "working away from home" in Japanese, it has come to mean Latin Americans who have migrated to Japan to do manual labor), this government project aimed to ameliorate a shortage in the factory labor force with foreigners "of Japanese blood." At the *dekassegui* movement's peak, Japan had about 350,000 Japanese Brazilians, although by 2013 Japan's economic stagnation had led the number to drop to a little over two hundred thousand.

Contact between bossa nova artists and Japanese Brazilian factory workers went little beyond sharing flights between Brazil and Japan. Unlike the Ono family, *dekassegui* worked on the factory production line, not the musical stage. In her twenty-plus-year career, Lisa Ono never played a show specifically for the tens of thousands of Japanese Brazilians concentrated in cities such as Hamamatsu and Oizumi. Indeed, while she had practically no contact with the community, *dekassegui* demanded Brazilian music of other types. In 2013, the country music stars Luan Santana and Michel Teló—the latter known for the catchy and internationally successful "Ai, Se eu te pego" (Oh, If I Catch You)—played huge shows to Brazilian audiences in Japan. Meanwhile bossa nova musicians like Edu Lobo and Oscar Castro-Neves attract Japanese crowds, yet hardly make a ripple among Brazilian fans.

Why don't Japanese Brazilians, who often reaffirm their identities by importing Brazilian products and music to Japan, embrace the ever-present bossa nova? The Japanese Brazilian cultural activist Valéria Ohtsuki thinks that "the majority of *dekasseguis* have little interest in bossa nova because, at the time when these Brazilians were emigrating to Japan, the genre was all but forgotten in Brazil." But there may be other explanations. The Tokyo-based Japanese Brazilian journalist Ewerthon Tobace, for example, sees three reasons that *dekassegui* distance themselves from Bossa Nova. First, the immigrants come from the lower-middle class and as an "'other' ends up being discriminated against. It's like being a fan of bossa nova and living in the ghetto. You can listen to it in your house, but in the streets it's gotta be [Brazilian] funk." Second, Tobace asserts, expats from Brazil become more "patriotic" in Japan, often embracing music seen as more traditionally Brazilian, like country music, axé, and samba. Finally, "for the new generations in Brazil, bossa nova is an antiquated style of music that failed to evolve with time. The lyrics are the same, the themes and the rhythm don't change." Brazilians even gripe, according to Tobace, that there is too much bossa nova in Japan's public arena. "I've heard lots of people complain that Bossa Nova is overplayed in Japan. From elevators to cafes, supermarkets, restaurants, even medical clinics and health spas."

Another Brazilian journalist from Tokyo, Roberto Maxwell, believes that this distancing is slowly changing. According to Maxwell:

> Over time, especially after the 1990s, Japanese Brazilians began self-identifying as Brazilians, setting themselves apart from "native" Japanese. And in the early 2000s, they began getting into Brazilian music, often as students either of non-Japanese Brazilians, who had come to Japan as musicians, or of skilled Japanese artists. All of this was a means of finding their place within Japanese society, not, as many had hoped at the beginning of the migratory process, as the children of Japanese parents (and therefore themselves Japanese), but as Brazilians instead. I would even venture to say that Japanese Brazilians are only into samba music and bossa nova here in Japan. (E-mail correspondence, 10 May 2014)

While bossa nova was developing its own dynamic in Japan, Lisa Ono was gaining other audiences, primarily in China. Despite China's stringent rules for foreign artists—for example, the government demands a musician's set list and a Mandarin translation of all lyrics—Ono's concerts became more frequent after 2010. I had the opportunity to see Ono in front of a crowd of some thousands of Chinese in June 2011, during the Kama outdoor music festival in Beijing. Under a gray sky heavy with pollution, Lisa and a group of all-Japanese musicians sang a Mandarin number off the 2010 album *Asia* (which includes traditional tunes sung in Korean, Mongolian, Thai, Sinhalese, Malay, and Bengali), but half of their set was in Portuguese. Among the songs was "Maracangalha," a classic samba tune by Dorival Caymmi. As I sat imagining how the words would be translated into Mandarin, I asked a nearby group of girls where Lisa Ono came from. "She's Japanese," one of them replied. But what language did they think she sang in? "Italian!" I had similar conversations with others in the audience—no one mentioned Brazil or the Portuguese language.

In 2011, Lisa Ono (whose Japanese name is written Xiao Ye Li Sha in Mandarin) embarked on her first big tour in continental China, playing in no fewer than seventeen cities. Her last concert was on 31 December in Beijing; Ono packed the immense annex gymnasium of Workers' Stadium, located in an upper-class area of the Chinese capital. Just a year later, however, came a shock: Ono's career became entangled in the Beijing-Tokyo dispute over the Senkaku and Diaoya islands. Amid pervasive xenophobic sentiment in China, Ono's spot on *Asian Wave* (a Chinese version of *American Idol*) was canceled, along with several concerts. After all, to the Chinese, Lisa Ono is Japanese. Yet when the island crisis cooled, Ono returned to China for a few shows, which garnered her even more success. In February 2014, Ono's concert in Shanghai attracted more than eight thousand people. In 2015, she returned to China, performing twenty-two concerts in several cities.

The lack of a popular sense in China that there is a connection between bossa nova and Brazil has become a challenge for the Brazilian consulate in China's economic hub, Shanghai. The Brazilians want and need a well-known product since China has surpassed the United States as Brazil's primary commercial partner. Yet Brazilian exports were basically limited to iron ore, soy, and petroleum. Like bossa nova, these were "anonymous products." For the Brazilian former consul in Shanghai, Marcos Caramuru de Paiva, bossa nova had to be reclaimed as Brazilian music. In his article "The Chinese Don't Know It, but They Love Brazilian Music," in *Folha de S. Paulo,* he described how bossa nova can be heard throughout Asia. In Shanghai, "the

FIGURE 18.1. Japanese Brazilian singer Lisa Ono during a 2011 music festival in Beijing. Photo by Fabiano Maisonnave.

sound of the street belongs to Lisa Ono," he wrote. CD hawkers on the city's teeming street corners have turned Ono's voice into great profits. But connecting Ono to Brazil is a different story. As the former consul explained:

> Brazilian music is directly linked to contemporary Chinese musical tastes. The sound is sweet, sung with a certain softness. Take an artist like David Tao, who has been successful among young and middle-aged audiences here in the last few years. His style of singing is directly related to ours. But the Chinese don't associate the music with Brazil. Educated and well-informed people within the 25- to 50-year-old age group know that bossa nova is Brazilian. But the vast majority do not. (http://vistachinesa.blogfolha.uol. com.br/2012/07/02/os-chineses-nao-sabem-mas-adoram-musica-brasileira/)

During the World Expo in 2010, the consulate worked to promote bossa nova's identification as a Brazilian music genre by sponsoring concerts by the group Bossa Negra. The quintet/quartet unites Brazilian and Asian musicians, recording bossa nova tunes in both English and Mandarin. The following year, it was the Chinese singer Jasmine Chen's turn. Chen, who has recorded Brazilian classics in Mandarin since 2008, came to share the stage with the Brazilian guitarist Filó Machado in Shanghai and, like Ono, played under the sponsorship of the consulate.

"When it comes to Bossa Nova, the Chinese are an easy sell. First off, the melodies are so pretty and, in Chinese music, this quality is the most important," said Jasmine in an e-mail interview. "Second, bossa nova is rhythmic, it rings of happiness and freedom. It easily attracts Chinese listeners."

During my three years in China, I constantly heard Lisa Ono's voice. On each occasion, I would ask those around me who was singing. The word *Brazil* never came up. The funniest response I received to my question was from a bartender in Hangzhou who said that the singer was Chinese and that she was singing in English. When I told Lisa about the bartender, she responded, "I love the story of me becoming Chinese! Brazilian music is the root of all music. And that must be why I'm labeled a Chinese woman singing in English."

Bossa nova, for all that, is no simple case of misrecognition. It is much more than just Brazilian music confused as Chinese, Japanese, or American. In its global travels, this Latin American genre has taken root in each new destination. Bossa nova remains true to the sound of Rio in the early 1960s— but also to the sound of New York, Tokyo, and Beijing in the decades that followed. Brazil's global musical roots become more local as the journey continues.

Translated from Portuguese by Lauren Papalia

REFERENCES AND SUGGESTED READING

Castro, Ruy
  2003 *Bossa Nova: the Story of the Brazilian Music That Seduced the World.* Chicago: Chicago Review Press.

NINETEEN

"More than a Nationality"

AN INTERVIEW WITH GAEL GARCÍA BERNAL ABOUT
LATIN AMERICAN CINEMA AND THE WORLD

Alma Guillermoprieto

I

GAEL GARCÍA BERNAL, THIRTY-SIX, born 30 November 1978, is one of the handful of Mexican screen actors who have transcended their country's borders to become international stars. First there was Lupe Vélez, the long-forgotten "Mexican Spitfire" who got her start in silent movies. Later in the twentieth century came Cantinflas, Dolores del Rio, and María Félix. Today the list includes the likes of Demian Bichir, Salma Hayek, and Diego Luna. But beyond its individual stars, Mexican film has often had a significant international presence; during what is known as the Golden Epoch (Época de Oro) of Mexican cinema, the 1930s, 1940s, and early 1950s, Mexican movies, with their stark visual aesthetic and gorgeous protagonists, may have been almost unknown in the United States, but each new arrival at the local cinema was received with mesmerized attention from Guatemala on south. Stars like María Félix and directors like Emilio "El Indio" Fernández created a *muy mexicano* tradition in which long-suffering Indians and stupendous sinners always seemed to be shot in heroic profile. The comedies of Tin Tan and Cantinflas enthroned the scatty, sarcastic language of *el populacho,* or Everyman, while the modest dance gyrations of fleshy, sensuous *rumberas* relaxed the hold of a Catholic upbringing on men and women alike.

The Golden Epoch instructed whole generations in emerging countries on what it is to have a national identity, and what such identities might contain. But those decades of glory came to an end when Hollywood began to export its big-budget Technicolor movies, whose glitter and glamor, publicity machines and technological superiority, both hypnotized viewers throughout Latin America and helped to reinforce an ingrown inferiority complex regarding el Gigante del Norte. The audience for homegrown movies melted away, Mexican national studios shut down, and between 1950 and 1990 only a scattering of movies were made in Mexico in any given year. Other than a few laborious art-house efforts, those that were produced were hardly of note.

Mexican cinema came to international attention again in the 1990s, reincarnated as art film with box-office power. Remarkable directors, cinematographers, set designers, and actors came up through the ranks. Thanks to the arrival of big-budget advertising campaigns and the age of the creative director, many aspiring *cineastas* survived as filmmakers by directing television advertisements. Of the generation of performers who came of age in the 1990s, none has become so identified with the New Latin American Cinema as Gael García Bernal, who, out of the sense of familiarity his screen persona generates worldwide, is often referred to by his first name only.

Gael has, certainly, the most distinguished filmography of the current crop of Latin American actors. At age eighteen, he starred in an enchanting ten-minute short called *De tripas corazón,* directed by Antonio Urrutia: the shy, hungry, sexual curiosity Gael projected contributed greatly to the film's Oscar nomination. A year later he was the unforgettable face in the multicast *Amores perros,* which brought him stardom and gave the brash young director, Alejandro González Iñárritu, his own parting-of-the-seas moment. Then came Alfonso Cuarón's *Y tu mamá también,* also an international hit, and an Oscar nominee. *The Crime of Father Amaro, The Motorcycle Diaries,* and *Bad Education,* the last directed by Pedro Almodóvar, soon followed. With these films came a slew of awards and Oscar nominations.

He has appeared or starred in thirty-four additional films and sung in a few of them. He even has a mock-music video on YouTube, initially made for the Mexican box-office hit *Rudo y Cursi.* Together with Diego Luna, his childhood friend and costar in *Y tu mamá también* and *Rudo y Cursi,* he started the production company Canana, which has produced, among others, the rigorously unsentimental beauty-queen thriller *Miss Bala* (Miss Bullet) and Cary Fukunaga's debut feature film, *Sin nombre,* about a pair of Honduran migrants traveling north through Mexico, which garnered many international awards and nominations.

García Bernal likes to pretend that none of this is exceptional. It's his way of protecting himself from the burdens of stardom, although it's not clear if the trick actually works. When I met with him one late morning in the Canana headquarters in Mexico City's hipster-ish Colonia Roma, he was hiding behind eyeglasses and wearing torn jeans and a T-shirt. Unshaven and uncombed but with the trademark light-up-the-room smile at full wattage, he looked more like his screen image than ever—a buzzingly alive, vulnerable heartbreaker. García Bernal keeps a crowded schedule whenever he is in Mexico City, but he loves to talk, and our conversation ran overtime in Canana's overcrowded, hyperenergized headquarters, while mild chaos ruled all around us.

Gael always tell the same story: he really had no intention of being in film, headed as he was for a college degree in philosophy, or sociology—"or maybe even journalism"—when an eight-month-long strike at the National Autonomous University of Mexico brought his studies to a halt. Stranded, he decided he might as well go to London to study theater while he waited for a better option. It arrived in the form of a leading role in *Amores perros,* González Iñárritu's first feature film.

Iñárritu, who was in advertising before he made a movie, and was the best-known deejay in Mexico before that, had used Gael in an ad once. He had also seen him perform in Bernard-Marie Koltès *Roberto Zucco,* a play from the 1980s about an Italian serial killer. "The National Theater Company staged it here in Mexico, and it pulled out all the stops," Gael said, punctuating his sentences with a full complement of exclamation marks. "I mean, Alejandro Luna [father of the actor Diego Luna] created a gigantic stage set! So González Iñárritu called me for the movie and I thought, sure, I can do that on my vacation!"

Having accepted the role on a lark, the film's multiple dark nuances escaped the nineteen-year-old actor as the shoot went on. The plot, with its shifting perspective and overlapping stories about love and destruction, could have been dreamed up by a moody tango composer after several nights of too much wine. "But when I saw [the finished product], I said, 'Ahhh! This is cinema! And *we* made it!' It gave me an identity, a nationality as an actor. I'd say to myself, 'I was there!' How crazy is that? That movie galloped all over the world and changed the life of everyone who took part in it."

It certainly turned his life around. "I thought I'd be going back to England after *Amores perros,*" he says now, laughing. "My dream was to go to Mexico after graduation and found a theater company and, oh, I don't know, marry a Slovakian actress, something like that, and tour the world." Instead, he got a call from Alfonso Cuarón, a friend of González Iñárritu who had already made a few well-regarded films in both Mexico and Hollywood—*Sólo con tu pareja* (Love in the Time of Hysteria) and *A Little Princess* were the better known—and who now had financing for a movie about two hormonally addled teenagers and the desperate young woman who decides to join them on the road.

Cuarón offered the lead parts in what was to become *Y tu mamá también* to Gael and his childhood friend Diego Luna. The young woman was played by the Spanish actress Maribel Verdú. "They told Diego and me that there were four candidates for the woman's role," Gael recalled. "And that all of them were really good-looking, but when they told us that one was Maribel Verdú we started shouting, 'Maribel! Maribel!'" He laughed, leaving the impression that he'd be happy to shout "Maribel!" all over again, given the chance. "We'd seen her in *Huevos de oro* and in *Belle Époque,* in the days when you felt that each movie you liked was your own personal discovery, no? She could melt ice!"

In 2000, *Amores perros* won the Semaine de la Critique prize at Cannes, and the next year *Y tu mamá también* won an acting award for Diego Luna and a best script award for Cuarón and his cowriter younger brother, Carlos, in Venice. "And that's where the whole craziness began," Gael concludes. "That's when I began to sketch out a life for myself in films."

Gael's sudden stardom owed a great deal to his face, which is a jumble of separate features: lumpy nose, too-broad forehead, big, wavy mouth. When he is tired the combination can make him look like an ice-cream clown about to melt. But it is an extraordinarily open face; there is that vulnerable, hungry mouth and, above all, the fantastically expressive hazel eyes, which seem to shatter when he projects pain and light up from behind the irises when he laughs, which is often. As was apparent from his first appearance before a camera, as a child star in a *telenovela,* there is no such thing as too much of a Gael close-up.

It must not be easy for a well-brought-up young man to recognize that his triumph owes so much to how his face looks when projected on a screen, and so García Bernal is happy to let his entire career sound like an accident, as if he were ashamed of its success. But there was no accident: he is the son of two well-established Mexican actors. Like his buddy Luna, he grew up backstage. He starred in a *telenovela* when he was barely eleven, was knowledgeable about film from earliest adolescence, and at age fifteen had already managed to find himself a slot at Gabriel García Márquez's film school in Cuba. He is a delightful conversationalist partly because he seems so utterly uninterested in playing the star, but it would be foolish to think that an international career like his is achieved without great ambition. One only has to see him approach the set before an hourlong interview with David Frost, nervously flexing his hands, eyes shining, walking almost on tiptoe with excitement— This is me! I'm going to be interviewed by David Frost!—to see how deep that ambition runs.

His success is also inseparable from the rise of a new globalized Latin American cinema that is innovative, ambitious, and socially aware but almost militantly un-ideological and seductively eager to make audiences happy. In the Latin American New Wave of the 1960s, the Brazilian director Glauber Rocha made movies that sang the epic Song of the People, while in Cuba the work of directors like Tomás Guitérrez Alea and Humberto Solás called attention to Castro's dogmatisms and errors but first and foremost professed revolutionary faith. In contrast, in Gael García's most recent Oscar-nominated film, *No,* the director, Pablo Larraín, argued that in the 1988 referendum in Chile that ended the rule of Augusto Pinochet, the victory of the "No" vote against the dictatorship was the result not of a long struggle by the opposition but of a brilliant public relations campaign. García Bernal played the creator of the "No" campaign.

Things happened between, say, Pinochet's bloody coup against President Salvador Allende in 1973 and the decision to make a movie about a bunch of PR people with the semblance of a conscience. There was the final acceptance by all but the most diehard leftists that the Soviet Union and the People's Republic of China had been monstrous shams and the Cuban Revolution a dismal failure. The Internet set the world talking to and all around itself, with unquantifiable effects on both nationalism and cosmopolitanism, not to mention the movie industry.

The Zapatista rebellion in Chiapas and its superstar leader, "Subcomandante Marcos," brought international attention to the indigenous communities of southern Mexico, although it had an agenda that owed far more to University of California, Berkeley, activists than to Marx: gender equality, gay liberation, freedom of speech, and environmental decay were topics of concern next to the right of indigenous peasant communities to rule themselves according to their own laws and customs.

There were, simultaneously, a few financial crises that made clear the shaky construct of consumer capitalism. In a region where faith and ideology have always played a leading role, all the solid beliefs had shattered by century's end. The new reality was a world in which no one was saved.

It was during this time that the young and ambitious González Iñárritu first began work on the structure of *Amores perros,* whose three separate stories form an interlocking narrative puzzle. The restless camera films shards and split seconds of reality, and the only politicized character is a former guerrilla. By the time we meet him, however, he has devolved into an embittered wanderer, a drunken vagrant who takes on occasional jobs as a hitman. García Bernal was cast as Octavio, a lowlife teenager who runs a dog-fighting ring. The film's pessimism was global, its concerns with structure were modern, and its energy and temperament were unmistakably Mexican. Audiences around the world absorbed it like a dark drug.

The directors Cuarón and González Iñárritu were in the habit of exchanging ideas and opinions about their respective films-in-progress with a third upstart, a round-faced compulsive jokester from Guadalajara called Guillermo del Toro, who had already made seven horror movies in Mexico, Spain, and the United States and would soon start work on the first *Hellboy*. His longtime cinematographer, Guillermo Navarro, would subsequently win an Oscar for his work on del Toro's *Pan's Labyrinth*. Part of the group as well was Cuarón's director of photography, Emmanuel Lubezki, who has picked up cartfuls of awards and praise for his work, most recently, for Cuarón's *Gravity*. *Japón,* an unpleasant movie that managed to be embarrassingly narcissistic, exploitative, and highly original, brought its director, Carlos Reygadas, great prestige. Soon, Gael starred in yet another Oscar-nominated film, *El crímen del padre Amaro,* directed by Carlos Carrera. Suddenly, there was a Mexican film movement, but it is symptomatic of his generation's distrust of ideology that the ever-forthcoming Gael García Bernal was visibly irritated by my question on this topic.

"Fortunately, we haven't fallen into the temptation of trying to put a name on this moment," he said, frowning. "Once there was the New Mexican Cinema, and now we could call this the New New Mexican Cinema, but it doesn't have a name. It's just Mexican movies." Ecumenically, he included in his list of New New movies Eugenio Derbez' saccharine bilingual comedy *Instructions Not Included,* which was an enormous box-office hit on both sides of the border, although he immediately confessed he had not seen it. "But I should, I should," dutiful Gael said, before returning to his central point. "I'm glad we haven't fallen into the temptation of saying this is the thus-and-such movement, and this is the X group and this is the Y 'groupuscule,' and these are the parents and these are the grandparents of the movement. It's a good thing that we don't have that Latin American favorite; a manifesto. It's a reflection of everyone's desire to avoid the beaten path."

Throughout Latin America, young filmmakers—many of them former students at government-sponsored film schools in Mexico and/or the film school created by García Márquez in Cuba—also discovered around the same time that they had an endless stream of stories to tell, private stories. There would be no more grand declarative epics, no prophetic doom-saying— at least until González Iñárritu and Cuarón got their hands on epic Hollywood budgets. For the moment, there would be only stories. Stories about the directors' own lives, or their parents' lives, or their servants' lives, or perhaps even that of the desperately lonely teenager in *La teta asustada* (The Milk of Sorrow) surviving the restrictions and terrors of life in the consolidating shantytowns around Lima, Peru. For the Latin American film artists who got their start in the 1990s, the universe consisted of individuals, often eccentric, caught in the crazy, fantastically unequal, contradictory, and narratively incomparable world of Latin America. Although not everyone was as concerned as González Iñárritu with narrative structure, it was second nature for young artists who grew up during the collapse of revolutionary faith to tell stories with multiple angles, about characters who could not be examined through one lens only.

And so Tenoch, the teenage character played by Diego Luna in *Y tu mamá también,* lets a telephone across the room ring and ring without lifting a finger while his nanny climbs up the stairs to answer the call. But on the road days later, gazing out the backseat window while the character played by Gael García Bernal drives, Tenoch is pierced by the memory of his nanny, whom he deeply loves. In *Amores perros,* Octavio, the character played by García Bernal, tries to seduce his sister-in-law and runs a monstrous dog-fighting business. But the thing is, he is sincerely in love with his sister-in-law and nearly dies trying to protect his dog.

In the Peruvian director Claudia Llosa's *Madeinusa,* the pitiful, gentle heroine wins viewers' wholehearted sympathy before she commits a dreadful crime. In *La estrategia del caracol* (The Snail's Strategy), the Colombian director Sergio Cabrera chooses to tell the story of a community's eviction from an urban slum—a ripe subject for social realism—as a lighthearted comedy, almost of manners. With the exception of González Iñárritu, whose view of the world is grandly tragic, the postrevolutionary-era directors in Latin America have this in common: an affectionate attachment to their characters and an extreme reluctance to fill their work with messages. This is true of Alfonso Cuarón and Guillermo del Toro, both of whom work on a very large canvas indeed, as well as of those directors whose smaller-scale movies regularly win prizes at film festivals but which find only a modest audience in their afterlives as DVDs and Netflix downloads.

Sophisticated, cosmopolitan, technically brilliant, the new filmmakers of Latin America have won every conceivable international prize in the past fifteen years and made consistently entertaining and/or challenging movies. They are crossover acrobats; Cuarón, del Toro, and González Iñárritu—the Three Amigos—work more in Hollywood than they do at home. Salma Hayek is idolized in Europe and a star throughout the Americas. Oscar-nominated Demian Bichir is perhaps the first actor ever to have starred in upscale Mexican *telenovelas*, an ambitious U.S. television series (*Weeds*), and a Hollywood movie. Colombia's Sergio Cabrera directed many episodes of Spain's wildly successful historical *telenovela, Cuéntame cómo pasó* (Tell Me How It Happened). Gael has worked for directors from ten different countries. And for all that, it is the rare Latin American movie that can escape from the DVD/Netflix cage. The biggest challenge faced by García Bernal and Diego Luna is not acting but keeping their production company, Canana, alive.

Movies get produced very differently in Mexico and Hollywood, Gael pointed out. "In the United States there are lawyers, public relations firms, a whole series of steps and of people who get paid." There are also, he might have added, a great many different ways in which a Hollywood movie generates income: product placement, star tours, franchising, subsidiary rights. "Here," Gael said, "the great majority of films have been directors' projects, from scripts they've written themselves, and which they'll go out and find a producer for." In contrast, Canana looks for film projects it can develop and then passes the hat for financing around the small pool of people with money who are also interested in Latin American cinema.

Luna and García Bernal set up Canana with their business partner, Pablo Ruiz, in 2004, which, in terms of the evolution of the Internet and its impact on old media, is almost an eternity ago. "Economically, it's been very complicated, very difficult," García Bernal said. "We started at a time when Latin American movies were sold immediately in the United States. There was access, interest. But in Canana's fourth year, approximately, no more Mexican movies were shown in the U.S.—no more movies in any language other than English, in fact." García Bernal laughs and apologizes for what he calls the "Nescafé theories" he is about to put forward as explanation for the general decline. He cited the rise of television series, "which are increasingly cinematographic, with the added virtue of being viewable at any time," and of course the Internet, with its nonstop access to every form of moving media. "Also, the best writers migrated to cable television in the United States, because audiences were no longer going to a movie house to see a small movie, a melodrama.

The economics didn't work out. Middle-class movies—not too expensive, not too cheap—went over to television," Gael said. "One branch of this small, melodramatic genre was what people up North call foreign films. People stopped going to see them."

II

Filming on location at a theater at the arts center of Purchase State College in upstate New York on an early November afternoon, Gael had just translated himself into an English-language actor. The pilot for a television series, *Mozart in the Jungle,* about a promising young cellist, an older, traditionalist orchestra director, and his irreverent, sexy, far younger rival (that would be García Bernal) was being filmed that week, and someone had come up with the idea of braiding weird corkscrew hair extensions into García Bernal's hair to underline his character's fiery temperament. The sight took some getting used to, but once García Bernal was on camera, his enormous vitality bounced off a nearby monitor like an atomic particle gone mad. One wanted to look closely, but the dazzle interfered.

Backstage, in the whispery, half-dark atmosphere of the theater, assorted producers and crew chatted softly between takes. On stage, the main character, the young cellist, was supposed to be rehearsing. The fiery young orchestra conductor was supposed to be captivated by the sound just as he was enjoying an intimate moment with another musician. During breaks in what the trades like to call "a torrid sex scene," Gael made casual conversation with his young partner in the scene, until they were both relaxed enough to play it with some fervor.

Jason Schwartzmann (most recently seen in the Tom Hanks vehicle *Mr. Banks*), who was on the set not in his capacity as a musician, movie star, or producer but as the writer for the series pilot, had been observing Gael turn his own private lightworks off and on for the camera. "Exuberant, you know?," Schwartzmann said admiringly. "So keyed in to life . . . It's not like he's just watching it."

III

For all the glamor and jumping around the world it involves, Gael's private life is domestic and quiet. He lives in Buenos Aires with the Argentine-born actress Dolores Fonsi and their two children. Away from the set he tries to compensate for the career he missed when the national university went on strike.

"I love to study," he said, on one of his breaks. "I'm doing a master's in philosophy, media philosophy." "It's part of the idealism that burgeoned in me when I became a father," he explained. "I had been putting it off, but when we got pregnant [Dolores Fonsi and he], I said, now's the time. I always wanted to have a master's degree."

I asked him the difference between acting in Spanish and in English.

"I can fly a lot higher in Spanish," he said. "Physiologically, I've been molded to speak in Spanish. As a child you work out a certain vocal gymnastics that gradually turn into an accent. I feel much freer in Spanish, but in English [because of his accent] I feel I'm allowed to make more mistakes, and that's liberating too." "In Spanish," he added, smiling, "I'm held more accountable for what I say."

He thought for a moment. "There's another thing: English is an inflected language. That's why a Shakespeare sonnet can change its meaning according to the inflection you give it, whereas in Spanish you have to alter the order of the words to achieve the same result, or add more words. That's why Spanish is more baroque; it has more structural convolutions. For me English is somehow more impenetrable."

In the end, whatever magic, complexity, or riveting contradictions an actor brings to the screen reflects the life behind the face. Gael García Bernal belongs to the generation of the Free Trade Agreement, which forever changed—or benighted, depending on your view—Mexican culture. He came of age in the decade when Mexico, like much of Latin America, opened up to the world while at the same time its citizens streamed over the northern border in unprecedented numbers. His is also the generation that rose up to welcome the indigenous Zapatista movement in the southern state of Chiapas. Gael was among the thousands of teenagers who traveled there to express their solidarity, and his irreverent, intense personality bears the stamp of Subcomandante Marcos, a man who knows a thing or two about holding the spotlight. It is an optimistic generation; García Bernal experienced the final days of the soft dictatorship of the Partido Revolucionario Institucional (PRI), and he has lived through the bitter disappointment Mexicans feel about the political leaders who replaced the old party, but he has lived his life as an artist and film producer free from the insidious, hidden censorship that hobbled the work of his predecessors.

Gael has stayed true to the tradition of social activism among Latin American artists and intellectuals, but his activism is post-ideological, simultaneously local and transnational. Five years ago, even before the massacre of seventy-two Central American migrants in northern Mexico brought the migrant crisis to world attention, Amnesty International asked Gael if he would make a documentary short about the horrors inflicted on Central American migrants as they travel through Mexico on their way to the United States. García rode the migrant train known as "La Bestia" (the Beast)—at some risk to himself and the other three members of his crew—and made four little films. He was stunned by the appalling stories he heard from the migrants, and by the fact that a certain number of his fellow citizens should see fit to make a living kidnapping, raping, extorting, selling, or murdering their Central American neighbors.

Along the migrant trail he met the priests and religious workers who have set up shelters for the defenseless travelers. "As Mexicans, we're like, choking, on this pain about the things that are happening [to migrants]," Gael said. "And these people [who work with them] can give us a different way to read the story, to feel a certain hope. Obviously, because so many of them are church workers, they express themselves in religious, spiritual terms. I'm not religious, but through them I understood a lot more about what Christianity can mean, as something that can't be taken away from you but also as something that has to do simply with giving." An example of the global impact of those involved in Latin American cinema, Gael's documentary shorts for Amnesty International can be seen on YouTube by searching "The Invisibles, Amnesty."

I asked Gael how he saw himself as a Mexican actor, and the answer took some time, as he was once again reacting to the threat of a label.

"My family on my mother's side is from Sinaloa [a northern state known both as the principal source for the United States of imported tomatoes and as its principal source of drugs]. I've been going to Sinaloa since I was a child," Gael said. "I know what a ranch is; cows, tomatoes, the sea, and those unending stretches of beach, beaches that are all yours! But I was born in Guadalajara, and I grew up in Mexico City, and I know that world too, and the world beyond as well. Here in Mexico I knew a lot of the children of exile [mostly the sons and daughters of South Americans who fled from the region's Dirty Wars], and in the theater there were a lot of foreigners too. When we went on vacation our destination was often Cuba.

"So I never had the idea that I, as a Mexican actor, had to represent this or that identity. Instead I felt, I'm an actor! I'll go where I'm called and make the movie! As a universal actor! So I do defend that freedom: I'm an actor, man, I'm more than a nationality. As a person, I'm more than a nationality."

It would have made sense for someone so eager to forge a career in film to move to Hollywood following his first great success. "That was the established route," Gael agreed. "Everyone went to Hollywood to make it big. But I said to myself, let's see, *Amores perros* is showing all over the world, and I've just finished shooting *Y tu mamá también,* which I think is probably going to do well also. So where's the need? I didn't get it. From a practical point of view, what movie is there in the United States that's as good as *Amores* . . . or *Y tu mamá también*? So why should I go to Hollywood?"

"Besides," Gael went on, "I'd done my professional studies in England, and I knew I could get work in Spain—and, why not, in the rest of Latin America too!" In fact, he saw himself as someone who could and would make interesting films anywhere in the world, as indeed he has. "And that's part of the luck of being a Mexican actor. I don't have to follow the preestablished career path of U.S. actors. So, on the one hand, there is this thing of wanting to be a universal actor and not to be typecast"—Gael broke here into an excellent Speedy González accent—"as a Mexican, or as a race actor. But it's precisely because I'm Mexican that I didn't have to go to Hollywood. It frees me to do what I want."

He was about to add another thought to this one, but a stylist came up and said gently that they needed him over in makeup to fine-tune his hair extensions, and Gael García Bernal graciously said goodby and headed back to the set, the Mexican actor free to be whoever he wants on the international stage.

Mexico City, 2014.

ABOUT THE EDITORS AND CONTRIBUTORS

FLORENCE E. BABB is the Anthony Harrington Distinguished Professor in Anthropology at the University of North Carolina at Chapel Hill. Babb's books include *Between Field and Cooking Pot: The Political Economy of Marketwomen in Peru* ([1989] 1998) and *After Revolution: Mapping Gender and Cultural Politics in Neoliberal Nicaragua* (2001), with University of Texas Press. Her most recent book, *The Tourism Encounter: Fashioning Latin American Nations and Histories,* published by Stanford University Press in 2011, focuses on the cultural politics of tourism in postconflict and postrevolutionary Latin America.

O. HUGO BENAVIDES is Professor of Anthropology, Latin American and Latino Studies, and International Political Economy and Development at Fordham University, as well as Chair of the Sociology/Anthropology Department. He has published three books: *Making Ecuadorian Histories: Four Centuries of Defining the Past* (2004); *The Politics of Sentiment: Remembering and Imagining Guayaquil* (2006); and *Drugs, Thugs and Divas: Latin American Telenovelas and Narco-Dramas* (2008). He has written over forty articles, which have appeared in edited volumes and scholarly journals.

MICHELLE BIGENHO is Professor of Anthropology and Africana & Latin American Studies at Colgate University. Based on fieldwork in Bolivia, Peru, and Japan, her research has addressed indigeneity, cultural property, transnational cultural work, folklorization processes, and the politics of culture. Her work is published in scholarly articles and chapters as well as in two books, *Intimate Distance: Andean Music in Japan* and *Sounding Indigenous: Authenticity in Bolivian Music Performance.* She has coedited and co-curated (with Henry Stobart) a Spanish-English bilingual website, *Rethinking Creativity, Recognition, and Indigenous Heritage.* As a violinist, she has performed and recorded in the Bolivian ensemble Música de Maestros.

DENISE BRENNAN is Professor and Chair of the Department of Anthropology at Georgetown University. Her books include *Life Interrupted: Trafficking into Forced Labor in the United States* and *What's Love Got to Do with It? Transnational Desires and Sex Tourism in the Dominican Republic.* She is currently writing *Love and Heartache across Borders* about families separated by legal status. She is an adviser to the Best Practices Policy Project and has been a board member of Different Avenues and HIPS—organizations that advocate for sex worker rights. She also founded the Survivor Leadership Training Fund for trafficking survivor-advocates.

ANDREW BRITT is a Ph.D. candidate in Latin American history at Emory University focusing on spatial history, race/ethnicity, Brazil in global context, and cultural histories of production. His dissertation explores the making of spaces and racial and ethnic identification in three neighborhoods in the city of São Paulo. The project is supported by a Social Science Research Council Mellon International Dissertation Research Fellowship and the Fulbright-Hays Doctoral Dissertation Research Abroad program.

BRENDA ELSEY is Associate Professor of History at Hofstra University. She is the author of *Citizens and Sportsmen: Fútbol and Politics in Twentieth-Century Chile.* Her work has appeared in the *Journal of Social History,* the *International Journal of the History of Sport,* and *Radical History Review.* She has written on sports and politics for mainstream publications, including the *New Republic* and *Sports Illustrated.* Her current book, coauthored with Joshua Nadel, examines the history of women's sport, gender, and sexuality in Latin America.

PETER EVANS is Professor Emeritus in the Department of Sociology, University of California, Berkeley, and Senior Fellow in International Studies at the Watson Institute for International Studies, Brown University. He is best known for his work on the political economy of national development, exemplified by his 1995 book, *Embedded Autonomy: States and Industrial Transformation,* which sets the role of the Brazilian state in comparative perspective. In recent articles he has examined changing state-society relations and the role of labor.

PAJA FAUDREE is Associate Professor of Anthropology at Brown University. She is the author of *Singing for the Dead: The Politics of Indigenous Revival in Mexico,* which won the 2014 Book Prize from the Society for Latin American and Caribbean Anthropology (American Anthropological Association). She is also a published poet and playwright.

PAUL GOOTENBERG, SUNY Distinguished Professor of History and Sociology at Stony Brook University, is a leading scholar of the history of drugs in the Americas. He studied Latin American history at St. Antony's College, Oxford, and the University of Chicago, before turning to global drug history with works such as *Cocaine: Global Histories* (Routledge, 1999) and *Andean Cocaine: The Making of a Global Drug* (University of North Carolina Press, 2008). He is active in interdisciplinary initiatives for new perspectives on drug studies and drug reform such as the Drugs, Security, and Democracy (DSD) program of the Social Science Research Council and the Open Society Foundations.

GREG GRANDIN is Professor of History at New York University and a member of the American Academy of Arts and Sciences. He is the author of a number of books, including *Fordlandia: The Rise and Fall of Henry Ford's Forgotten Jungle City*, a finalist for the Pulitzer Prize for History, the National Book Award, and a National Book Critics Circle Award. He is the also the author of *Empire's Workshop; The Last Colonial Massacre; The Blood of Guatemala; The Empire of Necessity*, which won the Bancroft Prize in American History and the Albert J. Beveridge Award in American History; and, most recently, *Kissinger's Shadow*.

ALMA GUILLERMOPRIETO is a critically acclaimed journalist who has covered Latin American events for the *Washington Post*, the *New York Review of Books*, and the *New Yorker* and is the former South American bureau chief for *Newsweek*. She is a past recipient of a MacArthur Fellowship. Her work can also be found in three anthologies, *Samba, The Heart that Bleeds: Latin America Now*, and *Looking for History*.

MATTHEW GUTMANN is Professor of Anthropology and Director of the Brown International Advanced Research Institutes (BIARI) at Brown University. His books include *The Meanings of Macho: Being a Man in Mexico City; The Romance of Democracy: Compliant Defiance in Mexico City; Changing Men and Masculinities in Latin America; Fixing Men: Sex, Birth Control and AIDS in Mexico;* and *Breaking Ranks: Iraq Veterans Speak Out against the War* (with Catherine Lutz). From 2009 to 2013, he was vice president for international affairs at Brown. He has also been a visiting professor in China and Mexico.

GABRIEL HETLAND is Assistant Professor of Latin American Studies and Sociology (by courtesy) at University at Albany, SUNY. His research examines how ordinary people can influence the decisions that affect their lives through social movements, electoral politics, labor organizing, and the creation of participatory institutions. His work has been published in academic and popular venues such as *Qualitative Sociology, Work, Employment and Society, Latin American Perspectives, The Nation, NACLA,* and several edited volumes.

JENNIFER SCHEPER HUGHES is Associate Professor of History at the University of California, Riverside. She is also co-chair of the Religion in Latin America and Caribbean Group of the American Academy of Religion. She is the author of *Biography of a Mexican Crucifix: Lived Religion and Local Faith from the Conquest to the Present* (Oxford University Press, 2010).

KIYOSHI KONNO is the author of *Che Guevara: A Manga Biography.*

RICARDO LAGOS is a lawyer, economist, and social democrat politician who played a key role in bringing down the dictatorship that ruled Chile from 1973 to 1990 and later served as president of Chile (2000–2006). Since May 2007 he has served as a special envoy on climate change for the United Nations. He also teaches political and economic development at Brown University. Among his recent publications are *The Southern Tiger: Chile's Fight for a Democratic and Prosperous Future* and *Mi vida: De la infancia hasta la lucha contra la dictadura.*

JEFFREY LESSER is Samuel Candler Dobbs Professor and Chair, Department of History, at Emory University. He is the author of three prize-winning books published in English and Portuguese: *A Discontented Diaspora* (Duke University Press,

2007), *Negotiating National Identity: Immigrants, Minorities, and the Struggle for Ethnicity in Brazil* (Duke University Press, 1999), and *Welcoming the Undesirables: Brazil and the Jewish Question* (University of California Press, 1994). His newest book is *Immigration, Ethnicity and National Identity in Brazil* (Cambridge University Press, 2013; Editora UNESP, 2015).

MARCIA N. MACEDO is a scientist at the Woods Hole Research Center and Research Associate at the Instituto de Pesquisa Ambiental da Amazônia. She studies the trade-offs between forest conservation and food production in the tropics. Her research combines satellite data, field measurements, and modeling to understand how deforestation and agricultural expansion are changing tropical streams and global climate.

FABIANO MAISONNAVE is a senior reporter and editorial writer for the Brazilian newspaper *Folha de S. Paulo*. He has worked as a correspondent in Campo Grande (Brazil), Washington, Caracas, and Beijing and has reported from thirty countries on events including the Haitian earthquake and China's leadership change. A former Fulbright scholar, he holds a master's degree in history from the University of Connecticut and has been a fellow at the Nieman Foundation for Journalism at Harvard University.

RIGOBERTA MENCHÚ TUM is a Guatemalan human rights activist, winner of the 1992 Nobel Peace Prize, and UNESCO Goodwill Ambassador. She is a lifelong advocate for Latin America's indigenous peoples and women. Her experiences during the Guatemalan internal armed conflict are recorded in the acclaimed testimonial *I, Rigoberta Menchú, an Indian Woman in Guatemala*.

RYAN NEHRING is a Ph.D. student in Development Sociology at Cornell University. His research interests include the history and political economy of agricultural research in Brazil and alternative food systems in Latin America. He has recently published articles in the *Journal of Peasant Studies* and the *Canadian Journal of Development Studies*.

CHRISTOPHER NEILL is Director of the Ecosystems Center of the Marine Biological Laboratory and Associate Professor of Ecology and Evolutionary Biology at Brown University. He researches the environmental consequences of deforestation and the expansion and intensification of agriculture in the Brazilian Amazon.

RUBEN GEORGE OLIVEN is Professor of Anthropology at the Federal University of Rio Grande do Sul in Porto Alegre, Brazil, and member of the Brazilian Academy of Sciences. He received his PhD from the University of London and has been a visiting professor at several universities, among them the University of California, Berkeley, Dartmouth College, Brown University, and the University of Paris. He was president of the Brazilian Anthropological Association and the Brazilian Association for Graduate Studies and Research in Social Sciences. He won the Erico Vannucci Mendes Prize for Distinguished Contribution to the Study of Brazilian Culture.

JEFFREY M. PILCHER is Professor of History at the University of Toronto. He is the author of *Planet Taco: A Global History of Mexican Food* and *¡Que vivan los tamales! Food and the Making of Mexican Identity*. He is the articles editor of the peer-reviewed journal *Global Food History* and is currently writing a book on how beer traveled the world.

SARAH PORTNOY teaches courses on Latino food culture and food justice at the University of Southern California. She is working on a book titled *Food, Health, and Culture in Latino Los Angeles* for Rowman & Littlefield Publishers.

RENATO ROSALDO is Professor Emeritus of Anthropology at New York University and a member of the American Academy of Arts and Sciences. He is the author of *Ilongot Headhunting, 1883–1974: A Study in Society and History* and *Culture and Truth: The Remaking of Social Analysis*. Rosaldo has won numerous awards for his poetry. He has also written the libretto for a comic opera, *Notes on the Balinese Cockfight*, featuring the famous anthropologists Clifford Geertz and Margaret Mead as main characters.

NANCY SCHEPER-HUGHES is Chancellor's Professor and Chair of Medical Anthropology at the University of California, Berkeley. She is the author of *Death without Weeping: The Violence of Everyday Life in Brazil* (University of California Press, 1993) and "No More Angel-Babies on the Alto do Cruzeiro: The Reproductive Revolution in Northeast Brazil," *Natural History Magazine* (2013). Beginning with *Saints, Scholars, and Schizophenics* (University of California Press, [1979] 1999), she has written about the impact of the Catholic Church on the lives of small communities in Ireland, South Boston, Brazil, and Argentina. In April 2015 she was invited by the Vatican as a member of the final plenary meeting on Human Trafficking at the Pontifical Institute of Social Science.

CHIE SHIMANO is a Japanese Manga artist and the illustrator of *Che Guevara: A Manga Biography*.

ILAN STAVANS is the Lewis-Sebring Professor in Latin American and Latino Culture at Amherst College. Among his recent titles are the graphic novel *El Iluminado* (2012), the children's book *Golemito* (2013), the cartoon volume *A Most Imperfect Union: A Contrarian History of the United States* (2014), and the cultural biography *Quixote: The Novel and the World* (2015). He has translated Pablo Neruda, Juan Rulfo, and Mariano Azuela into English, Isaac Bashevis Singer from the Yiddish, Yehuda Amichai from the Hebrew, and *Don Quixote* into Spanglish. The recipient of many international awards, his work, translated into fifteen languages, has been adapted for theater and film.

DANIEL SUSLAK is Associate professor of Anthropology at Indiana University and affiliated with the IU Center for Latin American and Caribbean Studies. He has done two decades of research on Mixe-Zoquean languages and the traditions and histories of their speakers. His research interests also include verbal art and the changing lives of indigenous youth.

WENDY WOLFORD is the Robert A. and Ruth E. Polson Professor of Development Sociology at Cornell University. She has written extensively on social mobilization, land reform, and state formation in Brazil and, increasingly, in Mozambique. She is the author of *To Inherit the Earth* (with Angus Wright; Food First Press, 2003) and *This Land Is Ours Now* (Duke University Press, 2010).

INDEX

2008 financial crisis, 20–21, 22–23, 73, 146–47, 152, 153

Abidjan, 94, 123
Afro-descendant Americans, 231, 232; and Brazil, 31, 104, 114–15, 132–33, 138–39, 274, 276–77, 280–81, 283–84; in Cuba, 123–24; Edson Arantes do Nascimento (Pelé), 138–39, 141; in Guatemala, 237; incarceration in U.S., 217; Laba Sosseh, 123–24; language, 104; music and dance, 114–15, 123–24; Rodney King assault, 153; slavery, 32, 103–4, 275–76; soccer, 135–36, 138–39, 143; U.S. black tourism to Brazil, 274; U.S. presidential politics and, 25; W.E.B. DuBois and U.S. black immigration to Brazil, 276; in Uruguay, 136
Alfonsín, Raúl, 20, 35n3, 78
Allende, Isabel, 299
Allende, Salvador, 8, 26, 118, 330
Almodóvar, Pedro, 327
Amado, Jorge, 291, 294
Amazon region, 5, 167–186; environmental destruction, 11, 33, 165, 171–172, 177–86; food and cuisine, 156, 157; of Peru, 105–6; plant-drugs, 207–8, 209, 210, 213; Theodore Roosevelt's journey through, 273
Anderson, Benedict, 223
antipoverty programs, 22, 27–28, 85, 188; Bolsa Escola, 22; Bolsa Família, 188, 282–3; Chile Solidario, 22

Arabic, 102, 302
Araucanians, 118
Arcade Fire, 289
Argentina, 25, 82, 86, 105, 293; Afro-Brazilian religions, 280–81; Che Guevara, 1, 102–3; dictatorship, 9, 36n8, 40, 42–45, 48–52, 140; literature, 97, 291–92, 295, 297, 299, 300; Marcella Althaus-Reid, 40; mate, 213; music, 114, 115, 117, 118, 120, 124, 137; on the global political stage, 4, 23; Pope Francis, 9, 37, 42–45, 47–52, 106, 108; redemocratization, 20, 24; sex work, 240, 243, 244; soccer, 136–38, 140, 142, 143; tango, 120, 137; truth commissions, 77–80; trade, 176; variety of Spanish, 32, 102–3, 106
authenticity, 93–95; Cinema Novo and national, 279–80; food, 148, 150–51, 156, 159; gaucho, 292; language, 300; "peasant essentialism," 150; *telenovelas*, 303, 308, 309; tourism, 260–262
Aylwin, Patricio, 24, 25, 26

Balcells, Carmen, 293–294
Baldwin, James, 312
Black Orpheus, 289
Bolaño, Roberto, 300
Bolivia: Che Guevara's death, 1, 31; climate change politics, 73, 82–84; dance, 119–20; drug politics, 215, 217, 218; immigration from to Brazil, 278–79;

Global South: appropriation of cultural forms from, 116, 124; circulation of Latin American democracy and social change within, 8, 24, 73, 79, 81; climate change, 82–84; development projects, 11, 187–88, 189, 192, 195, 200–1; drug culture, 207; first pope from, 9, 45, 46; sex worker activism and labor, 222, 241; soccer, 139; *telenovelas*, 288, 302, 312; tourism, 262
globalization: anti-globalization, 81; Brazil, 278; diffusion of participatory budgeting, 74; Flat World theory, 6; food and cuisine, 151; language, 113; literature, 296; origin of term, 15; soccer, 142, 144*fig.;* soybeans, 175–77; *telenovelas*, 302–3, 304, 311
Guatemala: 1954 coup, 59, 234; civil war in, 221, 234; drug policy, 217; human rights in, 234–36; liberation theology in, 40; Maya in, 101, 105, 229–30; Mennonites in, 105; migrants from, 110, 236; Rigoberta Menchú's Nobel acceptance speech, 225–39
guerrilla war: the Catholic Church, 51; Che Guevara, 2, 10; Dilma Rousseff, 25; drug policy in Colombia, 217; in Guatemala, 235; *Amores perros,* 331
Guevara, Ernesto "Che," 1–3, 4, 30–31, 34, 102; as icon, 1–3, 4, 17, 30, 89–93; in manga, 10, 17, 89–93; U.S. politics, 62, 63–64

Haiti (Saint-Domingue), 238, 281, 289; Alejo Carpentier's novel *The Kingdom of the This World*, 296; Landless Workers Movement in, 81; migrants from, 109, 278; Revolution, 4, 211; slavery, 211
Haitian Kreyòl, 98, 104
Havana: Miami's "Little Havana," 64; music, 94, 115, 123; tobacco, 210; tourism, 257*fig.,* 259–60, 266; U.S. politics, 59, 60, 62, 64, 65n11
Hernández, José, 292
HIV/AIDS, 5, 244, 246, 250
Honduras, 217, 229, 327
human trafficking, 45, 222, 241, 243–45, 250, 310

icon, 17, 31, 89–92, 133, 262
immigrants and immigration: in Argentina, 108; assimilation, 155; to and from Brazil, 108,110, 212, 271–72, 277, 278, 288, 317–18, 321, 322; food and cuisine, 94, 146–48, 152–53, 155, 160; language, 108–12; music, 116, 122, 123; soccer, 132, 133; to the U.S., 63, 108–12, 129, 152–53, 155, 160, 336; U.S. Immigration and Customs Enforcement (ICE), 129
imports: agriculture, 164, 170, 173–74, 176, 177, 184, 198; food and cuisine, 149, 336; of ideologies from the Global North, 72, 272–73; language, 102; manufactured goods, 278, 322; plant-drugs, 213, 336; soccer, 142; the transatlantic slave trade, 276
Iñárritu, Alejandro González, 327–333
indigenous languages, 10, 97–98, 99–103, 105–7, 111, 113
indigenous peoples: Araucanians, 118; in Bolivia, 82, 84, 125; in Brazil, 271, 273, 279; Catholicism, 47, 53; early colonial expansion and conquest, 3–4; environment and climate change, 183, 227, 231, 236; food, 150–51, 156; "imagined Andean indigenism," 94; 121; Inca, 98, 100, 114, 118–19, 156, 211, 212; *indigenismo*, 117, 291–92; language, 10, 11, 97–98, 99–107, 111, 113; Maya, 99, 100, 101, 105, 107, 151, 208, 211, 229–230, 268; *mestizaje*, 31–32, 147, 292; Mexica (Aztecs), 17, 68, 69, 98, 100, 151, 208, 211, 229; music, 118–19, 279; Olmec, 208; plant-drugs, 5, 165, 208–211; Roberta Menchú, 12, 221, 225–239; soccer, 135–36; Zapatista uprising, 262, 330, 335
International Monetary Fund, 21, 23, 36n5
internationalization: of Brazilian symbolic goods, 280; film, 326, 333; language, 113; literature, 13, 287, 293, 296, 300–1; soccer, 142–45
internet and social media, 330, 333; and Flat World theory, 6; food trucks, 152, 154, 154, 155; migration and transnationalism, 11; protest, 285;

Nacala Corridor, 191–94, 199
Narcos, 216, 288
neoliberalism, 35n4, 36n6, 72, 140, 160, 295
Neruda, Pablo, 9, 296
New Wave cinema (Cinema Novo), 330
Nicaragua, 238; Rubén Darío, 292; liberation theology in, 40; Sandinistas, 57n4, 62, 262; tourism, 256, 259, 266
Nobel Prize: for literature, 9, 17, 35n1, 296, 300, 301; for peace, 12, 225–26, 227–39
nongovernmental organizations, 12, 45, 77, 78, 232, 240–241
North-South relations, 86, 165, 288, 309; development partnerships, 187, 192, 195; Landless Workers Movement, 81; tourism, 257; sex worker activism, 222, 241. *See also* Global North; Global South

Official Development Assistance (ODA), 192
Operation Condor, 215
Organization of American States (OAS), 216, 217
Ortiz, Fernando, 148–49

Panama, 99, 122–23, 238
Paraguay: colonial trade in, 213; Guaraní as official language of, 100; Mennonites in, 105; sex workers, 243; soccer, 132, 140; social movements, 82
Paris: coffee shops, 211; DASPU fashion, 240; El Boom authors in, 295, 296; Latin American music in, 117, 120; Mesoamerican codices in, 101; training of Gastón Acurio, 151
participatory budgeting, 29, 73, 74–77, 85, 86
Partido dos Trabalhadores (Brazil), 29, 74, 282
Partido Revolucionario Institucional (PRI), 335
Paz, Octavio, 9, 296, 298, 301
Peña Nieto, Enrique, 29
Perón, Evita, 25
Perón, Isabelita, 25
Perón, Juan, 25, 49

Peronism, 295
Peru: economic growth, 265; food and cuisine, 10, 19, 105, 151; Gustavo Gutiérrez, 38, 52; language, 105–6, 107; *mestizaje*, 31; migration to and from, 108, 133; music, 114, 117, 118, 121, 125; plant-drugs and drug policy, 207, 211, 215, 218; political participation, 28, 74; Ricardo Zárate, 146–149, 155–61; *La teta asustada* (The Milk of Sorrow), 332; tourism, 259, 260, 263, 267*fig.*, 268
peyote, 208–9
Pinochet, Augusto: 1973 military coup, 8, 118; arrest of, 79; dictatorship, 24, 36n6, 118, 122, 140, 300; plebiscite, 24, 36n9, 330; Ricardo Lagos and, 26, 27*fig.*, 36n12
political parties, 234, 285; Brazilian Communist Party, 138; Frelimo (Mozambique), 196; Liberals and Conservatives, 262; Partido Revolucionario Institucional (PRI), 335; Partido dos Trabalhadores (Brazil), 29, 74, 282; soccer, 140
Pope Francis (Jorge Mario Bergoglio), 9, 16, 37–57, 106–7, 108, 112; relationship to military dictatorship in Argentina, 42–45, 48–51
Portugal: Brazilian independence from, 195, 272; colonial expansion and conquest, 3, 10 99–100, 271–72; dictatorship in, 79, 195; language, 32, 98–99, 102–4, 106, 110, 112, 113; Lusophone Africa, 187, 189, 194–95; lusotropicalism, 194, 277; merchants from, 148–49; migration to and from, 108, 110, 277; the slave trade and slavery, 115, 310
positivism, 272–3
poverty: liberation theology critique of, 40, 41, 42, 52; in Mozambique, 197; perspective on by Flat Worlders, 6; Pope Francis and, 54; Rigoberta Menchú comments on, 229, 230, 231, 233, 236, 238; soccer, 133, 139. *See also* antipoverty programs
ProCerrado, 189–90
ProSAVANA, 189–201

União Nacional de Camponeses (UNAC), 200

United States, 4, 6, 8; climate change, 33–34, 82–83; colonial settlement patterns in North America, 32; Cuba, 46, 52, 58–65, 120; food and cuisine, 11, 146, 150, 151, 159, 160; global leadership, 23, 72, 243; Hollywood, 115, 118, 279, 280, 326, 332–33, 337; international development projects, 190–91, 195; literature, 298, 299; language, 108–13; migration to and from, 278, 336; music, 119, 120, 122, 123, 137, 317, 319, 320; participatory budgeting, 75–77; plant-drugs and drug policy, 213, 215, 218; presidential politics, 25; race relations in, 276, 284; sex worker activists in, 241; the slave trade and slavery, 276–77; soccer, 139; soybeans, 171, 173, 175; Spanish American War of 1898, 294; torture prosecutions, 79–80; tourism from U.S. to Latin America, 256–70; trade with Latin America, 5, 323. *See also* Latino Population in the U.S.

Uruguay: Afro-Brazilian religions in, 280; Borge's story "Funes, the Memorious," 297; drug policy, 217; Eduardo Galeano, 4; language, 109; soccer, 135–37, 140

USAID, 188, 190, 191, 194, 199, 244

Vasconcelos, José, 8, 292

Venezuela: migrants from, 108; origins of salsa, 120; participatory budgeting in, 74, 75–77; political system, 28, 29; role in addressing global problems, 4; social movements, 82; and U.S. politics, 64

Watanabe, Sadao, 319

working class: in Chile, 28; food and cuisine, 146, 148, 150–51, 160; immigrants in London, 122; soccer, 133, 138–39; *telenovelas*, 304

World Bank; Chile Solidario, 21, 22; participatory budgeting, 73, 74, 75; support for South-South development, 187, 190, 192, 194, 199

World Cup, 136–41, 143, 241–43, 246, 281

World Trade Organization, 281

World War I, 292

World War II, 38, 115, 120, 276, 293, 300

YouTube, 26, 125, 327, 336

Zambia, 191

Zapatista rebellion, 262, 330, 335

Zimbabwe, 198